Ian Cawood is Head of History at Newman University College, Birmingham. He holds a PhD from the University of Leicester. He is a regular contributor to the *Times Literary Supplement* and his previous publications include *The First World War* and *Britain in the Twentieth Century*.

THE LIBERAL UNIONIST PARTY

A History

IAN CAWOOD

I.B. TAURIS

LONDON · NEW YORK

This book is dedicated to the memory of my mother who died during the final stages of its completion.

Published in 2012 by I.B.Tauris & Co Ltd
6 Salem Road, London W2 4BU
175 Fifth Avenue, New York NY 10010
www.ibtauris.com

Distributed in the United States and Canada
Exclusively by Palgrave Macmillan
175 Fifth Avenue, New York NY 10010

International Library of Political Studies 53

ISBN 978 1 84885 917 3

A full CIP record for this book is available from the British Library
A full CIP record for this book is available from the Library of Congress

Library of Congress catalog card: available

Typeset by Newgen Publishers, Chennai
Printed and bound by CPI Group (UK) Ltd, Croydon, CR0 4YY

MIX
Paper from
responsible sources
FSC
www.fsc.org   FSC® C013604

CONTENTS

LIST OF ILLUSTRATIONS

41. Such was the popularity of Unionism in the 1890s that products were marketed using the imagery of the alliance, adapted from political posters.

42. Carruthers Gould identifies the bitterness with which Chamberlain's support for the Education Bill of 1896 was received by his nonconformist supporters. *Westminster Gazette*, 4 May 1896.

43. The *Westminster Gazette* comments on the lack of substantial progress on Old Age Pensions in 1898, despite Chamberlain's earlier promises. *Westminster Gazette*, 7 January 1898.

44. The *Westminster Gazette* highlights the growing irrelevance of the Liberal Unionist Party. *Westminster Gazette*, 15 March 1901.

45. The conflict between Devonshire and Chamberlain over the position of the Liberal Unionist Association on the tariff reform question is publicly revealed in *The Times*, 11 January 1904.

46. A postcard reproduction of a *Westminster Gazette* cartoon implying Chamberlain's dominance of the Birmingham Liberal Unionist Association after the tariff reform split. Uncatalogued item, Cadbury Research Room, University of Birmingham.

47. J. West Ridgeway's article announcing, prematurely, the death of the Liberal Unionist Party as a result of the tariff reform split. J. W. Ridgeway, 'The Liberal Unionist Party', *Nineteenth Century and After*, 342 (August 1905), p.182.

48. By the 1906 election, Chamberlain had ensured that the troubled position of Liberal Unionism had been firmly replaced by the question of 'fair trade vs free trade'. Postcard, uncatalogued item, Cadbury Research Room, University of Birmingham.

49. The Liberal *Daily News and Leader* reports the fusion of the two Unionist Parties. *Daily News and Leader*, 10 May 1912.

50. W.T. Stead's *Pall Mall Gazette* attempts to distinguish between the different branches of Liberal Unionism. 'The Black Book', *Pall Mall Gazette*, 14 September 1887.

ACKNOWLEDGEMENTS

I am indebted to Dr Stuart Ball for his patient encouragement, guidance and painstaking proof-reading of the bulk of the material in this book. I would also like to thank Professor Yahya Nakeeb, director of research at Newman University College, who has unhesitatingly supported this project through many years. I am also grateful to Dr Matthew Cragoe, Dr James Owen, Dr Victoria Barbery, Dr Nick Crowson, Professor Jonathan Parry, Professor Eric Evans, Dr Angus Hawkins and Dr Noelle Plack for their advice and assistance. I would also like to extend my thanks to the staff of the Modern Political Records Room at the Bodleian Library in Oxford, the Cadbury Research Archive at the University of Birmingham, the Mitchell Library in Glasgow, the National Library of Scotland, the Women's Library in London, the Local History and Archives service at Birmingham Central Library and the archives of the London School of Economics, all of whom have made a significant contribution to this study with their professionalism and scholarly assistance. I am particularly grateful to Lord Clifford of Ugbrooke House for his permission to reproduce the political propaganda found in his archive. I must thank my editor at I.B Tauris, Joanna Godfrey, for her enthusiastic commitment to the book and the three anonymous reviewers who did much to improve the final manuscript. Any errors of presentation, content and understanding that remain are therefore entirely my own fault. Finally, I would like to thank my wife and my children for their patience and forbearance over the many years it took to complete this text.

INTRODUCTION

LADY BRACKNELL:	What are your politics?
JACK:	Well, I am afraid I really have none.
	I am a Liberal Unionist.
LADY BRACKNELL:	Oh, they count as Tories. They dine
	with us. Or come in the evening, at any
	rate.

(Oscar Wilde, *The Importance of Being Earnest*, 1895)

Lady Bracknell's witticism, though politely laughed at by audiences for over a hundred years, has, of course, lost any political meaning for most theatre-goers. As she suggests, after 1895 the Liberal Unionists quickly became socially and politically allied with the Tories and ever since there has been a tendency to forget that they were a separate party. This book intends to examine whether the absorption of the Liberal Unionists into the Conservative and Unionist Party was inevitable by examining the ideology, organisation and electoral performance of the Liberal Unionists, as well as the troubled relationship between the two branches of the Unionist alliance from 1886 until 1912.

The division of the Liberal Party in 1886, which became permanent after the failure of the 'Round Table' conference of 1887, is perhaps unique in British political history for a number of reasons: It was the biggest defection from any political party (at its height, the Party boasted seventy-eight MPs who refused to obey the Gladstonian whip); it was the longest lived breakaway political force in modern British political history, lasting for twenty-six years as an independent party, with its own associations, leadership, whips, agents, funds and publications (including a newspaper from 1887 until 1892 and a Party newsletter for the next twenty years); it was, arguably, the bitterest division in nineteenth-century political life, matched only in modern history by the split of the Labour Party in 1931. In 1886, fathers and sons, friends and club members parted company over the issue. Some, like William Harcourt and Joseph Chamberlain, managed to remain on good terms (in private at least), but others, such as Lady Stanley, president of the Women's Liberal Unionist Association, and her daughter the Countess of Carlisle, opened a breach that lasted beyond the death of one or other party.[1] As John St. Loe Strachey, leader writer for the *Spectator* wrote in his autobiography, this applied to middle class families as well; 'My father and my elder brother remained Liberals and followed Mr Gladstone, I followed Lord Hartington, Mr Chamberlain and Mr Goschen.'[2] Mary Jeune later commented:

> The Home Rule question absolutely divided London society into two factions, and the cleavage was distinct. The Home Rule Party were virtually ostracised by their own friends and relations … the cleavage between the two parties and the intensity of feeling surpassed anything in the memory even of those people who remembered the bitterness which existed at the time of the Reform Bill [of 1832].[3]

The division between the Gladstonians and Unionists was in most cases social as well as political. Alfred Pease recorded in May 1887: 'they [the Liberal Unionists] are more viciously bitter than our Conservative opponents. Give me every time a Tory, who can speak with civility at least when he has time to meet such social outcasts as ourselves.'[4] Henry James considered that party feeling in social circles was at its strongest from 1886 until 1890, that he had never experienced anything like it and that no political event since the Great Reform Act of 1832 had so divided the nation.[5] The *British Weekly's* correspondent at the Liberal Unionist conference of December 1886 confirmed the anger felt by some towards those who, it was felt, had betrayed their principles for their party. When William Harcourt's name was mentioned, it 'provoked the strongest manifestations of contempt and disgust – two gentlemen beside me relieving their feelings by spitting.'[6] Lord Spencer's behaviour provoked similar reactions and Henry James recorded that if any Unionist wished to invite Spencer or Harcourt to dine, he had to ask all his other guests to agree to meet him.[7] As R. B. Brett commented, 'all the argument, all the authority, all the social influence' was in favour of the Unionists' cause,[8] and the result was, according to the *Inverness Courier*, 'on a small scale, the outbreak of civil war.'[9]

The study of the Home Rule crisis has largely been dominated by those who look at the crisis as a missed opportunity for peaceful Irish self-government and those whose primary interest has been to investigate the decline of the Liberal Party. In both cases, the interpretation of 1886 is clouded by the attempt to find antecedents for an event that occurred after the First World War. Beginning with Morley's official *Life of Gladstone* in 1903 and developed by J. L. Hammond in 1938, there has been a tendency among the former to regard Gladstone as a far-sighted, humane politician, defeated by the careerism, timidity, self-interest and bigotry of his opponents, with devastating consequences for Ireland in the twentieth century.[10] There is of course no way of knowing whether the Easter Rising, the Irish Civil War or the 'Troubles' of the later twentieth century would have been avoided by the achievement of Home Rule or, indeed, whether a more destructive Civil War between Ulster and the rest of Ireland would have been the consequence had it been achieved. For Hammond, the split among Liberals in 1886 was a harbinger of the devastating division between Asquith and Lloyd George during the First World War, as well as the moment that large aristocratic sources of political funding moved away from the Liberals, never to be replaced. In short, Liberal Unionism is studied as a negative force and often caricatured as a 'revolt of the Whigs' or at best 'a progressive wing of the Conservative Party.'[11]

Those interested in Unionism have tended to view the issue from an Irish perspective, or more particularly an Ulster one. The largest number of studies published recently on British attitudes towards Ireland in the period and on British support for the Union, have tended to focus on the personalities, ideologies and events of the island of Ireland. D. George Boyce and Alan O'Day have largely regarded Liberal Unionism as mere 'dissident Liberals', ciphers for Conservative opposition to devolution, not worthy of the attention that they give the Ulster Unionist movement.[12] J. Loughlin has been the most savage in his condemnation of the 'racism' (as he perceives it) of the English Unionists, though he is frequently weak on the complexities of the British political narrative at this time.[13] Frank Thompson and Graham Walker have also written studies that briefly address the Liberal Unionists' role in 1886, but they are all more interested in the rise of Carson's Ulster Unionist Party, which dominated Northern Irish politics in the twentieth century, despite the fact that there was no connection between T. W. Russell's Ulster Liberal Unionists and Colonel Edward Saunderson's Irish Unionist Alliance, from which the UUP evolved.[14]

The most recent study of the Ulster question confirmed that historians continue to overlook the Liberal Unionists, stating that the Home Rule debate polarised the British polity 'into two blocs, for and against Irish autonomy.'[15] With this assumption, the study of late nineteenth-century Unionist politics outside Ireland has been dominated by work on the Conservative Party in the period, such as that of Professors Peter Marsh,[16] Richard Shannon,[17] Michael Bentley,[18] and in particular by E. H. H. Green's study of late Victorian and

Edwardian Conservatism.[19] As the titles of these studies suggest, the role of
the Conservatives, and especially that of Salisbury, has been the main focus
of analysis and their theme has been the fashion in which Salisbury adapted
his Party very successfully to the political circumstances of the period, using
imperialism, patriotism, moderate reform and, most effectively, defence of
the Union with Ireland to out-manoeuvre the increasingly divided Liberal
Party.[20] Salisbury's sure-footed avoidance of the issues of social reform and
the costs of aggressive imperialism are also well documented by David
Steele,[21] and in Robert Blake and Hugh Cecil's often over-looked collection
of essays.[22]

Salisbury's success was in winning the support of the large numbers of
Liberal peers and members of parliament who left the Liberal Party in 1886.
Reluctantly at first, this disparate group of landed aristocrats, wealthy businessmen and radical professional politicians gradually coalesced into a political party of sorts and attempted to maintain an independent policy whilst
remaining part of the Unionist alliance. The role and influence of the Liberal
Unionist Party on a period of remarkable transformation in British politics
has largely been ignored in recent years. A series of articles written in the
late 1950s and early 1960s attributed the 1886 schism in Liberalism to the
growing fear of socialism among the upper-class Whigs, one even going so
far as to describe the Liberal Unionist Party as 'a half-way house' between the
Liberals of Gladstone and Salisbury's Conservatives.[23] By the 1970s, this view
had become so orthodox that historians could describe Liberal Unionism
as 'the means whereby many Whigs and moderate Liberals could gradually move into the Conservative Party without feeling they had betrayed
their commitment to Liberalism.'[24] As late as 1998, Angus Hawkins was
still asserting that 'wealth and status in all forms, became overwhelmingly Unionist in opinion during the 1890s.'[25] Even W. C. Lubenow partly
sustained the orthodox view in stating that 'class conflict was ... the consequence,' of the 1886 Liberal split.[26] This was perhaps an unsurprising conclusion, given the class focus of most political studies of the period and the
behaviour of the Liberal Lords. Of the 183 Liberal members of the House of
Lords in 1886, 120 became Liberal Unionists according to *Dod's Parliamentary
Companion*, thus virtually ending the Liberals' aristocratic representation.[27]
Unfortunately this interpretation largely ignored the role of the radical
Unionists, chiefly concentrated in the West Midlands and around Glasgow,
who left the Gladstonians at the same time and over the same issue, as well
as the behaviour of moderate Liberals from more humble backgrounds than
the Cavendishes, Fitzwilliams and Foljambes. Recently, in a much neglected
study, Robert F. Haggard has demonstrated that there was no sudden shift to

radicalism among the Gladstonian Liberals and that Chamberlain's defection was, in many ways, born of frustration at the failure of the Party in general, and the National Liberal Federation in particular, to adopt the 'unauthorised programme'. Haggard concludes that 'classical liberalism', in other words concepts of individualism, 'character' and self-help, remained the dominant philosophy of the Liberal Party until after the Boer War.[28] Unfortunately, as Jonathan Parry has commented, 'most historians have not been sufficiently sensitive to the Liberal Unionists' distinctive and powerful tradition.'[29] Study of the work of the three chief ideologues of the Party: the Professor of Law, A. V. Dicey; the historian and Liberal Unionist MP, W. E. H. Lecky; and the historian Goldwin Smith, a disciple of John Bright, soon confirms that the principles which Haggard detected among Gladstonian Liberals after 1886 were still championed by the Liberal Unionist Party, long into the twentieth century.[30] What motivated Liberal Unionists was more than a mere 'fear of socialism' and arose from a contrasting interpretation of Liberalism and nationalism to that of Gladstone.[31]

In the large number of biographies of Joseph Chamberlain, few are successful in pinpointing the radical Unionist leader's difficulties after 1886 in maintaining an alliance with Whig land-owners on one side and the Conservatives on the other.[32] T. A. Jenkins' article in 1990 revealed the existence of a secret electoral fund controlled by Hartington and Lord Wolmer, the Party whip, which, Jenkins asserted, was deliberately kept secret from Chamberlain, even after he became the Party leader in the Commons in 1892.[33] This indicated that Liberal Unionism was itself not a particularly cohesive force, yet this particular issue has not been significantly addressed in any of the subsequent monographs or biographies. There has been no major study of the role of Lord Hartington (later 8th Duke of Devonshire), the moderates' leader, since 1911,[34] and the biographies of important Liberal Unionists such as Henry James,[35] George Goschen,[36] W. S. Caine[37] and Jesse Collings[38] are equally dated. Perhaps the only major study of Liberal Unionism ever published is M. C. Hurst's extremely detailed narrative of the 'Round Table' conference of 1887, which nearly brought the radical Unionists back into the Gladstonian Party. Whilst an impressive piece of historical reconstruction, the study failed to connect the events to the wider position of the Liberal Unionists in relation to the other political parties or of the MPs concerned to their constituents and local party officials.[39] The most recent studies of grass-roots Unionism fail to see the Liberal Unionists as anything more than an adjunct of the Conservatives with no distinct, separate identity of their own. Matthew Roberts even described Chamberlain's Birmingham as 'a bastion of Conservatism.'[40] Like the elephant in the room, the true nature of the Liberal secession of 1886 has been overlooked and the motives of the electorate in ending the period of Liberal dominance have been neglected.

The only study to have considered the Liberal Unionists as a genuine political grouping, was, if not dismissive, certainly disdainful. Cooke and Vincent saw the Liberal Unionist Party as largely neglected by its own leaders and composed of 'unimportant members of the leisured class,' who 'needed the crisis [of 1886] more than the crisis needed them' and who displayed all the features of the 'pathology of political virginity.' They may have seemed influential, largely due to their support from the press in general and *The Times* in particular, but in reality they had little influence over both high politics and the general public, occupying instead 'a closed system of self co-opting articulateness.'[41]

W. C. Lubenow's study of the Home Rule crisis, published in 1988, suggested that the Party was a more complex entity than Cooke and Vincent concluded. By closely analysing the social background of the Unionist lobby on 8 June 1886, he proved that class was not 'the cause or the explanation of political behaviour.'[42] He was the first to suggest that the initial split was chiefly on principle and focused on the particular issue of the Union, even though he said little of the varied motivations of the individual MPs. This work led to a re-evaluation of Liberalism as a Party of conflicting and disputing ideologies which had already suffered less serious splits in 1866, 1873, 1881 and 1882. Lubenow revisited the Party in 2010 in the last chapters of his otherwise excellent study of political culture in the nineteenth century. He offered a number of interesting insights into the Party's merger with the Conservatives in 1912, but failed to offer any new understanding of the Party other than from perspective of Parliament and clubland.[43] Similarly, in 2007 Eugenio Biagini produced a useful chapter on the position of the radical Unionists which proposed some plausible explanations of Chamberlain's motivation, as well as useful descriptions of the role of Ulster Liberals such as Isabella Tod and T. W. Russell, but it did little to explain the long-term electoral success of the Party as a whole.[44]

There have been a number of influential journal articles on the Liberal Unionists, none of which have ever been developed into full historical monographs. The ideology of the Liberal Unionist leaders was investigated further by T. A. Jenkins, who perceived a growing closeness developing between Chamberlain and Hartington in 1886.[45] Peter Davis's article investigated Liberal Unionist influence on the second Salisbury administration over the particular issue of Ireland and, perhaps unsurprisingly, found that the Party's Liberalism in this area soon proved difficult to sustain.[46] In contrast to the bulk of studies of Conservatism, John D. Fair's statistical analysis of the 'cohesiveness' of parliamentary voting between the Liberal and Conservative Unionists revealed that there continued to be distinctive differences of political behaviour on issues other than Irish Home Rule between those who agreed the 1886 electoral 'compact'.[47] Gregory Phillips also questioned Goodman's 'half-way house' thesis in his study of the Liberal Unionist peers. Rather than rushing into 'fusion' with the Conservatives, his study of the voting patterns of the Unionist peers led him to conclude that 'they formed a separate political unit in the House of Lords, not merely a nominal grouping of Tories-in-all-but-name.'[48] G. R. Searle was the first to suggest that Liberal Unionism was more than a 'transit camp' for those en-route to the Conservative Party. He argued that 'Liberal Unionism retained a quite strong identity of its own … especially … in Scotland.'[49] Despite the admirable focus on the Liberal Unionists as a party, almost all these studies concentrated either on the Party's leadership (based on their surviving correspondence) or the events at Westminster (based on parliamentary speeches and voting behaviour). Although a study of Conservatism, Jon Lawrence's examination of Wolverhampton politics provided an alternative approach to the traditional analysis, by suggesting that in the late nineteenth century the influence of local circumstances, publications and personalities could be just as effective in explaining the outcomes of regional political upheavals as the national influences of Westminster, Fleet Street and the clubs of Mayfair.[50] Lawrence's further study of political campaigns and local party activity in this period suggested that two aspects of the traditional approach to Victorian politics need to be challenged. Firstly, the primacy of ideology as a motivation for political action needs to be fully tested as religion, gender and national and local identity all played a crucial role in explaining political behaviour. Secondly, the assumption that political parties were monolithic, capable of centrally organising their activists and party members to obey the diktat of the caucus, is particularly untenable and based on ahistoric readings of nineteenth-century politics from late twentieth-century perspectives.[51]

Recently, in the wake of Lawrence's study, a few important new approaches to research into this aspect of the period have been added. In a penetrating case study of Paisley between 1886 and 1910, Catriona MacDonald has argued for the crucial importance of traditions within political communities. She concluded that the Liberal Unionist principles of constitutionalism and abhorrence of class-based politics were based on earlier radical commitments.[52] James Moore's studies of the failure of Liberal Unionism in Manchester and Leicester suggested that the appeal of Unionism was based on the attitudes of crucial local leaders and that the Party could not prosper without influential patronage.[53] He pointed out that, where no such leadership existed, the Liberal Unionists were frequently 'generals without an army', a conclusion partly borne out by my own research in Warwick and Leamington.[54] Graham Goodlad similarly suggested that the creation of local Liberal Unionist Associations depended upon 'local men prepared to take the initiative.'[55] Although rather limited in its scope, Catriona Burness's recent study of Unionism in Scotland clearly indicated that local factors must be examined to investigate why some pockets of Liberal Unionism continued to flourish into the twentieth century, while others had a more fleeting popularity, losing their grip on whole regions as early as 1892.[56]

In her detailed study of the Scottish press, Burness continued the excellent work begun by Stephen Koss, whose unmatched account of the role of the political press in Britain did much to reveal the relationship between the public appearance of a harmonious Unionist alliance and the private in-fighting and mutual mistrust.[57] Victoria Barbery, in a highly detailed and reflective thesis, attempted to place the Liberal Unionists of Lancashire into their local context, in particular relying heavily on the press coverage of the experiences of Henry James in Bury. A student of Jon Lawrence, she also considered that the impact of national politics took a long time to affect the behaviour of associations and candidates in individual seats. Perhaps uniquely, she regarded Liberal Unionism as 'a vibrant and independent movement', at least in Bury.[58]

My own work has sought to explore the strains in the relationship between the Liberal and Conservative Unionists following the accession of Chamberlain as leader of the Liberal Unionists in the Commons in 1892.[59] In particular, I investigated Chamberlain's motives for joining Salisbury's Cabinet in the subordinate position of Colonial Secretary, having been offered the posts of Chancellor of the Exchequer or Home Secretary. The reason for this decision lay, I felt, in the deep suspicion that some senior Conservatives and many grass-roots activists still felt for Chamberlain and his radical Unionists, which was manifested during the 1895 candidature dispute in the united borough of Warwick and Leamington Spa.[60] It was clear that the original 'compact' agreed between Liberal Unionists and the Conservative leadership in 1886 had not been an entirely equal arrangement and that it did not reflect the distribution of forces within Liberal Unionism. It is therefore possible to explore the nature of Liberal Unionism in terms of local, as well as national, political discourse, psephological behaviour and the political material culture that was evolving in this period, rather than simply in terms of monolithic ideologies, as Marsh, Bentley, Green and most others have suggested.[61] As Miles Taylor recently commented, the advent of the 'New Political History' has meant that 'the life has gone out of traditional historical debates' such as that surrounding the Liberal schism of 1886.[62] I feel that an investigation of the origins, identity, organisation and electoral performance of the Liberal Unionist Party and of the relations between the two branches of Unionism, may well help to refute, for once and for all, the sociological view of the Party as one born entirely out of class fear which was swiftly and effortlessly absorbed into the Conservatives after 1895.[63] I do not intend to offer a mere description of the Liberal Unionists, however. Lawrence has suggested that local politics merely 'played their part in cementing political allegiance – but we cannot hope to understand the genesis of political allegiance by focusing on such factors.'[64] This book seeks to go further than this and to demonstrate just how important local identity, regional difference and contrasting concepts of national character were in the emergence, the unexpected thriving and the sudden disappearance of Liberal Unionism. I intend to demonstrate that the patchwork nature of the political culture of late nineteenth-century Britain helped to foster a highly unusual political party which eschewed political office for nine years and then collapsed in a battle between local factions and its own leaders. This study will thus illustrate the tension in this much neglected period between an increasingly monolithic party political structure and a culture of civic behaviour and public character which emphasised an individual's higher duty to one's conscience. It will not seek to conjecture as to whether a 'national politics' had emerged by 1912, but it will offer some reflections on the persistence of principle and regional identity as the British polity sought to tame the impulses of a mass electorate.

As well as the papers and memoirs of the chief personae of the Unionist Parties, I have used the records of local Liberal Unionist and Conservative Associations and the official publications and Party journals of all branches of Unionism, in which there is frequent reference to the struggles for influence and independence of both individuals and parties. In those constitutions where tensions did become public, the local press, diligent and detailed in their investigation of local political activity, are a valuable source of evidence, especially as the editorial influence on such reports is frequently breathtakingly candid. *The Times*, perhaps at its most partisan during the Home Rule crisis, is a valuable source of information on the progress of the new Party.[65] *Punch*, also at the height of its influence, was frequently indiscreet in its revelations of dissension among Unionists. A number of other journals, both national and provincial, were consistently used by Liberals and Conservatives to voice their positions on the emergence and decline of this third force in British politics,[66] most significantly in 1905 when the death of the Party was announced.[67] For examples of local Party organisation, the bulk of those papers that survive (outside Scotland at least) date from the years 1895 to 1912, so the study of the Party's organisation will extend beyond the formation of the Unionist government of 1895 in order to make use of these.

This book will attempt to understand those politicians who opposed the political mission of William Gladstone and frustrated his ambitions for a lasting constitutional settlement for Great Britain until long after his death. Gladstone was deeply offended by the Liberal Unionists, referring to them as 'that unhappy, unfortunate, ill-starred abortion of a party.'[68] In less vindictive mode, he accused them of a fatal weakness for any new party: 'I do not admit that that they are a political party in the country. I will tell you what they are. They are officers without an army, they are clergymen without a church.'[69] There must have been some truth in this allegation as, during the crisis caused by the resignation of Randolph Churchill in December 1886, Alfred Milner wrote to his chief, George Goschen, advising him to take Churchill's place as Chancellor, 'I remain impenitently of the opinion, of deep conviction rather, that your place is with the army that wants a leader, rather than with the leaders who want an army.'[70] Having attended the first conference of the Liberal Unionists earlier that month, one of the many intellectual adherents of the new Party, Henry Sidgwick, noted that although the conference was 'a decided success ... we were like a regiment of officers without common soldiers, and with little prospect of finding any "rank and file."'[71] Clearly one of the Party's priorities if it was to survive beyond a single parliament would be to find an electorate willing to support it.

Secondly, the question arises as to whether the Liberal Unionists were genuinely Liberal. *Punch's* parliamentary satirist, 'Toby' (Henry Lucy) reckoned there was only one true Liberal Unionist, Leonard Courtney, MP for Bodmin, 'ever in a party of one',[72] who was eventually forced by his constituents to retire in 1899 due to his opposition to the Boer War. Alfred Hopkinson was a little more generous, believing there to have been three true apostles:

> There were three of us who used to tell each other that we really represented the pure Liberal Unionist faith: the late Lewis Fry of Bristol, J. W. Wilson and myself. It is worthwhile noting that the first two came of Quaker families and had some of the characteristics of political outlook which were probably due to that origin, and that the third, in his early days had had a Quaker governess and been to a Quaker school.[73]

Liberal Unionism was for many a position of political compromise, forced on them by the competing demands of support for reforming policies and free trade economics and an opposition to Gladstone's policy and method of introducing Home Rule for Ireland. Not surprisingly, as Liberals, many found it hard when forced to support Conservative policies and so retired from politics as soon as they were able or returned to the Liberal Party. For the others, some willingly renounced their Liberal values, as in the case of George Goschen, who eventually joined the Carlton Club in 1893, and who swiftly 'had become so "moderate" that a political microscope was necessary to distinguish themselves from Conservatives born and bred.'[74] However, Goschen was the only leading Liberal Unionist to join the Tories in the first seventeen years of the Party's history. Even if they voted for the Conservative government against their former colleagues, Hartington's Party stood as Liberals. With varying degrees of enthusiasm, they attempted to use their position as progressive allies of the Conservatives, to persuade the senior partner in the 'compact' (as the electoral alliance was known) to carry out Liberal reforms in areas such as education, land purchase, local government and protection for working people. Of course, indirect influence was no guarantee of ultimate success. Chamberlain, the greatest source of such persuasion, reckoned that he only succeeded on one in every four occasions he tried to introduce legislation. Unsurprisingly therefore, such attempts to influence policy are frequently over-looked or dismissed by the historians of Conservatism and Liberalism and their influence needs to be re-assessed in order to understand the relative success and failure of the two main parties in the early decades of the twentieth century.

The challenge of establishing a new political party is, of course, extremely revealing for those who wish to understand the political culture of late Victorian Britain. As an article in the Party newspaper exhorted its members in May 1887, passive support was no longer enough and 'it is the plain duty of every man possessing [Liberal Unionist] opinions to assist in defeating the wrong, and in speeding the triumph of the right. Every one can do something. A silent vote is of great service, but it is not enough.' The article went on to encourage membership of associations, canvassing of friends and acquaintances, distribution of literature and (rather self-servingly), 'spreading the circulation of the *Liberal Unionist*, a paper which gives expression to the best thoughts of the best men of the Party.'[75] Such an approach, motivated by a concept of duty that implied membership of an elite patrician group and which presumed membership of a certain professional or kinship group, appears wildly misjudged for the new politics of the period. The failure to adapt to the changing needs of an emergent democracy was almost a badge of honour among some Liberal Unionists. The Party also trumpeted the sacrifice of its leaders in jeopardising their political careers for the protection of the Union. No other political party can have said to have contained a man who turned down the premiership three times (Lord Hartington), a man who refused the Home Secretaryship (Sir Henry James) and a man who preferred to be Colonial Secretary rather than Chancellor of the Exchequer (Joseph Chamberlain). But in this constant self-sacrifice lies the origins and the ideology of Liberal Unionism, as well as the causes of its political failure.

This study therefore attempts to identify the varying ideological strands of Liberal Unionism and to explain how these were gradually recast into a national political language and forms of behaviour which, before the 1895 Unionist coalition, owed precious little to the Conservative ideology of Salisbury and Arthur Balfour. Secondly, the book addresses the period of Unionist alliance between 1886 and the Party's acceptance of office in 1895 in Salisbury's Unionist coalition administration. It intends to explore the Liberal Unionists' peculiar difficulties as an opposition party between 1886 and 1892 who largely supported the Tory government and then as an opposition who sat alongside the Tories from 1892 to 1895. As a minority group, the Party sought to influence the policy of others (chiefly the Conservatives), whilst simultaneously seeking to portray themselves as a party committed to a distinct set of principles. This created unique challenges which the Party had managed successfully to overcome by 1895, but which provoked a hostile reaction from their own allies that would prove the Party's downfall.

It is often assumed that the Party declined as an independent force after 1895 and this study offers evidence that the inactivity of the Party organisation and its electoral machine was a deliberate act by the Party's national leaders and resisted by its grass roots. It therefore extends the study of the Party's organisation and its appeal to the electorate to 1903 to establish the ways in which Liberal Unionism remained (in some regions at least) a vibrant political culture, with considerable activism and cross-class electoral support. By contrast, after the 1903–6 tariff reform campaign, it was so fundamentally divided that it only avoided electoral oblivion by a whisker in 1906 and became a branch of the Conservatives in all but name after Chamberlain's debilitating stroke of that year. That it took until 1912 for the Party to merge with the Conservatives speaks more of the lack of leadership among the Conservatives in this period and the confusion caused by the challenges of Lloyd George's aggressive 'peers vs the people' campaign of 1909 to 1912, than it does of any desire for independence on the part of the few remaining Liberal Unionists. That is not to say that individual MPs and, as in the case of Birmingham, individual areas, did not continue to identify themselves as Liberal Unionist, at least until the Second World War, when the Chamberlain family's dominance of the second city was finally broken.[76]

CHAPTER 1

'DAGON MUST BE THROWN DOWN': THE ORIGINS OF THE LIBERAL UNIONIST PARTY

Gerald Goodman first claimed that 'Liberal Unionism in its origins was a movement of political leadership. Uninstructed by the electorate, the Whig leaders refused to accept Gladstone's Home Rule Bill; in company with a section of radicalism, defeated it in parliament; and then, as an independent political party allied with the Conservatives, won a general election.'[1] Thirty years later, W. C. Lubenow agreed, 'policy on Ireland, like other policy, had its origins at Westminster, not in constituency pressure. Therefore it is in the parliamentary Liberal Party in 1886 that the origins of the great separation in the Party are to be found.'[2] Cooke and Vincent similarly explain the crisis entirely in terms of activity in the parliamentary lobbies.[3] This chapter seeks to prove that while the debate was centred on Westminster, it was influenced by electoral concerns and organised political support in the localities. Secondly, while the split certainly took place in Westminster, it would never have developed into a full political movement without strong bases of support in the constituencies and would have remained a parliamentary rebellion. The split was, as Peter Ghosh puts it, 'a party issue' in which rival interpretations of the Liberal tradition were mobilised to justify the parliamentary behaviour of the combatants, but it was not one solely confined to Westminster in either its conception or its realisation.[4]

The 'Skeleton' and the Queen

The origin of the Liberal Unionist Party has conventionally been seen as the issuing of the 'Hawarden Kite' simultaneously in the *Standard* and the *Leeds Mercury* in December 1885. The shock and surprise caused by this event, the 'earthquake and eclipse' as J. L. Garvin has it, goes some way to explaining the nature of the opposition that emerged once Gladstone's commitment to Home Rule was confirmed.[5] Gladstone's sudden public conversion to Home Rule in December 1885 actually came from his long-term, traditionally Liberal attitude to national self-determination. He had been troubled by his own government's actions in Egypt in 1882 and later in Sudan.[6] By adopting a policy of Home Rule while in opposition, he felt he was returning to a truer, more moral form of Liberalism after the compromises of his second administration.[7] He had not, however, shared his moral struggle with his Cabinet colleagues, many of whom consequently interpreted the Liberal Party's duty towards Ireland (and the wider Empire) in a very different fashion, although he was supported by Earl Spencer who had, as Lord Lieutenant in Ireland, implemented a coercive regime from 1882 to 1885.[8]

On the other hand, the support that Parnell had offered to the Conservatives in the general election of 1885 meant, in Angus Hawkins' memorable phrase, that 'an extraordinary fluidity prevailed over the political situation.'[9] In these circumstances, with Churchill and Carnarvon wooing Parnell, while Chamberlain floated his central board scheme, some type of political reorientation seemed inevitable. The only question was the extent and origin of the alteration.

The splits within the Liberal Party that had been problematic before 1886 became intolerable, once the election result of December 1885, which gave the balance of power to the Nationalists, became known. Lord Derby wrote in his diary:

> The state of things I imagine to be this – Gladstone has no time to spare and wants to get back to Downing St. The Whigs or moderate section, incline in that direction, but with less eagerness. On the other hand, the Radicals, Chamberlain and co., are not in a hurry. They had rather wait to get rid of Gladstone, Granville and the Whig party in general, thinking themselves strong enough to form a purely Radical cabinet.[10]

Most Liberals felt ambivalent about Gladstone's method of announcing the new policy, even if they supported the principle. Moreover, the announcement had been so unexpected that those who felt inclined to resist this strategy took a long time to organise their forces as they needed to assess the policy itself and the best cause of affecting, adjusting or aborting it.[11] Secondly, Liberals of all hues needed time to assess the attitudes of their followers. Even Chamberlain, who might have been expected to have led the revolt openly, given his role as the alternative figurehead of Liberalism between 1880 and 1885, chose to bide his time and actually to join Gladstone's third Cabinet, while promoting his own alternative approach to the Irish problem.

If the Liberal Unionist movement was to be anything more than a refusal to vote for a particular measure by disgruntled back-benchers, it needed a leader of national reputation and unquestioned political seniority around whom dissenting Liberals could coalesce. Although Hartington's position as this leader may seem to be inevitable in light of his early denunciation of the policy of Home Rule at Waterfoot on 29 August 1885,[12] he had, at this point, been more inclined to consider resignation and retirement from politics.[13] In November he expressed the same intention to Gladstone himself. 'More than ever, it would be the happiest moment of my life if I could see ... the possibility of my giving up any further part in politics.' On this occasion he revealed the cause for his feelings, asking Gladstone to take a 'strong and decided line against the Radicals' to prevent a 'state of disruption' once the G.O.M. retired.[14] As late as January 1886 he had expressed to Derby a willingness to allow an Irish Parliament, as long as the Westminster Parliament had the power to overrule when it chose. As Derby noted in his diary, 'in short he would restore the Irish parliament as it was before Grattan and 1780.'[15] It was, however, precisely this flex- ibility and willingness to consider (if not necessarily endorse) reform on its merits, combined with a proven competence in high office, that made this quintessentially Whig figure able to act as a figurehead for radicals as well as moderates.

The task of persuading Hartington to take on the task of leadership of a rebellion fell to George Goschen, described by Cooke and Vincent as 'the creative manipulator.'[16] In September 1885, while Hartington was still regarded as Chamberlain's chief opponent in the battle to succeed Gladstone, and Chamberlain and John Morley were still close radical allies, Morley informed Chamberlain of Goschen's influence. 'I suspect from one or two casual phrases that Goschen is working Hartington's "sourdement."'[17] The genesis of the Liberal Unionist Party was written when Chamberlain, for quite different reasons to Hartington, also came out against Home Rule at Warrington on 9 September.[18] Chamberlain regarded Ireland as an unneces- sary distraction from the 'unauthorised programme' of reform, but Gladstone had by this point made it clear both in public and in private to those such as Lord Derby, that 'his demand that the party shall adopt his programme [was] unreasonable.'[19] As Derby noted himself in January 1886:

> I strongly suspect that Chamberlain's attitude is not solely due to dislike of Home Rule, or fear of what the constituencies may say; but that he does not wish to come into office again under circumstances where his section of the party will be, as he thinks, inadequately represented.[20]

Goschen himself was unable to take on the role of leader for, as Mary Jeune put it, 'though in earlier life he had joined the Liberal party, I think his sympathies were always on the other side.'[21] Goschen was also unable to lead the Party due to his distance from the Liberals since 1874 and because of his unstinting opposition to any aspect of Chamberlain's radicalism.[22] As an indication of his lack of Liberalism, Goschen was one of the very few Liberals (outside Scotland) willing to attend meetings organised by the Orange Lodge-dominated Irish Loyal and Patriotic Union.[23] In his more expressive moments, Goschen foresaw the breaking up of the Liberal Party and a situation emerging where 'I should be able to act and come forward in defence of Moderate Liberalism, as one of the joint heirs of Gladstone and his "sound economic school" instead of as malcontent and outsider', but he was deluding himself.[24] As Northbrook noted to Hartington when Goschen was being considered as Randolph Churchill's replacement as Chancellor in January 1887, 'Goschen has always been in some respects something of a Conservative' and as far as the radicals in the Party were concerned, Goschen was hardly considered a Liberal at all.[25]

If Morley had discounted Goschen's ability to persuade Hartington, this was because he was unaware of the force behind Goschen's influence. Queen Victoria was united with Goschen in her suspicion of Gladstone who she regarded as 'a half-mad ... ridiculous old man' and she had refused to open Parliament throughout Gladstone's second administration.[26] She now bombarded Goschen with letters demanding that he persuade Hartington to act decisively.[27] 'You must keep Lord Hartington up to the mark and not let him slide back (as so often before) into following Mr Gladstone and trying to keep the party together.'[28] Victoria knew both Hartington and Gladstone well enough for this to be a genuine concern. Cooke and Vincent concur, believing the two figures not to have fallen out over Home Rule until late in March 1886.[29] This is usually explained as due to Gladstone's deliberate decision to keep the policy hidden, both in essence before the 'Hawarden Kite' and in detail afterwards. As late as 16 December 1885, Hartington was writing to ask Gladstone to respond to the rumours in 'all the newspapers ... about the existence of some plan which you have in preparation' and complaining that 'I am entirely ignorant of what may be going on.'[30] Gladstone cannot be accused of dissembling on this occasion, for he immediately responded and told Hartington that 'I consider that Ireland has now spoken' and that as a consequence an effort should be made 'to meet the demands for the management by an Irish legislative body of Irish as opposed to Imperial affairs.'[31] Hartington's reply was brusque, simply stating that he was 'unable to share your [Gladstone's] opinions,' but he failed to begin to prepare any resistance. Goschen unknowingly confirmed Hartington's apathetic reaction and revealed that he himself was given no indication of the thunderbolt about to be hurled from Hawarden, writing to Albert Grey on 20 December 1885, 'I saw Hartington yesterday. He was not combative at all.'[32]

Once the 'Harwarden Kite' was flown by Herbert Gladstone, Victoria's partisan attitude became clearer. She encouraged Goschen to appeal to 'moderate, loyal and patriotic men' and urged him to consider 'an amalgamation or rather juncture of Conservatives and Whigs.'[33] She never forgave the Nationalists for their refusal to participate in the Prince of Wales' Irish tour of April 1885, when he had been abused and threatened.[34] Salisbury now encouraged her as well, describing Home Rule to her as 'a concession to the forces of disorder' and 'a betrayal of the Loyalists of Ulster.'[35] Goschen was clearly more determined than ever to enforce the Royal Will, as he revealed in a letter to his wife in January: 'I spoke to Hartington in the strongest terms. I said it would be disastrous if he disappointed the Liberals in giving then a lead against Home Rule; that we must not think of the party.'[36] Hartington also received encouragement from Edward Watkin, maverick Liberal MP for Hythe, who urged him to form an alliance with Salisbury, with the rousing (if rather self-serving) exhortation, 'while you will have saved your country, you will be Prime Minister by the summer.'[37] Edward Heneage, Watkin's bitter business rival, began to act as go-between for Hartington and the radical Unionists, informing the Marquess in January that Chamberlain would support him.[38] Albert Grey, under Goschen's direction, began to sound out Liberal MPs who might form a faction to oppose Home Rule, but, as he wrote to his uncle, 'we are drifting on a flood tide to Home Rule. I am at present engaged in trying to work up a few Liberal M.P.s to get up and make a declaration against Home Rule but there is a curious timidity.'[39] He therefore made the first attempt to persuade Hartington through force of numbers, writing of '100 signatures' to a 'memorial' to persuade Gladstone to abandon the principle of Home Rule.[40] He was clearly concerned as he wrote to his uncle five days later, 'I should not be very much surprised if he [Hartington] agrees to serve under Gladstone.'[41]

There was also the possibility that the campaign against Home Rule might become associated with the landowning elite in Ireland, or at least fall into the hands of the Conservatives. On 9 January, Colonel Edward Saunderson, a former Liberal MP, and the Duke of Abercorn, a leading Irish landowner, refounded the Irish Loyal and Patriotic Union and organised a series of cross-party demonstrations in favour of the Union.[42] The first of these was at Chester on 29 January 1886, when Tories, Whigs and radicals condemned Home Rule. He liaised with the Duke of Westminster to find 'how far the Whigs will go with us' – the result had been a united platform and the meeting was deemed 'a great success.'[43] Ponsonby, on the Queen's behalf, began floating a scheme to keep Gladstone from office, in which Salisbury would resign the premiership, but remain Foreign Secretary, while Hartington took over at No. 10. Derby described this as 'eccentric' and suggested that Salisbury was behind it, in order to separate Hartington and Chamberlain.[44] Hartington responded to all this advice, but true to form, he failed to announce his decision to take the lead immediately. On 25 January, he voted with Salisbury's government against a radical amendment to introduce the 'three f's' for land leases into Great Britain, according to Goschen's biographer 'without having let anyone know what he was going to do.'[45] Hartington's 'faithful and useful adherent',[46] Henry James, began to exert his influence over the moderate Liberals, requesting that they vote with the Government and a further eighteen Liberals entered the government lobby on the following day.[47] That the amendment was Jesse Collings' demand for allotments probably added strength to Hartington's determination to act, as in doing so he could not only oppose Gladstone's scheme but also Chamberlain's radical ambitions. The rest of the Liberals, not party to Hartington's decision to act, merely regarded this as a Whig protest and voted for the amendment, defeating Salisbury's government and pushing the crisis within the Liberal Party into the open.

Once the possibility of a Home Rule Bill under Gladstone became a reality, however, individuals were faced with a more clear-cut dilemma. On 27 January, James went to Devonshire House to discuss whether Hartington should join such a ministry. Typically, Hartington now seemed unsure.[48] By 30 January, however, Hartington decided not to accept Gladstone's offer and James refused to join as well.[49] The Marquis reported to his father, 'I have not promised him any support, but I think that now the thing has gone so far he thought to have a fair trial and let the countryside see what he has really to propose.'[50] He still refused to lead an open opposition to Gladstone's Irish policy, on the grounds that, as he told James:

> I am not all sure that it is not the best thing to give a favourable condemnation to Mr Gladstone's schemes. I do not like HR and never

shall – but as things are now, if I oppose Mr Gladstone and am called on for an alternative policy I have not got one except the bayonet and I do not think the Liberal Party will stand that.[51]

And so, as Cooke and Vincent put it, 'Hartington was led by his followers, and his followers were led by Goschen.'[52] Goschen formed a moderate faction discrete from Hartington's Whigs, compromising Alexander Craig Sellar, Arthur Elliot, Albert Grey, Viscount Ebrington, Viscount Lymington and Sir John Lubbock with support from Henry Brand and Leonard Courtney.[53] Early in 1886 this group began to contact those who might be able to organise an alternative Liberal campaign at a grass-roots level. The best example of this is in a February letter from Albert Grey to James Parker Smith, an active Liberal in Glasgow. Grey asked him to compile two lists:

> (1) A list of Liberals who you think wd. join a sound Liberal association
> (2) A list of fighting Whigs who wd be glad to contest a constituency at the next G. E. against a Radical if the Tories step aside & allow the duel to be fought out.[54]

On 2 February Goschen began to sound out Salisbury on the possibility of an electoral truce. While he was sympathetic, Salisbury would not commit himself unless there was some guarantee that the split was permanent and that the rebels would not simply rejoin the Liberal Party once their seats were won.[55]

The first attempts were also made to define the relative positions of MPs, as Ebrington revealed in a letter written to persuade Hartington to act on 1 March 1886. Based on 159 election addresses of English, Welsh and Scottish Liberal MPs, it identified that thirteen MPs, including Hartington, had declared themselves opposed to a separate parliament for Ireland. Intriguingly, while some of these figures became leading members of the Liberal Unionist Party, such as Elliot, Courtney and the banker Michael Biddulph, many of these finally supported the Bill in June 1886. Sixty-six MPs had not mentioned the Irish Question at all, including many of the radicals, such as Bright, Chamberlain and Collings, but some future Liberal Unionists such as Lewis Fry, John Corbett and Joseph Powell Williams had been among twenty-three MPs who had promised 'to give the Irish as much local government as ourselves.' Some had been a little more circumspect, such as Heneage who had been among those who agreed to grant as much local government 'as is consistent with the unity of the Empire.' Only five MPs had openly advocated Home Rule (unsurprisingly, as the policy had not been seriously discussed by the Party or its leaders).[56] John Bright was contacted directly by James, but refused to commit himself.[57]

This was not very helpful to Goschen's group in identifying a body of MPs who were prepared to vote against a Home Rule bill. When faced with the offer of government position under a leader committed to a separate Irish legislature, a number of figures chose, purely from the bidding of their consciences, not to enter Gladstone's government. Craig Sellar refused the offer of the Surveyor-Generalship and Edmond Wodehouse, MP for Bath, refused the under-secretaryship for the Foreign Office.[58] As the Liberal Unionist Association (hereafter LUA) record for 1886 put it, 'it should be observed that the following Liberals who had generally hitherto worked in harmony with Mr Gladstone did not take office in the ministry viz: -

> Marquis of Hartington
> Lord Cowper
> Lord Northbrook
> Sir Henry James
> Mr Goschen
> Lord Selborne
> Duke of Argyll
> Lord Richard Grosvenor'[59]

Chamberlain and George Trevelyan joined the government, publicly stating that they made no commitment to Home Rule, but that they were willing to serve as long as the policy was to be one of 'inquiry and examination' of the various alternatives.[60] In that event, they reserved the right to resign. Chamberlain appeared willing to compromise with Parnell, however, publicly stating that 'I am convinced that it will be necessary to concede to the Irish people much more extended control of their own domestic business.'[61] Far more unexpected was the agreement of out-spoken opponents of Home Rule, such as Rosebery, Granville, Kimberley and Campbell-Bannerman. As *The Times*, now emerging as the chief mouthpiece for Liberal Unionism, commented acerbically, 'what faith can any longer be placed in English statesmen?'[62] The *Manchester Guardian* regarded the formation of such a broadly based government as a sign that no 'revolutionary' changes were envisaged by Gladstone.[63] Those closer to Westminster were less sure, as Wolmer wrote to his father in early February, 'the Government is a queer one in some ways. I cannot help strongly suspecting that they will fall to pieces when they begin to discuss Ireland.'[64] For those not asked to join the government, even more in the dark about Gladstone's intentions than the poorly informed Cabinet, there was a challenge over what statements to make in public at this time. Lubbock admitted to Derby that he was 'much perplexed as to what he shall say.' Derby could only advise him 'not to assume ... that the Government are going to give way to the Home Rulers ... but to maintain his intention to support the Union.'[65]

Hartington still refused to act as the moderates wished, despite numerous visits from Lubbock and Goschen.[66] Between January and March he repeatedly appeared willing to reach a compromise with Gladstone. He was perhaps persuaded by the strong performance of the Gladstonian ministers in their by-elections on appointment to the government. Only at the end of February did he agree to meet regularly with Goschen, Lubbock, James, Elliot, Brand and Wodehouse, but still refused to commit himself beyond this gesture and may simply have been attempting to prevent the moderate faction from being too outspoken too early.[67] He did meet with Salisbury on 2 March, who fished for an alliance between Conservatives and moderates, but, unlike Goschen, Hartington merely suggested a parliamentary alliance in order to defeat Home Rule.'[68] Lubbock began to host dinners with leading national and local figures on the radical side of the Party in late February and early March, whom the survey of election addresses had revealed were unsympathetic to Home Rule. These informal meetings help, in part, to explain the strong Cornish presence in the rebellion, as they included Ebrington, F. B. Mildmay and Courtney.

Image 1: *Judy* comments on the motives of Hartington's supporters for breaking with Gladstone. Note the use of 'Moderate Liberalism' rather than 'Whig'. *Judy*, 17 March 1886.

Chamberlain's 'frankness'

It was at this point that Chamberlain played his role in the creation of the Liberal Unionist Party. He resigned on 15 March, having finally realised that a scheme far closer to Parnell's than his own was being drafted, but Gladstone asked him not to reveal his resignation until 26 March in the hope of finding a compromise that he and Trevelyan could accept.[69] Chamberlain saw the opportunity to take a lead on the issue that would allow him to resurrect his claim to be an alternative leader to Hartington which seemed to have faded with the relative failure of the 'unauthorised programme' in the urban seats in 1885. Although the resignation is often explained as the result of Chamberlain's frustrated ambition,[70] the most recent biographer of A. V. Dicey suggests that Chamberlain may have been persuaded by revelations as to Parnell's character. Already chagrined by Parnell's abrupt rejection of his central board scheme, Chamberlain was apparently told by Dicey that 'Parnell was a liar and a traitor when he claimed that he only wanted Home Rule by constitutional means.'[71] Ford portrays Dicey's intervention as crucial in Chamberlain's journey from radicalism to Unionism, finally made decisive in March when a speech by W. E. H. Lecky, hitherto a favourite academic of the Nationalists, attacked the idea of a separate Parliament.[72] Chamberlain's policy was a dangerous one for himself, as Granville told Derby, 'he (C.) had not convinced the Caucus, thought he had lost control of that agency.'[73] On the other hand, he was rewarded with a panegyric in *The Times* that concluded that 'he will vindicate the faith of those who have discerned in his Radicalism a strong leaven of imperial instincts and patriotic spirit.'[74]

Chamberlain now began to discuss future action with his long-term opponents. On 22 March he met with Albert Grey and Balfour. Balfour wrote to his uncle, that 'Chamberlain talked with his usual "engaging frankness"' and that he got 'a better idea of the real Chamberlain' as a result. He reported that Chamberlain wanted to keep opposition free from the accusation that it was a 'Tory-Whig maneouvre' so that he could take his caucus in Birmingham with him. Chamberlain had been persuaded that his role was crucial as 'a Moderate Liberal' had told him that '"if you stand firm, 70 or 80 Moderate Liberals will vote against Gladstone."'[75] Gladstone had, of course, given Chamberlain two ideal opportunities for opposing Home Rule, without being accused of abandoning his principles. As the Home Rule Bill required the exclusion of Irish members (largely to remove the on-going issue of Irish obstruction in the Commons), yet still demanded that Ireland should pay £4,500,000 p.a. to Westminster, the radicals could argue that the principle of 'no taxation without representation' was breached by the Bill. Secondly, the land purchase measure which bought out the landowners of Ireland, was repugnant to them, as it rewarded those whose neglect and exploitation of their tenants had reduced Ireland to poverty and law-breaking.

On 22 March, James heard from Hartington that Chamberlain had also called upon him and encouraged him to form a new government if Gladstone resigned. Other aristocratic Liberals now urged Hartington to act to prevent Chamberlain seizing the initiative. The Dukes of Argyll, Bedford and Abercorn all wrote, promising to bring their influence and funds to Hartington's assistance if he acted now.[76] Queen Victoria wrote to Goschen, revealing not only her deep distrust of Chamberlain, but also her larger motive in opposing Home Rule. She disliked Chamberlain's involvement in the anti-Home Rule movement as 'the object to be attained for the safety of the country is a union with the Conservatives to put a check on revolutionary changes' and the Conservatives would not wish to form any alliance with 'Jack Cade.'[77]

Hartington had this one great advantage over Chamberlain, of course. As a former leader of the Liberal Party and an acknowledged moderate, Hartington could more easily build an alliance with the Conservatives, based on opposition to Home Rule without needing to articulate any clear alternative. As early as March, he was seen as the most likely next Prime Minister if Gladstone resigned after the anticipated defeat of the Home Rule Bill in the Commons.[78] Chamberlain, as a radical, had to offer some practical alternative to a separate legislature and, as he noted in his letter to Hartington of 3 April 1886, 'there must be some kind of legislative body or bodies in Ireland,' which was a position not shared by most moderates and almost all Conservatives.[79] James Bryce believed that 'Chamberlain could not work with Hartington and did not mean to' while Henry Sidgwick felt 'to me it seems that Chamberlain mistakes the situation and his own position.'[80]

Hartington still refused to reveal his position publicly, however, and was supported by others such as the Earl of Radnor who believed that it would be best to wait until the Bill was announced, otherwise Hartington would be accused of being prejudiced against all local government reform. Radnor's role in advising Hartington has been overshadowed by that of Goschen in most studies of the period, yet it was he who recommended a committee of consultation between the Conservatives and the Liberal Unionists to discuss tactics, a large public meeting in the west end of London and a series of further meetings across the country.[81] As a result, Salisbury wrote to Hartington in early April proposing 'conversations' on future tactics and thus began a correspondence that was to last until Salisbury's death.[82] Derby advised

Hartington to support a Conservative cabinet but to avoid a coalition, on the grounds that they 'were always unpopular and seldom lasted long.' Instead he recommended that Hartington should 'come to an understanding with Chamberlain.'[83] The course of future party composition and parliamentary tactics were beginning to take shape.

Goschen meanwhile continued to gather support in preparation for the revelation of the Home Rule Bill on 8 April. He called a breakfast meeting at Portland Place and invited Craig Sellar, Sir Rowland Blennerhassett, Sir John St. Aubyn, Grey, Lymington and Lord Arthur Russell. He sent his personal secretary, Alfred Milner, to gather opinion from beyond Hartington's circle, reporting the feelings of Scottish and Ulster Liberals and taking the views of such figures of Lord Rosebery and Lord Derby in mid-March.[84] The three figures who now emerged as the organisers of Liberal Unionist opinion were Milner, Albert Grey and Craig Sellar, all members of Goschen's moderate faction. As Milner later wrote, 'for the Liberal Unionist propaganda we slaved ourselves to shreds. We poured out pamphlets and leaflets. When we were all nearly dead we used to say to each other, "Never mind; go on. Dagon must be thrown down."'[85] There was some assistance from a couple of well-connected aristocrats. Lord Camperdown was 'active from the very beginning' and remained in London to help and Lord Monteagle 'rendered valuable assistance.'[86] Monteagle's assistance took the form of acting as an intermediary between Hartington and the Ulster Liberals, who were needing reassurance that they would receive support from senior figures in the Party if Gladstone's bill did amount to Home Rule for the whole of Ireland as an undifferentiated country.[87]

In these uncertain times, the public got some inkling of the crisis among Liberals in the by-election at Barrow-in-Furness. The official Liberal candidate was W. S. Caine, a leading advocate of the temperance movement but a known enemy of Parnell, so a second Liberal, a Mr Edmunds, was nominated by local Liberals loyal to Gladstone and announced he would fight against the traitor to Gladstone. Caine was perturbed, not only by Edmunds' candidature, but also by the refusal of the Party hierarchy to support him more fully. As he wrote to Chamberlain, 'MPs whom I have asked [for support] are stopped by the whips and I am and will be to the end, absolutely alone.'[88] By the following day, a meeting with Edmunds had confirmed his suspicions that some Liberal MPs and members of the Eighty Club had been behind the challenge: 'More than one front bench man is in it ... I fear Arnold Morley set the stone rolling.'[89]

Due to his known personal connection with Caine, Chamberlain clearly saw the by-election as a means of putting himself at the head of the emerging

Liberal Unionist movement, writing to the editor of the *Birmingham Daily Post*, 'it is an emphatic warning to the gentlemen who "sit on the fence".'[90] During the election Caine used the name 'stalwart' to describe those who questioned the new direction in Irish policy, to counter the Gladstonian label of 'dissentient.'[91] In the event the Conservative chief agent, Richard Middleton, possibly under the direction of Salisbury, paid off the Conservative candidate and Caine was returned with a comfortable majority. It was clear to Henry Sidgwick that 'Chamberlain is thoroughly aware that he must either crush Gladstone or be crushed.'[92] When the Home Rule Bill was introduced on 8 April, Chamberlain swiftly rose in the Commons to outline the radical Unionists' objections.

Image 2: *Punch*'s view of the meeting at Her Majesty's Theatre, 14 April 1886 with W. H. Smith, Goschen, Hartington, Salisbury and Rylands prominent. Although shown in the box, Chamberlain was not present. *Punch*, 24 April 1886.

The Debate Beyond Westminster

Not to be outdone, the moderate faction finally staged their joint public meeting with the Conservatives on 14 April, six days after Gladstone had finally revealed the details of the Home Rule Bill. Hartington finally committed himself to a policy of action outside Parliamentary opposition and attended the meeting, held at Her Majesty's Theatre in the Haymarket (later referred to as the 'Opera House meeting'). The presence of Salisbury and Hartington prompted one journalist to reach into classical metaphor: 'Agamemnon, King of men and Achilles, swift of foot, after many year of heart-gnawing strife, declared before the assembled Greeks that it must have been the darkness-haunting fury who had caused them to quarrel and that henceforth their wrath should cease.'[93] However, Hartington was clearly uncomfortable in the fervid atmosphere at the theatre, criticising the audience when they booed Gladstone's name. Such delicacy was lost on the press though and *Punch* depicted the meeting as an anti-Gladstone demonstration.[94] This impression was seemingly confirmed by the presence of Gladstone's harshest critic from the radicals, Peter Rylands, on the stage.[95]

Goschen had finally succeeded and the Queen was delighted: 'Organise as many such meetings, large and small all over England and Scotland as you can.'[96] Moderates still loyal to Gladstone were appalled by Goschen's successful manoeuvring, however, and sought to use the meeting to persuade others not to flirt with Salisbury. When Derby called a meeting of Liberal Unionist peers on 16 April at Camperdown's request, only forty-eight attended and fifteen sent apologies.[97] Harcourt tried to use the Opera House meeting to persuade Chamberlain not to join the rebellion, writing that 'nothing could have been more distressing to me in politics than to find myself politically separated from you.' He despaired of Hartington, however, believing he 'is past praying for since his operatic performance, and the skeleton [Goschen] has him fast in his arms.'[98] Liberals of every hue queued to pour opprobrium on Rylands' and Hartington's 'tactical mistake' in attending a Tory meeting.[99] Hartington refused to take part in such an open demonstration of co-operation again and other dissenting Liberals now refused to openly identify themselves for fear of alienating their own local Associations. Hartington received a far less positive response in his constituency than he had at Her Majesty's, as can be judged by the reaction to his speech to the Rossendale caucus:

> I desire to work, he said, not with our Tory opponents, but with men like Mr Chamberlain and Mr Trevelyan (groans) or like Mr Goschen or Sir Henry James (groans) in the Commons.

When Hartington sat down a trimming resolution was passed, which Hartington disassociated himself from. Eventually the Rossendale 300 deselected Hartington as their candidate by 138 to forty-five.[100]

The failure of the joint Unionist meeting did galvanise Hartington into organising a more strictly Liberal body to resist Home Rule. As Milner wrote to Phillip Gell on 18 April, 'we have at last constrained H. to be a little bit more business-like. He has appointed Brand, Grey and Craig Sellar as a Committee to organise our rebellion.'[101] Biddulph lent the Committee his office at 35 Spring Gardens. The choice of the honorary secretaries reveals the reluctance of the leading Liberals to be closely associated with the rebellion at this stage, however, as only Brand, Albert Grey, Craig Sellar and F. W. Maude were appointed.[102] As Milner commented to Gell in exasperation, 'characteristically – oh these Whigs – the first thing they are all going to do is to leave town.'[103] Any communication between the rebels and the Conservative leaders was thus left to inconspicuous figures such as Brand, who was in communication with the Conservative chief whip, Aretas Akers-Douglas, during April 1886.[104] The first indication of the reality of power relations in the Unionist alliance emerged, however, as the Liberal Unionist Committee prepared Evelyn Ashley to contest the by-election in Bradford that was held on 21 April, but Salisbury put pressure on Hartington to force them to withdraw him.[105] Brand was also given the task of persuading Chamberlain to join the Liberal Unionist Committee, writing to inform him of the change of tactics a week after the Opera House meeting:

> There is a desire prevalent to prevent the opposition [to Home Rule] from drifting towards coalition with the Conservatives and there is a general belief that any further action similar to that taken at the Opera House will be a mistake. If you should finally find it to be your duty to oppose the second reading of the Home Rule Bill, the support of your name will give great strength to the Committee.[106]

Milner reported to Goschen that Brand's overtures were accompanied by those of himself and Albert Grey. Although Chamberlain took his time in replying, he eventually declared his position. 'He will not join the Committee, but his letter to Maude is anything but unsympathetic.'[107]

Chamberlain had kept his distance from the moderates as he had still to secure support from his caucus in Birmingham. He met his divisional council on 21 April and defended his actions. He attacked the Land Bill unequivocally, but claimed that his opposition to the Government of Ireland Bill was conditional and based on the exclusion of the Irish members from Westminster.[108] He announced his willingness to support the Bill if his objections were addressed, but if they were not he still declared that he would neither join a 'cave' of rebels, nor enter an anti-Home Rule coalition.[109] Chamberlain's careful strategy succeeded and the meeting passed a vote of confidence in him by a huge majority. Then, however, a proposal was put to adjourn the meeting in order to consider the council's position on Home Rule. Chamberlain and Collings knew that this might be fatal as it would gradually become clear that no other council opposed Gladstone and so pressed for a decisive vote that night.[110] R. W. Dale, the influential radical Congregational minister, put forward a resolution committing the 'two thousand' to Chamberlain's position and it was carried overwhelmingly.[111]

Despite Milner's confidence, the difficulties that Chamberlain faced in retaining the confidence of the Birmingham caucus had led him to begin to negotiate with Gladstone via Henry Labouchere. He claimed that only the question of the retention of the Irish members and that of limitations on any new legislature in Dublin prevented a rapprochement.[112] However, by early May Chamberlain had realised that compromise would not be forthcoming and he made clear his position in a private letter to Charles Dilke:

> To satisfy others I have talked about conciliation and have consented to make advances but on the whole I would rather vote against the Bill than not and the retention of the Irish members is only with me the flag that covers other objections. I want to see [the] whole Bill recast and brought back to the National Councils proposals, with the changes justified by the altered political opinion.[113]

Chamberlain's prevarication was no doubt caused by the lack of presence of any high profile supporters in the Liberal Unionist Committee about which Milner continued to complain to Goschen:

> Maude is meeting with a serious but not surprising difficulty. He has received considerable number of letters ... the most important put the very pertinent question 'who are you?'... Men of any position don't care to co-operate, especially in invidious work of this sort, except with men of some standing.

Milner believed it was time for the leaders to put their heads above the parapet and begged Goschen to make a public statement or, better still, to secure Hartington's unequivocal support.[114] As a result of Maude's anonymity, Albert Grey emerged as the crucial figure in persuading wavering Liberals to oppose the G.O.M, describing himself as undertaking 'the duties of an amateur whip.'[115] Cooke and Vincent refer to him as the leading back-bench figure, '[he] was a Liberal Unionist *contra mundum*, when no one else was.'[116] Even one who was not convinced, Alfred Pease, acknowledged his ability: 'Albert Grey was one of the most irresistible and charming of men, with tact, temper, humour; he had a most happy disposition, and his cease-less efforts told on the young, for he was always young himself.'[117] Despite Liberal Unionism's reputation as a party of the old and the conservative, as Pease explained, Grey had succeeded in recruiting active supporters among the young. A. C. Corbett and Savile Crossley were only twenty-eight, and F. B. Mildmay was twenty-four. Milner was clearly active in canvassing sup-port, complaining that 'I have been writing letters till I am quite sick, and so has the indefatigable Gell.'[118] Goschen's role in the canvassing of prominent young moderates is difficult to identify, as he destroyed his papers, but he certainly wrote to one young man who was to become prominent in the Party and crucial in the alliance with the Conservatives, the Earl of Selborne's son, and Salisbury's son-in-law, Lord Wolmer, himself only twenty-six years old at this time. Goschen was quite prepared to use Hartington's name as the chief mover of the Committee as he attempted to persuade Wolmer to use his influence 'among the new members to see things in the same light as you do.'[119]

On 23 April, Milner set out a four-point plan of action to Goschen. A reg-ister was to be made of all the constituencies, with the names of local Liberal Unionists and all the particulars that could be gathered; separate lists were to be made of members who were sure to vote against the bill, members who were doubtful, and as much local influence as possible was to be exerted to strengthen the former and to turn the latter; a circular was to be sent out to correspondents asking them to both bring pressure to bear upon their repre-sentatives and to organise meetings; finally there had to be a literature cam-paign.[120] This latter strategy suffered a short-term delay as the printers could not be persuaded to work through the Easter holiday period. The main prob-lem was lack of facilities. They only had two rooms in Spring Gardens, with no space for committee meetings or greeting visitors. Basic reference works such as the *London Directory* and the *Red Book* had not been acquired and they had no map of the constituencies. There was no clerk employed in keeping records of Liberal Unionist subscribers and their constituency of residence. Milner was not without hope, as the Committee was about to go public and it was hoped that funds from supporters would then begin to arrive. 'We ought to have by the end of next week a really imposing list of names, and plenty of money.'[121] But he was clear: 'Altogether we need apparatus, and as we have the money we ought to get it at once. Do please ask for these things, and encourage our fitting ourselves out properly in every way.'[122] Goschen himself had apparently funded the Committee almost single-handedly until this point.

In revealing the short-term needs of the Committee, Milner highlighted the on-going dominance of the aristocratic elite in funding any political movement in Victorian Britain:

> Where are the Dukes with the long purses? They will never have another chance of asserting themselves politically if they mean to be walked over now. They can't simply stand aside now ... £80 to save an Empire!! You know I don't mean yourself ... But oh! these Whigs, these Whigs![123]

Despite Milner's accusations of 'want of go' on the part of the Whigs, the following day he was forced to report rather contritely to Goschen that his prudence had been justified as he now could report the support of Northbrook, Ribblesdale, Cowper, Fife, St Albans and Grafton, as well as ten MPs. He still champed at the bit, however. 'Where are Bedford, Westminster, Derby, Selborne, their names and their money?'[124] Derby wrote to allow his name to be added to the Committee on 28 April.[125]

If the Committee wished to be more than a mere Parliamentary rebellion, however, the battle needed to be joined outside Westminster. On 8 April, many newspapers, hitherto Liberal, announced their resistance to Home Rule. The *Scotsman* simply announced 'this will never do' and, despite pressure put on him, Charles Cooper refused to back down: 'if I was to be ostracised for acting conscientiously, ostracised I would be.'[126] Chamberlain was clearly concerned about the attitude of the press as he had taken a canvass of opinion before he met Balfour in March. As he reported, perhaps optimistically in order to convince the Conservatives of the Liberal Unionists' strength: 'the great bulk of the London newspapers – of course, I am talking of the Liberal newspapers, including *Reynolds's* and *Lloyd's*, are going against Home Rule but the majority of the country newspapers are evidently preparing to support Gladstone.'[127] This opinion appeared to be confirmed next month when Caine informed Chamberlain that 'all the London working men's weekly papers are with you strongly.'[128] Among the Liberal publications that supported the Unionist cause in 1886 were the *Daily Telegraph* (circulation c.220,000), the *Scotsman* (c.70,000), the *Glasgow Herald* (c.70,000), the *Aberdeen Free Press*, the *Inverness Courier,* the *Spectator*, the *Economist*, the *Observer*, the *Daily Chronicle* and the *Northern Whig*.[129] Among regional papers, the *Birmingham Daily Post*, of course, stayed loyal to Chamberlain, while the

Western Morning News did likewise for Hartington, but, in general, the provincial press was far less positive than the London media.[130] The *York Herald* provided one of the few northern Liberal Unionist mouthpieces, along with the *Tyneside Echo*. Robert Bird estimated that in Scotland, 'out of 79 newspapers: 22 were Liberal Unionist; 13 were Conservative; 29 were Gladstonian and 15 were neutral.'[131]

Now there were some guarantees of funds, local organisation was begun, as Gell revealed to Parker Smith:

> The Committee have just been in council about the Scotch prospects and Craig Sellar has strongly recommended that local committees shall be at once formed at Edinburgh, Glasgow and Inverness.[132]

Craig Sellar, MP for Partick, found a positive response when he visited his constituency and was very encouraged by his experience in Scotland.[133] He did face more problems with his Party organisation, as he found his caucus split over the issue.[134] Maude sent Parker Smith a list of west of Scotland Liberals who should be asked to join the Liberal Unionist Committee as well as a list of 'Liberals who it is believed can be influenced' with details of the size of the majorities of the latter group.[135] In due course, a West of Scotland branch of the Liberal Committee for the Maintenance of the Legislative Union between Great Britain and Ireland was founded on 10 May. Milner made it clear that the struggle for the Bill would be fought outside Westminster as he wrote to Goschen the night before the announcement of the Committee, 'we must set the constituencies in a blaze of dissension right and left and frighten the party men thoroughly as to the consequences of passing these measures.'[136] As he told Gell, the Committee intended to target those seats where the sitting Liberal MP had a small majority and to 'stir up agitation' among Unionist Liberals in order to force the MP to abstain or vote against the Home Rule Bill.[137]

At Westminster, Brand was recalled to London to write to the wavering Liberal MPs.[138] The chief problem at this late stage was the position of Hartington. The Committee were under no illusions as to the caution that Henry James was urging on his leader.[139] Goschen clearly overcame James's blandishments, for on Friday 30 April, the Liberal Committee for the Maintenance of the Legislative Union was announced to the press with Hartington as its President, Maude as secretary and the two bankers, Lubbock and Biddulph, as honorary treasurers.[140] The initial list of subscribers, as found on the only list extant, demonstrates that Brand's letters had clearly begun to have an impact, as there were forty-three named MPs. There were, in total, 461 officially declared members of the Committee, including

thirty-eight baronets, twenty lords, fourteen earls, five viscounts, four mar-
quises and five dukes (Argyll, Bedford, Grafton, St Albans and Westminster).
There were nine senior military signatories (including two admirals), eight
professors (including T. H. Huxley and J. R. Seeley), sixteen clergymen and
six Queen's Counsels, as well as such prominent individuals as the Dean
of Gloucester Cathedral, the former Surgeon General, James Mouat, the
President of Corpus Christi College, Oxford and the German revolutionary,
Karl Blind.[141] This list was later described as containing 'a large proportion of
whom were well known for their service to the Liberal Party.'[142] One should
not underestimate this list as merely reflecting the views of the old-fashioned,
the antiquated or the aristocratic. The views of elite groups still carried huge
weight in all sections of society, partly as they were well reported, but mainly
due to their influence in setting the moral, cultural and ethical standards of
the age. As Jeune commented, 'the Liberal Party lost a great deal more than
political support by the rupture, for the Duke of Westminster's defection was
followed by many other rich and important people.'[143]

Hartington chose to launch the campaign against the Home Rule Bill
in the area that had been most suspicious of radicalism, east Scotland. As
Goschen had his seat in Edinburgh, the two Liberal leaders first publicly
denounced Gladstone's policy at a large public meeting in the Music Hall in
George Street on the same day that the Committee went public. Supported
by the Marquis of Tweedale and the Earl of Stair, the Scottish aspect of the
rebellion seemed considerable. Arthur Elliot, John Wilson, William Jacks,
Ernest Noel, John Ramsay were all present on the platform and six other
Scottish MPs sent letters of support.[144]

The Defeat of the Bill

Chamberlain, in a letter to Labouchere, estimated that 111 Liberal MPs
now opposed the Government of Ireland Bill and that fifty-nine had publicly committed themselves to vote against it.[145] By 2 May, he could inform
Harcourt that 119 were opposed and seventy were committed.[146] By 4 May,
he told Labouchere that 134 were opposed, with eighty-four certainties.[147]
The Liberal Unionists had more compelling arguments than Grey's personal charm, Milner's persistence and Brand's correspondence. As Henry
Broadhurst, Parliamentary Secretary of the Trades Union Congress, recalled
in his memoirs:

> Our opponents, quick to seize their advantage and skilled in political
> manoeuvring, employed all the arts of social life to capture the waverers.

The great London mansions were continuously ablaze with brilliant entertainments designed to attract the rank and file of the party. On the other hand, no adequate measures for counteracting these insidious temptations were taken by the Liberals. With other members, I undertook the task of attending to some of the waverers.[148]

It is clear that the close social (and kinship) bonds between the leading Liberal families made the decision over Home Rule extremely difficult and painful. In a letter to Hartington after the Bill was defeated, William Harcourt commented, with apparent sincerity, 'if there is to be war between us it will be to me the saddest thing which has befallen me in public life.'[149] Harcourt himself, who regarded Home Rule as 'wholly impracticable', chose to remain in the Gladstonian camp, as he felt that 'the question at issue like that between the Northern and the Southern States in America will only be finally settled by fighting,' but knew that the English position would be strengthened if there had been a genuine attempt to offer a constitutional solution.[150] Powell Williams, inclined to abstain, felt duty bound to support Chamberlain: "I would not be guilty, whatever may be my own opinion upon the particular point at issue, of the meanness of standing aloof from you in the critical moment.'[151] John Morley recorded that coaxing, bullying, managing and all the other arts of political emergency went on at an unprecedented rate during this period, with neither section of the Party having a monopoly.[152] Clearly the idea that the decision to vote for or against the Bill was made merely on the bidding of the consciences of individual MPs is unsustainable. This may have been the case among those asked to join the government in February, but now the full force of the party machine was being brought to bear on MPs. The Liberal Unionists could offer the promise of an uncontested election in the anticipated contest, as, on 11 May, Grey wrote that 'we are at work with the Conservative whips in organising election contests in view of an early dissolution,' and on 21 May he revealed that he was already collecting funds, with one donor already contributing £2,000 and a target of £50,000 set for the end of the month.[153] On 9 June, the *Birmingham Daily Post* reported that the Committee had already raised £30,000.[154]

Chamberlain, however, believed that his willingness to negotiate had proved successful and was convinced that Gladstone was on the point of capitulating on the issue of retention of the Irish members. When Gladstone moved the second reading of the Bill on 10 May, he had written to Collings, 'I am assured that there is a complete surrender to me.'[155] However, as Kate Courtney recorded in her diary, what Gladstone announced was merely the admission of Irish members to the Imperial Parliament when it dealt with Irish customs and excise. Caine, now acting as the Chamberlainites' whip, turned to Leonard Courtney and told him, 'we are as we were – only more so'.[156] Chamberlain made it clear to Labouchere that negotiations were now at an end.[157]

Chamberlain's position in his constituency was almost as delicate as that of Hartington. His lieutenant in Birmingham, Powell Williams, warned him of dangers in his heartland:

> The people are stark mad about the G.O.M. and if they get the idea that we were working against Home Rule – and they would get it if we declared for the withdrawal of the Bill – it would be impossible to hold them.

He went on to advise Chamberlain to avoid being seen with Hartington and to stick to the single issue of opposition to the exclusion of the Irish MPs under the proposed Government of Ireland Bill.[158] Chamberlain did invite fifty MPs in favour of granting autonomy to Ireland but opposed to the Government measure as it stood, to his house in London on 12 May. But, aware of his weakened position now negotiations with Gladstone had failed, he ignored Powell Williams' advice as *The Times* reported: 'Lord Hartington's name was greeted with great warmth and a desire expressed of bringing the Whigs and Radicals together.'[159] The meeting prompted John Bunce to conjecture that sixty members would 'probably' support Chamberlain, with 'between fifty and sixty' following Hartington, predicting an overall majority of 'between 50 and 70' against the second reading of the Home Rule Bill.[160]

Hartington held his own meeting two days later and Chamberlain, to the astonishment of many (and no doubt to Powell Williams' despair), was true to his word and attended with twenty of his supporters. On invitation from Sir Henry Meysey-Thompson, Chamberlain addressed the meeting and declared his opposition to both Home Rule Bills. *The Times* concluded that Home Rule was dead and predicted a Hartington ministry with Chamberlain offered a senior position.[161] Even Bunce was taken aback. 'It was understood that the two sections of Liberal members who are adverse to the Irish government bill would offer their opposition on different and practically irreconcilable grounds.'[162] Chamberlain explained his action in a letter to his brother Arthur:

> I went to Hartington's yesterday:
> 1st To show that we were a united party of opponents and not heterogeneous atoms.
> 2nd Because Hartington has frankly come over to my view and will finally adopt my policy of Federal Local Government as an alternative to Separation.

3rd Because it strengthens our party in the House to know that we are solid – and that one section is not likely at the last moment to leave the other in the lurch.

4th Because Mr G has burned his boats on the question of the retention of Irish members and does not intend to make any further attempt to conciliate me.[163]

Of course, this paid no attention to the attitude of Chamberlain's caucus in Birmingham and was either misleading or deluded in its second assertion.[164] Labouchere warned Chamberlain, 'the Whigs are all running about, boasting how they have you in their coils.'[165]

The meeting was hardly an irrevocable breach though, as Edward Hamilton met with Henry James and other moderates and attempted to find a reconciliation, as they were aware that otherwise they would be reduced to 'mere "catspaws" of the Tory Party.' Hamilton reported to Gladstone that 'they abhorred the idea of parting from you' and it was perhaps this letter which emboldened Gladstone into calling the rebels' bluff in June, believing that they would lack the confidence to finally break with him.[166] Similarly, Chamberlain spent the following few days trying to persuade Hartington to allow Gladstone to withdraw the Government of Ireland Bill and to replace it with a general resolution in favour of some greater degree of Irish autonomy.[167]

In Ulster, the fear that the principle of Irish Home Rule was to be conceded provoked the Mayor of Belfast, Sir Edward Harland, to call a public meeting in Ulster Hall which 5,000 'of every class and creed' attended to voice their disapproval and to communicate this to the Liberal Unionist leadership.[168] In response, Hartington, by now in a much stronger position with Chamberlain's public support for his leadership, gave a speech in Bradford in which he firmly opposed Chamberlain's idea, pushing for unconditional surrender from Gladstone.[169] He was strengthened by the first indication that the Conservative leadership would call upon its membership to leave Unionist Liberals unchallenged in any future election. Salisbury, at the annual meeting of the Primrose League, announced that he was willing to put aside party difference 'for this great purpose' and, crucially, that the Conservatives 'desire that no Liberal shall suffer in his electoral prospects by reason of the part which he has taken in the defence of the unity of the Empire.'[170]

When a full meeting of the Liberal Unionist Committee was arranged for 22 May, Chamberlain tried to organise his radical faction to form a bloc within the Committee, but the other radicals demurred, preferring to leave the matter to the decision of each individual and his caucus.[171] When the Committee meeting took place at Westminster Palace Hotel, Hartington's success in out-manoeuvring Chamberlain was evident. Chamberlain, not his supporters, attended, so there was no discussion of amendments to the Home Rule Bills or propositions of alternative schemes of Irish self-government. The Committee pledged itself to defeating the Bills and nothing else. A general committee with fifty-nine members, including nineteen MPs, was appointed, although true power lay in the hands of the executive committee, comprising Goschen and his coterie: Lord Camperdown, Grey, Brand, Craig Sellar, Arthur Elliot, Henry Hobhouse, Blennerhasset, Biddulph, Lubbock, Robert Finlay, Meysey-Thompson, Milner, Lord Monteagle and Lord Richard Grosvenor.[172] Only Rylands spoke for the radicals, while the meeting was dominated by Goschen, Argyll, Derby and Hartington.[173] The *Manchester Guardian* recognised 'that the reported Hartington/Chamberlain agreement [was] a delusion – on any positive policy for the settlement of the Irish Question.'[174] The meeting was largely for the purpose of encouraging resistance to the Home Rule Bill by demonstrating that there would be a party apparatus established to support those who would surely provoke a general election by their actions.[175] Although the differences within the Unionists were creating problems for the leadership, Hartington believed they were surmountable:

> I do not think that it is necessary to take up a position of antagonism towards Mr Chamberlain and the section of the party which he leads. I believe our objects are the same, the difference between us being sim-ply that he sees less difficulty than I do in framing a measure which would give satisfaction to reasonable Irish aspirations.[176]

Some of the radicals were nervous, however, and attended a meeting that Gladstone called at the Foreign Office on 27 May, looking for a way of avoid-ing voting against the Bills and being associated with the negative policy of Hartington and the Tories.[177] Much to Chamberlain's horror, twenty of them now claimed to be satisfied with Gladstone's promise to delay the third reading of the Bill. Gladstone now estimated that there were only eight Chamberlainites and sixty-six moderates and Hartingtonians.[178] Chamberlain immediately called a meeting, but his authority over the group was clearly slipping following his presence at Devonshire House on 14 May, as only thirty-three attended.[179] Caine later reported that thirty of Chamberlain's supporters were either 'shaky' or had declared their intention to vote for the Bill.[180] Chamberlain adjourned the meeting for four days and begged Hartington to persuade his followers and the Conservatives merely to abstain on the second reading but both Salisbury and the Liberal Unionist leader rejected the idea.[181] Hartington now revealed his trump card and announced that he was able to offer an electoral guarantee to encourage his supporters to break with Gladstone completely. At a meeting on 28 May, a letter from Akers-Douglas was read with an absolute undertaking from the Conservatives that they would not contest the seat of any Liberal member who voted against the Bill.[182] It was this guarantee of electoral advantage that persuaded the Liberal Unionists to finally cross the Rubicon and vote against Home Rule, as any accusations of treachery towards the G.O.M in their constituencies could be countered, not only by statements of personal integrity, but also by the mathematics of electoral probability.

Chamberlain was now faced with a very poor choice. To return, defeated, to Gladstone's side was clearly impossible for him, so he could either abstain and hand the leadership of the movement to Hartington, or enter the lobby alongside the Tories with very few radicals at his side. He was aided by the decisive action of the Glasgow Unionists who wrote to their MPs, threatening them that 'the members voting for the second reading will be held responsible by their Unionist constituents.'[183] This, together with a guarantee of support from the West of Scotland Committee and the prospect of an uncontested election, stiffened the nerves of the nine west of Scotland MPs who eventually entered the opposition lobby on 8 June.[184]

When a meeting of fifty MPs was held on 31 May in committee room 15 (including between fifteen and twenty of those who had been at Devonshire House on 14 May),[185] Chamberlain resorted to a desperate stratagem in order to stem the haemorrhage of his supporters. He had, on Caine's advice, written to Bright, imploring him to attend the meeting. Bright had refused, stating that 'I am not willing to take the responsibility of advising others as to their course' but he sent a letter explaining his position.[186] Bright clearly did not want the letter to be used by Chamberlain and Bright had, of course, been conspicuously silent during the Home Rule debate.[187] In order to retain his credibility with the radicals in the audience, Chamberlain implied that personally he would prefer to abstain and claimed that he would simply follow whatever choice the meeting made. He then read Bright's letter, with its unequivocal declaration to vote against the second reading.[188] Chamberlain then announced he would vote against the Bill and those at the meeting opposed to the Bill voted by forty-eight to four against merely abstaining.[189] Caine made sure that the press received the version of the meeting that stressed Chamberlain's (and his) reluctance to take such a step:

> We did our best ... to induce them to abstain, but it was felt that if the policy of abstention were to be pursued it must be adopted by a

Image 3: Edward Sambourne correctly identifies the stratagem whereby Chamberlain persuaded sufficient radicals to follow him in order to defeat the second reading of the Home Rule Bill. *Punch*, 12 June 1886.

considerable body of members ... If we could have got thirty who would pledge themselves to abstain we were prepared to have recommended that course, but we could not.[190]

Unsurprisingly, Bright was alarmed that his letter had been used in a fashion that virtually guaranteed the defeat of the Bill. He wrote to Chamberlain the next day:

If I had thought I should do harm, I should have said something more
or less. Even now, if it is not too late, I could join you in abstaining if
we could save the House and country from a dissolution which may
for the Liberal party turn out a catastrophe the magnitude of which
cannot be measured.[191]

Of course, Chamberlain had managed to hang onto his radical credentials
through his misuse of Bright's letter and so had no intention of meeting with
the old radical at this stage. Parnell, for one, was not fooled by Chamberlain's
public protestations and careful management of his opposition. On seeing
Chamberlain after the Bill's defeat, Parnell remarked, 'there goes the man
who killed the Home Rule Bill.'[192] Gladstone too, realised that the events in
committee room 15 had condemned his Bill.[193]

Frantic canvassing now took place, with Craig Sellar informing Hartington
on 3 June: 'These are Liberals certain to vote against: 79; who will abstain:
25'. Craig Sellar predicted a majority of eighteen against the Bill but admitted that his estimate of the abstainers was uncertain and that they held the
balance. He concluded, however, that 'I consider the rejection of the bill is
certain.'[194] Goschen had expressed similar concerns about the '20 or 30 doubt-
fuls' to Milner and had named those he considered most possible for members of the Committee to influence. They included several MPs who went on
to serve as Liberal Unionists for at least a Parliament, after voting against the
second reading, such as Henry Beaumont, Savile Crossley, Donald Currie,
George Dixon, G. W. Hastings, Mildmay and Cuthbert Quilter. Milner was
advised to give these men 'systematic, thorough and tactful attention.'[195] In
reply, Milner added the names of those radicals 'whom I would despair of',
including F. W. Maclean.[196] Albert Grey, using his aristocratic charm to the
last, reporting to his uncle that he had spoke to each 'doubtful' individually,
believed that, as a result, 'I did more good in the lobby talking to Members
than I should have done in the House listening to Gladstone.'[197]

In his diary, Alfred Pease noted that even on the day of the vote, there
were still '"waverers and shufflers" who remained undecided.'[198] Labouchere
was contemptuous of these MPs: 'Half of these people are like women,
who are pleased to keep up the "I will and I won't" as long as possible in
order to be courted,' yet he believed that the decisive influence lay outside
Westminster as such waverers usually followed their caucuses and supported
the Bill.[199] Kate Courtney recorded that 'guesses range from a majority of 6
for to a majority of 30 against.'[200] Chamberlain was now very confident and
commented the same day to a Conservative MP who was also escaping the
stink from the Commons' drains, that the majority against the Bill would be

"HOW'S THAT?"

Image 4: The Birmingham Gladstonian periodical, *The Owl*, comments on the defeat of the second reading of the Home Rule Bill. Note the cricket ball marked as '30' and Chamberlain as bowler. *The Owl*, 11 June 1886.

thirty.[201] His information was clearly better than that of the Liberal Unionist Committee, as Albert Grey was expecting a majority of at least thirty-six and was amazed when the Bill was defeated at 1 a.m. by 341 to 311 with moderate MPs such as William Rathbone, Joseph Pease, C. M. Palmer and Miles MacInnes supporting the Bill, despite having spoken to him of their objections to the Bill in its entirety.[202]

The bulk of those newly elected in 1885 followed Gladstone. Of the 129 new Liberal MPs, only twenty-seven joined Hartington in the lobby against the second reading of the Home Rule Bill on 8 June. But the strength of the Party lay in its regional centres. Seven out of nine Liberal MPs in Birmingham, eight out of thirteen Liberal MPs in Devon and Cornwall, six out of twelve East Anglia Liberals and twenty-four out of sixty-two Scottish MPs voted against the Bill. In Scotland, Home Rule cut across the two most divisive issues of the last Liberal administration, with churchmen and dis-establishers, crofters' supporters and aristocrats entering the lobby together. Of the 131 acknowledged 'radicals', thirty-two followed Chamberlain, mostly from the West Midlands and the west of Scotland.[203] In the other areas of radicalism, however, there was scarcely any revolt against Gladstone's leadership at all in Manchester, Leeds and Hull. The future pattern for the Party's bases of support was thus laid. As Christopher Harvie has noted, although personal considerations were important in the decision as to which lobby to enter on 8 June, 'professional reputation, institutional developments and the nature of the [electoral] audience' had a much greater influence on the crucial choice that had to be made.[204] The events at Westminster had produced a split (or rather a series of splits) in the Liberal Party, but had not yet produced a formal division between two rival interpretations of Liberalism. Liberal Unionism, as opposed to Liberal dissension, was born at the general election of 1886.

CHAPTER 2

WHIGGERY OR SOCIALISM? THE IDEOLOGIES OF LIBERAL UNIONISM

Increasingly, the acceptance of an *a priori* meaning of a term such as 'Unionist' has been questioned by those who seek to examine the ability of language to shape, as well as reflect, the behaviour of the actors in the wider political environment.[1] This chapter seeks to examine the conflicting, over-lapping and complementary definitions of the phrase 'Liberal Unionist' for, as Biagini has noted, the campaign against Home Rule 'was part of the broader debate on imperialism, liberty and democracy.'[2] Although the political realities of the first era of mass politics required the existence of a unified 'Liberal Unionist Party', there were in fact many varieties of Liberal Unionism. There *was* a struggle for ideological primacy within the Party, but historians of the Liberal and Conservative Parties have shown that there was nothing unique in this. This chapter aims to demonstrate that, contrary to most interpretations, there was a unity of principle, purpose and practice in the behaviour of the Liberal Unionists, at least until the formation of the Unionist coalition government in July 1895. This may not have amounted to what so many modern political historians desperately seek, a coherent and consistent 'ideology', but it was far more than just a loose amalgam of the politically disaffected and the intellectually moribund.

John Bew has recently established that 'Unionism is most accurately seen as the *de facto* creed of the British state.'[3] Although 'Unionist' is a label that is now associated with the Conservative Party in the early twentieth century and with Ulster's sectarian politics, to a reader in 1886, the associations were far more positive. One of the greatest affirmations of Liberal Unionism was the support of so many Scottish MPs, including such solidly non-English figures as the crofter MP, Charles Fraser Mackintosh, and the editor of the *Scotsman*, Charles Cooper. The positive view of the benefits of the Union was shared by many lowland Scots and some highland Scots, who even referred to themselves on occasions as 'north Britons.'[4] Not only did 'Unionism' imply a support for the integrity of Great Britain and a belief in the benefits this brought, it also deliberately had historical connotations, with a cause popular among working-class radicals. It was not lost on many that Goldwin Smith, the great Liberal supporter of Lincoln's cause in the American Civil War, was a strong supporter of Hartington's Party.[5] In 1893, Dicey warned that the Nationalists were risking Civil War, by ignoring the will of the majority, just as the Confederate states had done thirty-two years earlier.[6]

For some, the job of the Liberal Unionists was simply to defeat Home Rule and then to return to the old party lines. As Milner himself wrote to Goschen, following his six-week visit to Ireland prior to the 1886 general election, 'the people of Ireland ... are praying for a "little wholesome neglect." If only the House of Commons could be shut up for ten years ... what a transformation scene we should witness in poor politician-ridden Ireland.'[7] The Party's chief propagandist, John St. Loe Strachey, revealed that, for many, the Party had but one purpose, to defeat Home Rule so comprehensively that it would no longer be raised as a proposal by any party. In January 1892, he admitted that 'after that has been done ... the Liberal Unionist Party will have performed its allotted task.'[8]

The intellectual defence of the Union

The place of ideology in later Victorian politics has been strongly asserted by those such as E. H. H. Green and Matthew Fforde who see the emergence of a new coalition of the 'propertied' who could resist the imprecations of 'New Liberalism' and Socialism. However, they have tended to ignore the significance of the defence of the Union in providing what Jeremy Smith describes as a 'totem',[9] preferring to read the Liberal Unionists' existence in orthodox class terms.[10] In fact, intellectual support ensured that the Liberal Unionists' stance was carefully articulated to appeal across class boundaries.

As Christopher Harvie has noted, 'academic opinion on the whole tended towards Unionism.'[11] On 4 May 1886, *The Times* had listed 'eminent men outside the political arena, who are ... thorough-going Liberals and who have declared themselves hostile to the disruption of the United Kingdom' to include Sir Frederick Leighton, Herbert Spencer, Goldwin Smith, Matthew Arnold, Henry Sidgwick, J. A. Froude, John Tyndall, W. E. H. Lecky, J. R. Seeley, T. H. Huxley and Lord Tennyson.[12] The support of Catholic intellectuals such as Lecky and Thomas Maguire, the first Catholic to become a fellow of Trinity College, Dublin, was crucial in enabling the Liberal Unionists to present themselves as immune from sectarian Protestantism and representative of the whole community of the United Kingdom.[13] The botanist, Sir John Lubbock, MP for London University, was treasurer of the initial Liberal Committee for the Maintenance of the Legislative Union between Great Britain and Ireland. Sir William Thomson (later Lord Kelvin) had joined the Liberal Unionist Committee by 24 May; scientists may have been inclined to Unionism, suggests Greta Jones, due to the Catholic Church's implacable opposition to the theory of evolution.[14]

As well as Henry Sidgwick at Cambridge, Millicent Fawcett was a leading member of the Women's Liberal Unionist Association, together with Emily Davies, the founder of Girton College, Cambridge.[15] More generally, the university seats proved very supportive of Liberal Unionism with London, Oxford, Dublin and Edinburgh and St. Andrews all returning Liberal Unionists in the period. As Burness has noted, six professors of Glasgow University were vice presidents of the West of Scotland Association, as well as the Chancellor, the Earl of Stair.[16] In July 1887, the combined Universities of England presented an address to Hartington, signed by 'a number of resident graduates of the two universities ... eminent in either literary or scientific or classical studies.'[17] Shortly after the 1892 election, William Miller, the new secretary of the Liberal Unionist Club, wrote to Phillip Gell looking for new speakers 'among undergraduates at Oxford who would be of service to us as soon as they have taken their degree.'[18] The Oxford Liberal Unionist Association had two professors as vice-presidents: Rev. Professor Thomas Fowler, professor of logic and President of Corpus Christi College, and the legal professor, T. E. Holland; and there were ten further professors on the Committee.[19]

The Liberal Unionists arguably benefited more, in the first age of mass politics, from the influence of writers, capable of spreading the message through popular history. T. B. Macaulay, although dead for twenty-six years at the time of the first Home Rule Bill, had been a prophet of imperial British identity in his *History of England from the Accession of James II*, published between 1848 and 1855. Froude, whose 1870 *History of England* had made him, to his biographer at least, 'the most famous of living English historians,' attacked the prospect of Catholic persecution of both peasants and Protestants under a Home Rule parliament, based on his reading of Irish history and became the chief inspiration for the patriotic radicals, of whom Chamberlain eventually became the unquestioned leader.[20] Froude's later novel, *The Two Chiefs of Dunboy* (1889), popularised his Liberal criticisms of Gladstone's schemes still further, as did *Hurrish* (1886) by Emily Lawless.[21] As a believer in the inclusive potential of a liberal Protestant state in which sectarianism could best be minimised, Froude now began to articulate the movement towards large states in which nationalist self-interest had to be sacrificed for the benefits of economic strength, civil freedoms and political liberty.[22] This was a cause of great appeal to the British electorate between 1886 and 1903 as the jurist Alfred Venn Dicey put it at the centenary of Trafalgar:

> The yearly crowning of Nelson's column, the influence exerted by the writings of Froude, of Seeley, and above all of [Alfred] Mahan, the tales and the verses of Rudyard Kipling, with their glorification of British imperial sway, and the echo which the teaching of all these writers finds in the hearts of the English people throughout the United Kingdom and our self-governing colonies, all tell their own tale.[23]

Dicey, Vinerian Professor of Law at Oxford University and author of *Law of the Constitution*, 'the most influential constitutional textbook of the last century',[24] emerged as the Party's leading ideologue. In addition to his academic excellence, he also had political credibility as he had argued in favour of better treatment of Irish Catholics during Gladstone's second administration, while refusing to accept that either Home Rule or coercion provided the solution.[25] In this, he followed the lead of the great Victorian constitutionalist, Walter Bagehot, who had feared that Home Rule would challenge respect for the law and authority.[26] Dicey continued with this nuanced position after the 'Hawarden Kite', arguing that Ireland, rather than being separated from English rule, needed to enjoy the full benefits of English law, which it had been so far denied.[27] In Scotland, the Union had preserved the best of the indigenous institutions, but in Ireland, only the worst elements remained.[28] Dicey rejected the paradigm of the parliamentary discussions of spring 1886 that posited a choice between coercion and Home Rule and believed that the Union with Ireland was both possible and desirable. For him the only two possible solutions to Ireland's problems were: a more sympathetic and non-sectarian implementation of the Union; or complete independence for Ireland. Any other suggestion was a mere chimera, including any suggestion of a devolved assembly in Ulster. As he put it:

> The fullest legislative assembly meeting in Dublin would rightly claim to speak for the Irish people. A town council, whether of Birmingham

Image 5: The cover of Frankfort Moore's comic novel shows Unionists' view of a
cabinet meeting of the Irish Parliament following Home Rule. F. Frankfort Moore,
*The Diary of an Irish Cabinet Minister: being the history of the first (and only) Irish
National Administration, 1893*, London: John Reed & co., 1893.

or Belfast, springs from, and is kept alive by the will of Parliament and
cannot pretend that its powers, however extensive, compete with the
authority of its creator.[29]

Having established a reputation among academics and politicians as a dispassionate commentator, the enthusiasm with which Dicey took up the defence of the Union had a significant effect. Trowbridge Ford gives him credit for recruiting W. E. H. Lecky to the Liberal Unionist cause as well as changing the editorial policy of the *Spectator*.[30] Dicey had always believed in the historic potency of nationalism as identified by J. S. Mill, seeing in the recent developments in Italy, Germany and the United States the desire for integration leading to a moral and political regeneration.[31] For him, as for most Liberal Unionists, Irish nationalism, with its negative approach, disruptive parliamentary methods and disdain for the rule of law, was the greatest threat to the integration of Great Britain and implied a collapse of the imperial mission, economic decline and a fracturing of the most effective political and legal structure in the world.[32] He wrote to Bryce in April 1886, 'I feel it more strongly than I can tell you & more strongly than people would believe of me.'[33] Although, as a staunch Liberal, he found it hard to join an alliance with the Tories, such was his belief in the cause, he was prepared to tolerate 'strange and very uncongenial political company.'[34] In order to support the Liberal Unionist cause, Dicey wrote *England's Case Against Home Rule* during the election campaign in June 1886. In it, he laid out the moderate Liberal cause most explicitly. He admitted that he had no particular knowledge of Ireland or Irish history and that, as the book's title suggested, he was only concerned with 'the advantages and disadvantages from an English point of view, of either maintaining the Union or of separation from Ireland.'[35]

As a Liberal, he accepted that the Nationalists were honest in their view that Home Rule was a first step on the road towards complete separation, but regarded the English Home Rulers as duplicitous in stating the Home Rule was a final solution as it could only inflame demands for complete independence. His opposition to Home Rule was thus summarised in three points:

1. Home Rule would arrest and reverse the historic expansion of the British Empire which had begun in the sixteenth century and would threaten the political institutions of the country.
2. As a constitutional revolution, Home Rule would threaten the integrity of the United Kingdom as had evolved since the Union of England and Wales.
3. Home Rule would never satisfy the Nationalists, as they called for the repeal of the Act of Union and not a 'Union of Hearts' envisaged by Gladstone once Home Rule had been passed.

For Dicey, Home Rule meant 'the endowment of Ireland with representative institutions and responsible government' and, as such, he believed this would cause a number of constitutional difficulties between Dublin and

Image 6: A LUA poster from 1893 pours scorn on Gladstone's promise that a 'Union of Hearts' would persist in the event of Home Rule for Ireland. Clifford 3(2).

Westminster.[36] He criticised Home Rulers in the Liberal Party for presenting Home Rule as merely an extension of local self government, while Irish Nationalists claimed it to mean virtual independence for Ireland. This, Dicey believed, would lead to significantly poorer relations between the two countries. Ireland was a vulnerable point in Britain's island defences and an unsympathetic Irish government might encourage other powers to use the island as a base to attack the British mainland. This may seem far fetched today, but the fear of French attack had resulted in the creation of a line of sea forts in Sussex and Kent between 1859 and 1860 and the memory of the Directory's landings in Ireland and Wales in 1797 still influenced attitudes.[37] In Scotland, in particular, this was a genuine concern and in 1886 the Glasgow Chamber of Commerce passed a resolution expressing the fear that Ireland would 'become the choice refuge of all the dynamitards of Europe.'[38]

Dicey's argument then extended, revealingly, to the political structures that had created the Home Rule crisis. The growing democracy of the British political system was, he felt, no guarantee of sensible or effective government, a view which was shared by Salisbury and most Conservatives.[39] He accused the Liberal Party of abdicating its responsibility by hiding behind the electoral results in Ireland of 1885, when, in reality they were giving in to the threat of violence and parliamentary opposition. 'Cowardice masks itself under the show of compromise, and men of eminent respectability yield to the terror of being bored, concessions which their forefathers would have refused to the threat of armed rebellion.'[40] As he apparently commented parenthetically, suicide was not an acceptable solution to toothache.

Dicey's book was fundamentally a creed of negative Unionism. It opposed the idea of Home Rule as Ireland was too close to the rest of Britain and thus too much of a security risk to allow control over its own affairs. It posited the growth of larger multi-ethnic states as inevitable and thus saw Home Rule as ahistoric. It rejected the right of three million Irishmen to overrule the rest of the British electorate and regarded English civilisation as more advanced than the Irish. It did accept that Irish grievances needed to be addressed, but denied that these could be best resolved through a Dublin parliament. Oddly for an academic, Dicey discounted the significance of Irish history in the Home Rule crisis. In his rebuttal, Justin McCarthy attacked this weakness:

> All that history teaches is to be ignored, to be wiped away, and a quarrel as old as the hills to be investigated as if were a mushroom that only came into existence the week before last.[41]

Dicey analysed Ireland's fundamental difficulty as economic and concluded that only the resources of the United Kingdom could resolve this. Of course, this ran entirely counter to Gladstone's reading of the 1885 Irish vote.[42] For Dicey, as for so many other Unionists, the Union was ultimately of greater significance than the principle of democracy. Parry sees the Liberal Unionists as losing confidence in Gladstone's ability to distinguish between 'the material wishes of seasoning opinion and unconditional section clamour' and consequently having become 'a soft touch for any well-organised minority who could persuade him of their morality.'[43] Consequently, the Liberal Unionists claimed that the 1891 'Newcastle Programme' marked Gladstone's surrender to 'faddists' such as temperance reformers, trade unionists and disestablishers. Ultimately, this attitude led many one-time champions of franchise reform, including Dicey, to defend the House of Lords' right to veto the decisions of the Commons.[44]

Finally Dicey acknowledged, as so few Home Rulers did, the problematic religious, cultural and ethnic divisions in Ireland and argued that only the Union, if it was reformed on an non-sectarian basis, could resolve these issues.[45] There had to be a single paramount legislative body, in which were represented the various cultural, ethnic and social groupings of the United Kingdom, which would 'equalise conditions as far as practicable throughout the three kingdoms.[46] That said, Dicey was quite prepared to use the apparent threat to Ulster prosperity and civil rights that Home Rule seemed to offer, to bolster his argument. In his mind, Home Rule would betray those 'loyal' Irishmen who wished to retain their British citizenship:

> [Home Rule] whilst not freeing England from moral responsibility for protecting the rights of every British subject, does virtually give up the attempt to ensure that those rights have more than a nominal existence and thus gives up the endeavour to enforce legal and equal justice between man and man.[47]

Such a disgrace, he felt, would haunt the politics of the mainland and would provoke a wave of demands for similar treatment throughout the Empire, which would hasten the collapse of Britain's world power status and its decline into a minor European state, nearly as impoverished as its Irish neighbour. This was an effective attack, as the Home Rule scheme's greatest weakness was its refusal to confront the distinctive religious, economic and cultural character of Ulster.[48] Ulster was, after all, the wealthiest region of Ireland, with a wage rate so high that its population had quadrupled in the last half century. The success of its shipyards, linen factories, ropeworks and tobacco factories were used by many, including Chamberlain, to demonstrate that the Union could bring prosperity to regions outside the British mainland.[49]

However, despite encouragement by figures in the Party such as T. W. Russell and Isabella Tod and those outside such as Colonel Saunderson and Lord Randolph Churchill, the 'Ulster Question' was not especially emphasised in the Party's literature, at least before 1892, when the issue grew desperate as the Party seemed to be heading for electoral disaster.[50] It was only in September 1890 that the Party officially sanctioned mention of the risk of 'civil war' in Ulster if Home Rule was forced upon the country.[51] To many, such as Dicey, such talk was provocative and the very purpose of Liberal Unionism was to ensure the supremacy of the law over party political concerns.[52] To threaten to break the law when it did not suit a political group's interests would be to lower oneself to the moral standards of Parnell and the Nationalists.[53] Instead, the Party preferred to emphasise the positive benefits from an inclusive and united British identity which appealed to lowland Scots, Ulster tenant farmers, Cornish Wesleyans and Birmingham radicals. As a Catholic Unionist announced at a Unionist meeting at Leinster Hall on 11 November 1886:

> The Unionists ... believed in ... union between all classes and sections of the community; union between Catholics and Protestants; union between the rich and the poor; union between landlords and tenants; and union between Great Britain and Ireland.[54]

The Liberal Unionist Party only resorted to appeals based on Protestant distrust of clericalism when their electoral oblivion appeared to beckon in the early 1890s. With the Irish episcopacy's direct intervention in Nationalist politics in the condemnation of Parnell, Henry James warned the Liberal Unionist Club in April 1891 that, 'if the government of Ireland is given to the Irish people, it will, in fact be given into the hands of the Roman Catholic priesthood.'[55] The following month, the Party newspaper included a number of anti-clerical statements and began a series of articles entitled 'The Clerical Conspiracy in Ireland.'[56] Such policies were risky: ideologically, as Liberalism had traditionally attempted to appeal across sectarian lines; and electorally, as many Unionists in southern Ireland were Catholic.[57] Although Glasgow is traditionally associated with sectarian politics, Edinburgh seems to have also been susceptible to the anti-clerical argument. Lewis McIver although a confirmed radical, was faced with a tough challenge in South Edinburgh in 1892 and turned to religion in his speeches, accusing the Liberals of tolerating 'the priest in politics'. He was clearly determined to have his cake and eat it, for he demurred any accusation that he was 'endeavouring to stir up religious animosity', preferring to brandish 'the true Liberal's feeling for religious freedom, religious tolerance, of respect for every man's religious opinions sincerely held' and to use the names of Bright and Spurgeon freely.[58] As a more prominent radical, restrained by the Unionist alliance, facing electoral oblivion in a much larger scale, the new Party leader endorsed McIver's approach in an address to the Nonconformist Unionist Association at the end of March 1892. Chamberlain was far less subtle than McIver in his appeal to sectarian instincts:

> Irish Protestants will be left entirely at the mercy of a Parliament in Dublin, which will be, as far as its majority are concerned, filled with delegates and creatures of the Irish Roman Catholic priesthood. I do not believe that Irish Protestants will accept this proposal.[59]

The *Liberal Unionist* continued to complain of clerical interference in the general election in Ireland, claiming that 'the priestly functions have been forgotten for the last three weeks, and the religious minister has become a political haranguer and an electioneering agent,'[60] although this was exactly the role of the Irish nonconformist clergy in the Unionist alliance. T. W. Russell, despite his radical principles, was quite prepared to threaten 'the distinct menace of civil war' in May 1892.[61]

With the announcement of a Home Rule Bill in the Queen's Speech in January 1893, Hugh Arnold-Forster, who represented an Ulster seat, introduced an amendment attacking the 'vast amount of clerical influence.'[62] This was soon followed by detailed (if selective) summary of nonconformist reaction to the second Home Bill in June 1893 in *Liberal Unionist Association Memoranda*. The Presbyterian Church leadership was quoted as believing that 'the measure seriously impairs our civil and religious liberties.' The Methodist Conference had declared that 'far from being a message of peace to Ireland, [it] would be a fruitful occasion of more distressing discord and strife.' The Quakers apparently declared that 'the Bill ... will, of necessity, be extremely injurious to the moral and material prosperity of this country.'[63] Even a Roman Catholic manifesto against the Bill was being circulated, signed by the Party's single Catholic MP, William Kenny, together with Daniel O'Connell's son, the Earl of Fingall, the Earl of Kenmare, the Earl of Westmeath and Lord Louth.[64]

The Party was, however, keen to distance itself from accusations that it was playing the Orange Card, as Churchill had done with such violent consequences in 1886. Any contact between the Orange Order and the Liberal rebels was organised through the Irish Loyal and Patriotic Union, co-ordinated by Rowland Blennerhassett, one of Goschen's circle.[65] The only recent study of the Orange-Unionist alliance in Scotland states that 'a discreet public distance was [usually] maintained.'[66] Asked to take the position of president of the Irish Unionist Alliance, Hartington wrote to Wolmer that he was reluctant as 'I thought the thing had an Orange appearance which would not be acceptable to some of my friends in Ireland.'[67] When the Ulster Convention of 1892 was organised, it was emphasised that it comprised 'descendants of Scotch Covenanters ... descendants of leaders of Volunteers ... descendants of United Irishmen ... sons of old fighters for Catholic Emancipation ... advocates of ... the rights of the tillers of the soil' and that 'Orangemen are only one element in this movement'. Even those Orangemen present, as a result of their involvement with more Liberal Unionists, demonstrated 'a calmness and moderation of spirit which is new in their history.'[68] The Convention itself passed off without any riot or violent incident, a deliberate contrast with the ethnic cleansing of areas of Belfast in June 1886. There were, it was said, all creeds present at the event which attracted around 100,000 people, 'Episcopalians, Presbyterians, Roman Catholics, Methodists, Unitarians, Independents, Baptists, Jews and Friends.'[69] Peter Gibbon goes as far as to suggest that this event, organised by the Liberal Unionists, marked the birth of 'the Ulsterman.'[70]

With the Liberals' electoral victory in 1892 and the introduction of the second Home Rule Bill, the argument that Parliament was supreme needed some adjustment and here the position of the Ulster Protestants did become crucial. As the *Liberal Unionist Association Memoranda* put it in a supplement, 'Parliament has no moral right to cast off and repudiate the allegiance of the loyalists of Ulster.'[71] There was also a perfect opportunity to attack the

Liberals for failing to adhere to the principles in which they claimed to believe, with the increased use of the 'guillotine' (now nicknamed 'Gladstone's gag') limiting the freedom of speech at Westminster itself:

> This injustice was perpetuated by a government calling itself Liberal! By a party which professes to be the champion of free speech, and by the majority of a House of Commons which has no mandate from the people of Great Britain either for this revolution of the British constitution, or for the revolutionary method by which it has been sought to establish this great wrong.[72]

Discontent with the attitude of both Liberals and Nationalists towards Parliament and due procedure clearly animated the Lords in their decisive vote against the second Home Rule Bill in 1893, following the 'Judas' outburst aimed at Chamberlain in the House of Commons. It also led to a defection, when George Doughty, who had won Heneage's seat at Grimsby for the Liberals in 1895, crossed the floor in July 1898, expressing anger at the behaviour of Redmond's MPs.[73] He fought a by-election on the issue and demonstrated the continuing anti-Catholic attitude of the town by securing his return with a comfortable majority of 1,751 votes.[74]

Much of Dicey's 1886 book had been taken up with dystopian visions of the consequences of an independent Ireland and damning critiques of the constitutional short-comings of any scheme of Home Rule, chiefly because they would all challenge the crucial element of the British polity, the sovereignty of the Westminster parliament. His ultimately negative interpretation of Unionism was only partly shared in Birmingham and the other, more radical areas.

Radical Unionists regarded themselves as 'advanced Liberals' much as they had done before 1886 and viewed Hartington's moderates as necessary but unfortunate allies. The radical Unionist ideology was expressed most succinctly in *Home Rule from a Liberal Unionist's Point of View* by Richard Parkes. In this, although there was a strict insistence that 'there must be persistent enforcement of the law of the land', there was a traditionally radical attitude in the pamphlet's conclusion: 'Landlordism must go and ... Land Acts of the future must tend in the direction of peasant proprietorship.' The pamphlet hinted that Liberal reunion was possible by calling on the Gladstonians to postpone indefinitely Home Rule and the extension of local government to Ireland as the prelude to reconstruction.[75] Other radical Unionists emphasised that the 'unauthorised programme' had been abandoned by Gladstone's fixation with Parnell and that now 'Ireland blocks the way.' This view had been expressed by Chamberlain early in 1887, when he first expressed his disgust that 'thirty two millions of people must go without much needed legislation because three million are disloyal.'[76] In this way, Unionism could act as a source of constructive economic and social reform and a means of improving the humanitarian achievements of the imperial mission. Of course, this attitude was shared by other independently-minded Liberals, who were not associated with Chamberlain, such as Lubbock, Courtney and Lewis Fry. In 1886, Lubbock also voiced a concern that would return in the Edwardian Age, that there was a danger in surrendering to the violence of Nationalist Ireland, for 'if the people only proved themselves sufficiently turbulent they would be rewarded by having half their taxes off and being relieved from contributing to any national emergency.'[77]

In some ways, however, Parkes' pamphlet demonstrated that radical Unionism appeared to be more akin to Salisbury's Conservatism with its description of 'the character of the average Irish peasant' matching the Conservative leader's famous 'Hottentot' remarks at St James Hall on 15 May 1886. In contrast to the principled, legalistic opposition of the moderate Liberal Unionists, Parkes resorted to an English prejudice, believing that 'he [the Irishman] has the ignorance, superstition, cunning and a large admixture of that happy-go-lucky element which in England is called idleness ... [with] an utter want of self-reliance.' For Parkes, such idleness also affected the Irish people's political and religious behaviour, clinging to Roman Catholicism because of its demand for complete surrender of the individual's conscience and joining secret societies for the power of intimidation that this would bring them.[78] In one of '30 Reasons against Home Rule', the *Liberal Unionist Association Memoranda Supplement* claimed that 'the Irishman, sufficiently inclined to drink already, will drink as a patriotic duty.'[79] Such an attitude could sometimes translate into apparent callousness, as is evident in the *Liberal Unionist*'s leader on the failure of the potato harvest of summer 1890:

> the death rate is very low and fewer young children and more very old people die than elsewhere in the three kingdoms.[80]

Biagini suggests that this was not, as Loughlin might have it, race propaganda, but rather an attempt to use the language of Darwin to condemn those who, respectable society felt, had put themselves in a class of their own, through acts of terror or poverty. As they were beyond the reach of civilisation, terms such as 'bestial' and 'sub-human' were felt to be entirely appropriate.[81] Any grievances that the Irish had were exaggerated by opportunistic Nationalists and were probably the result of the indolence and fecklessness of the Irish themselves.[82] This did not amount to a condemnation of the Irish on racial grounds.

In July 1886, John Bright significantly contributed to the radical rebellion against Gladstone by claiming that the Irish lacked the political maturity which the northern English working class had demonstrated during the 'cotton famine' of the 1860s.[83] However, unlike the Conservatives, the radical (and the moderate) Unionists believed that a nuanced combination of coercion and reform could improve the Irish character so that some degree of self-government would be possible in the distant future.[84] Of course, many Liberal Unionists differentiated between the humble Irish cottager and the Fenian terrorist. Since 1882 and the murder of Cavendish and Burke and the Maamtrasna massacre, many Liberals had accepted that there must be no concessions to violence and threats of disorder, otherwise the rule of law itself might be in jeopardy. As Trevelyan had put it in 1883, when Chief Secretary for Ireland, if British rule was abandoned in Ireland, 'we should have a mutual massacre.'[85] There was also the belief that there was no strong popular support for the 'land war' despite Gladstone's and the Nationalists' claims, as only 2–4% of the tenant farmers joined the 'Plan of Campaign', and that intimidation and corruption explained the massive Nationalist majorities in rural Ireland.[86] Such genuinely Liberal concerns as to the motives and behaviour of the Nationalists explain the majority of the Liberal Unionist Party's willingness to accept coercion in 1887 and the *Liberal Unionist* continuously fed this attitude with its 'Latest Outrages in Ireland' feature, which ran for every one of the paper's eighty issues. Chamberlain consistently argued that, far from oppressing the average Irishman, the Crimes Act was a guarantee of freedom from intimidation. In this way, coercion was, in the words of a letter writer to the *Baptist Magazine*, both 'just and Christian.'[87]

As Stephen Koss has written, there was no natural alliance between the Free churches and the Liberal Party, merely the acceptance that 'Liberalism was ... the less unsatisfactory of the rival parties.'[88] As a consequence, although the 1886 division within Liberalism was shared by nonconformist Protestantism, it was not on the same lines. The nonconformist alliance at first refused to take part in politics.[89] The Methodist Conference in London in August 1886 passed a resolution condemning the introduction of party politics into Methodist buildings or meetings.[90] The historian of Congregationalism records that prior to Home Rule when the denomination was almost entirely Liberal it had been easy to introduce political resolutions at the Annual Congregational Union, but that afterwards the situation was quite different.[91] No Free Church denomination (outside Ireland) attempted a resolution on Home Rule at any of the annual denominational conferences and any resolution of support for Gladstone and his attempts to resolve Irish grievances never referred to the specifics of the 1886 Bill.[92] Even in the resolutions condemning coercion as a policy, which were passed at such conferences during the next few years, Home Rule was never referred to directly.[93]

If not nationally then, but in certain regions, as Raphael Samuel wrote, in 'the 1890s ... Nonconformity reached some kind of zenith of political influence.'[94] This was certainly true in Birmingham where the leadership of Dale and Chamberlain led the Birmingham nonconformists to join the Unionist cause. Dale's opposition was based on opposition to the Home Rule Bill's clause which excluded the Irish from Westminster, but would continue to extract taxation from Ireland. The other influential Free Churchman who became Unionist was Charles Spurgeon, a Baptist who was the best known British preacher of the day.[95] Spurgeon's opposition was, however, based on the fears for future treatment of Irish Protestants under a largely Catholic parliament. As will be seen in Chapter Four, the Liberal Unionists attempted to make the long-established nonconformist distrust of Catholicism into a political movement through the Nonconformist Unionist Association, which reached the peak of its activity in 1892. This was not simply historical prejudice against a rival faith: Nonconformity stood for the principles of humanitarianism, self-help, sobriety and, above all, resistance to the confessional state. The announcement of papal infallibility in 1870 that helped to trigger the Kulturkampf in Germany and Gambetta's 'Voila l'ennemi!' campaign in France, alienated many Liberals in Britain as well. As the *Christian World* put it, 'centuries of Popish rule have taught us that we can never trust them when once they have power in their hands.'[96]

The fear of 'Rome Rule' was shared by almost all the Protestants of Ireland, both those who feared specific measures of injustice, such as the endowment of Catholic schools, and those who spoke wildly of pogroms of Protestants. Other nonconformist Unionists identified by D. W. Bebbington include Congregationalists such as Christopher Newman Hall, Henry Allon, Robert Bruce and John Stoughton and Presbyterians like Oswald Sykes and John Monro Gibson.[97] Koss also suggests that Wesleyan Methodists, predominant in Cornish nonconformity, were far more 'middle-class and traditionalist' than both Primitive Methodists or the other dissenters.[98] On the other hand, such was the appeal of Gladstone's reputation among chapel-goers that, in the words of the *Baptist*, 'men ... were overawed by the stature of the Liberal leader and so lost their power of independent judgement.'[99] The experience of Wales demonstrated that it is impossible to support any bland claim that the nonconformist middle class were able to salve their consciences by voting for Liberal Unionists instead of Conservatives, as they became increasingly concerned by the rise of socialism and 'New' Liberalism.[100] It will be shown later, however, that in certain regions and, for different reasons, the Liberal Unionist Party was highly effective in bringing dissenters into the Unionist camp, at least until 1902.

As early as December 1885, Edward Watkin had claimed that Home Rule was a perversion of 'true Liberalism.'[101] William Cartwright, campaigning in Northamptonshire had denied being 'a seceder from my political principles.'[102] Craig Sellar, when writing to advise Hartington to sit on the opposition benches in July 1886, had referred to the Liberal Unionists as 'the true church of Liberalism.'[103] Edward Heneage had expressed the sentiment most fully, writing to his (separatist) agent in January 1887:

> I deny that we are Dissentient Liberals; we are consistent Liberals and Unionists; the others are Radicals and Home Rulers who dissent on every part of the Bills among themselves and include Unionists like Herschell and Rosebery and Separatists like Parnell and Labouchere in their ranks.[104]

Colonel Henry Hozier, the first secretary of the Liberal Unionist Association, took this attitude still further, when he addressed the West of Scotland Association in October 1886:

> They were not dissenters, they were the True Church. He claimed that they held those noble Liberal principles that had been handed down from generation to generation of Liberals to all Liberal statesmen since the Great Reform Act.[105]

Writing in the Party organ in October 1888, the poet Ernest Myers claimed that the break over Home Rule was 'a calamity which contains the promise of a purer and more vigorous revival.' Like Dicey, he saw the Liberal Unionists as the standard bearers for the true values of Liberalism, as it had been defined by the Party during the 1860s (largely through the work of Mill), and he saw the attempt by Gladstone to deviate from these principles as something akin to apostasy. It was not by accident that he used biblical language to express his hopes for the future of the Party:

> When the stock of true Liberalism has again borne fruit upward, when the party has purged itself of the false crew who have conspired to trail our flag in the mire ... although the Liberals may be for a time a less numerous host, they will not be ... a weaker one.[106]

As W. C. Lubenow has demonstrated, the voting behaviour of the Liberal Unionists in the 1886–1892 parliament showed considerable similarity between them and their former colleagues on all issues apart from Home Rule.[107] Like a radical religious sect breaking away from the body of an established church, many Liberal Unionists saw themselves as a righteous

minority persecuted by the sinful and ignorant, but assured of an ultimate
victory in the political paradise to come.

What, then, were the 'principles of 1885' around which the Party had
once united, which the Gladstonians had abandoned and to which the Liberal
Unionists claimed to be the true heirs?[108] First, as Dicey himself frequently
reminded audiences, was the demand that the law had to be obeyed and that, by
breaching the law and encouraging others to do so, the Nationalists had lost the
right to demand political reform from Parliament. As *Liberal Unionist Association
Memoranda*, in a specially produced supplement to coincide with the introduction of the second Home Rule Bill, expressed it, there were benefits to be had:

> The history of the past seven years has shown that Ireland can be
> tranquil and prosperous under the rule of the Imperial Parliament in
> which she is adequately, if not excessively represented, that the rights
> of individuals and of minorities are represented and enforced; and that
> her mutual resources can be developed.[109]

Liberal Unionists believed that the liberal constitution that had evolved by
1867 acted as a bulwark against despotism and sectarianism. All the ref-
erences to 'upholding the rule of law' which may appear to many modern
scholars to be mere English cant which overlooked the suffering of the Irish
people, were in fact based on the principle that true freedom of action was
only possible when the law, rather than a class, race or denomination, ruled
the country.[110] As Liberals, Hartington's Party believed that 'justice for
Ireland' could be delivered, but only within the British constitutional frame-
work that had taken such historic struggle to erect. Liberal Unionism was
based on the principle of civic inclusivity; tolerance of other interest groups
whether political, social or religious was to be enshrined in the legal frame-
work overseen and regulated by an inclusive legislature.

Secondly, the 'principles of 1885' alluded to a belief in a quasi-Spencerian
form of political evolution from fear, inequality and reaction towards trust,
liberty and progress. This was best summarised in Andrew Reid's celebrated
collection of answers from leading Liberals to the apparently simple question 'why are you a Liberal?' Although Chamberlain and Gladstone's succinct
answers are perhaps the most famous, the response of Lubbock, a behavioural
scientist as well as a banker and a politician, perhaps summarised the traditional principles of Liberalism most completely:

> I have been a Liberal because the Liberal Party has been contending for
> principles ... among the most important of which may be mentioned

civil and religious liberty, peace abroad, economy at home, free trade, a fairer distribution of seats, the extension of the franchise and last but not least, the general education of the people.[111]

Therefore it was not a surprise to find T. H. Huxley and Herbert Spencer as active supporters of the Liberal Unionist Party, as it attempted to persuade the Conservatives to make elementary education free of charge, resisted the perceived threat of clericalism in a devolved Ireland and promoted a politics of conscience, collaboration and compromise over one of party discipline, confrontation and dogmatism.

There were of course some disputed principles in the legacy of mid-Victorian Liberalism which the Liberal Unionists laid claim to and which disrupted the new Party to some degree as they had the Liberal Party as a whole since 1865. The issue of temperance was a major feature of late Victorian Liberalism and support for the 'local option' was an article of faith among some radicals. Isabella Tod, certainly the most tireless of all the Party's female speakers, complained in 1889 that 'it has been a constant distress to us that at many of the by-elections the Unionist candidate has been ... sometimes infriendly, when asked for his opinion on temperance questions.'[112] A 'Scottish Radical Unionist' went so far as to suggest that 'no inconsiderable number of Radical Unionists ... deem the drink evil a much greater danger to the country than the separatism of Messrs Parnell and Gladstone.'[113] Another 'Scottish Radical Unionist' offered an alternative explanation for the by-election defeats at Ayr and Govan, suggesting that, 'a candidate who temporises in regard to the drink question simply courts defeat.'[114] In a move clearly designed to influence the outcome of the Partick by-election in 1890, the *Glasgow Herald* asserted that 'the Unionist candidate [Parker Smith] is sounder on the liquor question.'[115] In the end, though, the Conservatives' decision not only to ignore the demands for reform from their Liberal allies, but even to introduce a compensation clause into the 1890 Licensing Bill, drove the most active of all Party's organisers, W. S. Caine, to resign in protest and force a by-election in 1890.[116] Caine's mutiny was a source of some embarrassment to a Party nominally Liberal as a whole and radical in part, but was mitigated by the refusal of other such committed temperance campaigners as T. W. Russell to join Caine's protest.[117] On the other hand, the secretary of the radical WSLUA confessed at the AGM in 1890 that 'the question of the licensing clauses caused a temporary but very deep disturbance throughout our Association ... the severe shock shook the loyalty of not a few.'[118] Caine's dramatic decision must have been motivated by personal discomfort as much as by principle, though. Henry James recorded that 'he [Caine] could not much longer stand being hissed at and hated at every temperance meeting he attended and should probably go back to Gladstonian Liberalism.'[119] It was, however, a dramatic, sudden and very public rejection of the Party by a figure often seen as one of Chamberlain's chief lieutenants. Yet his resignation speech did not simply criticise the government on the Licensing Clauses of Goschen's Local Taxation (Customs and Excise Duties) Bill, but went much further, announcing that he would do all he could to defeat the government and formally declaring himself no longer a member of the Liberal Unionist Party.[120] Within months, he had subscribed £20 to the British Fund in Aid of the Irish National Struggle.[121] Such a dramatic *volte face* demonstrated the great passion that the temperance movement inspired in later Victorian political culture and the bewilderment among those less concerned. As the *Manchester Guardian* commented, 'if merely talking about beer can make a man forget his strongest principles, what must drinking it do?'[122]

If temperance was the issue on which the Party was most divided, the issue of free trade appeared to be a shibboleth for all Liberals. Accusations that a Home Rule government, dominated by the Nationalists would introduce tariffs to protect Irish agriculture, added to the concern about Gladstone's alliance with Parnell among Liberal voters.[123] The advent of Labour candidates in the late 1880s, with their demands for greater collectivism and defense of British employment in the face of cheap foreign imports, had been gleefully derided by the Liberal Unionists, who could accuse the Gladstonians of having abandoned the great financial policy of Cobden and Bright. If there was to be closer commercial union with the Empire, it would be on the basis of free trade.[124] It was therefore with some dismay that the *Liberal Unionist* reported Salisbury's speech at Hastings in May 1892, in which he hinted that the agricultural sector, suffering the worst depression of the century, might be stimulated by some measure of Protection. St. Loe Strachey complained that the speech was 'most unwise.' The Liberal Unionist Party 'is a Free trade party', he claimed and Salisbury threatened the stability of the 'compact' if this was not respected, for 'any attempt to tamper with Free trade must break up the alliance with the Conservatives.' The terms of the alliance had to be evenly observed, especially in light of the recent Welsh Bill, 'while Radical Unionists refrain from attacking the Church, the Protectionist Tories should surely keep their hands off Free Trade.'[125] Not all Liberal Unionists agreed, such as W. V. Jacklin, an organiser in Glasgow, who criticised free trade as 'delusive and treasonable' and claimed that the policy was the cause of the disruptions in Ireland.[126] The divisions over the issue remained hidden within the Party until 1903, though, when Chamberlain's sudden conversion to tariff reform convulsed both his Party and Balfour's Conservatives.

Perhaps the most difficult issue for the Liberal Unionists was the question of the established church. Of course, in raising the issue of disestablishment, as he did in 1891–2, Chamberlain trod on some very important toes. It is clear that the threat of disestablishment had nearly caused a secession of moderate Liberals in Scotland as early as 1885 and had contributed to the scale of the Unionist revolt in the west of the country. For Salisbury and the bulk of his Party, maintenance of the established church was part of the Conservatives' apostolic creed. As David Steele has convincingly described, Lord Salisbury devoted a huge amount of his precious time between 1886 and 1892 struggling to pass a Tithe Bill (which failed) and a Clergy Discipline Bill (which succeeded in 1892), neither of which did much to aid the alliance with the nonconformist Liberal Unionists. His intention in these cases, as in the introduction of free elementary education in 1891, was to reform the Church in order to protect it from attack.[127] When he no longer relied on Liberal Unionist votes, his attitude towards the church became clearer both in the Education Bill of 1896 and the Clerical Tithes Bill of 1899, which provoked a back-bench Liberal Unionist revolt led by Leonard Courtney.[128]

A crucial element of the Liberal Unionist ethos was the freedom of personal conscience and political action, which had been increasingly challenged by the growth of party structures and the increased power of party organisers in general and party leaders in particular. The broadening of the electorate in 1867 was clearly the crucial event in determining the future of the British political system, what H. J. Hanham has described as 'the first decisive event in ... the "transition to democracy."'[129] The evolution of party apparatus from 1867 to 1885 was largely a response to the substantially enlarged electorate, which, in turn required the work of substantial professional organisations to canvas, cajole and co-opt. Nationally, both Liberals and Conservatives created a central organisation which brought the local party bodies under varying degrees of control. On a constituency level, paid party agents organised sophisticated political associations and recruited activists who checked the electoral register, door-to-door, raised funds and held formal and social meetings. The 1883 Corrupt Practices Act placed strict limits on the expenditure that associations could deploy and thus required the use of volunteer workers, which brought middle-class women (those with the time and means to play this role) into national political life.[130] Successive political leaders also appealed over the head of parliament to the electorate (most recently Gladstone in the Midlothian campaign) through public speeches and electoral campaigns. Popular support, not parliamentary support, became the crucial measure of political success and this led to Chamberlain's attempt to seize the political initiative by issuing the 'unauthorised programme' in

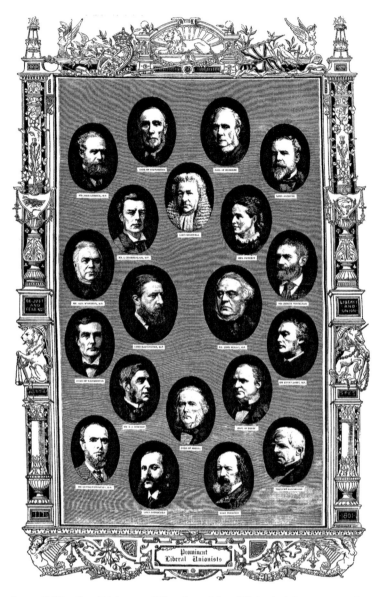

Image 7: The *Graphic*'s image of 'Prominent Liberal Unionists' demonstrates that Liberals of every hue supported the new party. Note that John Bright's image is the only one of an equal size to Hartington's. George Trevelyan would leave the party within months. The *Graphic*, 15 January 1887.

1885. Most historians agree with Angus Hawkins that by 1886, 'parliamentary government had gone ... parties and their leadership ... incontestably exercised that sovereignty formerly belonging to parliament itself.'[131] This was recognised by other commentators, who bemoaned the passing of 'an assembly where gentlemen gathered to exercise their independent prerogative and reason.'[132]

As Hawkins has also illustrated, the achievement of reform in 1867 had been the result of a parliamentary battle with MPs dictating their terms successively to Gladstone and Disraeli, whereas the 1884 Reform Act had merely been rubber-stamped by Parliament after it had been agreed privately between the Conservative and Liberal leaders.[133] Criticism of the emerging rigid party structure was most effectively expressed by Sir Henry Maine, a year before the Home Rule crisis, who condemned the reduction of independent MPs to the role of mere delegates.[134] It was dissatisfaction with this trend, opposition to an illiberal development, and the loss of influence of traditional aristocratic and local gentry families that explains the composition of much of the Liberal Unionist Party, not a natural affinity with the Conservatives. Goschen was the exception, not the rule (and Goschen, of course, had failed to support the 'party of 1885'). Hence, as the *Liberal Unionist* put it, 'no small proportion of those Liberals whose sympathies were entirely Unionist were men who had never been in the habit of taking an active share in party politics.'[135] In 1891, one Association even declared that 'the Unionists were not party politicians.'[136] This is why Wilde had his hero Jack Worthing, declare that he had no politics, and was thus a Liberal Unionist. Liberal Unionists were those who regarded themselves as supporters of enlightened principles and remained aloof from the squalid business of party dispute.

Liberal Unionism was therefore as much a reaction against the growing power of party machinery in general and Gladstone's arbitrary attempt to impose a new Liberal orthodoxy in particular, as a dismissal of the principle of Irish autonomy. Hartington complained of Gladstone in 1886, 'did any leader ever treat a party in the way that he has done?'[137] One former Liberal MP, Duncan McLaren, resigned his presidency of the Edinburgh South Liberal Association on the grounds that Gladstone had attempted 'a virtual assumption of political autocracy or dictatorship.'[138] Lord Selborne condemned Gladstone as 'a revolutionary demagogue.'[139] Victoria Barbery has shown how Sir Henry James was able to undermine Gladstone's position as the 'people's tribune' by highlighting his own consistency on the Home Rule issue and thus to offer himself as 'a strong, alternative lead[er].'[140] Gladstone's political ability was unquestioned, as was the respect for his achievements in the past, but now the Liberal Unionists considered that he had abandoned his statesman-like concern for the whole community in favour of the pursuit of power, whatever the cost to his principles.

Gladstone's lack of consideration for the stated principles of his own Party was probably crucial in provoking John Bright to join the Unionists. As he wrote to Caine, 'what will be the value of a party when its whole power is laid at the disposal of a leader from whose authority no appeal is allowed?'[142] It was this dislike of the Party leadership's dictatorial tendencies which could unite the leader of the moderate Unionists, Lord Hartington, with the leader of the radical Unionists, Joseph Chamberlain. As T. A. Jenkins has observed, the authoritarian approach which Gladstone appeared to be taking to the Irish question was regarded by many, such as Bright and Arthur Elliot, as contrary to the principles of a Party founded to protect the right of individuals to hold firm to their principles.[143] A Liberal was distinguished, according to Andrew Reid, by his 'love of his own conscience more than the approval of the conscience of the people'[144] and Gladstone's capitulation to the conscience of Nationalist Ireland led many to reject their revered leader, as the cartoons of the day reflected.[145] Of course, the only aspect of Parliament that still expressed views not dictated by the party whips and not based on the appeal to popular sentiment, the House of Lords, was almost fully united against the concept of Home Rule, as can be seen by the revolt of the Liberal Lords in 1886 and the devastating scale of the defeat of the second Home Rule Bill in 1893. This in turn led to Rosebery's tentative criticisms of the position of the Lords, which would eventually flourish into the constitutional crisis of 1910.

Many individual MPs had felt, since the creation of a mass electorate in 1867, that they had lost their independence as the need for party structure had resulted in an increase in the power of the party leaders or 'wire-pullers' who were now able to 'boss' their votes and personal manifestoes.[141] In Grimsby, Heneage denounced the 'caucus wire-pulling' as the Liberal Association sought to disown him in July 1886, even though they had endorsed him during the election.

The dislike of the limitations on the autonomy of MPs in Parliament, which many moderate Liberals already felt was compounded by the obstructive tactics of the Irish Nationalists between 1877 and 1885, provided many Liberals with a connection between the distaste for 'wire-pulling' and the distaste for Irish politicians. A desire to preserve the independence of MPs was perhaps the single most common motivating factor in the decision of most of the 1886 rebels to join the breakaway Liberal Unionist Association on 5 August. The attitude of moderate Unionists towards their caucuses is perhaps best epitomised by F. W. Maude, honorary secretary of the Liberal Unionist Committee. When the South Oxfordshire Liberal Association deselected him, he wrote to the *Oxford Chronicle* angrily asserting the right of candidates not to behave like 'clockwork voting machines, of which the party whip shall be entrusted with the keys.'[146] The behaviour of some caucuses towards long-sitting MPs may have played a role in temporarily driving some Liberals away from the Party, unused as they were to being addressed in the fashion that Sir Henry Hussey Vivian's constituency Association adopted when they met at Neath:

> He [S.T. Evans] did not know whether they were to call Sir Hussey a representative or a delegate (A Voice – 'Delegate!'). He would not parley with words, but if he did not vote with Mr Gladstone, he would be misrepresenting them, and his course should be to place his seat in the hands of his constituents (Applause).[147]

Perhaps far more typical of the initial relationship between the Liberal Unionist MPs and their caucuses was the experience of Edward Heneage and the Grimsby Liberal Association. Here 'the 300' clearly disagreed with Heneage's strongly expressed opposition to Home Rule, but refused to de-select him because, as Heneage put it, 'I imagine that they still believe in my honesty and Liberalism.'[148] Local Liberal Associations, aware of the affection that long-standing MPs enjoyed among their constituents, were reluctant at this early stage to risk damaging what had been hitherto a working relationship profitable for both sides over an issue that would, most likely only last as long as Gladstone's surely short, remaining career. Heneage's own agent and his chief confidant and correspondent, James Wintringham, was a supporter of Home Rule, who successfully demanded that the Association continue to select Heneage as the Liberal candidate in 1886, as he 'truly represents us in nine points out of ten.'[149]

This reluctance to accept the party system cannot merely be regarded as a resistance among moderates to give up their cherished freedom of action, however. Three prominent members of the Party, Gell, Courtney and Lubbock, regarded the party system as the unfortunate result of the nature of British democracy as it had evolved over the century and continued to campaign for proportional representation, though there is little evidence for popular support for this cause in the movement, despite Gell's belief that 'proportional representation would have saved us from the present misfortune.'[150] As Dicey put it in a letter to St. Loe Strachey in 1894, 'sham parliamentary government means a very vicious form of government by party.'[151] Millicent Fawcett, herself invoking her late husband's support for a 'national' party, wrote of her dislike of party influence on public behaviour, 'witness the hissing of Mr

Caine by his former friends in the temperance movement, and the rancour with which the Liberal Unionists in Dorsetshire and in the Eighty Club have been drummed out of the Party.'[152] Part of the Liberal Unionists' discontent with party politics was the reduction of MPs from the role of local representatives, to mere lobby fodder, ordered into action by cracking of the party whip. Many Liberal Unionists prided themselves on their strong connections with, and consequent representation of, the distinct regional identity and local needs of their constituencies. This helps to explain the survival of isolated MPs such as Henry Hobhouse in Somerset, Cuthbert Quilter in Suffolk, Harry Anstruther in St. Andrews and even Edward Watkin in Hythe, as well as the regional powerbases of the Party, in areas with a strong sense of local distinctiveness, such as Cornwall, Glasgow and Birmingham.

However, campaigns such as Home Rule helped to turn politics in late Victorian England from a patchwork of local variety into a black and white division on national issues. Voters, studies have suggested, began to vote for national parties in these circumstances (or abstain as did many Liberals in 1886), rather than local candidates.[153] As a result, parties rather than individual MPs became increasingly powerful and the battle for party leadership and control of the political agenda became the chief struggle for political success. In this way, the local Liberal Unionist MP was constantly required to accept issues advocated by his Party (or his Party's allies) that his conscience rebelled against. The decision to support coercion in 1887 produced the first revolt against the Party's leadership, followed by the growing exasperation with the lack of constructive reform (especially in Ireland) as the Conservative government struggled on. The exclusion from office (and the frustration of Chamberlain's social programme) prevented any further walk-outs between 1892 and 1895, but once a Unionist coalition was formed, a series of MPs with a strong sense of regional identity and political autonomy (most notably T. W. Russell and Leonard Courtney) left the Party.

Of course, this anti-caucus ideology was not shared by Chamberlain's Birmingham radicals and herein lay the fundamental problem of the Liberal Unionist Party. The very principles that motivated a revolt against the perceived tyranny of Gladstone's forced policy change (anti-Irish sentiment notwithstanding) were not shared by an important element of those who formed the Liberal Unionist Party. As the Divisional Council of the West Birmingham LUA put it in December 1888, 'we are not only Unionist, but we are radical Unionist and though we welcome the Conservatives when they come up to our standard, we do not go to Toryism.'[154] Unlike LUAs elsewhere, the West Birmingham branch sent copies of its resolutions in favour of 'improvements in local government and land tenure' to the Liberal Unionist

Party leadership and to Balfour and Salisbury.[155] Although the moderates may have nostalgically regarded the period before 1885 as an age when MPs were freer to act as they saw fit (and Parliament, not the executive or the party, held true power), to attempt to reverse the process was to defy the tide of political change that had become a tidal wave with the 1884 Act, when 58% of the adult male population gained the right to vote. In truth, these attitudes revealed a deliberate refusal to accept that politics in an age of democracy required the work of professional organisers. In an extraordinary attack, Thomas Raleigh, candidate for Edinburgh West in 1888 epitomised this view in an article on 'Democracy' in 1889, in which he dismissed the urging of his own Party's leaders such as Lord Wolmer and W. S. Caine:

> Party managers are always imploring us to organise, and it is true that nothing can be done without organisation. But it is not for the interest of the people that they should be strictly drilled and definitely brigaded to suit the convenience of party managers ... there must be large bodies of men prepared to vote on the merits of a great question, without regard to party interests.[156]

This view was shared by many Liberal Unionists, according to Argyll as 'all the most independent members of the Liberal Party repudiated and opposed [Home Rule].'[157] This nuanced view, in a period of increasingly polarised national politics was difficult to explain without a sophisticated propaganda machine and after its failures before 1892, the Party turned to the one man who had most embraced and embodied the new politics of the 1880s: Joseph Chamberlain. It is an indication of how desperate the Party's position had become that most of the moderates were prepared to abandon their fastidious dislike of the machinery of modern politics and hand their future to a man who neither respected their politics nor sympathised with their romantic yearning for a political world of individual MPs acting according to their consciences and mediated through bonds of kinship instead of caucuses, mass meetings and door to door canvassing.

As a believer in Liberalism as the gospel of individualism, the growing interest in social legislation profoundly alarmed Dicey, as it did others in the Party, but the fear of socialism, emphasised by many historians of the Liberal Unionist Party as the motive behind the split of 1886, does not appear to have figured very strongly in the writings of the Party's leaders before 1890. In January 1890, in response to the announcement of the 'Newcastle Programme', the *Liberal Unionist* declared 'we shall not consent to the erection of fresh inequalities in the name of Socialism' and gave its front page to an attack by Montague Crackenthorpe on 'the deadening methods of state socialism.' The article read almost like a line by line repudiation of the 'unauthorised programme' of 1885, in the name of orthodox Liberalism. 'The state,' Crackenthorpe wrote, 'cannot undertake to provide sanitary dwellings at the expense of the taxpayers. That would be to do injustice to the class that would not share the benefit, and to demoralise the class that would.' In this way, he still exhorted the rugged individual to seize opportunity and to overcome adversity in a fashion that J. S. Mill and the recently deceased Matthew Arnold would have found wholly acceptable. He also recorded his objection to the Eight Hours Bill, which Hartington opposed and, in a choice of issue possibly designed to provoke the reaction of those such as George Dixon, free education.[158] Instead, the typically mid-Victorian solution of 'philanthropy' was favoured. In this way, Biagini's claim that 'there was a link between the Union and social reform', is, at least until 1891, untenable.[159] Less contentiously, the article recorded the Party's objection to the 'New Unionism' on the grounds that self-interest was the trade unions' main motivation, not a concern for the success of their industry.[160] As the issue of Home Rule receded, however, and working men were increasingly exposed to propaganda from the Labour movement, through Robert Blatchford's *Clarion* and Joseph Burgess' *Workman's Times,* the Liberal Unionists were forced to offer their model of gradualist reform in opposition to more expansive and utopian appeals. The Party newspaper warned that 'socialism ... based as it must be on compulsion would diminish the wealth of the world', which would perhaps have been somewhat ineffective as a disincentive to the 30% of the population that Booth estimated lived in a state of 'chronic want.'[161] Chamberlain was careful to appeal to consistent Liberal principles when he advocated old age pensions at the Aston by-election in 1891, assuring middle class voters that he favoured a policy of insurance and rejecting compulsion.[162] He was, however, coming under pressure from his own constituency Association in West Birmingham, who intended to hold him to his promise that 'more attention [would be] given to the great social questions which directly affect the interests of the working classes.'[163] He recognised that a refusal to countenance any state intervention in the hours of labour would lead to disaster in the East Midlands and South Yorkshire: 'I doubt if any candidate has a chance in mining districts other than the northern coalfields unless he is willing to accept at all events the second reading of the [8 hours] Bill.'[164] W. H. Smith and Hartington attempted to defuse the Eight Hours issue by appointing a Royal Commission on Labour in March 1891. Derby accepted Smith's invitation to serve on the commission and Hartington told him frankly that 'the one main object ... is to gain time, and avoid the necessity of acting on the dangerous eight hours question until after the general election.'[165] Once the general election was safely disposed of, Chamberlain was clearly determined to push the issue, as he strove to expand the Party's cross-class appeal. He wrote to James in October 1892, announcing his intention to create a programme of social legislation: 'the only doubtful item is the 8 hours bill for miners' but he reassured Hartington's retainer that 'it cannot possibly do harm, and may do good.'[166]

With the announcement of the 'Newcastle Programme' in 1890 and the constant repetition of Gladstone's assertion that he stood for 'the masses' against 'the classes', it was incumbent upon the Liberal Unionists to demonstrate their commitment to constructive reform, whilst stressing their desire to legislate in favour of the whole community rather than the sectarian interests of any particular class. The Party's gradual acceptance of a more collectivist approach is normally associated with the take-over of Chamberlain as leader in January 1892 when Hartington succeeded to the Dukedom of Devonshire. There is some evidence that the Party was influenced by the work of the social investigators who would later influence Hobson and Leonard Hobhouse in the change of Liberal Party policy after 1895 and which is usually referred to as 'New Liberalism.' In 1889, the *Liberal Unionist* printed a lengthy and detailed summary of Booth's *Life and Labour of the People*.[167] Hartington himself acknowledged the need for a more reforming approach when he complemented the work that Chamberlain had achieved in free education and allotments. He acknowledged that more could be done, but used the convenient scapegoat of 'Irish obstruction' to justify the lack of substantial progress on social issues.[168]

The influence of D. G. Ritchie's 1891 work, *The Principles of State Interference*, which advocated broadening the role of the state in removing obstacles to an individual's life chances, was particularly felt among the radical Unionists. Of course, radical Unionism had been a very muted philosophy until then, confined to the constituencies of individual MPs, Birmingham and the west of Scotland. Constructive Unionism was genuinely accepted by 'Englishmen of ordinary common sense [who] ... have no objection ... to secure by Tory aid, solid legislative benefits.'[169] At first, however, the benefits (and the 'Tory aid') seemed limited. Proposals such as the 1887 Land Transfer Bill and the Tithes Bill had been lost in the 'Massacre of the Innocents' caused by the debate on the Crimes Bill, while ideas such as 'Home Rule All Round' were diluted in the face of Conservative and Scottish and Ulster Liberal Unionist opposition, to form the basis of the granting of county councils through the Local Government Act of 1888 (for Scotland in 1889).

As had been demonstrated in their pressure on Salisbury to pass an Irish Land Bill in 1887, land purchase was the preferred Liberal Unionist solution to land issues on both sides of the Irish Sea. Chamberlain had chaired the 1888 Select Committee on Small Holdings and eventually, after much pressure from both Chamberlain and Collings' Rural Labourers' League, the Small Agricultural Holdings Act was passed, just before the dissolution of parliament. After the failure to convince Gladstone to accept the 'unauthorised programme', much was made of this measure (despite Collings' concern that it lacked any compulsory element), in demonstrating how the needs of British workers were more effectively resolved under a Unionist, rather than a Home Rule, administration.[170]

It was only with the disastrous defeats at South Molton and Rossendale that senior moderate Party figures began to accept the need for a more positive manifesto. In February 1892, Henry Hobhouse proposed a scheme for Irish local government, 'acceptable to all Liberal Unionists' and followed this with a demand for a parish and district council reform.[171] On the other hand, aristocrats like Argyll warned Salisbury that 'Chamberlainism is an unstable element – and an image which may require "bloody sacrifices".'[172] Argyll's view was not shared in the west of Scotland where the regional Liberal Unionist Association pressed their demands for land reform in order to reduce the flood of emigration from the Highlands. Admittedly, the defection of James Caldwell in 1890 and the defeat of Fraser Mackintosh in 1892 blunted the Association's influence, but their constant pressure for procedural as well as administrative reform, both before and after the 1892 election, allowed Chamberlain to claim that there was a demand for a less timorous policy across Great Britain. The campaign for free elementary education, granted before the election, had been assisted by the advocacy of Cameron Corbett, MP for Glasgow Tradeston, who had introduced a private members bill to this effect in 1881.[173]

As the 1892 election drew close, Chamberlain wrote to James illustrating the weakness of the moderates in winnable seats, with Lichfield as an example. 'I told Wolmer that the candidate must go for the 8 hours miners' bill. Yet [Major] Darwin who knows nothing and cares little about the question is sent without instructions and goes awry. Consequently what would have been a safe seat for us is very doubtful.'[174] Exasperated, Chamberlain washed his hands of the moderate Liberal Unionist MPs in rural seats (despite the fact that he was their leader), writing to Wolmer that 'I cannot answer for the Dodos in the country.'[175] Chamberlain, leader of a Party which had very nearly been obliterated in the general election, with his personal electoral triumph in Birmingham as evidence, now sought to convert the Liberal

Unionists to a policy of constructive reform in almost every aspect of government and administration. Although Matthew Fforde is quite right to describe Chamberlain's motivation as chiefly political, 'a response to a threat, not the product of inner conviction', the enthusiasm with which the social programme was taken up in Glasgow, Birmingham and Cornwall and also by the Women's LUA, demonstrates that it built on Liberal traditions of humanitarian reform, designed to prevent the vagaries of fate from limiting a worker's access to opportunity and self-advancement.[176] What resulted was a constructive, reformist Unionism, designed to out-flank socialist claims of class bias. Radicals might demand a more collectivist approach, and Tories and Whigs might jib at the sacrifices that had to be made by their aristocratic allies, but most Conservatives and Liberal Unionists could accept this new approach. Now the Unionist alliance could truly claim to be acting in the interest of the whole community and not merely as an alliance of negation. As this domestic policy was allied to a defence of British interests abroad and, after 1895, a policy of aggressive imperial expansion, the way was paved for the twentieth-century electoral success of the Conservative and Unionist Party.

G. R. Searle believes that by 1894 Chamberlain's new direction had led to a new division in the Unionist alliance. Less significant by now, he claims, was the distinction between Liberal Unionists and Conservatives. Instead one could delineate between the 'moderate' and the 'advanced' Unionists.[177] In 1894 Chamberlain had devised a clever strategy to try to win Devonshire's support for his programme of social reform. When Rosebery, desperate for a political lifeline for his foundering government launched his attack on the House of Lords at Bradford, Chamberlain wrote to his leader, claiming that the best way to prevent Rosebery's crusade catching fire among working-class voters was to offer them constructive alternatives. 'Information obtained from a great number of constituencies by Powell Williams ... show that the electors are much more interested at the present time in social questions and the problems connected with the agitation of the Labour Party.' He now made a highly ambitious claim: 'I have reason to know that ... Lord S. is favourable in principle to all the proposals which I submitted in my Birmingham speech [12 October 1894]

- Amendment to Artisans' Dwellings Act
- House Purchase
- Courts of Arbitration
- General Provision for Accidents,

Chamberlain was careful not to trouble Devonshire 'with the matters in detail', but raised the spectre of 'the wild schemes of confiscation and revolutionary change' to try to frighten the increasingly timorous Duke into publicly advocating his own 'practical' policies or at least offering 'the expression of willingness' to seek such reforms.[178] Chamberlain had, in fact, merely asked Wolmer to ask his father-in-law 'whether it might not be possible for the House of Lords to spoil the game of the Gladstonians by itself dealing with some of the important social questions by means of bills?' Chamberlain had assumed that 'Lord Salisbury is not opposed to any of them' and had suggested 'as especially worthy of attention the House Purchase Bill, the extension of the Artizans' Dwellings Act, the establishment of Courts of Arbitration, Compensation for Injuries and Aliens Immigration.'[179] In reply Salisbury had informed Wolmer that he saw 'his way pretty clearly to the introduction of an Aliens Immigration Bill and of an Arbitration Bill ... he is afraid that any attempt to deal with the question of the purchase of working men's dwellings ... would be held to be an infringement of the privileges of the Commons.' In the area of Employers' Liability, Salisbury felt constrained by two problems: 'the domestic servants one' and 'the susceptibility of the employers generally.' He even claimed that the Bills could not be introduced into the Lords as he lacked colleagues competent to do so. While he did tell Wolmer, as Chamberlain told Devonshire, 'that these criticisms are not to be taken as indicating any want of sympathy on his part with your general views on these subjects', one cannot escape the conclusion that Salisbury was attempting to string Chamberlain along and that Chamberlain was attempting to do the same to Devonshire.[180]

Chamberlain again tried to use the grass-roots Conservative organisations to promote his more progressive policies, as he had once attempted to enlist them through their architect, Randolph Churchill. He wrote to James, no doubt hoping to influence him to work on the Duke: 'I hope you read the resolution of the National Scottish Conservative Association supporting every one of my proposals and urging the peers to initiate the legislation.'[181] At the same time, it was clear that he was prepared to compromise his long-held position on the upper chamber and to defend it against Rosebery's attack. He may have stated at a meeting at the Coliseum that 'I am ready to view with favour any reasonable proposal which would add an elective element to the House of Lords', but he made it clear at the Liberal Unionist conference at Durham on 16 October, in the presence of Lord Londonderry and Lord Durham, that 'until you can find me a better, I am going to stick to the House of Lords.' As for Rosebery's attack on the peers, 'it is merely a device to give a fillip to the jaded spirits of a pumped out party.'[182]

Once Chamberlain's programme was out-manouevred by Salisbury, Akers-Douglas and Middleton in 1895, the possibility returned of the divisions within Liberal Unionism reasserting themselves and crippling the Party as they had in 1892. In these circumstances, Chamberlain's choice of the Colonial Office was natural. Not only was the defense of the Empire shared among most Liberal Unionists but Alfred Dicey had always stressed the historic mission of the British Empire and the centrality of the United Kingdom within the Empire. Any threat to the Union threatened the Empire and Dicey believed that Home Rule would ruin England and Ireland. He was supported in this view by J. R. Seeley, who had first developed a historical narrative of the positive benefits of the expansion of British identity in *The Expansion of England* (1883) and whose work is acknowledged to have influenced Chamberlain's imperial views.[183] The interest and concern for Empire, which had so troubled Gladstone in his third administration, could now be defended as the export of British liberties and freedoms and, as such, could appeal to a working-class audience, encouraged to support the cause of the imperial mission through popular newspapers and music hall.[184] It could also unite the varieties of ideology within the Unionist alliance, as those such as Lubbock could rationalise that 'a majority of Englishmen, Scotchmen and Irishmen [were] determined to maintain the integrity of the Empire' for solidly Liberal values such as 'the cause of law and order, of liberty and patriotism.'[185]

The threat that Home Rule presented to the British Empire had first been expressed by Lord Wolseley, speaking in London on 10 April 1886, when he urged the nation 'to say with one voice "hands off" to that man, no matter who he may be, who would dare break up and dismember this Empire and in doing so ruthlessly destroy it.'[186] It was also clear that in some working-class constituencies the issue of Empire could be equally important. During the election, a speaker addressing a large radical meeting asked 'why should anyone object to home rule?' and was answered by a number of voices 'because it will lead to the break up of the Empire.' The speaker, rather unwisely, responded 'who cares whether it will or not?' From that point, noted the Gladstonian *Inquirer,* the speaker lost his hold on the meeting and the paper concluded that British people clearly did care about the integrity of the Empire.[187] The cause of Empire could accommodate Liberals with very different views of its structure and operation, from the supporter of devolution, Lord Lansdowne, to federalists such as Lord Selborne and Earl Grey. It was also, of course, valuable common ground to share with the Conservatives, especially the illiberal figure of Salisbury, who claimed in June 1886 that he was fighting the election on 'one great issue ... the ... empire.'[188] The issue of Empire, although by no means a crucial matter in

JOEY AND THE LORDS.

JOEY :—"They toll not, neither do they spin, but —— they ARE useful sometimes, even to an Old Radical!"

Image 8: *The Dart* satirises Chamberlain's new found affection for the House of
Lords following Lord Rosebery's attacks. *The Dart*, 25 August 1894.

1886, increased in importance during the history of the Party, achieving its
apogee between the Diamond Jubilee and the Boer War, a war fought, in
theory at least, over the constitutional rights of Englishmen abroad. In some
ways this was inevitable, as, when Chamberlain spoke to Balfour in March
1886, he used this aspect of radicalism as the bridge in any future alliance
with the Conservatives. As he put it, 'my Radicalism at all events desires
to see established strong Government and an Imperial Government.'[189] In
1887, speaking at Ayr, he made his attitude public; Home Rule, he believed,
would 'pave the way for the dissolution of the Great Empire which has been
the envy and admiration of the world.'[190] Of course, the Liberal Unionists,
radicals and moderates alike, supported the concept of a 'Liberal Empire', the
chief exports of which were the rule of law, the promotion of representative
government, religious tolerance and the benefits of free trade.[191] This belief
in the moral purpose of Empire was, as Parry has convincingly demonstrated,
a key feature of nineteenth-century Liberal ideology.[192] It was, of course, in

marked contrast to Salisbury's view of Empire as an economic resource and strategic weapon, to be exploited by 'white people [who] possessed a special pedigree and played a privileged part in the world order.'[193] Nevertheless, as an advocate of a 'National Party' and an ardent imperialist, Chamberlain's growing support for closer ties between the metropolis, the dominions and the colonies could be read as an attempt to find common areas of agreement between the British political classes.[194] It must not be forgotten that 'Joe's war' was fought ostensibly over the issue of the civil rights of the Uitlanders, the British who were denied citizenship in the Transvaal, a republic notorious for its bigotry, race politics and lack of religious tolerance.[195]

As imperialism could appear very distant, one of the great achievements of the two Unionist Parties was to present the cause of Empire in a fashion which could excite and activate working-class voters. It is barely ever noted by historians that both Victoria's Golden and Diamond Jubilees took place during periods of Unionist dominance. In 1887, with the alliance tottering after Churchill had resigned and as Chamberlain and Trevelyan discussed reunion with Harcourt and Herschell, the Golden Jubilee was designed as an assertion of a united nation, in marked contrast to the alternate vision of devolution that Gladstone had proposed the previous year. Loughlin describes the event as 'a crucial landmark in the developing imperial identity of the British "race".'[196] Lady Monkswell recorded being 'sick with nervousness ... whether the Irishmen would take the opportunity of blowing us all up together – Queen, Lords and Commons in [Westminster] Abbey', noting the exclusion of Nationalist Ireland from the celebrations and a popular association between Catholicism and insurrection that had a clear parallel with the Gunpowder Plot of 1605.[197] In 1897, with the Unionist alliance secured, Home Rule defeated and the Empire at its zenith, the Diamond Jubilee was a celebration of the new politics of patriotism, organised by Chamberlain to test the consciences of those Liberals worried by the rise of anarchic republicanism, internationalist socialism and little-Englander Liberalism.[198] It was this Jubilee that was an opportunity for Chamberlain to begin to articulate a more openly 'racial' ideology of imperial unity which continued in his speeches (and those of other radical Unionists) until it became a central feature of the discourse of tariff reform.[199] On the occasion of both Jubilees, national bank holidays were supplemented with special acts of thanksgiving, reviving a mid-century custom of thanking God for his protection of Britain and its monarchy. The Queen's barely hidden support for the Unionists provided a means whereby Salisbury and Chamberlain could create a profitable association between the defense of the united nation and royal celebration.[200]

Liberal Unionism was, therefore, a deliberate political position, not a mere half-way stop on a journey from Liberal to Conservative. It was designed to appeal to those moderates, radicals and Free Churchmen who wished to oppose Home Rule without having to join with their historic opponents, the Tories. As with the Liberals before 1885, the Liberal Unionists were 'a party of ideas and ideals, much given to discussion and argument' on issues such as female suffrage, proportional representation, temperance and, above all, the role of the state.[201] Victoria Barbery over-states her case when she concludes, on the basis of her examination of the politics of Bury, that, '[Liberal Unionism] had a distinctive ideology; neither Whiggism, nor Conservatism' as there was no single set of principles to which all Liberal Unionists adhered, apart from support for the Union.[202] The dominant socio-economic interest in Liberal Unionism and the exact nature of the Party's ideology varied from region to region and, in some cases, from MP to MP.[203] Looking back in 1912, Viscount Wolmer (by now Earl of Selborne) restated his belief that the Liberal Unionists were 'the natural heirs of mid-Victorian Liberalism.'[204] He convincingly asserted that the Liberal Unionists had maintained the principles of constitutionalism, the defence of minorities and the benefit of the nation as a whole rather than self-interest, as well as the tenets of protestant Christianity through educational reform, electoral reform and social protection for the least wealthy.[205]

That the Party faced the challenge of organised Labour with a new programme after its bare electoral survival in 1892, demonstrated that it, like the Liberal Party before 1885, was capable of adapting to changed circumstances. As Jeremy Smith has demonstrated for the Conservative Party in the same period, to do so was not to compromise ideological principles, merely to alter the 'selection, emphasis and prioritizing of its assorted aims and beliefs.'[206] However, the failure of that new programme to be fully articulated and accepted and the ultimate demise of the Liberal Unionists as a party with a set of distinct ideologies, rather than a party of individuals with distinct principles, was a result of the divisions within Unionism, which were expertly manipulated by the Conservative leadership, who feared the consequences of such political experimentation.

CHAPTER 3

'LIBERAL YEAST TO LEAVEN THE CONSERVATIVE LUMP': THE UNIONIST ALLIANCE

The Birth of the Alliance

In light of the distinctively Liberal attitudes of Hartington's Party, Jonathan Parry has shown, 'few [of the Liberal Unionists] were enamoured of the Conservatives' apparently irrational, prejudiced, unintelligent governing style.'[1] When considering their future in August 1886, some Liberal Unionists, while admitting that the Conservatives were no longer the reactionary party of the past, still baulked at the prospect of joining them, as 'we hold it still to be to too great an extent a party of landlords.'[2] It is, therefore, ahistoric to regard, as most historians do, the Liberal Unionists and Conservatives as suitable candidates for an alliance or the eventual fusion between the Parties as inevitable.[3] What emerged was an electoral arrangement, created to serve the short-term needs of both Parties that gradually developed into a pact of mutual assistance, which both Parties attempted to exploit for their own profit. As Parry concludes, 'the Liberal Unionists reassured themselves that at least ... Salisbury might make a better fist of defending endangered values than the unprincipled, irresponsible, unEnglish Gladstone.'[4] The alliance was, at least until 1895, a marriage of convenience, not one born of mutual admiration.

Negotiations between the Tories and the Liberals opposing Gladstone's Home Rule Bill began with tentative proposals to George Goschen in February 1886. Lord Salisbury was keen, seeing an opportunity of ending a period of nearly forty years in which there had only been one Conservative majority government, and he restrained his Party from interfering in the Home Rule debate at Westminster, so that the opposition to Gladstone's Bill would come from within his own Party. On 16 May 1886, with the prospect of a snap election looming, Salisbury and Hicks Beach unveiled the electoral truce when they told the National Union of Conservative Associations that Conservatives must support Liberal Unionist candidates in constituencies where the Conservatives would have had no chance of defeating a Liberal in normal circumstances.[5] The Conservatives were therefore carefully responding to the concerns of the Liberals who did not wish to be publicly associated with 'their hateful allies' and were keeping their profile as low as possible.[6]

After the defeat of the Bill, Salisbury wrote to Goschen on 20 June to make arrangements for the forthcoming election. On the following day, Salisbury wrote directly to Lord Hartington asking for his intervention in seats where Conservatives were fighting Gladstonians. Although Hartington was reluctant to endorse Conservatives with whom he disagreed on a myriad of historic issues, against Liberals with whom he disagreed on one, he did respond to Salisbury's pleas and eventually agreed to advise Liberal Unionist voters to support Conservatives in seats where no Liberal Unionist was standing.

Prominent Liberal Unionists, such as Edward Heneage in Grimsby, were supported by the local Conservatives and felt no restrictions on their expression of Liberalism. One Conservative demanded, 'let no member of the Tory Party assist in returning to Parliament any Liberal',[7] but it appeared that in most constituencies the Liberal Unionists enjoyed considerable Conservative support for their principled stand against Home Rule. Under the terms of the informal agreement, a few leading Liberal Unionists were forced to stand aside for Conservatives. The nascent alliance did manage a more co-operative approach in four double constituencies, running Conservatives in harness with Liberal Unionists in Newcastle-upon-Tyne, York, Northampton and Portsmouth.

Once the 1886 election had produced a hung Parliament (albeit with a Unionist majority), the Liberal Unionists held the position of kingmakers. When Hartington asked Chamberlain his advice on whether or not to join a coalition, Chamberlain was quite adamant in his refusal and was supported by Lord Derby, who distrusted the Conservative leader. When he met Hartington on 24 July, Lord Salisbury found that the Liberal Unionist leader was determined **not** to enter a government as it would jeopardise his standing as a Liberal. Hartington had to consider the effect that twenty years of Conservative-Liberal antagonism had had on his own supporters. The Liberal Unionists were determined that they should be an independent Liberal group and resolved at an executive committee meeting on 24 July to maintain a separate headquarters, with subscriptions to local Liberal Associations to be broken off. Chamberlain, Lord Wolmer, James and Derby also advised

PUNCH, OR THE LONDON CHARIVARI.—JULY 31, 1886.

CROSS-ROADS.

S-L-sb-ry. " HULLO! AREN'T YOU FELLOWS GOING FURTHER WITH ME?"

Image 9: *Punch* detects strains in the Unionist alliance as soon as the 1886 election is over. *Punch*, 31 July 1886.

Hartington that the Party should continue to sit with the Gladstonians, now on the opposition benches.

The Liberal Unionists' choice masked serious ideological divisions. As early as May 1886, the *Birmingham Daily Post* described Chamberlain's faction as 'for Mr Gladstone, if he will but modify his plan' and Hartington's as those who 'would refuse, at any time or under any circumstances, to concede autonomy to Ireland.' The article concluded, pessimistically, 'the two sections ... can have no continuous ground of common action.'[8] Hartington himself confided to James that he could 'never ... be sure how far Chamberlain and I will be able to go on together.'[9] Once appointed as Chancellor and Leader of the Commons, Randolph Churchill attempted to appease the Liberal Unionists' conscience over Ireland, promising to implement local government reform. When Churchill unexpectedly resigned in December 1886, the pressure for a Hartington-led coalition government grew. However, the Tory chief whip, Aretas Akers-Douglas, played his first hand in his on-going attempt to keep Liberal Unionist influence to a minimum, warning that 'he

THE DRAFT HOUND.

Master of Hounds, loquitur :—

Hump! So he's here! Will he ever go back? Call him the pick of the opposite pack, Lent me awhile. It's exceedingly kind! Know him of old; wasn't quite to my mind Not so long since. Thought him most unreliable. Still, I've had losses, and so must be pliable. Looks a bit lonely! Would like to have had One or two kennel-mates, eh, my old lad?

Somehow, however, that couldn't be squared; Others hung back, but thought *you* could be spared. Compliment, truly! Your points they could never Appreciate fully. And yet you *are* clever! Promising pups, like the one I've just lost, Bring heaps of bother, involve lots of cost. You'll fill his place in a steadier style. Hope you'll get on with my kennel awhile.

Should have liked "Harty"; such hounds are so few! [do! Still, you *have* points, and—I think you may

At the annual Twelfth Night festivity given on the stage of Old Drury last Thursday, a Shakspearian actor cautiously declined the proffered slice. Quoting the reply of *Hubert*, he exclaimed, "Baddeley I fear!" And he did not "take the cake."

Image 10: *Punch*'s comment on the appointment of George Goschen as Chancellor of the Exchequer following Randolph Churchill''s resignation. *Punch,* 15 January 1887.

could not whip up the [Conservative] men for Hartington.'[10] The perception that the government was tottering was quelled by the appointment of Goschen as Chancellor of the Exchequer in January 1887, encouraged by Queen Victoria, Hartington and Heneage. Goschen was chosen as he was

ELEVENTH Year, No. 532.   THE   DART.   Friday, Dec. 31st, 1886.

ME AND RANDY.

Image 11: The Birmingham Tory periodical, *The Dart*, comments on Chamberlain and Randolph Churchill's isolation in the political arena after Churchill's resignation as Chancellor of the Exchequer. *The Dart*, 31 December 1886.

a Liberal barely distinguishable from the Conservatives in his economic outlook.

Of course, this was actually another coup for Salisbury and another blow for Chamberlain. Now the Birmingham leader had lost his most useful ally in the Conservative Cabinet, one who had expressed sympathy with the idea of a new party comprising the 'advanced' sections of both Unionist Parties. He was also now a member of a Party which was in an alliance with the previously derided Conservatives, and one that would most likely last for the remainder of the Parliament. As he put it, 'we may be face to face with a Tory government whose proposals no consistent Liberal will be able to support.'[11] The fall of Churchill meant that a Crimes Bill, which Chamberlain had openly denounced, would now be introduced. William Harcourt spotted that Chamberlain's position was uncomfortable, if not untenable, and responded positively to Chamberlain's suggestion of a meeting at the end of 1886 which eventually led to the 'Round Table' conference which has been described in such minute detail by Michael Hurst.[12]

When the Crimes Bill was introduced in March 1887, Hartington began to write to Salisbury, not to criticise the measure, but to ensure the distribution of honours among Liberal Unionists in exchange for their support. Chamberlain and his followers were the crucial problem, but here Hartington and Salisbury had a rare moment of good fortune. John Bright roused himself to offer his support to the Crimes Bill to Wolmer on the grounds that 'Mr Gladstone ought to have suppressed the Land League five years ago.'[13] As the Liberal Unionists had the choice of whether to support the Bill or bring the government down, the Conservatives could safely call their bluff and the Bill was passed with sixty-four Liberal Unionists voting in favour of it. For many Liberals, this was the issue which finally made the breach in the Liberal Party irreversible. Henry James in Bury had managed to weather the storm of criticism that followed his vote against the Home Rule Bill in 1886 and had been re-adopted at the Liberal candidate in Bury. However, a meeting to condemn the Crimes Bill in April 1887 produced 'sulphur in the air' and the sight of Liberal Unionists 'hissing at old friends.'[14]

For some Liberal Unionists who had made pledges against coercion, the alliance had served its purpose in defeating the Home Rule Bill, but it was now being distorted by the Salisbury–Hartington alliance. Arthur Winterbotham spoke out for this group during the debate in March 1887 and led three other radicals back to the Liberals. It looked as if Chamberlain would be left completely isolated, until W. S. Caine, the champion of the temperance movement, came to his rescue and stood firm. Others, such as F. W. Maclean, MP for Woodstock, voted in favour of the Crimes Bill, for the solidly Liberal reason that it was 'paving the way for the introduction of reme-dial measures [including] very wide measure of self-government.'[15] Salisbury realised that he had tested the patience of his allies too far and as a token of his constructive intentions, introduced a hastily devised Land Bill. The Bill was only allowed to pass the Lords having been emasculated, however, leaving the land issue largely unresolved until the Wyndham Act of 1903.

The alliance that emerged between the Parties after 1887 was then one of electoral and political pragmatism, not born out of any natural affinity between the Parties. In the subsequent eight years of the alliance, before the two Parties finally formed a coalition government in 1895, a number of ideo-logical and operational difficulties therefore challenged a relationship that had been forged by Party leaders at Westminster.

The Alliance Tested 1887–1889

Firstly, there were clear political divisions between the Parties. When the Land League was finally proscribed in 1887, the need to offer a constructive alternative to Home Rule became paramount. Chamberlain attempted to pre-empt the damage this would cause to the radical Unionists by estab-lishing a national Association distinct from Hartington's in London and with a speech in which he suggested the formation of a national progres-sive party to implement land and local government reform in Ireland. Of course, for Salisbury and Balfour, there was nothing to gain and much to lose from such a re-organisation. This issue was only resolved by Hartington's *ex cathedra* pronouncement at Greenwich on 5 August, when he announced 'that the time is not yet ripe for such closer union.'[16] Constantly frustrated, Chamberlain tried to put pressure on Hartington, on the ground that 'every day brings me letters from Liberal Unionists in all parts of the country ask-ing me what the issue is and where we still differ from our old colleagues ... I am at my wit's end to know ... what to say to prevent the disappearance of our followers in the country.' It was at this juncture, with his allies deserting him and his constituents questioning his stance on coercion, that Salisbury handed Chamberlain a life-line, or at least a breathing space. The opportu-nity to represent Britain in the fisheries dispute between Canada and United States would give Chamberlain the chance to prove his skill as a statesman and avoid association with the implementation of the Crimes Bill.

Prior to Chamberlain's return, Hartington took the trouble to re-define the Liberal Unionists' position in a speech at Ipswich on 7 March 1888. He finally stated that he could not see how a reconciliation between the two branches of Liberalism could be achieved and, therefore (nearly two years after the formation of the first party organisation), conceded that 'we have no alternative before us except to do all that is in our power to constitute a 3rd party.' He made clear that 'while we adhere to the opinions we have always held on the Irish question we have not renounced one single Liberal opinion or Liberal principle.' Finally, to appease Chamberlain, he stated that 'there is room within the Liberal Unionist Party ... for the extremest radical as well

Image 12: The Gladstonian periodical, *Fun*, illustrates the dissensions in the Unionist Alliance. Goschen, on the right of the Liberal Unionist Party, is kept quiet with a comforter marked 'office' but Chamberlain, on the left, continues to interrupt Hartington's sleep. None of this disturbs the 'Tory Party.' *Fun*, 29 August 1888.

as for the most moderate whig' and that the Unionist policy was not 'simply one of obstruction and resistance to reform.'[17] The tactic appeared to have worked, for Chamberlain at least, as he wrote to Wolmer on his return to England later that month, 'I shall be glad to be able once more to take my place amongst you.'[18] The Liberal Unionist Party would remain allied with the Tories, but they would remain Liberals as well.

Writing in the Party newspaper, Ebenezer Le Riche blamed the Party's defeats in the 1892 election on the overly close relationship with the Conservatives: 'At meetings the relative merits of the Conservative and Liberal parties were pointed out, the Conservative big drum was beaten, the party colours and sentiments flaunted wholly regardless of the 10 to 40% of radicals who were thereby alienated and whose votes lost us the seat.'[19] As will be demonstrated below, it took until 1895 for the Liberal Unionists to find an opportunity to portray themselves as more authentically Liberal than Rosebery's shambolic government and a strong case can be made that it was the Liberal Unionists who made the decisive contribution to the Unionist landslide of that year.[20]

'Certain Local Difficulties'

At a local level in Britain in the late nineteenth century Liberal–Conservative animosities were enforced by religious, social and working allegiances and these proved remarkably resilient, even when the cause of Union and empire offered a bridge between them. The first of many disputes which was to hamper the Unionist alliance until the 'fusion' of 1912, took place at St Ives in June 1887. Here, as in so many of the later cases, the issue of disagreement was disestablishment. Salisbury correctly commented, 'I generally find that it is that question that makes the difficulty.'[21] Local party leaders, accustomed to a simple divide between Liberal and Conservative, became increasingly restive of having to support a local Conservative candidate. As the position of the Liberal Unionists became more fragile in the aftermath of the Crimes Bill, this problem became more serious. Some, who found their Liberalism under question, chose to remind their electorate of their principles by criticising their Tory allies, such as Henry James who attended a dinner at the Manchester Reform Club and gave a speech attacking the Primrose League.[22]

Between 1887 and 1892, the Liberal Unionist Party lost nineteen out of twenty-three by-elections, including ones in their stronghold of western Scotland, and the Associations began to demand what they perceived as their side of the electoral bargain from the Conservatives. The growing divisions between Conservatives and Liberal Unionists at constituency

THE FIGHTING COCKS.
Grand Ruction between the Paddington Woodcock and the Cock of Highbury Barn Door.

Image 13: *The Dart* comments on the proposed candidature of Randolph Churchill
for John Bright's old seat of Central Birmingham, *The Dart*, 19 April, 1889.

level finally found public expression in the dispute over the candidate for
Birmingham Central in 1889. Chamberlain regarded the seat as his to allo-
cate, but the local Conservatives, bitter opponents of Chamberlain long
before 1886, saw an opportunity to make trouble. [23] This reflected a dis-
trust of radicalism that was certainly still felt by many local Conservatives.
In the North Buckinghamshire by-election in October 1889, one of Evelyn
Hubbard's Conservative supporters 'began his speech in the following style.
"Chapter xv.. verse 7 of the book of common sense – 'never trust a radical.'"[24]
The rapidly shrinking radical Unionist section of the Party felt that the
Birmingham seat was a vital test of the Party's credibility as an independ-
ent force. A hastily organised Party conference was held in Birmingham at
the end of April with Hartington, Lord Camperdown and the Duke of St
Albans all attending. The Conservative candidate withdrew, under pressure
from Balfour and John Bright's son won the subsequent by-election with a
majority of nearly 3,000.

To ease relations on a local level, Wolmer now urged Liberal Unionist
Associations to regulate their relations with their Conservative allies by

the creation of joint committees. In West Derbyshire, for example, a joint Unionist committee was organised, comprising two members of the Liberal Unionist Association and three members of the Conservative Association. This committee became the chief organising body in the constituency, meeting in 1892 before the election and in 1893 and 1895. Joint Unionist meetings regularly took place within the constituency and at every election until 1900, a joint Unionist manifesto was issued by the committee. In some areas, however, such as the west of Scotland, the Liberal Unionists were aware that any hint of co-operation with the Tories would be electoral suicide and here the relations between the Parties were as bitter as ever. Wolmer, unsympathetic to the regional priorities of local Associations despaired. 'Scotland gives us more trouble than the rest of the United Kingdom put together.'[25]

The problematic issue of disestablishment resurfaced, however, with the ill-advised attempt to debate the position of the Welsh church in 1891. On 1 January 1892, a correspondent of *The Times* noted that although 'there is at the present time complete harmony so far as the leaders are concerned,' this was not the case in the rank and file of both parties, amongst whom 'there is a certain amount of jealousy and suspicion.'[26] Shortly after becoming Party leader in the Commons, this jealousy was expressed in an area doubly close to Chamberlain himself. At East Worcestershire, the unexpected resignation of Hastings, on a charge of fraud, had led Chamberlain to persuade his eldest son, Austen, to stand as a Liberal Unionist for the constituency that included the Chamberlain home at Highbury. Unfortunately, the chairman of the local Conservative Association, Victor Milward, insisted that Austen Chamberlain must pledge not to vote for disestablishment in order to receive the support of local Conservatives. The Conservatives were eventually faced down when Chamberlain suggested that if pledges against disestablishment were to be asked from Liberal Unionists, pledges in favour of disestablishment might be asked from Conservatives by Liberal Unionists. Following the crisis, Lord Salisbury held the first joint meeting of the Unionist leadership that year, but the issue of disestablishment continued to hinder the relations between the radical Unionists and the moderates and Conservatives. As Chamberlain noted in 1892:

> The position of the Liberal Unionists in the country was not a pleasant one. They were reviled by their own former friends, and did not thoroughly trust, nor were they trusted by their new allies.[27]

At Warwick and Leamington, just outside Chamberlain's duchy, the most serious local crisis between the Parties of the Unionist alliance took place in

A BLACK SHEEP!

Image 14: *The Dart* comments on Austen Chamberlain's selection as Unionist candidate for the vacant seat of East Worcestershire. *The Dart*, 12 February 1892.

1895. Here the Speaker, Arthur Peel, had represented the seat since 1865 and he had been counted among the Liberal Unionists as he had been opposed by the local Conservatives in 1885 (despite the speakership), but not in 1886 or 1892. On the announcement of his retirement in March 1895, the local Conservatives claimed the right to contest the seat. Chamberlain stuck to the terms of the 1889 'compact' and extracted from the Conservative leader in the Commons, Balfour, a letter of support for his chosen candidate, the Speaker's son, George.[28] Alfred Austin in the *Standard* and George Curzon in the *New Review*, with at least the tacit consent of Salisbury, took the opportunity to launch attacks on Chamberlain's behaviour and character.[29] When a public meeting was held at Leamington Town Hall to launch Peel's campaign, he was humiliated,[30] and Chamberlain hurriedly dropped him and adopted Alfred Lyttelton, the sporting hero and a friend of Balfour's, as a compromise candidate acceptable to the local Conservatives.[31] While historians have investigated the example of Warwick and Leamington, the case of Hythe is less well-known.[32] Sir Edward Watkin, MP for Hythe, was seriously ill in 1894 and looked unlikely to stand again, and the Liberal

A POLITICAL MORMON.
ELDER JOSEPH:—She too is sealed to me.

Image 15: *The Dart* comments on Chamberlain's appropriation of Warwick and Leamington. *The Dart*, 5 April 1895.

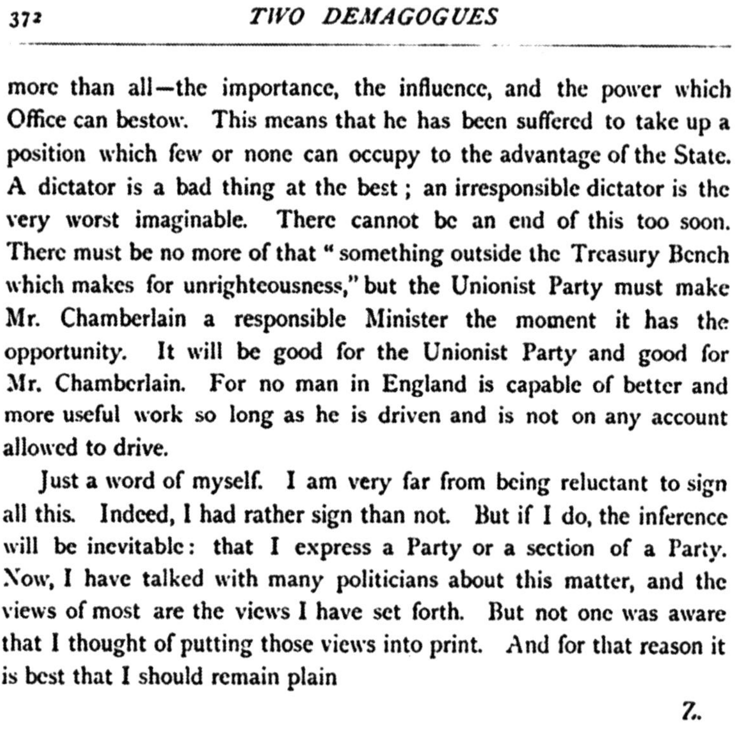

more than all—the importance, the influence, and the power which
Office can bestow. This means that he has been suffered to take up a
position which few or none can occupy to the advantage of the State.
A dictator is a bad thing at the best ; an irresponsible dictator is the
very worst imaginable. There cannot be an end of this too soon.
There must be no more of that " something outside the Treasury Bench
which makes for unrighteousness," but the Unionist Party must make
Mr. Chamberlain a responsible Minister the moment it has the
opportunity. It will be good for the Unionist Party and good for
Mr. Chamberlain. For no man in England is capable of better and
more useful work so long as he is driven and is not on any account
allowed to drive.

Just a word of myself. I am very far from being reluctant to sign
all this. Indeed, I had rather sign than not. But if I do, the inference
will be inevitable: that I express a Party or a section of a Party.
Now, I have talked with many politicians about this matter, and the
views of most are the views I have set forth. But not one was aware
that I thought of putting those views into print. And for that reason it
is best that I should remain plain

                                                                  Z.

Image 16: The final page of the anonymously authored article attacking
Chamberlain's position in the Unionist alliance. Anon. ('Z'), 'Two Demagogues: A
Parallel and a Moral', *New Review*, 12 (April 1895), p. 372.

Unionist chief agent, John Boraston, complained that the local Conservative
leader had forced their candidate forward against the wishes of the local
Liberal Unionists. When Devonshire approached Salisbury, the Conservative
leader was a little taken aback. 'Mr Boraston's information to you is in hopeless disagreement with the information which has been furnished to me by
Douglas.'[33] As far as Salisbury was concerned, Bevan Edwards, the chairman
of the Hythe Conservative Association, was now adopted as the Unionist
candidate for Hythe. The rival Liberal Unionist was ordered to withdraw his
candidature once a Unionist cabinet had been formed and Edwards won the
seat at the general election.

   The co-incidence of the Hythe and Leamington disputes seemed to signal that a genuine Unionist crisis was underway and Boraston was keen to

encourage Chamberlain's sense of grievance. He sent Chamberlain a letter from the honorary secretary of a northern Association: 'There is an intensely strong feeling as to the questions which have arisen at Hythe and Leamington. If the matter is not settled soon and in our favour you may rest assured that a good many Liberal Unionists will not stir one peg at the next General Election.'[34] Boraston continued to worry Chamberlain by telling him of the experiences of Liberal Unionists in Barnstaple and Tavistock where the local Liberal Unionists were 'soured at the mutinous spirit that the Conservatives are showing.'[35] *Punch* was quick to spot the common problems that both crises illustrated.[36] These quickly receded once the election campaign of 1895 was under way, but the antipathy between certain Unionist Associations continued to trouble the alliance even when the central Associations merged in May 1912. The Birmingham Liberal Unionist Association held aloof and refused to amalgamate until January 1918.

The 'Skipper' and the Chief Whip

The Parties' managers and organisers, imbued with far greater authority since the expansion of the franchise in 1884, were charged with enforcing a Westminster electoral pact in the constituencies and they too proved less than enthusiastic in working harmoniously with those who had previously been their bitterest allies. After the 1886 election, in which there were remarkably few disagreements over candidatures, disputes over the allocations of seats emerged and the Conservatives' managers were clearly intent on serving the interests of their own Party. In the first dispute at St Ives, Hartington wrote to Salisbury complaining about the behaviour of the Conservative chief agent, Richard Middleton. Middleton thought little of his new allies, observing in mid-1887, 'without the Conservative Party ... no Liberal Unionist can secure his seat in any future election'.[37] The actions of the *Birmingham Gazette* in provoking the crises in Birmingham in 1889 look particularly significant when one considers that Richard Middleton was chairman of the syndicate that controlled the *Gazette*, a newspaper which was the rival of the pro-Chamberlain *Birmingham Daily Post*. When Middleton was finally forced to disown Randolph Churchill's attempt to contest the seat and order the Birmingham Conservatives to back down, for the sake of future relations, the dispute was presented as merely the work of the ill-informed and malicious.

In the wake of the crisis, however, there was now a need to define exactly what the relationship between the two Unionist Parties should be and to turn the verbal 'compact' of 1886 into a more formal document. Hartington was forced to ask Wolmer, the newly appointed Party whip, whether any

agreement existed in writing. It clearly did not and Salisbury only reluctantly agreed to extend the agreement to include the crucial issue of candidate vacancies. Three heads were agreed so as to avoid any repetition of the
Central Birmingham dispute (see Appendix 1). It is notable that in the event
of dispute over the choice of candidate, the Party leaders in the Commons,
W. H. Smith and Hartington, would be consulted, not the Party managers,
who were usually responsible for the selection of candidates. Although not
explicit, it is possible to imagine that the Liberal Unionists now distrusted
Middleton to act in a disinterested fashion, especially where west midland
seats were concerned.

Despite this document, *realpolitik* meant that the choice of candidate was
largely determined by Salisbury, no doubt advised by Akers-Douglas and
Middleton to give as little away as possible. In Cambridge in 1892, where there
was a strong Liberal Unionist presence among academics, Hartington tried
to have Albert Grey adopted for the University and Montagu Crackenthorpe
adopted for the city constituency. Despite the aristocratic lineage of the
former and the strongly anti-socialist beliefs of the latter, Salisbury refused
to give way. In 1892, when the Liberal Unionists lost 37% of their parliamentary strength overall, while the Conservatives lost only 19% of theirs,
Chamberlain complained bitterly to Heneage, 'I am afraid we get put off
with all the hopeless seats and in this way we are slowly edged out of existence as a separate party.'[38]

The impact of the 1892 general election results distinctly altered the relationship between the two Parties. From Salisbury's perspective the result
was perhaps as good as he might have expected. His Party was in need of a
rest after the unusual experience of minority administration for seven years.
The Conservative dominance of the House of Lords and the small size of the
Gladstonian majority (dependent on Irish votes) told Salisbury that a second
Home Rule Bill could be successfully resisted and that any Liberal administration was likely to be short-lived. The dramatic decline of the Liberal
Unionists now raised the prospect of a Conservative majority in a future
election, rather than a Unionist one, and this appeared to cause little concern
to the Conservative managers. As this likelihood drew nearer in early 1895,
the malicious influence of Akers–Douglas and Middleton on the alliance
became apparent in the Hythe and Leamington disputes. At Hythe, adjacent
to Akers-Douglas' Kentish fiefdom, the Conservative chief whip was brazenly
partisan. Devonshire wrote to Chamberlain complaining that 'A. Douglas
seems to have been acting in a very extraordinary manner.'[39] Chamberlain
was clearly concerned about the behaviour of the Conservative whip, as he
now began to keep detailed notes of Akers-Douglas' role in the crisis.[40]

Image 17: *The Owl* interprets Chamberlain's appointment as Liberal Unionist leader as revealing the true power relationship among the Party leadership.
The Owl, 1 January 1892.

Middleton's role in stirring up the Conservatives in Leamington was revealed in my article on the dispute,[41] and he also played a role in stiffening Conservative resolve at Hythe. Less well known is that a second dispute arose at his behest in Central Birmingham in July 1895 when Lord Charles Beresford offered himself as a Conservative candidate, once Albert Bright's intention to stand down became public. It was reported to Chamberlain that Middleton took a keen interest in the affairs of Birmingham and Powell Williams was in no doubt that the crisis was once again of Middleton's doing, but all he could suggest was that Bright should fight the general election and then resign. In the end, a compromise Liberal Unionist candidate was selected, to demonstrate Chamberlain's willingness to meet the Conservatives' concerns about the proposed candidate, Grosvenor Lee. Beresford was forced to withdraw his candidature after he came under pressure from Salisbury, who was, as at Leamington, forced to intervene to undo his principal agent's mischief. These events did not do Middleton's or Akers Douglas' careers any harm, however. After the election, a banquet was held in Middleton's honour at the Constitutional Club where he was presented with an inscribed silver casket inside which he found a cheque for £10,000.[42] Akers–Douglas was appointed to the Cabinet in 1895 as Commissioner of Works.

Salisbury Triumphant

The precise nature of the legislative programme that the alliance wished to see enacted presented the most serious challenge, especially with such a contrast in the ideological heritage of the Parties. Without a document of agreed policy, the struggle for influence continually unsettled the alliance. The Liberal Unionist Party could point to two solidly Liberal achievements in the period, with the introduction of free elementary education and the 1888 Local Government Act, both of which Chamberlain had demanded in the 'unauthorised programme' three years earlier, but there was scant achievement in Ireland and friction over the Church. As Chamberlain warned Balfour, 'you cannot ... keep Radicals in the sound faith of Unionism by tickling them with whiggery.' Hartington knew that Chamberlain could only demand so much, as 'he knows too well that the Gladstonians hate him too much ever to take him back again'.[43] When Hartington succeeded to the Dukedom of Devonshire at the end of 1891, however, the Party took a gamble, appointing Chamberlain as leader in the Commons, in the hope of restraining his radical instincts, whilst retaining his undoubted electoral appeal. At a meeting to endorse his leadership at Devonshire House on 8 February 1892, rather than avoiding the difficult issue of disestablishment, Chamberlain made

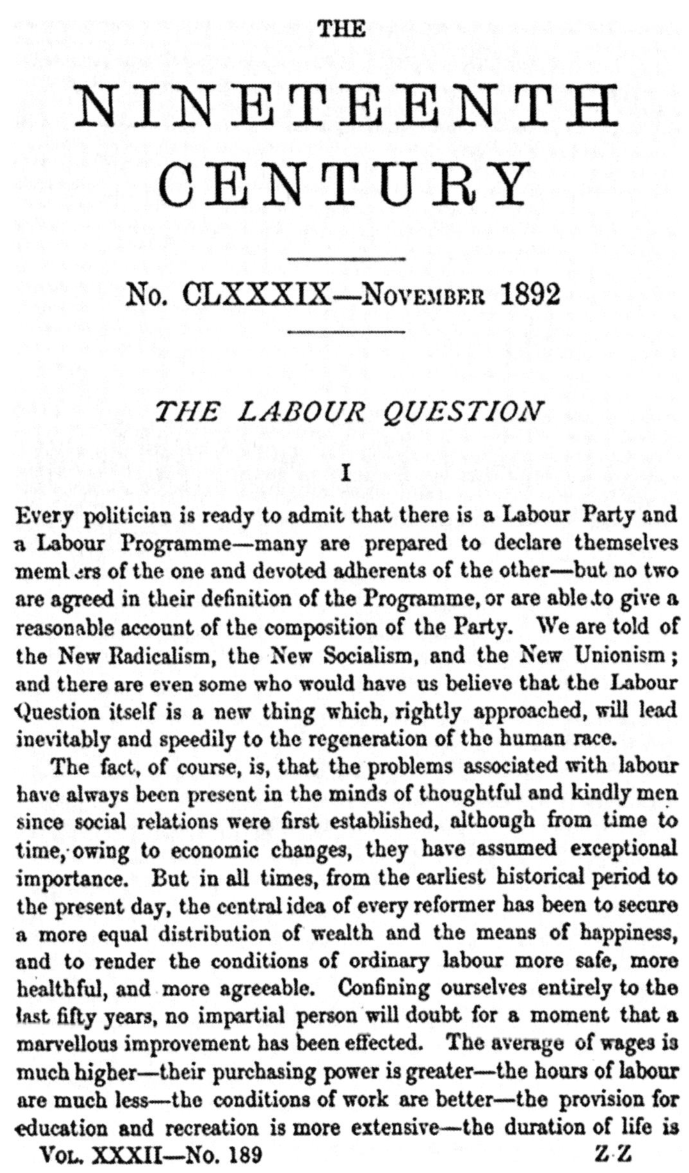

THE

NINETEENTH CENTURY

No. CLXXXIX—NOVEMBER 1892

THE LABOUR QUESTION

I

Every politician is ready to admit that there is a Labour Party and a Labour Programme—many are prepared to declare themselves meml ers of the one and devoted adherents of the other—but no two are agreed in their definition of the Programme, or are able to give a reasonable account of the composition of the Party. We are told of the New Radicalism, the New Socialism, and the New Unionism; and there are even some who would have us believe that the Labour Question itself is a new thing which, rightly approached, will lead inevitably and speedily to the regeneration of the human race.

The fact, of course, is, that the problems associated with labour have always been present in the minds of thoughtful and kindly men since social relations were first established, although from time to time, owing to economic changes, they have assumed exceptional importance. But in all times, from the earliest historical period to the present day, the central idea of every reformer has been to secure a more equal distribution of wealth and the means of happiness, and to render the conditions of ordinary labour more safe, more healthful, and more agreeable. Confining ourselves entirely to the last fifty years, no impartial person will doubt for a moment that a marvellous improvement has been effected. The average of wages is much higher—their purchasing power is greater—the hours of labour are much less—the conditions of work are better—the provision for education and recreation is more extensive—the duration of life is

Image 18: The title page of Chamberlain's article, 'The Labour Question', *The Nineteenth Century*, 189 (November 1892), p. 677.

his position clear: 'I stated my intention of continuing to support by vote, and in any other way that seemed fitting, the disestablishment of the State church.'[44]

Chamberlain attempted to exploit his association with radicalism in the few months before the election in 1892, by returning to the issue of social reform that had proved so successful at the Aston by-election the previous

Image 19: *The Owl* imagines the reactions of the leading Labour politicians to Chamberlain's article, 'The Labour Question'. *The Owl*, 4 November 1892.

218   PUNCH, OR THE LONDON CHARIVARI.   [November 12, 1892.

THE BRUMMAGEM BIRDCATCHER.
(*A Lay of a Labour Programme.*)   AIR—"*The Ratcatcher's Daughter.*"

Brummagem Birdcatcher (aside). 'AH! I FANCY I SHALL HAVE THEM PRESENTLY!"

In Vestminster not long ago there dwelt a lad named JOEY;
He vos not raised in Vestminster, but in a place more goey.
At snaring birds he vos a dab, of eggs (and plots) a hatcher;
And he vos called young Vistling JOE, the Brummagem Birdcatcher.

Young JOE of Grand Old VILL-I-AM, at fust vos pal most chummy,
But second fiddle vos not quite *the* instrument for Brummy.
Says he, "Old VILL vants his own vay, the vicked old vote-snatcher!
But that arrangement vill not suit the Brummagem Birdcatcher!

Image 20: *Punch* comments on the opportunism of Chamberlain's article, 'The Labour Question'. *Punch*, 12 November 1892.

year. Bolstered by the increase in the majorities of the six Liberal Unionist seats in Birmingham and the four in neighbouring areas in 1892, he stepped up his attempts to persuade his Party and the Tories to accept a programme of social reform, writing to James, 'our Unionist programme of the last 5 years is nearly exhausted ... If we attempt to win on a policy of negation, the fate of the moderates on the London County Council will be ours.'[45] In

November 1892, Chamberlain published an article, 'The Labour Question' in the *Nineteenth Century,* advocating an increasingly collectivist approach from the Unionists in order to prevent the emergence of class-based politics, which the election of Kier Hardie seemed to presage. At first the reaction from the Conservatives was lukewarm. Although Balfour expressed his sympathy in a speech at Sheffield in December, he was unwilling to commit to specific policies. Salisbury was, however, having none of it, writing to Balfour in 1892 that if the Conservatives took up Chamberlain's ideas, 'we must in so doing alarm a good many people who have always been with us', adding that, 'I fear these social questions are destined to break up our party.'[46] After Gladstone's retirement, Rosebery had signalled a new direction for the Liberal Party with the introduction of an Employers' Liability Bill in 1893, swiftly followed by the Mines Eight Hours Bill. Chamberlain firstly strove to distance his programme from that of the Liberals, accusing them of issuing 'appeals to class prejudice.'[47] This could not disguise the fact that Rosebery was attempting to occupy the same collectivist ground as the Liberal Unionists and that the actions of the Lords in blocking these reforms would undermine Chamberlain's own programme. When Rosebery's Employers' Liability Bill was thrown out by the upper house, Powell Williams warned Wolmer of the consequences: 'The effect of the loss of the Bill on the north is very bad indeed ... This is not an opinion. I can give you proof.'[48] Powell Williams, now the Party's chief manager, encouraged local Associations in the north of England, the west of Scotland, Ulster and Cornwall to pledge their support for a sustained campaign of Unionist reform. Although criticised in the Tory press continuously, the campaign was supported by such solidly Liberal figures as Millicent Fawcett, a prime mover in the Women's Liberal Unionist Association.

When, after the Second Home Rule Bill, Chamberlain demanded an alternative Unionist reform programme at Bradford on 2 June 1894, Balfour responded more positively, increasingly convinced by Chamberlain's argument that such pledges were necessary for the Unionists to break through in the north and in Wales. By the time Chamberlain spoke to his constituents in West Birmingham in October, as well as an extension to the Artisans' Dwellings Act, a House Purchase Act, employers' liability and alien immigration, there was a call to enact temperance reform and a tribunal of industrial arbitration. In his on-going attempt to win Salisbury's approval, the restriction of labour hours was explicitly limited to miners and shopkeepers (therefore excluding domestic servants and agricultural labourers as Salisbury and his Party wanted). As for old age pensions, Chamberlain now stated that 'I do not propose to give everyone a pension as a matter of right; I propose to help the working classes to help themselves.'[49] The first response from Hatfield was eventually made public in a speech at Edinburgh at the end of October. Salisbury admitted that he had sympathy for Chamberlain's 'general objectives' but claimed to have no knowledge of the detailed programme that the Liberal Unionists were preparing.[50] Chamberlain vented his frustration to James:

> In my opinion a Unionist government should, from the outset, declare its settled intention to ... devote itself entirely to the study and prosecution of social legislation. Unfortunately the Conservative Party is weak in constructive statesmanship, but the Govt., must contain men capable of giving practical application to the principles on which such legislation is to be based.[51]

Balfour appeared far more eager to endorse Chamberlain's proposals wholeheartedly, claiming in November that the Unionists would have 'a monopoly of [social] legislation.'[52] Buoyed by this, Chamberlain suddenly ceased his caution, perhaps realising that he would never win over Salisbury and began to make a number of wild promises to the electorate. Speaking at Heywood in Lancashire later that month, he made the choice for working-class voters clear:

> You may as I have said, try to disestablish the Welsh church, or you may, on the other hand, try to become the owners of your own houses. You may attempt to pass an Irish Land Bill, or you may attempt to get old age pensions for yourselves.[53]

Balfour continued to encourage Chamberlain's campaign at a speech in January 1895 at Manchester at which he claimed that social reform came second to the maintenance of the Union in the alliance's priorities. Emboldened by this, Chamberlain became even more open in his programme, even referring to social issues as 'the primary policy' in his response to the Queen's Speech in the Commons in February.[54]

The campaign to convince the Conservative leadership to accept Chamberlain's programme was terminated, however, by the local crises at Hythe, Leamington and Birmingham which broke out in spring 1895 as the prospect of election victory drew close. The *Standard* warned Chamberlain that 'the alliance ... may be terminated soon.'[55] Chamberlain threatened to resign over the issue, complaining to Akers-Douglas, Wolmer and Balfour of having been 'stabbed in the back by my friends'[56] but he soon realised that Salisbury would be, if anything, quite pleased at the prospect of Chamberlain's departure.[57] Chamberlain withdrew his threat and quickly distanced himself from any specific programme. His first opportunity came when Millicent

Fawcett spoke at a meeting of the Metropolitan Liberal Unionist Federation in May and proposed a motion urging the Party leadership to press forward measures of social reform. Chamberlain, chastened by his treatment by the Conservative press, failed to respond to Mrs Fawcett's invitation and instead spoke of his priority as 'the expansion of the empire.' On the same day, Salisbury spoke at Bradford, making it clear that 'nothing would induce me to adopt the socialistic [sic] remedies', but he acknowledged, 'there is an evil.'[58] When Chamberlain issued his personal manifesto, although he claimed that 'Unionist leaders are absolutely agreed in their determination ... to devote their principal attention to a policy of constructive social reform', he no longer enunciated specific policies.[59] It cannot be denied, however, that support for elements of the social programme was widespread among Liberal voters and the Party's achievement of seventy seats, including nine in the north of England and one in Wales, owed much to popular expectation of substantial reform.

It is important to understand that the creation of the coalition government of 1895 was, ironically, encouraged by the 'friction' that had arisen. Devonshire, speaking at the annual banquet of the National Union of Conservative and Constitutional Associations in June 1895, rather than ignoring the recent problems, advised his Conservative audience that 'I do not know ... whether it would be wise that we should forget them.' Warming to his theme, he continued,

> where there is smoke, there is generally fire and even if that small smoke had not made itself manifest, a very small amount of reflection and consideration would convince any sensible men that in an alliance such as that has existed for nine years between the Conservative and Unionist parties, there are elements of difficulty which might have become elements of weakness or even of danger.

He concluded that the only way to finally resolve disputes was to make the common cause of the Unionists explicit through a government composed of Liberal and Conservatives.[60] Chamberlain, speaking after the Duke, was remarkably (if understandably) restrained and, instead of enunciating a programme of reform, blandly spoke of his hopes for 'constructive legislation.'[61]

Of course, he was in no position to go as far as to suggest that there ought to be a fusion of the two Parties as a result of the formation of the Unionist government. The Party immediately began to debate the issue, though, with two articles under the title, 'Alliance or Fusion' appearing in June's *Nineteenth Century*, with St. Loe Strachey supporting a separate identity for the Party and Edward Dicey arguing in favour of merger. Strachey's argument was that the continued existence of the Party ensured that, even with the defeat of Home Rule legislation, the continued commitment of the government to the Union was recognised and simply to coalesce would be to risk the votes of Liberals, who could not bring themselves to vote for a Conservative candidate. By contrast, Dicey's criticism was that the division between the Parties had 'become a distinction without a difference.'[62]

The allocation of offices in the Unionist coalition made Salisbury's power clear. While Chamberlain was offered the Treasury but turned it down in favour of 'the minor, non-controversial post of the Colonies'[63] and Devonshire was satisfied with the Lord Presidency as it would not interfere with his time at Newmarket, Sir Henry James was treated in a fairly dismissive fashion. Having already been overlooked in December 1890 for the

XI.—ON THE ALTAR OF THE COALITION.

[*From* PICTURE POLITICS.]

Image 21: The *Westminster Gazette* reflects on the relative sacrifices that had to be made for the formation of the Unionist Coalition government of 1895. *Westminster Gazette*, 5 July 1895.

post of Lord of Appeal, Salisbury attempted to fob James off with a judicial post, until he was eventually granted the Chancellorship of the Duchy of Lancaster at the behest of Chamberlain and Devonshire.[64] With the election over, Salisbury made it clear that the 'evil' he had spoken of would not be eagerly confronted under his premiership and that the priorities of government, stated by Chamberlain in May, were shared by himself. The Queen's Speech of August 1895 contained no mention of domestic reform at all and he did nothing to prevent an amendment to the speech asking for measures to address unemployment to be defeated by 211 to seventy-nine. Speaking at Brighton in November, he suggested that 'our legislation should be careful and tentative ... however much you may desire to benefit your neighbour, do not benefit him by taking money out of the pockets of another man.' Five months after Chamberlain's manifesto, he stated that 'the sufferings under which agriculture is groaning are the first evils to which we must apply ourselves.'[65] It is difficult to dissent from David Steele's conclusion that unlike Gladstone, Salisbury had now 'tamed' Chamberlain.[66] Chamberlain at the Colonial Office was no longer the Liberal Unionist spokesman on this issue and it was left to an equally quiescent Devonshire, as Lord President, to attend a conference on the Poor Law at Derby in September, where he stated that 'anything which may be proposed in [the direction of state-aided insurance] ... must be of an extremely tentative character ... We must make up our minds to the fact that for a long time to come a great proportion of even the industrious aged poor must be dependent for their support ... from the Poor Law.'[67] When attacked by Rosebery for explaining away promises made by the Unionists at the election, Devonshire responded in Leeds in October that the government was receptive to the principle of reform but was committed to a policy of 'prudence, caution and moderation' as laid down by the Conservative leadership.[68] For those such as Alfred Pease, who had considered joining the Liberal Unionists in 1886, this behaviour confirmed his suspicions of any collaboration between Liberals and Tories:

> I have often thought of a story I was told as a child of a Russian family flying before a pack of wolves, in their sledge with four horses. To save themselves they tried sacrificing one horse, then another, each victim reprieving then for a short time from a terrible fate, and in their desperation finally sacrificing their children, and all in vain ... [Liberal] principles, their promises ... all had to be thrown away to defeat the policy of conciliation and justice.[69]

XLIV.—SUGGESTED TO TORY HOUSEHOLDERS.

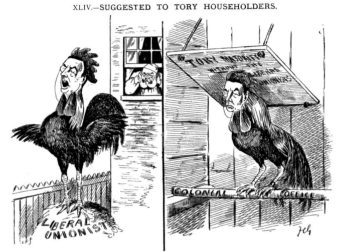

" Confound that bird ! I must cure him of that crowing ! "   " That'll keep him quiet ! "

[WESTMINSTER GAZETTE, July 27.]

Image 22: The *Westminster Gazette* comments on Salisbury's successful taming of Chamberlain after the 1895 election result gave the Conservatives a majority without the need for Liberal Unionist support, *Westminster Gazette*, 27 July 1895.

From a Conservative perspective, John Bridges encapsulated the cultural differences that prevented the Unionist alliance from being any more than a parliamentary electoral arrangement:

> Our ways were not often their ways. Smoking concerts, for instance, which we found so serviceable, were, I feel sure, an abomination to the Liberal Unionists. I have seen a few of them there, but if not always like skeletons at the feast, they never seemed comfortable. They gave the idea of condescending to what they considered a regrettable waste of their valuable time. We, on the other hand, thought their political tea parties, attended by those we did not know, and perhaps had never heard of, and their wives and daughters (who would have laughed to scorn the idea of developing into political personages like our Primrose dames) jejune affairs. It appears there is something in the professing of Liberal politics that makes a man averse to joviality; or rather perhaps, people of a saturnine or melancholy complexion are irresistibly

IV.—THE COLD WATER CURE.

The DUKE OF DEVONSHIRE: "Wretched little things! There's nothing like cold water for them."—
(*Vide* recent speeches.)

Image 23: The *Westminster Gazette* comments on Devonshire's post-election rejection of Chamberlain's promises of social reform. *Westminster Gazette*, 2 November 1895.

drawn towards Liberalism; and certainly all work and no play makes Jack an exceedingly dull boy.[70]

As Rohan McWilliam has described, 'bloody-minded, tub-thumping, beer barrel jingoism … characterised Toryism in later Victorian years.'[71]

The principled Liberal Unionists, with their disdain for the politics of the public house and the street corner, were naturally uncomfortable with this culture of aggressive nationalism, as they were with the honest vulgarity of the Primrose League's concert parties. Although W. T. Stead waspishly commented, 'scratch a Liberal Unionist and you will find a Tory',[72] Gregory Phillips concluded from his study of the Liberal Unionist peers that 'contrary to received opinion, the Whigs did not sink gratefully and immediately into the Tory embrace.'[73] Some more radical policies, such as temperance, non-denominational education, increased collectivisation, further franchise reform (including the enfranchisement of women) and disestablishment continued to divide the Liberal Unionists as they had done 'the party of 1885.' Of course, these policies posed a particular threat to the Party of the Church, the farmer and the businessman – the Conservatives – and were, as a result, a significant stumbling block in the Unionist alliance. What emerged instead was a commitment to the rule of law and the defence of the historic mission of the British Empire. These issues were used to disguise the divisions within the alliance, but in 1895 Chamberlain learnt just how flimsy this disguise was. It was, therefore, a political decision on his part, to use the imperial mission between 1895 and 1903 to bring a genuine affinity to the two wings of Unionism. Some radicals and committed Liberals refused to go along with this and grumbled, resigned or returned to the Liberal Party, but Chamberlain no longer needed the Liberal Unionists as much as he needed to prove his acceptability to the Tories.

CHAPTER 4

PARTY ORGANISATION – CAVE OR CAUCUS?

Initial Reluctance 1886–1889

The impact of the Corrupt and Illegal Practices Prevention Act of 1883 is still debated, with evidence of the 'nursing' of constituencies, outright bribery and deferential behaviour at the ballot surviving into the twentieth century.[1] One element of consensus has emerged, however. All agree that the Act, together with the Reform Act of 1884 which significantly enlarged the electorate, provided a huge challenge to political parties in terms of management, organisation and central over-sight. Rix quite rightly denies a 'straightforward transition to professional agency',[2] but a survey of the Liberal Unionist organisation reveals a complex picture with the survival of traditional practices, attempts to engage a wide range of volunteers and the sustained influence of regional (rather than central) organisations. The traditional interpretation of the orderly spread of central party organisation to the constituencies in the last quarter of the nineteenth century has been increasingly challenged by historians and the example of the Liberal Unionists confirms the interpretation of Conservative Party organisation in London recently offered by Alex Windscheffel: 'The absence of systematic central control over grass-roots structures and strategies ... is striking.'[3]

On 5 May 1886, the general committee of the National Liberal Federation met at Westminster Palace Hotel in London and voted its confidence in Gladstone by an overwhelming majority. All the dissentient Liberals promptly resigned.[4] The *Annual Register* recorded that most local

Liberal Associations were more strongly in favour of Gladstone's policy than the members who had been returned a few months earlier. As Cooke and Vincent comment caustically, Chamberlain 'wanted not less than everything and ended up with Birmingham.'[5] Kate Courtney noted that 'Chamberlain is completely worsted in his struggle with Mr Gladstone – hoist with his own petard with a vengeance.'[6] The loss of the caucus (outside Birmingham) was a severe blow for the Unionists' prospects, but for many of the dissentient MPs it was almost a relief to be free of its pressure and demands, as was made clear by the attitudes expressed at Chamberlain's meeting on 12 May.[7]

As a result of this ambivalence, extra-parliamentary organisation was limited among the Liberal Unionists in 1886. The public meeting at the Westminster Palace Hotel on 22 May 1886 formally created the Liberal Union, the prime purposes of which were, according to Hartington, to counter the pressure of the caucuses to support the Government of Ireland Bill's second reading and to prepare to contest the general election that would probably follow the Bill's defeat. Goschen explained that local committees of the Liberal Union had already been formed in Glasgow, Nottingham, Liverpool, Derby and elsewhere and that others should now be established, for the purpose of publishing and circulating literature and raising funds. A general committee of fifty-eight was then appointed, including nineteen MPs and thirteen peers.[8] A Metropolitan Committee was formed to organise the Party's London campaign, led by Lubbock, and a finance committee of six of the wealthiest Liberal Unionists was created.[9]

Milner and Goschen decided that, in the circumstances, a strict division of activity would be the best action, revealing just how divided the Liberal Unionists were. Scotland and Ireland were left to deal with their own affairs (and Wales was left to individual candidates).[10] England's constituencies were parcelled up between the two branches of the Liberal Unionists. 'I think the Radicals ought to do the Midlands, but in the East and South West, you would be more effective', Milner informed Goschen.[11] In this way, the candidates in each region were forced to rely on one or other organisation, becoming beholden to one of two very different leaders. The shortcomings of this approach were identified by the Committee in the aftermath of the 1886 election.

Having been forced into a closer embrace with Hartington than was politically advisable for a radical leader during the election campaign, Chamberlain now chose to organise an alternative force to that of the Liberal Unionist Committee. He wrote to his brother the day after the defeat of the Home Rule Bill suggesting a 'National Radical Union.' Caine and Kenrick were to be the leading vice-presidents and all the forty-six radicals who had opposed the Bill were invited to join.[12] Within ten days, the first meeting of the National Radical Union was held, unsurprisingly, in Birmingham. Such was Chamberlain's haste to put distance between himself and Hartington that he had not waited to secure the consent of the forty-six radicals he had asked Arthur to contact. Even the *Birmingham Daily Post* had to admit that 'the room was but partially filled' and when the vice-presidential posts to support Chamberlain's presidency were announced, only twelve MPs were named (and eight of these sent apologies!).[13]

In fact, twelve of Arthur Chamberlain's list of forty-six radicals had already joined the Liberal Unionist Committee. Eventually seventeen MPs put their names to the NRU.[14] Unlike the other Liberal Unionist organisations, the NRU refused all assistance from their Conservative allies, largely because it was not needed, as the Liberals had chosen not to contest any of the Liberal Unionist seats in the city apart from that of Bordesley, for which Collings was standing.[15] Chamberlain, by carefully presenting his opposition as being based on the few, illiberal elements of the Bill and continuing to stress his commitment to greater autonomy for Ireland, had even managed to recruit Gladstonians to the Union. All his supporters were convinced that the split among the radicals was only temporary and would be healed once the election was over.

Once Churchill had resigned and the 'Round Table' talks collapsed, Chamberlain began the monumental job of building his own party machine, by calling a conference of the NRU in Birmingham on 1 June 1887 (see Appendix 3). This event began with a resolution, proposed by Jesse Collings 'declaring its desire for the unity of the Liberal Party,' but making it clear that any future 'reunion' was to be on Chamberlain's terms.[16] In July 1887, when the *Liberal Unionist* reviewed the Party's organisation, it had to admit that the National Radical Union had 'hitherto acted as a separate, though friendly, organisation.'[17] Caught between loyalty to Hartington and admiration for Chamberlain, MPs faced the dilemma of which body to affiliate to. Heneage in Grimsby felt as early as July 1886 that, in the light of the slanders that the Liberal Association were spreading about him and the fact that he was increasingly being made unwelcome in the Liberal Club, 'it would be a very good thing to form a branch [of the National Radical Union] in Grimsby', but he also knew that he had to obtain Hartington's approval before he could become a vice-president.[18]

Image 24: *The Owl* mocks Chamberlain's National Radical Union. *The Owl*,
18 March 1887.

Although considerable effort had been made in creating the Committee, many believed that the organisation had served its purpose in defeating Home Rule. As Chamberlain wrote to Heneage in July, 'I expect … that after a year or so, the Gladstonians will come to their senses.'[19] The future Party whip, Lord Wolmer, wrote a letter of commiseration to J. T. Brunner, who had lost his Northwich seat to a Liberal Unionist, in which he expressed that he was 'awfully sorry to see you were beaten,' and sighed 'Oh! When and how will this split be healed!!'[20] Even Milner was uncommitted beyond the immediate future and concurred with Goschen as to 'the wisdom, nay the absolute necessity of keeping up the Liberal Unionist Party, for the time at least, as a separate organisation.'[21]

However even as the Committee organised the defeat of the Home Rule Bill, Milner was unsure about its future:

> Somehow or other I am not easy about it [the Committee] and to say an arrogant thing, don't believe it has progressed so much in proportion of late days as it did during the first week. But of course, it is always easier to begin a thing than to keep a steady head of steam up afterwards.[22]

In the words of J. P. Grant, later honorary secretary of the East and North Scotland Association, 'it was not easy to overcome at once the apathy that succeeds a period of political turmoil.'[23] This was, in part, caused by the retirement of a large number of those who voted against the second reading, either out of fear of rejection by their caucuses, or a reluctance to take any further part in the rebellion against their still much-admired leader.[24] The immediate circumstances of the defeat of Home Rule at the polls still left the Party's future in doubt, as there was still the possibility of Gladstone's retirement and the subsequent re-union of the Liberals under a Unionist leader such as Chamberlain or Hartington.

Maude, Milner, Grey and Brand had no intention of allowing the new Party to collapse and on 24 July the Committee was re-constituted as the Liberal Unionist Association. A circular was sent on 28 July to all the original members of the Committee appealing for the names of prominent supporters and sympathetic newspapers in as many constituencies as could be identified.[25] Gladstone's refusal either to consider retirement or dropping his commitment to Home Rule meant that the party apparatus would now be needed indefinitely. On 1 August 1886, the Liberal Unionist MPs met at Devonshire House and formally constituted the premises at 35 Spring Gardens as the offices of the Liberal Unionist Association, appointing

Colonel H. M. Hozier as the first secretary. Hozier had already filled this role during the election, as Robert Bickersteth acknowledged in February 1888.[26] Craig Sellar was appointed as Liberal Unionist whip.[27] On 8 August, Chamberlain finally agreed to form some official connection with the rest of the Party and joined the Liberal Unionist Committee together with Caine, Collings and other radicals.[28] Only on 9 August was the die cast, when the NLF formally announced its commitment to Home Rule and the expulsion of members who refused to support this. The Association record book notes that 'this proved the urgent necessity of organising the Liberal Unionist Party throughout the country.'[29]

The Association swiftly began to establish regional branches (carefully avoiding the West Midlands), concentrating on Scotland, Lancashire and the north of England. Outside these areas of Liberal Unionist representation, the task of organising was largely left to MPs, as Northbrook revealed in his letter to Wolmer, isolated in Hampshire. Northbrook admitted that 'I hardly think we are strong enough to establish local organisations in each country division, but we should show a very respectable front for the whole county including the I[sle] of Wight.' He went on to suggest that a 'County Liberal Unionist Association' be established and to encourage membership by setting a 'a very low subscription, indeed a nominal one, say 5/0.'[30] There was no initial organisation of the main area of Liberal Unionism, Devon and Cornwall and it was admitted that the organisation in Ireland was 'independent of England.' There appeared to be limited enthusiasm for centralised organisation among the Party's leaders, for, although invitations to a proposed Liberal Unionist national conference were sent to members in September, the executive committee did not actually meet until 3 November to fix the date for 7 December. The executive committee also fixed the subscription rate for membership of the central Association at the relatively high level of two guineas, although the committee also suggested the creation of a lower level of supporter, the 'associate', who would be allowed to join 'without payment of any subscription.'[31] Although the *Liberal Unionist* claimed in July 1887 that over 200 constituencies now had Associations, it had to admit two years later that the Association had faced severe difficulties at this time, as 'the very success with which the danger had been averted tended to make the LUs over-confident.' Once the actual crisis was over, 'the old indifference to party organisation and party machinery began to reassert itself.'[32] In this way, the traditional, moderate Liberal dislike of 'wire-pulling' was a major hindrance to the formal establishment of a third party in its earliest, most crucial years.

Perhaps as a consequence of this distaste for committee work and canvassing, Hozier was given full responsibility for organising the first

Liberal Unionist conference. This public gathering of the Party's leaders was symptomatic of the out-dated approach that the Party took. Although the *Liberal Unionist* later claimed that 'the names of the delegates present, made it evident that the Association was not only firmly established, but that it had a right to take its place amongst the chief political organisations in the country,' in truth the series of speeches reported in newspapers and the subsequent banquet did little more than reassure the Party's wealthy donors that it was a going concern and an alternative focus for social activity. Chamberlain failed to attend and there is little or no evidence of the conference making any impression in the provinces, outside the Unionist press.

It had already been noted that F. W. Maude, the Party's first secretary, was considered to be too obscure a figure for the initial recruitment drive to the Liberal Unionist Committee. Maude's lack of passion for the cause was also clearly evident on the hustings, for he had failed to win at Sheffield Attercliffe at the General Election. Despite this, he had kept the position of Party secretary, but proceeded to demonstrate an approach to party organisation that was congenial to the Liberal Unionist hierarchy but less effective in a new age of mass democracy. In Milner's eyes, he was simply too passive and he wrote to Goschen urging him to press Maude to be bolder in both policy and expenditure. Unlike Milner, Maude regarded his role as that of a general manager, not a 'restlessly aggressive' political activist.[33] He was praised for his work in setting up the Liberal Union Club, to accommodate those expelled from the Eighty Club, but he showed little enthusiasm for the Party's work.[34] The Association's failings were candidly reported by the *Liberal Unionist* in the aftermath of the failure at the St Austell by-election in May 1887, when it was noted that 'the Liberal Unionists were absolutely unorganised.' Caine, always keen to attack his moderate colleagues, commented that 'a good LU organisation would have given the Gladstonians a crushing defeat.'[35]

After several months of such criticism, Maude fell ill in summer 1887 and his deputy, Colonel Oliver Duke, took over his responsibilities in running the Liberal Unionist Club.[36] The Party's lack of progress was clearly shown by the overwhelming defeat of Evelyn Ashley at Glasgow Bridgeton in August. Gell wrote to Milner complaining that 'Spring Gardens exists to let things slide.'[37] Milner replied, agreeing that 'we want a chief of staff badly.'[38] Maude then unexpectedly rejoined the Gladstonian Party in 1887 when coercion was introduced.[39] Much to the Unionists' embarrassment, he immediately appeared at a demonstration organised by the Liberal League, asserting that 'the hour had arrived when every Radical Unionist and every

Liberal Unionist who did not look forward with complacency to finding his final resting place in the slough of Toryism, should seek salvation by joining the Liberal Party.[40] Oliver Duke was appointed secretary in Maude's place but did little more than oversee the Liberal Union Club's gradual eclipse by the LUA. He eventually resigned in December 1890 to further his political ambitions by standing as a Liberal Unionist candidate.[41] Duke was succeeded by the chairman of the Wigtownshire LUA, Sir Andrew Agnew, who was chiefly responsible for the launching of the Union Jack vans prior to the 1892 General Election. It was a mark of the diminishing status of the Club that when Agnew resigned in April 1892, 'a young barrister', William Miller, was thought sufficiently qualified to fill the role for the general election.[42]

Once Milner had departed to be Goschen's private secretary at the Treasury and the parliamentary negotiations of 1887 were complete, the more committed Liberal Unionists, such as Caine, urged greater activity from Liberal Unionist leaders in the provinces. Speaking of the defeat of the Conservative candidate in Ilkeston in 1887, he wrote of the lack of effective organisation in the first issue of the *Liberal Unionist*, under the title 'Organise – Educate!':

> The Liberal Unionist Association must take a fresh departure. Hitherto, it has accomplished useful work in conserving Unionist force in Parliament and in a few constituencies, where Unionist principles are strong. Now, it must become an aggressive power, organising its adherents from John O'Groats House to Land's End; and, having organised them, it must find them the materials and speakers to carry a steady and persistent propaganda.[43]

Those MPs who prided themselves on their commitment to Liberal principles, such as Leonard Courtney, also urged greater action on Arthur Elliot, who was now emerging as one of the leading activists at 35 Spring Gardens. Courtney particularly stressed the need for 'a responsible man to be there all day.' He recommended his political agent, John Boraston, 'known to Hobhouse as well as to myself' and Caine was duly impressed by his abilities.[44] Thus Boraston's career was launched, which culminated in his appointment as principal agent of the united Party in 1912.

Despite Hozier's achievements in 1886 and his continued work as he toured the newly founded branch Associations in Liverpool, Manchester, Glasgow, Edinburgh, Dundee, Aberdeen, Darlington and Nottingham, Caine for one soon came to believe he was not sufficiently committed to the post. In February 1887 he wrote to John Fell:

I am very anxious about our organisation. 35 Spring Gardens is not
doing its work. Hozier is only there for ½ an hour a day, and although
a very exceptional man, we want more than that.[45]

Although Courtney had an interest in the Party's organisation, as newly
appointed Chairman of Committees at Westminster he did not have the time
to commit to the task that Caine did. Behind Hozier's back, Caine set to
work building a new team to replace Milner's:

I have got a small organising committee formed at 35 S. G. consisting
of Arthur Elliot, Hy Hobhouse, and myself, and as soon as our Asst.
Sec. arrives, we will get to work as vigorously as possible.[46]

Unlike Hozier, Boraston was referred to as 'zealous' in the review of the
Association's first year and, with the organising committee's help, he began
plotting Hozier's removal. [47] Caine made sure that news of Hozier's shortcomings reached Hartington's ears.[48] In the meantime, as the work of co-
ordinating the growing Association developed, Biddulph's office at Spring
Gardens became unsuitable and the Party transferred its business to 31 Great
George Street in Westminster on 29 September 1887.[49] The executive committee also began to appoint paid agents in constituencies where no voluntary body had yet been formed.[50] The introduction of the Crimes Bill and
the crisis this provoked meant that many, hitherto distant from practical
organising, now urged a re-evaluation of the Association's activity. J. Boyd
Kinnear, defeated candidate for East Fifeshire in 1886, criticised current
activity as 'merely joining associations and celebrating banquets' which was
surely a criticism of Hozier's tactics to date. He called instead for canvassing, especially of the working classes, 'no hamlet should be left unvisited, no
workmen's club without a lecture.' The duty of the Party's sponsors was made
clear, 'those who have pecuniary means must pay the necessary expenses.'[51]
Kinnear's criticism was echoed by Heneage, who reported to Chamberlain
the lack of strategic direction in the establishment of the party organisation,
'I get spasmodic communications suggesting LUAs in Tory or Separatist
strongholds.'[52] Richard Chamberlain, as the only Liberal Unionist MP with
a largely working-class constituency in London, suggested that the Party
officially advocate free libraries, technical education, labourers' allotments
and municipal, local and school board elections.[53] Shaken by the defection
of those such as Trevelyan, Maude, Buchanan and Winterbotham, the Party
leaders responded and Hartington, Chamberlain, Selborne, James, Courtney,
Finlay and Elliot all addressed 'not far short of one hundred meetings' in the

next month to challenge the view that the Party was 'declining', 'dispirited' and 'practically extinct.'[54]

Increasing Professionalism 1889–1892

Pressure was put on those reluctant to spend time away from their estates to participate in the Party's activities. Henry Hobhouse, the head of the literature department, had stepped up his efforts and the Party had 102 different leaflets available by the end of November.[55] By the following year 'the number of separate leaflets, apart from pamphlets, issued by the Association amount[ed] to 143, and that the number of copies distributed since the work commenced may literally be reckoned by millions.'[56] The literature department was assisted by the defection of a large proportion of the Liberal press. As Edward Porritt noted in 1906, 'after the Home Rule split, the Liberal sustained disastrous losses in the newspaper world.'[57] *Sell's Dictionary of the World's Press* put it in 1893, 'no political question which ever agitated the country brought more changes in the press world than the controversy in regard to Home Rule for Ireland.'[58] Koss agrees, 'the weight of newspaper opinion had indeed abruptly shifted.'[59] *The Times*'s conversion to the cause of Liberal Unionism was part of a wider revolt against Gladstone's policy by the print media, which also played a role in maintaining the Party over such a long period. Although attempts to sustain new newspapers such as the *Liberal Unionist* and *Yr Undebwr Cymreig* and to re-launch the *Manchester Examiner*, the *York Herald* and the *Leeds Mercury* as Liberal Unionist titles all failed after initial optimism, much of the Liberal press followed Hartington and Chamberlain, including the *Daily Telegraph*, the *Daily Chronicle*, the *Graphic*, the *Irish Times* and of course, the *Birmingham Daily Post*. Arthur Elliot, MP twice for the Party, became editor of the *Edinburgh Review* after 1895. In Scotland, press support was strong with Charles Cooper, editor of the *Scotsman,* and Charles Russell, of the *Glasgow Herald,* vice-presidents of the WSLUA. Among the religious press the non-denominational *Christian World*, the largest circulation religious journal with 120,000 copies, the radical *Baptist*, the Unitarian *Christian Life*, the Anglican moderate Liberal *Guardian* and Spurgeon's *Sword and the Trowel* all became Unionist as did the *Methodist Recorder*. Perhaps most importantly for the Party's attempt to reach the urban working class, *Lloyd's Weekly Newspaper*, the *Weekly Times & Echo* and the *Weekly Dispatch* followed Edward Dicey's lead at the *Observer*. These penny papers, often passed around working men's clubs and workplaces, had opposed the 'land war' and regarded Home Rule as 'seditious' since 1880.[60] The *Weekly Times & Echo* finally abandoned Unionism in 1894 and endorsed the redistributive elements of Harcourt's budget of that year, giving greater urgency to Chamberlain's social reform programme as he sought to repair the loss of trust among radicals that this seemed to indicate.[61]

The Times remained a strong advocate of Unionism, attempting to bolster the tottering government in early 1887, as it suffered the resignation of Churchill and the threat of a mass return to the Liberal Party by the radical Unionists, with the publication of the 'Parnellism and Crime' articles. Salisbury went so far as to suggest that the owner, John Walter, should receive a knighthood, even as the articles were appearing. Hartington, influenced by Henry James, who had seen the correspondence on which some of the most serious allegations were based and was unconvinced of their veracity, advised Salisbury against this. 'If anything should happen to discredit the authenticity of the Parnell letters, *which is not impossible*, the effect would be almost disastrous.'[62] That the disaster was not as terrible as it might have been, must be said to have been due to Hartington's circumspection.

The Party did, however, attempt the unusual move of launching an official party newspaper, the *Liberal Unionist,* edited by John St. Loe Strachey, leader writer of the *Spectator.* The paper was specifically introduced to encourage the formation of new branches of the LUA across the constituencies. The first edition was served to members at the first meeting of the Liberal Union Club.[63] In it Hartington paid tribute to 'the services which have been rendered to our cause by the powerful and able journals in the metropolis and the provinces,' but explained that,

> at the present time, Irish political questions seem to be involved in so much obscurity, and to be confused by so many side issues, that there is a special necessity for a journal which shall endeavour forcibly to present the main facts of the case and the real aims of the respective parties to the controversy.[64]

The paper started as a weekly in March 1887, but was clearly facing difficulties quite soon as, after nineteen issues, it became a monthly in August 1887. As a propaganda sheet it was clearly well organised with a stirring, if highly selective account of 'latest outrages' from Ireland in every issue and, after February 1890 a rebuttal column of 'recent deviations from veracity.' As a newspaper though, it was frankly appalling, with a leaden tone and a failure to present anything other than the official party line on a series of reported speeches and ponderous articles on party organisation that even the Party's own officials must have struggled to read. Publicly, Strachey proclaimed that 'in entering upon our second year of issue as a monthly publication ... the circulation is above 10,000 copies, and there seems every reason to look forward to a further increase',[65] but in private he knew that the public were, in his view, 'suspicious of papers started or bought for the purpose of backing up particular views.'[66] Strachey did his best, introducing foreign news in July 1888 and even a 'Humours of the Fray' column in poor imitation of *Punch* and *Fun,* but it remained essentially a party newsletter, with little detailed coverage of difficult questions. A subscriber who only read the *Liberal Unionist* may have either missed major issues such as the outcome of the Parnell Commission and the Welsh disestablishment debate, or, at best, had a very peculiar view of these. In a desperate attempt to broaden the paper's appeal in January 1889, the *Liberal Unionist* was effectively re-launched as 'a monthly political magazine' to include 'matters of more general interest,' such as 'matters of Home, Colonial and Foreign policy.' As one of the major new features was a book review column in which obscure academic titles were reviewed at inordinate length, the content of the *Liberal Unionist* reveals the failure of Liberal Unionists to understand the nature of the increasingly literate if unsophisticated new electors, with the launch of Harmondsworth's *Daily Mail* only four years away. The increase in price to 3d in January 1889 can hardly have helped circulation figures among working class voters.

The paper struggled to survive without generous handouts from the Liberal Unionist Club as it could 'literally get no advertisements at all, not even £10 worth a month … the fact that it was the organ of the Liberal Unionist Party was absolutely fatal to it with advertisers.'[67] The defeat of the Party in the general election spelled the end of the paper and the final issue appeared in September 1892. In her biography of her husband, Amy Strachey explained the reason behind this decision. 'The fusion between the Liberal Unionists and the Conservatives seeming too complete for so technical a paper to be carried on:'[68] The *Liberal Unionist* was replaced by *Liberal Unionist Association Memoranda* (hereafter *LUAM)* which was merely a collection of speeches and reports of official party meetings rather than a genuine newspaper.

It took another six months to finally depose Colonel Hozier, while the LUA had expanded gradually, reaching 115 branches covering 257 constituencies by 1888. The *Liberal Unionist* acknowledged that it was an impossible task for anyone such as Hozier, 'who was unable to devote his whole time to it.'[69] In February 1888 Courtney informed his wife:

Caine has just told me that Hozier has resigned, having capitulated before Caine's attack. Caine hopes to follow up the blow by re-installing our friend [Boraston], perhaps not in exactly the same position but heading to the same or better in the end. Don't say anything about this to anyone.[70]

As it was, Caine was outmanoeuvred by the more moderate executive committee and Robert Bickersteth, MP for Newport (North Shropshire) between 1885 and 1886, was appointed as the new secretary, with Boraston retained as his assistant.[71] The plotters were given lesser rewards to secure their support. Caine became chairman of the Metropolitan Committee, comprising himself, Lubbock and Richard Chamberlain, which was made responsible for the Party's organisation and activity in the capital with Boraston appointed as honorary secretary to this Committee as well. When the new Committee visited their offices at 74 Palace Chambers, Bridge Street, on 26 March 1888, they found the existing organisations 'if not beyond benefit of clergy ... at least in a condition of suspended animation.'[72] Formal weekly meetings were introduced and Caine quickly set to work establishing branch Associations in north-east Bethnal Green, east Finsbury, Fulham, north Hackney, Haggerston and Enfield, Holborn, south Kensington, north and south Paddington, north-east and west St Pancras and Tottenham in the space of six months.[73] The attempt to reach working-class voters was clearly Caine's intention, as he held meetings in November at the Hammersmith Radical Club, the Woolwich Radical Club and the Walthamstow Working Men's Institute. He recruited H. T. Anstruther and Leedham White to his Committee and a substantial registration drive was also carried out; and 'in the case of one division alone, claims have been put in on behalf of 115 Liberal Unionists.'[74] By autumn 1888, the Metropolitan Committee felt that 'there is now in each ward a compact body of Unionists whose influence must be reckoned with.'[75] By April 1890, there were forty-four Associations in London and Caine organised a meeting at the Westminster Palace Hotel on 25 April to form a Federation. Surprisingly, Hartington's deputy, Henry James was elected President.[76]

With Caine now enjoying a position of even greater authority within the Party and Hartington promising that the Party could accommodate 'the extremest [sic] Radical', Chamberlain felt his interests were best served by drawing closer to Hartington. The National Radical Union was re-named the National Liberal Union in October 1888, demonstrating greater if not complete accord among the Party leaders. As Powell Williams later explained:

It soon became apparent that the term 'radical' had its disadvantages when the object in view was to make an appeal to the Liberal Party generally. It has only a sectional not a general signification. All

Radicals are Liberals, but not all Liberals are Radicals … for these
reasons the name of the Union has recently been altered to that which
it now bears, namely the 'National Liberal Union.'[77]

However, the Party at Great George Street was becoming concerned with
the independence of the NLU. The National Liberal Union, recognised as
a separate section of the Party's organisation, was often in competition with
the rest of the Party.[78] It was, in contrast to the LUA, committed to more
than just preserving the Union. As Powell Williams noted, 'the attention
of the new body was confined to one object only: promoting a system of
local government in England, Scotland, Ireland and Wales, and under the
supreme authority of one parliament for the United Kingdom.'[79] In June
1889, it organised its own conferences of radical Unionists in Huddersfield,
Newcastle and Plymouth. In April 1891, an even larger conference was held
in Portsmouth attended by representatives from Hampshire, Berkshire,
Dorset, Surrey, Sussex and Wiltshire, with Powell Williams presiding and
Chamberlain the chief speaker. In those seats where there had been sympathy
towards Chamberlain's brand of Liberalism before 1886, the Union sought
to expand its interests, using the more professional methods employed in
Birmingham. In Bradford, for example, a radical was appointed as agent
very soon after the defeat of C. M. Norwood in Bradford Central in 1886.
Registration work was undertaken independent of the Conservatives and a
series of public lectures was held at times convenient to working men, and a
debate organised with a prominent Gladstonian. Finally, the NLU organised
a conference in the city and appointed a general secretary to the Bradford
Liberal Unionist Association, E. C. Baily, to take charge of initiating other
Yorkshire Associations under the Radical, not Liberal, Unionist banner.[80]
All this activity seems to contradict Michael Barker's assertion that 'Radical
Unionism was a transitory and essentially a localized phenomenon.'[81]

In 1889, Hartington was forced to visit Birmingham to attempt to settle the areas of responsibility of the LUA and the NLU, after Chamberlain
had refused to obey the summons to Chatsworth in October when there
arose a dispute over who should represent the Liberal Unionist interest in
Huddersfield.[82] Hartington was clearly deeply offended by the quasi-independent actions of the NLU, writing a letter of unusual length (for him) in
May 1890:

We don't want to have anything to do with Mr Baily or the
Birmingham crew. They raise no money and I do not believe that
except in Birmingham and perhaps in the west of Scotland, they

have any influence. But what can be done to satisfy Chamberlain? He
attaches extraordinary importance to this National Liberal Union. I
know that in one or two places where he went last year he suggested to
the local Liberal Unionist Association that they should affiliate themselves to the NLU and when after some correspondent points out the
difficulties I saw him and talked it over with him at Birmingham I
altogether failed to make an impression on him. Now, as you see he has
been at Wolmer again about it.[83]

The rift in party organisation was not even healed when Chamberlain
became Party leader in the Commons in February 1892. While Chamberlain
was appointed as vice-chair of the Organising Council, the National Liberal
Union remained an entirely separate body and Chamberlain made no
attempt to amalgamate it to the LUA.[84] Only in 1894, when Chamberlain
tried for a second time to convert the Party to the cause of social reform,
did he re-organise the NLU in the Midlands. Now, the NLU was refounded
as the Midland Liberal Unionist Association. It was claimed at this meeting that the total membership of the Association outside Birmingham was
21,707, approximately 10% of the electorate. In Birmingham the proportion was even higher with 13.75% of the electorate belonging to the group.
The Association proudly claimed that 'no friction between the Conservative
and Liberal Unionist organisations had resulted' in the previous eight years,
a claim that was neither historically accurate, in light of the Birmingham
Central and East Worcestershire disputes, nor far-sighted, considering the
storm cloud that lay in wait over Leamington.[85] The Midland LUA remained,
however, entirely free from Boraston's control. The Yorkshire Liberal Unionist
Federation, meanwhile, became even more of a mouthpiece for Chamberlain's
policy statements. In September 1894, a motion was passed calling on the
Party 'to devote attention to measures calculated to improve the relationship between employers and employed, to protect the thrifty labourer from
destitute old age and to give effective agricultural education in rural schools,
and generally to better the condition of the working classes in town and
country.'[86] Meetings and conferences continued to be held under the title of
National Liberal Union until at least 1898, when a conference was held in
Manchester and Chamberlain re-animated the debate on old age pensions,
promising that 'we may be able to do something ... before this Government
goes out of office.'[87]

The attempts which Caine had made to reach out to a wider audience
were now copied elsewhere. In London, Edward Bruce Low organised con-
versaziones to appeal to 'friends of members and ladies.' Although political

speeches took place, these were limited and, 'lest the succession of speeches should become tiresome, the ladies were invited between each speech to contribute their share by supplying music and singing' and as a consequence, numbers attending rose from 180 to over 400.[88] Boraston agreed with this approach, noting that any initial meetings of provisional committees 'prove more successful in every way when something of a social character is given to them and the experiment of introducing coffee and cigarettes has on many occasions operated very happily to remove that feeling of restraint or diffidence which so often robs meetings of much of their practical value.'[89] The Metropolitan Committee, of which he was honorary secretary, took this less formal approach further still in St. Pancras South, where 'arrangements have been made for first class Smoking Concerts every Monday at 8.30, and dances once a fortnight. The Club is well fitted with billiard tables, reading room, smoking and card rooms.'[90]

By 1889, the organising committee of the LUA was no longer sufficiently professional to cope with the growing Party. There was concern that Prange, the organising agent, was failing to establish sufficient Associations.[91] In October, Hobhouse and Story Maskelyne (MP for Cricklade) called for the creation of a council of Associations for the counties of the west of England, in an attempt to create a more democratic system in emulation of the NLF and NUCCA. T. G. P. Hallett, secretary of the Somerset Association, had argued in the pages of the *Liberal Unionist* that a 'central representative Organising Council ... [would] give each county, or each county of a certain size, direct representation.' [92] Two months later, one of the most active regional organisers, Robert Bird, secretary of the West of Scotland LUA, which already had a strongly representative structure, wrote in the Party newspaper:

> A cry has gone up ... for a Federation of the whole Party, to be centred in London, and presided over by Lord Hartington; so that, by a chain of elective representation, the leaders may be ever within hearing of the voices of the constituencies, and the most belated and forlorn committees.[93]

In response, the Committee was re-established as the Liberal Unionist Organising Council of the Liberal Unionist Associations of the United Kingdom on 22 March 1889. There were to be fifty members, with forty elected by the branch Associations and ten nominated by the executive committee (see Appendix 2). It would seem that this was largely the work of Lord Wolmer, newly appointed whip to the moderate Unionists.[94] Chamberlain in his dismissal of the new Organising Council, revealed Wolmer's central role in Liberal Unionist organisation. When he wrote to Austen shortly before it was constituted, he commented that 'I do not believe in it – it is all organisation and nothing else ... let Wolmer have his little scheme and see what he can make of it.'[95]

There were now 124 district Associations, thirty-eight of which had been founded in the past year. There remained 150 constituencies outside London which had no LUA, but in all but twenty-two there were activists in correspondence. Hartington summarised the work of the LUA as being 'to raise and expend very considerable sums of money in the dissemination of political information, and by means of its organising agents to cover the whole country with branch associations.' Hartington and Lord Stalbridge were elected as chairman and vice-chairman respectively of the Council. Bickersteth and Boraston were automatically appointed as secretary and deputy, with the Party whips, the secretaries of the Metropolitan Committee and the NLU given ex-officio membership. A committee was set up for standing orders and rules and another for the revision of schedules.[96] By the time the Council met three months later, there were 157 branches of the LUA. One of these was in Portsmouth, where Arthur Conan Doyle took his first steps in what was to prove a frustrating political career.[97] It appears that he was identified as a useful supporter by the local MP, Sir William Crossman, as a result of his correspondence with the *Portsmouth News* in 1888, and Doyle hoped that by helping Crossman he would get in contact with, as he put it in a letter to Mary Doyle, 'the inner circle of Liberal Unionists.'[98]

At this point, the organisation of the Liberal Unionist Association appears to have become more professional and more centralised under Bickersteth's control. The weaknesses that Balfour had candidly noted to Salisbury, began to be eliminated.[99] Caine's Metropolitan Organising Committee was moved to the main Party headquarters in Great George Street in March and the publications department was moved to the Party's premises on 1 April.[100] In May, the *Liberal Unionist* called upon the branch Associations to perform their own registration work, as 'hitherto, we have had to mainly depend upon the Conservatives to do this work for us, but surely we are now able to stand upon our own bottom ... our leaders are active, it is time the rank and file asserted themselves.'[101] Bickersteth appears to have toured Britain, lecturing on how to improve their appeal to the electorate. The best record of his advice appears in the report of the talk he gave in Glasgow to the West of Scotland LUA in July 1888. Despite the high level of activity in the area and the support for many radical policies, the defeat of Ashley at Glasgow Bridgeton in 1887 meant that Bickersteth had a receptive audience. He told the Association that they needed to make

the executive committee more representative of the electorate as a whole
and that more consultation was needed on the choice of candidates. More
generally, he encouraged them to learn from their opponents and to apply
'something of the Gladstonian methods and energy to the conduct of elections.'[102] Unlike many of those he spoke to, the Association listened to
the advice and acted almost immediately, with Craig Sellar appointed to
the Liberal Unionist 'candidates committee' and affiliating a branch of
the Women's Liberal Unionist Association.[103] The reorganisation was not
entirely successful, as Sir John Pender was shortly afterwards adopted as
candidate for Govan on the advice of the 'candidates committee' and proceeded to lose the by-election in January 1889 by over a thousand votes,
prompting criticism from the radicals in the Association.

Despite the lists of meetings and newly-founded Associations in every
issue of the *Liberal Unionist,* just occasionally there were hints that all was not
as well as it seemed. A letter in the May 1890 issue claimed that:

> In some of the counties there is nothing more than a Liberal Unionist
> Association on paper, which distinguishes itself by doing nothing, and
> the members of which never come into contact with one another, and
> probably hardly know of each other's existence. The most that is done
> is perhaps once in two or three years to get up a joint Unionist meet-
> ing, at which the lion's share both of the platform and the audience is
> Conservative.[104]

The moderate leadership also appeared to regard the LUA as a nuisance.
Hartington wrote in 1889, 'I have no objection to be President of the Sussex
LUA, though I suppose it means a speech some day.'[105] Argyll similarly
showed a lack of awareness of the needs of politicians in an age of emerging
democracy when he candidly admitted that he had no idea of the extent of
Liberal Unionist support in Scotland.[106] Wolmer persisted, however, urging
the LUAs to take a more professional approach. A circular in his name was
sent in November 1889 to all LUAs:

> The *entirely altered* character which modern electioneering tactics have
> imparted to the conduct of contested elections, imposes upon me
> the duty of taking every step to make sure that the gentlemen to be
> entrusted with the interests of the Liberal Unionist candidates on these
> occasions are not only thoroughly efficient, but also so well acquainted
> with the machinery employed by our opponents, that they may be in a
> position to meet them on equal terms.

Wolmer went on to offer to train all the local agents and to appoint ones from lists of candidates if these were sent.[107]

At the LUA headquarters, Bickersteth was, like his predecessor, criticised by his own Party and daily faced with the ambition of his deputy. In early 1891, he chose to resign.[108] According to the minute book of the West of Scotland Association, he did so because Boraston had requested and received permission from the Party leadership to circulate the Irish Presbyterian manifesto of 29 December 1891, without consulting his superior.[109] Although W. S. Caine had dramatically departed the Party in the previous year, his protégé finally achieved his ambition and became the Association secretary.[110] After the 1892 defeat, Boraston continued as secretary, but he found his position increasingly challenged by the organiser of the National Liberal Union and the radical Unionist whip, Powell Williams, especially after Chamberlain's accession to Party leadership in the Commons. Henry James acknowledged that 'from 1892 to the G. Election of 1895, Mr Powell Williams occupied the position of manager.'[111] In October, Chamberlain informed James that he intended to re-found the Association, 'I hope to get every constituency in the 3 countries fairly started with a permanent organisation.'[112] The decision to continue the work of Boraston's Liberal Unionist Association after the 1895 election was made by Selborne and Powell Williams without any consultation and it was agreed that 'all points of importance' should be reserved 'for Williams' decision' and that Boraston should consult Williams 'who will give him an hour 2 or 3 times a week' on all other matters.[113] Harry Anstruther, who became whip to the moderates after Wolmer's elevation to the Lords in 1895, appears to have been entirely restricted to the management of Westminster matters.

The publications department was one aspect of the Liberal Unionist operation that seemed to lack neither funds nor efficacy. Taken over from Hobhouse by Boraston in 1888, by January 1891 it had produced 1,396,000 copies of eighty leaflets, 825,000 copies of eighteen pamphlets, 710,000 copies of the Liberal Unionist manifesto and 84,000 copies of the *Liberal Unionist*. In total, 2,305,000 copies of Liberal Unionist literature had been produced in less than five years.[114] The focus of these publications shifted as the Party's position altered. Between 1886 and 1889 the focus appears to have been on Parnell's inadequacies and the fearful consequences of separation. However, with the catastrophic performance of the Party in successive by-elections, after 1889 a less reflective tone and a more negative approach was discernable until the General Election of 1892. After that, the influence of Chamberlain's social programme was paramount until the creation of the

Unionist Cabinet when the focus again shifted, as the threat of Home Rule receded and the Party's leadership drew closer to the Tories.

Regional Organisation

As the central Association had been riven by in-fighting between Boraston, his sponsors and his successive superiors, it is not surprising that most of the work of organisation in these years was left to individual branches. As Holland notes, 'the life of the [Liberal Unionist] system lay in the local L.U.A.s.'[115] Although full records for only four constituency branches survive (Partick, Mid-Devon, W. Birmingham and W. Derbyshire) and Victoria Barbery has written that 'little is known about grass-roots Liberal Unionists',[116] it is possible, with the help of the local and national newspapers and the partial records of Associations in private papers, to construct a picture of the relative scale and significance of local activity. As Cooke and Vincent emphasise, in the nineteenth century there existed 'purely regional political patterns in which national politics could hardly get a foothold.'[117] In the studies of the rise of the Labour Party which dominated nineteenth-century British political history until the mid-1980s, it was eventually recognised that understanding the 'unevenness and ambiguity' of the patchwork of local political organisation and support was necessary before explaining parties as national organisations with their own programmes, principles and style.[118] In order to appreciate the varied fortunes of the Liberal Unionist Party on both a national and regional level, it is necessary to evaluate the organisational approaches and the local issues that mitigated the national Party's relationship with its supporters and the electorate. It is also essential to acknowledge Lawrence's clearly argued point that divisions among Liberals were well established and that the promotion of rival Liberal candidates after 1886 was, in numerous local cases, merely the confirmation of long-standing rivalries and antagonism *within* the Liberal Party.[119]

The West Midlands

Birmingham and the West Midlands became the unquestioned citadel of Liberal Unionism from 1886 until at least 1914, with many arguing that the Party, although officially merged with the Conservative Party from 1912, actually continued to control the parliamentary representation of the city until 1945. Chamberlain's hold over the city was not guaranteed, however. His difficult electoral campaign in 1886 was rescued when John Bright overcame his reluctance to speak out and made a major speech in the city on 1 July.[120]

Fearing the influence of Chamberlain and Bright and the popularity of Jesse Collings' campaign for land redistribution, Henry Broadhurst chose to fight in the East Midlands, where he successfully defeated the Liberal Unionist candidate for Nottingham West. As result, not a single Gladstonian was returned for Birmingham. Three Gladstonian candidates elsewhere in the country testified Chamberlain's position had cost their Party dear.[121] Once the election was over, Chamberlain kept his distance from Hartington, both ideologically and geographically, in the hope of retaining the support of the '2,000', the Birmingham Liberal Association. This eventually proved impossible with the proscription of the National Land League in August 1887 and, when he returned from his sojourn in Washington, Chamberlain was forced to inaugurate a Birmingham Liberal Unionist Association, in addition to the National Radical Union.[122]

For most historians, there is little doubt that the role of Joseph Chamberlain was crucial. His position as the leading radical of his day and his unique achievement in managing initially to win the support of the Liberal 'caucus' in 1886, are usually seen as sufficient explanation as to why Chamberlain won and retained the support of the city and its surrounding constituencies. However, this underestimates the influence of other crucial figures in the Liberal movement in the region, who for their own reasons chose to oppose Home Rule. Henry Sidgwick, after visiting George Dixon on 5 September 1886, wrote in his diary:

> I asked for an explanation of the Unionist phalanx in Birmingham ... He thought it was half an accident, the party was really divided here as elsewhere, just below the top, but that Bright and Chamberlain and himself ... happened to coincide on this question; and they, I gathered were the three recognised leaders. Bright by being the old time-honoured, political chief; Chamberlain the established 'boss' in the industrial action of the municipality and Dixon the educational boss.[123]

Perhaps one should add Collings to this list, who is often seen merely as Chamberlain's lieutenant. In fact Collings, with his passionate drive for land reform, was a potent political organiser and recruiter for the Unionist cause in particular. He founded the Rural Labourer's League in 1888 and his pressure helped to pass the Small Holdings Act of 1892, which was much trumpeted in rural constituencies and was declared to have saved the seats of many rural Unionists in 1892.[124]

The depth of Liberal Unionist support was revealed when the Birmingham Conservatives challenged Chamberlain's right to nominate John Bright's son, Albert, to contest his father's Central Birmingham seat in 1889. Chamberlain arranged for Powell Williams, Austen and other radical Unionists to canvass the constituency. So thorough was the survey of opinion that they even employed subterfuge, using a loyal farm worker to pose as a Gladstonian Liberal, to assess how reliable the promises of support they received were.[125] Powell Williams was jubilant at the results:

> One thing comes out most clearly ... that there are an immense number of Liberal Unionists in the division, and that the Tory estimate of their relative strength of the sections of the Unionist forces is all fudge.[126]

The almost unique achievement of the Birmingham Liberal Unionists was that, as well as being geographically concentrated, they were also ideologically coherent. Perceiving the inherent conservatism of any Liberal Unionist movement controlled by Goschen, Hartington, Lord Derby and the Duke of Argyll, Chamberlain had been at pains to establish a separate organisation in 1886, following the resignation of the Birmingham officers of the National Liberal Federation on 5 May 1886. Through the NRU Chamberlain built up a chain of support that stretched from the Welsh borders (both A. H. Brown for Mid Shropshire and Jasper More for Ludlow were avowed radicals) to North Staffordshire. Chamberlain's emergence as the unchallenged leader in the area of his 'fiefdom' was of course enabled by the death of other Unionist leaders like John Bright in 1889 and the passivity of alternative leaders such as George Dixon and C. P. Villiers, who never visited his seat in Wolverhampton at any point between 1886 and 1898.[127] The new MPs such as Wiggin, Meysey-Thompson and Kenrick, owed their seats to Chamberlain's patronage and were expected to remain loyal. If MPs failed to come up to Chamberlain's standards, such as Albert Bright, they were ruthlessly disposed of. Chamberlain, much to the annoyance of local Conservatives, was always on the look-out for opportunities to defend or even, on two occasions, in Central Birmingham in 1889 and in East Worcestershire in 1892, to expand his 'fiefdom'. As Chamberlain's on-going support enabled the Conservatives to appeal to a portion of the English working classes that had been hitherto outside their reach, with Balfour's support, he got his way.[128] On a third occasion in 1895, he received a clear warning from Middleton and (by association) Salisbury that he had exhausted the patience of the Conservative Party.[129]

The West of England

In the west, an Association had been formed in Bath in May 1886 and by the end of the year, Associations existed for Somerset and Bristol; Dorset formed an Association early in 1887. As a result of Hobhouse and Story Maskelyne's pressure, the Bristol and Western Counties LUA was set up, with a travelling agent employed and by the end of 1890 it had 1,157 members.[130] County Associations for Gloucester and Wiltshire were also soon established.[131] Serious organisation work did not begin immediately in Cornwall and Devon, largely due to the resistance to party organisation of the individual MPs, led by Leonard Courtney. This changed in 1888 after a narrow defeat at a by-election in St Austell. By April 1889, the local LUAs were joined into a central organisation, when a federation of the two counties under the presidency of Lord Revelstoke was established. This had offices at Plymouth with a paid secretary and it raised an income of over £1,000 p.a.[132] By 1889 Wolmer was referring to the Devon and Cornwall Liberal Unionist Federation as an example to the rest of the Party for its organisation and efficiency.[133] The Federation was certainly very active with over 300 meetings during the winter of 1889–90.

The strength of Liberal Unionism in Cornwall appears to have been focused around Courtney at Liskeard, T. B. Bolitho at St Ives and successive Liberal Unionist MPs at Truro. The Party seemed much less secure in Devon, where it had won four seats in 1886. Although F. B. Mildmay was unassailable at Totnes (which he held until 1922), the second safest seat, South Molton, was lost in a by-election in 1891, when the Gladstonians achieved a swing of 21.6% in their favour. This was followed by the capture of two of the remaining three Liberal Unionist seats in Devon at the General Election in 1892 and the reduction of majorities elsewhere. It appeared that some (if not all) of the Liberal abstainers in 1886 had chosen to vote for the G.O.M. one last time.

It is a matter of speculation whether the appeals of the Irish nonconformists, who almost unanimously opposed Home Rule and who organised the Nonconformist Unionist Association to send speakers from Ulster to persuade the nonconformists of England to vote likewise, found an audience willing to listen in a region where the majority were chapel-goers. Certainly the efforts of popular speakers, like H. M. Bompas and Isabella Tod and the illustrated lectures of the Liberal Unionist Club's Union Jack van were focused on the villages of Devon and Cornwall before the general elections of the 1890s. Even Chamberlain was not afraid of appealing to the sectarian interests of the largest nonconformist church, asking at Bodmin in October 1889, 'what answer the Methodists of Cornwall were going to make to the appeal of their brethren, the Methodists of Ireland?'[134]

Perhaps the best insight was given by *The Times*' special correspondent, who carried out a detailed survey of every electoral district, between October 1891 and March 1892. Of 'the Western counties' he wrote:

At one time a tendency was displayed by certain LU members to rely too much upon personal influence and too little upon active co-operation with the Conservatives. The lesson of South Molton, however, has not been thrown away and things are upon a much more satisfactory basis,

but he then went on to stress the importance of 'Mr Courtney's personality' in Bodmin, 'the personal influence of Mr Mildmay' in Totnes and the fact that the candidate in Truro, 'Mr J. C. Williams, comes from one of the most respected families in the west of England.'[135] Sometimes, old-fashioned paternalism funded from deep pockets was enough to win lasting affection, as was the case in North Bristol, where Lewis Fry won the seat twice between 1886 and 1895, partly as the result of actions such as the 'generous aid which you so willingly extended to the sufferers of the disastrous floods with which our city was visited some months ago.'[136]

In Cornwall, the support of prominent nonconformist Liberals, such as Courtney and T. B. Bolitho, and the Wesleyan community's distrust of the Irish Nationalists, created a strong Unionist centre which was able to retain a core of seats in the 1892 election and recover most of its losses in 1895. It was only with the treatment of Courtney himself after 1895 that the Party began to lose its grip in a region that could convincingly be described as exhibiting a truly Liberal form of Unionist culture.[137] The uncatalogued records held at Ugbrooke House in Devon demonstrate the influence that a committed local leader might make. Although Ashburton remained a solidly Conservative seat, the role of Lord Clifford in maintaining a Liberal Unionist presence was crucial.[138] Without a regional organisation, an Association had been established in 1886 with a turnover of over £80 a month in its first months.[139] The failure of the Liberal Unionists at the election in 1892 drove Clifford to contemplate winding up the LUA,[140] and a series of canvasses took place in the villages around Newton Abbott between 30 December 1893 and 28 July 1894 and revealed only eighty-six Liberal Unionists (of whom seventy-eight were unwilling to join a Liberal Unionist Association) from 1,858 enquiries.[141] Clifford endeavoured to keep the Liberal Unionist Party active, contributing £20 of the recorded £44 in the subscription book for 1904. In October 1904 he attempted to persuade the Unionist leadership to let a Liberal Unionist contest the seat at the forthcoming election, but without success.[142] It must be noted, that as a Catholic, Lord Clifford was probably unable to secure the mass support that such solidly nonconformist Liberal Unionists such as Mildmay and Courtney were able to enjoy.

Of course, the adherence of many of the old Liberal families to the Unionist cause was understandable, as this Party was the only one not to have fully replaced the old kinship bonds with a dominant central association. The influence of 'new' money and the new mass politics gradually began to tell in the 1890s, even in areas such as Devon and Cornwall, although this was still largely in the Liberal Unionists' favour, with the support of newspapers such as the *Western Morning News*, the *Devon and Exeter Daily Gazette*, the *Evening Post, Trewman's Exeter Flying Post*, the *Cornish Telegraph, Evening Tidings* and the *Cornish Post and Mining News*.[143] The latter was founded by Arthur Strauss, the mine owner, in order to counter-act the antipathy that had prevented his candidature in Camborne in 1886 and, although it cost him an estimated £40,000 to achieve, he eventually won the seat in 1895 (only to lose it again to W. S. Caine in 1900).[144] In a similar fashion, Edward Hain, the owner of the *Cornish Telegraph* and *Evening Tidings,* managed to succeed T. B. Bolitho in 1900 and held St Ives for the Liberal Unionists until he joined the Liberals as a protest against the take-over of the Party by the tariff reformers in July 1904.[145]

The North of England

In the north-east, there was a strong, radical organisation, with apparently mass support among working men. In February 1887 the Northern Counties LUA, consisting of Northumberland, Cumberland, Westmorland, Durham and the North Riding was established. In July a meeting of 5,000 demonstrated, in the words of the *Liberal Unionist,* 'that the army of Liberal Unionists in the north does not consist only of officers.'[146] Soon all these counties had their own Associations and it was decided at a meeting in Newcastle, that 'since there was no longer need for a nursing mother nearer than London, each county should be advised that for the future they were to act as independent organisations.' Durham was noted as being particularly strong with 'useful' Associations or Committees in all fifteen constituencies. The Liberal Unionists in Durham could claim to have forged strong links with organised labour, as the travelling agent for the Durham and North Riding LUA (and beaten candidate at Wansbeck in 1886), Mr Wright, was 'a popular and active member of the governing body of the Miners' Union.' In Stockton-on-Tees, where it was claimed there were 400 Liberal Unionists, they were said to be 'mainly working men.' The honorary secretary of the Durham and North Riding LUA, Jonathan Backhouse, even arranged a separate 'compact' for the area: 'we are determined to fight every constituency (though we shall recognise respectfully the miners' right to at least one of the Durham seats).'[147]

Backhouse was confident of success in the 1892 election, but no new seats were won and all the existing Liberal Unionist seats in the region were lost.

Image 25: The Liberal Unionist Club in Northgate, Darlington. Such institutions were a crucial part of the Liberal Unionist attempt to appeal to the electorate in the early 1890s. Durham Record Office DR10794, Durham County Council, http://ww2.durham.gov.uk/dre.

This may have been partly due to the increasingly erratic behaviour of Sir Henry Havelock-Allan, hero of Lucknow in 1857 and MP for Durham South East, who appeared to spend his time suffering imaginary slights from his colleagues at Westminster. In 1890, he considered that he had been 'cold-shouldered' by the Party and threatened to leave, warning that 'on his answer will depend ... the fate of Liberal Unionism in Durham and Northumberland.'[148] Clearly Havelock-Allen was not satisfied, for Chamberlain received a letter from Albert Grey on the eve of the election that prompted him to write despairingly to Wolmer: 'I agree that under the circumstances there is absolutely nothing to be done. The state of things is not very creditable to Northern Unionism.'[149] Due to the considerable financial support offered to the local Association by Lord Durham, the Party regrouped and began to build a social organisation to supplement the Party's political appeal to voters. Liberal Unionist Clubs were established for working men and hence some seats were taken in 1895.[150]

In Manchester, despite the efforts of Professor Alfred Hopkinson, the eminent bio-chemist, there was little improvement until a conference of Lancashire and Cheshire Liberal Unionists organised in February 1887 by Henry James. The central Association sent Percy Crosse to help to organise the area and the Manchester and District Liberal Unionist Association was founded, with Hopkinson as chairman. A number of other Lancashire Associations were formed but the Manchester Association secretary, H. T. Crook, reported that continued hopes for an eventual Liberal reunion and the popular support for Gladstone 'have caused the development of the organisation to proceed more slowly.'[151] James Moore has described how many prominent Unionists in the Manchester Liberal party were 'very reluctant' to openly oppose Gladstone and as result, by 1889, only three of Manchester's six constituency divisions had even a provisional Liberal Unionist committee.[152] Hopkinson was far more blunt: 'It was said at the time that the whole Liberal Unionist party in the Manchester district could drive to their meeting in a four-wheeled cab.'[153]

A circular from the Manchester and District LUA in June 1891, made it clear that although an appeal from the finance committee had succeeded in raising money from the existing members, the number of new subscriptions was admitted to be 'very small.' The Association's committee informed the members that 'to complete the work of the year in Manchester and Salford a sum of at least £700' was needed, pointing out that the Association had had debts of £310 at the beginning of the year.[154] In these circumstances, the Party was reluctantly forced into a closer relationship with the Manchester Conservatives, as evidenced by the joint Unionist meeting at the Free Trade Hall in March 1889.[155] Moore explains this failure to develop as due to the unfortunate death of Peter Rylands in 1887 which deprived the Lancashire region of a radical figurehead to match Chamberlain.[156]

As party manager, Lord Wolmer realised the need to promote the Liberal Unionist cause in the north of England if the Party was to have any hope of developing its limited base of support. As Koss comments, Salisbury was not keen to spend his Party's funds on risky newspaper ventures, but he did not object to his allies 'from whose prodigality he stood to benefit', taking such risks with their money.[157] Firstly, the Duke of Westminster had acquired a controlling interest in the *Chester Courant*. Secondly, Lord Durham and Henry Wentworth-Fitzwilliam gained control of the *York Herald* and turned it into 'the leading Liberal Unionist organ in Yorkshire.'[158] Thirdly, the Duke of Bedford had bought a large number of shares in the Central News press agency,[159] and finally, a paper with a strong Liberal heritage became available for purchase. The *Manchester Examiner* had been founded by John Bright and Edward Watkin in 1845 and under the editorship of Henry Dunkley it reached its dominant influence. By 1888, however, 'the paper had been going downhill for years' and in January 1889 it was announced at a meeting of the Manchester Liberal Unionist

Association that it had been bought by a Liberal Unionist group called the Manchester Press Company Ltd. Sir Joseph Lee, chairman of the Manchester Association, famous as the promoter of the Manchester Ship Canal, was chairman of the company. The directors of the company 'were of the opinion that no connection between Lord Hartington and the paper were necessary,' on the basis that their support for Hartington's policies was likely to have great influence in the area as long as it was not seen as a mere mouth-piece for the Liberal Unionist Party. Unlike the *Liberal Unionist,* it was hoped that the *Examiner* would be able pay its own way and operate as a genuine circulation rival to the Gladstonian *Manchester Guardian* and the Tory *Manchester Courier.*[160]

The project was presented to the Party as being an unalloyed success, with the readers of the *Liberal Unionist* informed that 'it has made a name for itself as the best English provincial newspaper ... It is now very largely read by all the professional classes and merchants in the district.'[161] Six months later, however, Wolmer sent Hartington 'the papers and documents revealing the present position of the *Manchester Examiner.*' He did so at the request of Lee and Hopkinson who were clearly having trouble raising advertising revenue or selling shares in their company. They wanted Hartington to persuade Lord Derby 'or some other rich men' to take up the present £25,000 worth of shares.[162] Although Hartington obliged, the Duke of Westminster only offered £1,000 as he was not keen to be purchasing 'another inefficient Conservative paper which we are trying to convert into an efficient "Unionist" journal.'[163] Hartington wrote gloomily to Wolmer, 'this won't help much.'[164] W. H. Smith kept encouraging Hartington to find subscribers, enclosing a positive report written by Henry Hunt, a 'competent newspaper expert.'[165] Derby was reluctant, however:

> I have not been able to learn much about the *Manchester Examiner* perhaps from not knowing the right people to refer to. I do not much believe in propping up a newspaper by subsidies, except at its first start, before it has had time to become known.[166]

The paper did have to be propped up, to an extravagant degree, to give the Liberal Unionists a voice in Manchester as £8,900 was spent from the special election fund towards the affairs of the *Manchester Examiner.*[167] After the election of 1892, Wolmer referred to the paper as no longer the Party's concern. 'That matter is now closed and the property sold.'[168] The sum recovered from the purchaser, Colonel Thomas Sowler, Conservative proprietor of the *Manchester Courier,* was a mere £390, but Sowler kept the paper going until 1894, when, in its final edition, it sadly announced 'that Liberal Unionism has never been appreciated, never thoroughly understood.'[169]

Elsewhere in Lancashire, the establishment of Associations took even longer, largely because the Liberal Associations attempted to prevent the split of 1886 from being formally recognised in party structures for as long as possible. In Bolton, for example, the Unionists only left the Liberal Association in 1892.[170] Only in February 1889 was any real attempt to appeal to working men made, when it was noted in the party organ that Unionist 'news rooms' had been established at Bacup and Rawtenstall, with the pointed comment that 'the need of some such rallying points has been greatly felt.'[171] Given Hartington's exposed position in the region, funding for the Party was lavish in the area. By July 1889, the first Liberal Union club was opened in Rawtenstall, with another planned for Bacup.[172] By the end of 1889 the Bacup club had 120 members.[173] As has been noted, the Crimes Bill was the source of the organisational breach in Bury, with the two Liberal papers taking opposite sides, the *Bury Guardian* standing by James and the *Bury Times*, which, according to James, 'denounced me as a representative of treachery and represented that my position was a disgrace to the Borough.'[174]

Perhaps realising the need to shore up their supporters in the region with the prospect of a general election close, the Liberal Unionist conference was held in Manchester in 1891, but this had little effect, as only James retained his seat and the eight other candidates in the area were defeated. By 1894, the party had become sufficiently organised to boast a properly organised Association, with a JP, Jonas Clarke, as chairman and nine further justices on the executive committee.[175] In Manchester, however, it continued to suffer from a lack of geographical concentration of its supporters, with many non-resident businessmen making up the Party's ranks and so was constantly forced into a reluctant alliance with the local Conservatives, which, apart from the victory of Argyll's son in South Manchester in 1895, bore little electoral fruit. Even Lorne's victory may, Moore suggests, have more to do with the Conservatives' organisational strength, which the Liberal Unionists benefited from, by means of a joint committee.[176]

In Yorkshire, Milner identified the lack of support for the position of Liberal Unionists as early as 1886. 'I said I was going to spend a week in the West Riding looking up Union Liberals and here I am as large as life. Where the Liberal Unionists are, is a more difficult question.'[177] Where Liberal Unionism did have a presence in the county, it was often confronted by a Conservative Party which was desperate for as many Unionist votes as possible for itself in a region of strong attachment to the G.O.M. Central Bradford was considered 'their own province' by the LUA, but the local Conservatives disliked this attitude. G. Hoffman, a vice-president of the Bradford LUA, wrote that 'the Conservatives would naturally like to have one of their own

party' but the Bradford Liberal Unionists were determined to hold onto the
seat.[178] In nearby Leeds, despite the claims that 'there were not a hundred
LUs to be found in the whole borough', an Association had been formed in
December 1886 but had not managed a significant breakthrough, largely
due to the need to build up finances (the subscription list in the entire city
had only raised £157 1s 6d in 1889), but also because of the negative policy
of the Party. In such a city of committed Liberalism, 'there is a very general
desire ... that some effort should be made to give to Ireland a scheme of
local self-government ... and thus take away all reasonable cause for dissatisfaction.'[179] Eventually a Yorkshire Liberal Unionist Federation was formed,
largely as a result of the tireless work of Walter Morrison, MP for Skipton.
At the inaugural conference in September 1890, it was embarrassingly clear
that Liberal Unionism had failed to take root in the county, as, in response
to a circular asking for information on organisation, some Associations had
not managed even to respond, while 'there are many centres where canvassing
and registration require to be more fully attended to' and many constituencies were unable to find anyone suitable to act as an agent.[180] The 1892 election proved the limitations of Morrison's Federation, as even he lost his seat
in the obliteration of all the Liberal Unionists in the ridings.

Here again, the Party sought to use the press to establish a Liberal
Unionist tradition. Following the establishment of the Unionist *Bradford
Argus* the previous year, in 1893 E. S. Talbot wrote to Devonshire on behalf
of W. Talbot Baines, asking for assistance in the purchase of an established
paper for the Unionist cause in the hitherto impregnable Gladstonian stronghold of Leeds:

> It would be a real gain to have if it be possible in the town, a paper
> whose action, on Liberal lines, should be such as to mitigate the deplor-
> able tendency to an ever sharpening partisan hostility of two camps on
> religious and educational as well as on purely political matters.[181]

The paper in question was the venerable *Leeds Mercury*, which Baines was
proposing to purchase for £80,000. The paper, in its Liberal heyday, had
enjoyed a circulation of 735,000 in 1854 but that had fallen to 28,000 by
1893.[182] The chief source of funds for the Liberal Unionists in the north,
Walter Morrison, was approached and although he believed that the purchase
might help in reviving Unionism in the north, he refused to commit himself
to help purchase the paper, as he saw 'no chance of a profit if the paper is
bought to begin a new policy.'[183] As far as can be ascertained, the Liberal
Unionists in the region chose instead to promote the cause of Chamberlain's

social programme through traditional canvassing and pamphleting. As the Party managed to win four seats in Yorkshire in the Liberal Unionist revival of 1895, despite the relative inactivity of the regional Federation, it seems likely that this had more to do with Chamberlain's policies and with exasperation with the Liberal government, than local organisation and grass-roots activism.

The East Midlands

In Nottingham in 1886, the newly formed Association had 'no formal machinery at its disposal, no organised committees at work, and all its servants voluntary and honorary workers.' The Association could not afford a Liberal Unionist registration agent and was forced to advertise in the local press and to send the names of supporters to the local Conservative agent who agreed to act as joint 'Unionist' agent. Such were the problems facing the small, under-funded and inexperienced Party in areas with fragmented support that issues of principle had to be sacrificed as Herbert Williams, the secretary of the Nottingham and Nottinghamshire Association, admitted. 'We must go in for that "closer bond or union" with the Conservative party' and he urged the Association to regard the prospects of reunion with the Gladstonians as hopeless. This alliance with the Conservatives proved catastrophic in a region where the Association was fully aware that its initial success was due to 'the support given to it by Dissenters.' Individual candidates were left to overcome the electoral consequences of an alliance formed due to Liberal Unionist organisational limitations rather than ideological affinity or electoral strategy. Colonel Charles Seely was eventually adopted as Liberal Unionist candidate in his former seat West Nottingham, where 'the division is a very Radical one, composed principally of working men, and not only working men, but trade unionists.'[184] Here Seely wisely kept his distance from the Tories and advocated the implementation of an Eight Hours Bill, which Hartington and the Conservatives opposed, and he successfully overcame Henry Broadhurst, former secretary of the parliamentary committee of the TUC, in 1892. He was assisted by the work of a branch of the Women's LUA, who 'thoroughly organised the women' of the Basford district in canvassing Seely's electorate with his position on the Bill.[185]

    In Leicestershire, there was a similar dependence on the role of a crucial individual. At first, the support for the Union among leading Liberals (including many radicals) in Leicester appeared to offer the hope that a kernel of Liberal Unionism would allow the Party to grow in the city, but as James Moore has ably demonstrated, 'Chamberlain's influence in Leicester was ultimately no stronger than that of Hartington on Manchester.'[186] The selection of Bickersteth, a moderate, angered the radical Unionists, who had hoped to persuade Richard Chamberlain to stand, failed to attract much Conservative support, and he was resoundingly defeated.[187] By 1888 Liberal Unionism had ceased to be a credible force in Leicester, following the defection of alderman Thomas Wright, the leading Party figure in the town.[188]

Wales

Cooke and Vincent comment that in Wales, 'shortly after the 1886 election, Liberal Unionism in Wales had sunk without trace.'[189] In the face of Gladstone's support for Welsh disestablishment and his pronouncement that 'Welsh Nationality is as great a reality as English nationality',[190] the attempt to found successful Associations struggled, as the lack of meetings in the principality recorded in the *Liberal Unionist* revealed. As Matthew Cragoe has shown, Gladstonian Liberals very effectively made the Home Rule campaign into a Welsh issue. The candidate for Anglesey in 1886, Thomas Lewis, stated that he supported Home Rule for Ireland so that education reform, land redistribution and disestablishment could be achieved in Wales.[191] The secretary of the Cardiganshire Liberal Unionist Association, Henry Evans, reassured the *Liberal Unionist's* readers that 'there are in almost every locality in Wales at the present moment large numbers of people who have deep convictions, and are strongly opposed to the Socialistic doctrines advocated by the Home Rulers', but offered no evidence of how he would convince the electorate to abandon their support for Gladstone.[192] The Party frankly admitted its weakness in the area, commenting that 'nothing has been done by Welsh Liberal Unionists to stem the poisonous flow [of Parnellism]',[193] and among female activists 'unfortunately, no footing has as yet been obtained.'[194] As well as apathy, the Party in Wales faced the obstacle of an entirely unsympathetic press and their unfriendly editors and publishers. There were only two Unionist weekly papers, both of them Conservative, as opposed to seventeen Welsh Gladstonian papers. [195] The Party was forced to attempt to whip up radical Unionism in Wales by founding a Welsh language monthly newspaper *Yr Undebwr Cymreig (The Welsh Unionist)* that openly advocated Welsh disestablishment even before the 'Newcastle Programme'. Spurred on by this, Unionists in Anglesey started a Welsh weekly paper called *Y Clorianydd* in August 1891, which survived until 1969. Welsh Liberal Unionists such as Henry Evans called vainly for more interest in the country from Wolmer, requesting a Liberal Unionist van for Wales, as 'at the present moment the inhabitants of Wales are only allowed to hear one side of the question.'[196] The attitude of the Welsh nonconformist press appears to have been in marked contrast to those of Ireland and Cornwall. Here, the Party complained, 'clerical intimidation as practised by the Irish priests has infected the English Nonconformist minister with a noble emulation ... and gallant little Wales is determined not to lag far behind. For it appears that the *Tyst* ... has informed its readers that those Methodists who may support Unionist candidates are to be "marked men."'[197] Without an influential Welsh-speaking Liberal Unionist leadership, Welsh voters appeared to regard Liberal Unionism to be as 'alien' as Conservatism.[198]

Scotland

As Rob Colls has persuasively argued, it was in Scotland where greatest enthusiasm for the concept of the Union of Great Britain was to be found. Unlike in England, where the Union may have been perceived as a means of exporting Liberal values to inhospitable climes, in Scotland there was a genuine intellectual case for the United Kingdom, made by writers as diverse as Adam Smith, David Hume and Sir Walter Scott. As Colls puts it, 'England made the Union but Scotland made it work.'[199] Despite assumptions that the split in 1886 was foreshadowed by divisions in 1885 between radicals and moderates on the disestablishment and crofter issues, Catriona Burness has conclusively shown that Liberal Unionism straddled both sides of these divides and the Scottish Liberal Unionists included committed churchmen such as Lord Wolmer and Robert Finlay, disestablishers such as Thomas Raleigh and Professor Calderwood, radicals such as Lewis McIver and Alexander Cross, temperance enthusiasts such as Cameron Corbett, landlords such as the Duke of Argyll ('the arch-enemy of land reform'[200]) and Harry Anstruther, businessmen like Sir William Arrol and crofters such as Charles Fraser Mackintosh.[201] The issue was clearly painful, as so many Scottish Liberals felt a personal affection for Gladstone and Gladstone regarded himself as a Scot.[202] The crucial factor in the Liberal Unionist success in Scotland was clearly organisation and the relative success rates of the Liberal Unionists in the east and west of Scotland was chiefly the result of the very different standards of effectiveness in the two organising bodies in Scotland. Here, uniquely, minute books for the two central organising bodies, the East and North of Scotland Liberal Unionist Association (E&NSLUA) and the WSLUA survive.

The organisation in Edinburgh, covering east and north Scotland, did not emerge until after the 1886 election. The East and North of Scotland Committee had collected £2,000 within five weeks of June 1886, which it used to support those MPs who had voted against the Home Rule Bill to fight their elections, but the E&NSLUA was not officially founded with an office until 10 November 1886.[203] By 1889 they had a paid secretary and clerks and ninety-four branches in forty constituencies.[204] This organisation was clearly dominated by aristocratic Whigs such as the Earl of Stair (who was president) and the Marquess of Tweedale. The minute book also reveals that the relations between the radical and moderate Unionists were, in this area, very poor. It appears that there was an entirely separate radical Unionist Committee for Edinburgh, which organised a visit by Chamberlain and Trevelyan in March 1887.[205] Although the E&NSLUA agreed on a joint invitation, before Chamberlain and Trevelyan came, the radicals demanded that the conference should pass resolutions on issues such as local self government for Scotland, land law reform and 'the largest possible extension of self-government in all the three kingdoms.' The moderates were appalled and refused to participate in the conference which was in fact, overshadowed by the 'Round Table' negotiations, which carried Trevelyan, and the only Liberal Unionist in Edinburgh, T. R. Buchanan, back to the Liberals.[206] Similar divisions were also evident at a constituency level in the region. Austen Chamberlain had been chosen to contest Trevelyan's old seat of Hawick in the Borders, which fell under the control of the E&NSLUA. Although the detail of the dispute is unclear, it appears that some of the moderates, either in the Hawick Association or the parent body, objected to Austen (perhaps due to his views on disestablishment). Joseph Chamberlain wrote to his son complaining of the 'jealousy and local prejudice of the Scotch Whigs' advising him to give them 'pointe de Chamberlain' and encouraging him to seek promotion from the 'Nat. R. Union and various [radical] local associations.'[207]

Relations remained poor, largely due to Chamberlain's influence. When arrangements were being made for his second visit, he made it clear that he would only agree to come if the event was organised from Birmingham in the name of the National Liberal Union.[208] In 1889, the E&NSLUA demanded that the resolution in favour of 'one man, one vote' should be removed from the National Liberal Unionist programme.[209] By contrast, a meeting in Edinburgh later that year attended by Balfour demonstrated very close co-operation between the E&NSLUA and the local Conservatives. These divisions may have contributed to the poor administration of the Association, but it is clear that its major weakness was its inability to attract numerous subscribers and the consequent struggles for control between the few individuals who dominated the Party. In November 1887, the accounts reveal that the treasurer, A. L. Bruce, had overseen a total spend of £1,068 in the last year,

with only £692 raised in subscriptions. A further £200 had been donated by
the LUA on request for 'additional assistance' from the honorary secretary,
J. P. Grant, but this still left the Association only £5 in the black.[210] The
following month a new secretary Adam Gifford, was appointed, whose
attempts to set the Association on a more professional footing were clearly
not to the tastes of the President, who promptly reduced his subscription
from £100 to £50.[211]

Worse was to follow, as on 17 March 1890, the Association chairman was
forced to resign for criticising members of the executive committee.[212] The
restored aristocratic leadership showed no signs of engaging with the new
methods of electioneering. Boraston was criticised for attempting to interfere
in the running of local Associations within the E&NSLUA's purview, when
he urged a more active canvass, and the suggestion of a Union Jack van for
east Scotland was turned down, on the grounds of expense (even though the
Association had, by then, a balance of over £400).[213] Despite this, Gifford
managed to persuade the Association to appoint four organising agents to
cover the area the Association was responsible for and had increased the
subscriptions to £2,000 by November 1891. He also managed to persuade
his executive committee to start a van, but by the time it began work in
April 1892, it faced an impossible task in countering Liberal propaganda.
The Association's leaders were still unable to build good relations with the
more radical WSLUA. When the Edinburgh body invited Chamberlain to
the capital in December 1891, the WSLUA failed to assist and 500 tickets
for the meeting remained unsold, leaving the E&NSLUA with a loss of £125
for what should have been a fund-raising event.[214] In April 1892, when the
WSLUA organised a conference in Edinburgh, the E&NSLUA refused to
participate.[215]

In the 1892 election, Middleton had clearly decided not to waste
Conservative efforts fighting hopeless seats in the area and left the E&NSLUA
to squander their own funds. An enormous number of candidates were put
in the field (thirty-one), some at the very last minute, such as in Kirkcaldy,
where a candidate had still not been found in April 1892, and many of them
in completely hopeless seats like Aberdeen, where one candidate, the hapless B.
P. Lee, managed to win 16% of the vote.[216] Huge sums were sent to struggling
candidates (£800 was sent to Dr Aitchison in Clackmann and Kinross) and the
Association soon found that it had spent the £6,250 that Gifford had raised in
a special election subscription. The Association, having attacked Boraston for
interference only eighteen months previously, was now forced to plead for extra
funding from headquarters in Spring Gardens. The famous 'special electoral
fund' duly provided £4,000, but the money was wasted as twenty-six of the

thirty-one candidates in the area lost. The policies which the Conservatives adopted, with little sympathy or understanding for Scottish politics, and the Liberal Unionists were forced to defend, were partly to blame. Chamberlain understood, as he listened to the views of Fraser Mackintosh on becoming leader, that the refusal to allow the Crofters' Bill 'will ruin our chances in the north of Scotland.'[217] Those, like R. B. Finlay, who adopted a 'cold, unsympathetic attitude towards the pressing popular reforms now so justly demanded by the working class' were punished by the voters.[218] Under the new whip, Anstruther, the Party was far less generous and the van's staff were paid off, the lecturer dismissed, one of the regional organisers was sacked and the others forced to travel third class.[219] The salary of the chief organiser was reduced (but as he was aware that the Party had no other agent, he simply stopped attending committee meetings until it was restored).[220] The Party did manage to fund a 'Scottish Liberal Union Club' and contributed to the launch of the *Edinburgh and Leith Advertiser*, but it increasingly shared the task of electioneering with the Conservatives.[221] In 1895, the E&NSLUA was forced to contest a mere seventeen seats (but managed to win eight of these), while the Conservatives contested nineteen of the seats in the area. It did still manage to spend money unwisely, for the candidature of R. M. Fullarton in Orkney and Shetland cost the Association £1,854.5.2, yet the seat was comfortably retained by the Liberals with 20% more votes than the Liberal Unionists.[222]

The contrast between the whiggish, aristocratic amateurism of the East of Scotland Association and the more radical, middle-class, professional Association in the west could not be more marked.[223] The West of Scotland Liberal Committee for the Maintenance of the Union of Great Britain (as it was initially called) was founded by Sir William Thomson and leading Glasgow businessmen and lawyers in 10 May 1886, following an anti-Home Rule rally at St. Andrews Halls on 21 April.[224] It was refounded as the WSLUA in November 1886, when the Scottish Liberal Association was taken over by the radical National Liberal Federation of Scotland.[225] With its central office in Glasgow, it was a highly professional and extremely active Association but suffered from divisions between radicals and moderates. Unlike the Liberal Unionist Association before the Organising Council was created in March 1889, the WSLUA had a printed constitution from its inception with every branch Association having the right to elect seven delegates to the Central Executive at Glasgow. It soon had twelve branches; by 1887 it had thirty-five, by December 1888 there were sixty-six.

Once the election was called in 1886; the Committee in Glasgow contacted Maude to ask for 'a distinct line' to take and proceeded with its own organisation when Maude's reply was not regarded as 'sufficiently definite' by the

Committee.[226] The Committee immediately raised £160, employed Robert Bird as agent, with paid clerks based at 224 Ingram Street, distributed 5,000 leaflets and put adverts in the *Glasgow Mail* and *Glasgow Herald*.[227] Demonstrating a degree of independence from London that was to mark out the Glasgow Liberal Unionists for the duration of their existence, *they* informed Maude who their candidates were, even though they took note of Maude's advice as to which constituencies should be allocated to the Conservatives to contest and which should be fought by Liberal Unionists.[228] The Committee successfully fought eight out of fourteen constituencies in the region, having distributed 736,750 leaflets, 6,125 pamphlets and 67,700 posters and spent well over a thousand pounds.[229] By the time of its third annual meeting on 6 December 1888, the WSLUA could boast of a membership of 6,000, with ninety honorary vice-presidents, including the editors of the *Scotsman* and the *Glasgow Herald*,[230] and the very first students' Liberal Unionist Club at Glasgow University, formed in March 1888. As Walker and Officer note, 'the economic elites [in the west of Scotland] tended to be Liberal Unionists, fearful of radicalism, but often contemptuous of the rural landed aristocracy.'[231] The tireless secretary of the WSLUA, Robert Bird, advocated a more constructive policy and, unlike the E&NSLUA, the organisation in Glasgow changed its constitution in December 1888 'from a mere negative "maintenance of the legislative union", to the affirmative "the promotion of Liberal Unionist principles."'[232]

The Association soon began to demand greater urgency from the leadership at Westminster, passing a resolution in favour of 'a wide measure of local self government for Ireland' in November 1887.[233] This was closely followed by James Caldwell (MP for Glasgow St Rollox) passing a resolution in favour of 'dealing in a thorough manner with the land question in Ireland.' This was eventually widened to a resolution, no doubt designed to embarrass not only Hartington but Chamberlain as well, which was unanimously endorsed by the Association, that 'the Liberal Unionists have no wish whatever to continue [Dublin] Castle Rule ... In Ireland freedom and liberty at present were completely crushed down.'[234] Clearly, support for Liberal Unionism in Glasgow was not built on Orange Order prejudice.[235] Some in the WSLUA saw greater affinity with Chamberlain's programme and helped to organise a National Radical Union conference at Ayr in April 1887. Bird attended the NRU conference in Birmingham in June 1887 and the leading vice-president, Thomson, attended Chamberlain's celebrated Ulster meeting in Belfast in October 1887.[236]

Following the defeats at the by-elections in Bridgeton, Edinburgh West, Dundee, Ayr and Govan, the WSLUA itself began to adopt a more radical programme. In April 1889, the radicals on the executive committee resolved that there was an 'urgent need for passing a large and final measure of land purchase for the settlement of the agrarian question in Ireland, and thereafter a liberal measure of reform of Irish Government'.[237] At the AGM in December, there was an attempt to introduce even more radicals onto the executive committee, when Bird nominated the radical former MP for Leith, William Jacks, as vice-president. This was despite the fact that, according to the minutes of the subsequent discussion, 'a great many men had considerable doubt as to where Mr Jacks really was.'[238] Unfortunately for Bird, Jacks turned down the invitation and rejoined the Gladstonian Liberals.

Bird's radical ambitions received a further blow when Caldwell, increasingly disillusioned with a leadership who showed precious little evidence of Liberalism in their behaviour at Westminster, resigned from the Party when a measure was introduced to the Free Schools Bill which would, in his opinion, have damaged the educational opportunities of poorer children in Scotland.[239] He affirmed that 'his hostility to Home Rule is undiminished', but felt better able to advocate a vigorous reform programme as an independent. In a desperate attempt to retain the WSLUA's radical credentials, Bird allowed him to remain a vice-president of the Association until January 1892.[240] He rejoined the Gladstonian Party in March 1892, stood for Glasgow Tradeston in 1892 and only failed to take Corbett's seat by 169 votes.[241] With the defection of Jacks and Caldwell, Bird now found that the moderates, led by Kelvin and the new Association president, held the upper hand. Kelvin declared that they should not force Devonshire to endorse any programme for the forthcoming election and decided to avoid a debate on policy by cancelling the Liberal Unionist conference due to be held when he visited the city on 27 May 1892.[242] Bird and five other radical members of the executive committee attacked this decision as 'a huge blunder.'[243] The chief organising agent, Tosh, appears to have been largely the choice of the moderates and oversaw a spend of £657 on the election, despite subscriptions of only £510. The Party was only able to contest nine seats, in contrast to the fourteen of 1886.[244] Two seats were lost, St Rollox and South Ayrshire and Bird and his fellow radical, Cameron Corbett, who had barely held onto his seat in Tradeston, made clear their support for 'an advanced Liberal programme' in the style of Chamberlain, on the basis of the 'astonishing results in and around Birmingham.'[245]

With Powell Williams' support, Bird forced Tosh to resign and began to try to persuade the Association's committee to reorganise the Association on a more professional level, and he was able to appoint a man who Caldwell had recommended back in February 1890, W. L. Blench.[246] This seemed vindicated as the Party's subscriptions shot up from £533 in 1891–2, to

£2,094 in 1892–3. In 1893 at the AGM, the Association was re-organised as Bird had suggested. The executive was re-constituted as a 'Liberal Unionist Council' and Bird was finally employed full-time with an office and staff.[247] The *Glasgow Herald* could remark, with some satisfaction, after the AGM on 29 November 1893 that the election defeats did not seem to have dampened the ardour of the WSLUA:

> That must have been something of a revelation to others besides ourselves who doubted if the Liberal Unionists in Scotland were keeping their rank in the race ... it may be questioned if any political association can show a better record of work done, or give a larger earnest of devotion to a cause that the Liberal Unionists of the west.[248]

The moderates had not surrendered, however. When the executive committee met to discuss Chamberlain's *Nineteenth Century* article in November 1892, Parker Smith admitted that 'they [the executive committee] might not all agree with the whole of Mr Chamberlain's views regarding social questions' which was clearly a reference to Kelvin and his supporters.[249] Although details were avoided to prevent divisions, the Association sent a resolution in favour of 'a general policy of progressive social reform' to both James and Chamberlain.[250]

These divisions did not hamper the Association's work, however, as it spent nearly £1,000 in grants to its branches, to keep them in readiness for an election that might come at any time as the Liberal government tottered. When Wolmer visited in February 1894, he was delighted with what he found. 'From all he heard, he believed that, if possible, the strength of the [WSLUA] was increased and the good work they were doing was intensified.'[251] When the Association met in August 1894 to review its organisation, Bird could report that there were sixty-six LUAs across the region. The Association worked closely with its members, with all seven Liberal Unionist MPs on the executive committee.[252] By October, Bird had managed to accrue a balance of £1,635.[253] In the following year, Bird and Blench had increased the number of branch Associations to 102, with nine new ones in Lanarkshire alone, and Bird had been forced to employ a 'literary assistant' to deal with the distribution of publications.[254] So effectively had Bird and Blench been in raising funds that the Association increased the number of Liberal Unionists MPs from five to six (with Sir William Arrol capturing South Ayrshire with a comfortable majority), while retaining a positive current account balance of £437 and with a further £4,550 held on deposit.[255]

Ireland

The one regional Association with the most justified claim to having stayed true to their beliefs of 1886 was that of the Irish Liberal Unionists. Despite Unionism's association with sectarian politics in Ulster, John Bew has convincingly demonstrated that Liberal Unionism had a strong tradition in and around Belfast throughout the nineteenth century.[256] Having failed to win a single seat in the 1885 general election, the Ulster Liberals organised a convention in St George's Hall, Belfast, after Randolph Churchill's speech at Ulster Hall and Hartington's speech to the Eighty Club. Around 700 attended, both Catholic and Protestant, and adopted the resolution of the leading Liberal businessman, Thomas Sinclair, that the Union should be maintained, but that 'an extended system of local self-government' should be adopted.[257] A further Liberal demonstration against the Bill was held on 30 April at the Ulster Hall, at which it was resolved that a committee should be formed.[258] The Ulster Liberal Unionist Committee finally met on 4 June, comprising the majority of Belfast Liberals but was clearly limited in its organisation, as it admitted that 'West Belfast was lost in 1886 merely by bad management and careless registration.'[259] They ran five candidates in the province (three other Liberal Unionists stood in the south). They hoped to win the support of Roman Catholic Unionists in areas where the Catholics would never vote Conservative because of the Conservative alliance with Orangeism, as typified by Colonel Saunderson, MP for North Armagh, and his Ulster Loyalist Anti-Repeal Union.[260] Secondly, they hoped to win the support of tenant farmers, as the candidates were clearly identified as opposing the landlord influence. Thirdly, they hoped to appeal to working-class voters by exposing the consequences of separation and, so many Liberals warned, the imposition of protectionist economic policies from a Nationalist government.[261] Their relationship with the local Conservatives was very difficult, as a result of these sectarian and class issues, and 1886 saw constant bickering in the pages of the *Northern Whig* as to the allocation of candidatures. This spread into municipal politics with Liberal Unionists (successfully) putting up candidates against Conservatives in the November 1887 municipal election.[262] Given the radical nature of the demands for land reform that T. W. Russell advocated forcefully both during and after the election, it was not surprising that the Association's Honorary Secretary, Thomas Harrison, noted the Ulster LUA's work 'in connection with [Caine's] London Liberal Union and the Birmingham Radical Union.'[263] It was also not surprising that the battle for the Unionist leadership in Ulster was fought in these years between Saunderson's Union of landowners and businessmen and Russell's Liberal Unionist tenant farmers' Association.

This group was seen as distinct a faction as Chamberlain's radicals by the *Pall Mall Gazette* in September 1887, though it was admitted by the official Party organ as early as July 1887, that both these MPs differed from the rest of the Party in the level of their discontent with the first Irish Land Bill that Balfour introduced in 1887.[264] Russell was clearly determined to push the views of the tenant farmers he represented, regardless of the problems this caused within the Unionist alliance, as Hartington complained to James: 'I am afraid the Ulster members will get us into trouble. The government will not agree to the inclusion of the rent revision clauses.'[265] Russell sent a letter to *The Times*, announcing his resignation from the Party when the Conservatives in the Lords attempted to remove the rent revision amendments he had included during the debate in the Commons.[266] Although supporting the Act of Union, Russell demanded substantial land reform and local government reform in Ireland on the same grounds as had been granted to England and Wales in 1888. On the issue of land reform he had influential allies in the Catholic community such as the poet, Aubrey de Vere, who championed the reforming Unionist cause in the *National* and *Edinburgh Review*s.[267] Under Arthur Balfour's secretaryship some significant agrarian measures were obtained, but a Land Purchase Act, which made £33 million available through the Congested Districts Board, took until 1891 to get past the obstinacy of Whig and Conservative Irish landlords. That it did so in time for the 1892 election, gave Russell the opportunity to expand his power-base and three of the Liberal Unionists seats were won with ease; the two sitting MPs increasing their majorities fourfold, in marked contrast to Liberal Unionist performance elsewhere, and Arnold-Forster was rewarded for his perseverance with the capture of West Belfast. With the Nationalists at each other's throats over Parnell's adultery, Russell cannily persuaded William Kenny QC ('a Roman Catholic Liberal Unionist and a leading member of the Irish bar') to stand for Dublin St Stephen's Green.[268] Here, two nationalist candidates, divided on Parnell's leadership, handed him the victory by fifteen votes. Although Kenny's election took advantage of the nationalist split, it proved the *Northern Whig* right when it wrote that support for the Union 'is shared by the most respectable Catholics.'[269]

Despite his success, Russell again came into conflict with the landlord influence in the Party over land reform while in opposition and actually had to resign from the Party to get his way in 1894.[270] He withdrew this resignation, but, as Chamberlain told Balfour, 'the relations between the landlord and Orange party and the tenant and Liberal Unionist sections are very much strained.'[271] William Kenny also criticised Chamberlain when he resorted once again to anti-Catholic rhetoric in October 1894, aware as he was of the damage that such language could do among his middle-class Catholic electorate.[272] When the Unionist coalition was being formally arranged in July 1895, Chamberlain pressed for Russell to receive a junior office, but Russell would only accept if his demands for land reform were acceded to. He was clearly distrusted by the Conservatives who blocked W. C. Trimble's attempt to fight Enniskillen as a Liberal Unionist in 1895.

However, Russell persevered, aiding Kenny in his triumphant retention of St Stephen's Green in the general election and the Irish Liberal Unionists then won a fifth seat when the historian W. E. H. Lecky was elected for Dublin University in December 1895, both of which demonstrated the Irish Party's continuing commitment to non-sectarian solutions to Ireland's problems. The Irish Liberal Unionists subsequently passed a resolution at their annual meeting in 1897 demanding democratic local government and a land purchase bill. The Land Bill introduced in 1897 was opposed by some moderate Liberal Unionists, such as Walter Morrison, on the grounds that it was interfering with the Liberal principle of the sanctity of property.[273] Russell had to threaten resignation for a third time to overcome Conservative and moderate Liberal Unionist opposition to the Bill and had to swallow a series of amendments. The Act that emerged did, however, achieve Russell's principal aim: protection for tenants' rights and improvements.[274]

Fulfilling the pledge to local government reform proved even more difficult as the moderate Liberal Unionists opposed any scheme for fear of it being monopolized by the National League, while Chamberlain's pet project of 'provincial councils' for Ireland was regarded with horror by Russell and his faction. The Irish Local Government Act was eventually introduced by the Irish Secretary, Gerald Balfour, in February 1898 and was perhaps the greatest triumph for progressive Unionism in the period. Although Gerald Balfour is usually credited with 'killing Home Rule by kindness', there is a case to be argued that the pressure that the Russellites brought to bear on the Cabinet was decisive. Russell attempted to resist the growing anti-Catholic bigotry in his constituency, South Tyrone, and voted in favour of a Catholic University for Ireland, which prompted other loyalists to oppose him with an independent Unionist, Major R. T. Howard, in 1900.[275] Russell triumphed, but resigned from the Party in 1902 in frustration over loyalist refusal to accept Wyndham's proposals for land purchase. He proceeded to field candidates against Saunderson's official Unionists at two by-elections, East Down (February 1902) and North Fermanagh (March 1903) and won both these and the crowning achievement of the Land Purchase Act of 1903 which finally enabled the tenant farmers of Ireland to buy their land.[276] His extraordinary career continued when he won a by-election in 1911 with Liberal support and he was appointed under-secretary for the Department of Agriculture and Technical Instruction for Ireland under Asquith.[277] The Unionists, rid of Russell's awkward radicalism, reunited under Long's leadership, ceased any serious efforts to sustain Unionism outside the north and formed the Ulster Unionist Council in 1905, pledged to resist Home Rule through violent, rather than legislative means. As Jackson concludes, 'by the time of the third Home Rule Bill, Unionism was to all intents and purposes an Ulster phenomenon.'[278] It had also lost much of its Liberal identity as Ireland increasingly polarised, politically and culturally.[279]

Affiliated Organisations

The Liberal Unionist Party contained other, more focused political organisations, structured on a national level, which also demonstrated a variety of influence and activity and in many ways were the fore-runners of the 'league of leagues' which E. H. H. Green drew attention to a decade ago.[280]

The Women's Liberal Unionist Association (WLUA)

As Jon Lawrence has noted, following the Corrupt Practices Act of 1883, 'women gradually began to assume a more prominent role in all aspects of public politics'[281] and the Liberal Unionist Party responded to the creation of the Women's Liberal Federation in 1886 by founding the Women's LUA in north Kensington in May 1888. Kate Courtney claimed the idea was Mrs Tod's, but the chief movers were unsurprisingly the wives of the senior Liberal Unionists, in particular, Lady Stanley, Kate Courtney, Mrs Biddulph and Mrs Caine. However, women from the whole Liberal spectrum belonged to the organisation in the same way that they did in the Party itself. Looking back fifteen years later, Millicent Fawcett noted that although the Association was formed mainly to resist Home Rule, 'we had from the first other and subsidiary objects which we have always described on our Programme as the promotion of Liberal principles and the development of local liberties.'[282] The first meeting of 'L.U. ladies' took place at the home of Kate Courtney in May 1888, even though some women had been forbidden to attend by their husbands.[283] Millicent Fawcett's dislike of party politics and mistrust of Gladstone had been acquired from her late husband Henry and she quoted his opposition to Home Rule in a letter to *The Times* at the height of the Home Rule debate.[284] She had spoken at the first Liberal Unionist conference in December 1886 and she now became one of the most active of the Association's speakers, giving a rousing denunciation of the prospects of a self-governing Ireland at the first meeting held in Lady Stanley's drawing room in the West End in July 1888.[285]

Perhaps the chief activist among the Association was the formidable Isabella Tod, secretary of the Ulster WLUA and founder member of the Ulster LUA, who, within two months of the WLUA's formation, had written the lead article for the *Liberal Unionist*.[286] Tod was a tireless campaigner, speaking at meetings across Britain, often facing hostile crowds, writing letters and articles for newspapers and organising and assisting branches of the LUA and WLUA.[287] Female political activists could offer services in a fashion that most men found difficult; as one of the organisers of the North London branch of the WLUA, Richardson, noted, 'women could work all the year round at times when there were no elections going on, as well as when there was all the excitement of a contest. Men could only arrange their business to give up time when elections were taking place. Women might influence voters by house-to-house visiting, or by quiet discussion.'[288] The WLUA had twenty-one branches within a year and began to demand official recognition from the Liberal Unionist Council. They set up offices at 92 Palace Chambers, Bridge Street in Westminster and advertised in the *Liberal Unionist*. As the rising star among the Party managers, with Caine's enthusiasm dimming, Wolmer was keen to encourage the Association in its efforts and attended the WLUA Council meetings.[289]

The role that Wolmer, probably in common with the rest of the Party's leadership, envisaged the WLUA playing was summarised by one of their officials:

> Women are for the most part rooted to the soil; they will never be a large guerrilla force, but they may be an excellent territorial militia. It is for this reason that we have been urging on the LUA the desirability of employing them to work among the voters in their own neighbourhoods, to influence the people whom they know, or whom they easily could know; so that when an election comes on, instead of fetching in strangers from a distance, who have to begin by learning their way about, we may have a corps of women workers on the spot, knowing the electors personally and living in permanently friendly relations with them.[290]

In particular, the Party's reliance on Conservative records and efforts in the crucial field of registration might be mitigated through the use of the WLUA volunteers. The WLUA came to be seen as a valuable electoral tool and became quite sophisticated in its approach to the electors. A lengthy article, 'Some Hints to Women on Canvassing', whilst epitomising the patronising tone often used when addressing female activists, gives an astonishing level of detail. Women canvassers are given advice on how to approach 'the stiff Conservative who will not vote for a Liberal Unionist' (and vice versa), the 'temperance man', the 'eccentric religionist', the 'indifferent man' and even the 'invalid' in order to win their vote. Although the canvassers may have been middle-class themselves, the guidance was clear where votes needed to be won, 'if you have the choice, you had better go among the working classes, you will be much more useful.'[291]

Despite the limited view of the Association's role among some of its own leaders, Kate Courtney, the WLUA secretary, was clearly intent on creating a radical organisation, in keeping with her and Fawcett's views on female suffrage and other social and political questions. The organisation's leaders were keen to stress that 'they were not only Unionists but Liberals, and should not allow themselves to be confused with Conservatives.'[292] Tellingly, 'the leading place' for the WLUAs was Birmingham, which had its first meeting on 9 October 1888 at 8 Corporation Street, with Mrs Herbert Chamberlain as president and Mrs Arthur Dixon as one of the vice-presidents. The Birmingham WLUA had established a membership of 1,000 within nine months and, by November 1891, it was nearly 2,000.[293] The Association was credited with 'a conspicuous part' in the success of the Party's candidates in the 1892 election, largely due to their work in tracing and canvassing voters who had removed.[294] In London, Caine's radical Metropolitan Committee took control of the North London branch of the Association through Richard Chamberlain. A Cornish branch was started in July 1888.[295] An attempt was made to spread the reach of the WLUA into the other heartland of Liberal Unionism, the west of Scotland, with Fawcett attending the inaugural meeting of the regional WLUA in Glasgow on 8 November 1888.[296] However, with their strictly conservative social attitudes, the Scots failed to develop a similar body of supporters, as 'the feelings against women joining in politics appears to be very strong.'[297] The Association, with branches in Glasgow, Ayr and Paisley was clearly of some help. J. Parker Smith's wife became its president, following his election victory in Partick in 1890, and in early 1892, it was promoting the candidature of Alexander Cross for Camlachie.[298] Parker-Smith's own increased majority in 1892 was a result of 'this very well-organised branch.'[299]

In Ireland, where Isabella Tod oversaw an active Association with branches in Leinster, Connaught, Munster, Waterford and Tipperary, membership although 'very numerous' was not always 'earnest' or even motivated by purely political impulses. A Tipperary Nationalist, in his account of a WLUA Clonmel public meeting on 7 September 1889, asserted that the meeting, in an area where 'no other Loyalist Association of any kind exists', was largely attended by those who were seeking to make more personal alliances: 'It was a great day for mothers with marriageable daughters.'[300] Elsewhere, the Association struggled to assert its identity. Although Phillip Gell managed to create an Association in Oxford, the lack of a Liberal Unionist candidate made the group less attractive to the socially-ambitious Oxford Unionist women (and their daughters) and by 1891 it was holding joint meetings with the previously derided Primrose League.[301]

As the 'Newcastle Programme' encouraged a wider debate of reform beyond Home Rule in the early 1890s, Lydia Becker, Fawcett and Courtney were keen to use the WLUA's influence to push for the Party to advocate female suffrage.[302] The less radical members of the executive committee and those concerned by the impact of such a policy on relations between Conservatives and Liberal Unionists were unenthusiastic and at the conference of WLUA secretaries on 4 June 1891, the organisation declared itself neutral on the issue of female suffrage.[303] This did not solve the problem, as Isabella Tod immediately wrote a lead article criticising the Party leadership for putting pressure on the WLUA. As most women were Unionists, she argued, surely there was much to be gained by a bolder approach to politics?[304] The issue flared up again as the election drew closer. When Mrs Fawcett refused to agree to Margaret Farrow's request not to mention women's suffrage at a meeting of the Birmingham WLUA scheduled for 20 January 1892, Mrs Farrow cancelled the meeting.[305] Mrs Fawcett therefore wrote an article entitled 'Women and Politics' in the January edition of the *Liberal Unionist* in which she lambasted the paper for having criticised a Conservative conference resolution in favour of women's suffrage. In a bitter tone, she commented that 'I am always sorry when I see Liberal Unionists justifying the taunt so often uttered against them in the Gladstonian press that they are *plus Royalistes que le Roi* i.e. that they are more Tory than the Tories', and she went on to make a chilling prediction: 'If the paragraph I have criticised represents fairly the mind of the Liberal Unionist, it is a symptom of death.'[306] St. Loe Strachey responded with the official Party line that was not designed to promote enthusiasm among the WLUA's more radical members:

> The Liberal Unionist Party, as far as we are aware, is not committed to Female Suffrage ... Mrs Fawcett appears to think we should be drummed out of the Party because we do not express a direct opinion in favour of female suffrage ... we cannot help thinking that we shall be most truly Liberal if we allow expression of opinion from all sides and do not assume that no one can be a Liberal Unionist who does not agree with us on Female Suffrage.[307]

Although Wolmer himself let Mrs Fawcett know that he would support a ballot for a suffrage bill at Westminster, there was clearly little unanimity in the WLUA on this issue.[308] Kate Courtney recorded that the issue 'made some of the ladies very hot and excited.'[309] At the AGM of the WLUA on 11 May, Fawcett was not invited to speak and the question of support for women's suffrage, if discussed at the event, was not reported. Mrs Fawcett explained her inaction in 1903: 'I and other suffragists always abstained from pressing it [women's suffrage] because ... we felt it would lead to the break up of the Assn. and we had suffrage societies on which to work for suffrage.'[310] There is clear evidence here of Liberal Unionists being able to continue to act according to their principles outside the formal party structures, with no external limitations being placed upon their freedom of action, but equally there is no evidence that they achieved 'a higher profile within a shrinking movement.'[311]

The Party was far more comfortable with the WLUA playing a supporting role and a largely decorous one at that. The report of the AGM emphasised a very traditional view of the priorities of such events: 'The platform was fringed with daisies, lilies and other flowers tastefully arranged.'[312] Despite this and despite the limited social reach of the body, by the Council meeting on 10 May 1892, Kate Courtney could report that the Association's membership stood at 7,000.[313] The body was clearly the work of a few committed activists, however, as the report on election activity for 1892 revealed. In it the Association reported that 'a band of Irish ladies' had travelled the country 'to press upon English voters the claims of the Irish loyalists.' This 'band' was found to number four, including the indefatigable Isabella Tod.[314] Most of the canvassing work was also done by a few volunteers. So rare was an effective activist that Agatha Richardson wrote to Mrs Fawcett in February 1894, recommending the services of a Miss Charlotte Jones as 'strong, energetic, methodical, bright, and thoroughly trustworthy.'[315] As Devonshire had commented at the AGM in May, 'a great deal had been done by it [the WLUA] on an extremely meagre income.'[316]

The refusal to support suffrage disheartened the Courtneys and was compounded by the Party's failure to respond to the WLUA meeting on proportional representation that was held at River House, Chelsea Embankment on 10 July 1894, at which Courtney and Lubbock argued passionately for electoral reform in Balfour's presence.[317] Finally, when the Conservative and Liberal Unionist leadership blocked Leonard's bid for the Speakership in March 1895, Kate and Lady Stanley considered resigning from the Association. Mrs Arnold-Forster wrote an urgent letter describing this prospect as 'like a nightmare' and managed to prevent any hasty action.[318] But as can be seen from the two volumes of Kate Courtney's diaries from 1895 to 1900, she now felt 'that the L.U. Party in Parliament are not as independent as we thought.' She felt particularly aggrieved at Chamberlain's influence as she felt he was 'too clever a wire-puller for a small party to be at all free under his leadership.' Unsurprisingly her activity with the WLUA dwindled, choosing to visit Germany from 31 May to 10 June at the height of preparation for the expected election and, as far as can be gleaned from her diary, holding no WLUA meetings and never speaking outside her husband's constituency during the election campaign.[319] The only other truly significant contribution of the WLUA was its support for Faithfull Begg's Women's Suffrage Bill in 1897, even though it was known that the Duke of Devonshire was personally opposed to such a measure. Although the Bill was defeated, it provides evidence of the on-going ideological divisions within the Party, as, even after the formation of the coalition government, twenty-five Liberal Unionists MPs voted for the bill and twenty against.[320]

The Nonconformist Unionist Association

The Party was also directly responsible for the creation of a supposedly independent pressure group, the Nonconformist Unionist Association. This body, established by a group of nonconformist lawyers, was inaugurated at the Cannon Street Hotel on 17 April 1888, in order to repudiate the claim that most nonconformists were Gladstonian.[321] As Parry has shown, nonconformist involvement in Liberal politics had not only been motivated by a dislike of state interference in religion and education, but also by a suspicion of Ultramontanism in Ireland. Fear of an over-mighty Catholic priesthood had been one of the chief causes of the politicisation of Nonconformist communities in the 1850s and their support for an English political culture that permitted liberty of conscience as well as encouraging individual responsibility.[322] It was therefore inevitable that, while entering into an alliance with the Tories, the Party needed an organisation to reassure chapel-goers that the Liberal Unionists had not sacrificed their commitment to the ethical values of dissenting Liberalism.

Although the group was always presented as the non-partisan voice of the nonconformist movement, it was in fact originally organised by the Ulster Liberal Unionist Association.[323] As the Liberal Unionist Party struggled that year with the burden of coercion, which drove many of its supporters back to the Liberals and the lack of any constructive policy that would appeal to working-class voters, the temptation to return to sectarian politics was clearly too great to resist. The body originally sent speakers such as Isabella Tod and T. W. Russell to speak at election campaigns in England to persuade voters that 'the whole body of Protestant opinion in Ireland [was] against Home Rule', but it soon became more ambitious.[324] It organised a highly publicised meeting between the non-Episcopalian minister and both Salisbury and Hartington and then held a banquet at the Hotel Metropole with the Moderator of General Assembly of the Irish Presbyterian Church (R. J. Lynd) present. The two Ulster Liberal Unionist MPs were of course in attendance, together with Havelock-Allan, Goldsmid, the Scottish MPs Corbett and Sinclair and, perhaps most notably, Chamberlain's lieutenant, Powell Williams. Senior Methodists, Baptists and Congregationalists attended and the names of Spurgeon and Dale were frequently referred to as prominent supporters. The purpose of the meeting was, as the chairman, G. Hayter Chubb, put it, 'a reply to the repeated insinuations of the Separatist Party to the effect that Nonconformists were necessarily Gladstonians.'[325] Shortly afterwards, the *Liberal Unionist*'s new column, 'Friends and Foes of the Union' began with a profile of the leading figure in the one nonconformist sect not represented at the Hotel Metropole banquet, the Quakers. The article on John Bright emphasised 'his desire to benefit the people' in all he did, arguing that there was consistency in his opposition to 'the policy of handing Ireland over to anarchy.'[326] Bright, although reluctant to work with the Party in any fashion, was unable to prevent his name being splashed across the Party's literature (a poster was even made up with his face and Charles Spurgeon's). When he died, the *Liberal Unionist* was printed with a black border on its front page.[327]

The Nonconformist Unionist Association increasingly revealed its links to the Party as the general election grew nearer. In September 1889, the *Liberal Unionist* published 'Some Reasons why Nonconformists should be Unionists', written by the Association's President, T. E. Winslow QC. This revealed the largely anti-Catholic nature of the organisation as two of the five heads were that Home Rule 'will lead to the endowment of Roman Catholic Religious Education in Ireland' and that it would give the 'Irish Roman Catholic parliament' the power to use taxes 'for the purposes of the establishment or endowment of any form of religion in Ireland.'[328] In March 1892, a meeting of the NUA was held with Joseph Chamberlain as guest speaker, at which he described himself as 'one of yourselves and a Nonconformist.'[329] Chubb, now president and described by Bebbington as 'the leading spirit in the NUA',[330] announced the opening of branches of the NUA outside London, but little activity took place. When interviewed by the *Pall Mall Gazette* in 1893, Chubb had to admit that there was little point in going to such expense as 'half the members of [LUAs] are Nonconformists.'[331] Bebbington concludes that 'the NUA was a one-man band', which 'did little effective work apart from holding banquets.'[332] With the threat of the second Home Rule Bill, the NUA was superseded by the Irish Presbyterian General Assembly's decision to hold a Unionist Convention in Belfast. Here, the support of prominent

Liberal Unionists such as Thomas Sinclair was significant in avoiding a sectarian or threatening appearance, as even Catholic priests were welcomed onto the stage. Following this success, the Liberal Unionists appeared to have gradually allowed Chubb's Association to decline, as they felt they could make much better Unionist capital out of the official nonconformist bodies of Ireland, rather than through an intermediary body. The only significant role the NUA appeared to play after 1892, in addition to organising a meeting in support of H. M. Stanley's candidature in North Lambeth, was to help H. M. Bompas organise his survey of 1,243 nonconformist laymen on their support for the second Home Rule Bill in 1894.[333] The organisation then appeared to lie dormant until it was resurrected by Bonar Law one last time in 1912 to contribute to the opposition to the third Home Rule Bill.[334]

The Rural Labourers' League

The other body organised to appeal to a particular group among the electorate which was far more independent of the central Party's control was Jesse Collings' Rural Labourers' League. Collings had been deposed as president of the Allotments and Smallholdings Association by Home Rulers and the National Agricultural League was tottering under Joseph Arch's poor leadership. [335] This seemed an ideal opportunity for the National Radical Union to re-assert its appeal to the rural electorate. Chamberlain was clearly the driving force behind it, having written to Wolmer in 1888 advising that, 'I think we ought to start at once a new Labourer's League and put Collings at the head of it.'[336] Their motivation was to force upon the Conservatives something less of a token gesture than the extremely limited 1887 Allotments Act, which, David Steele admits, 'Tories hoped ... might stave off a demand for something more.'[337] The League was founded on 12 May 1888 in Birmingham and went on to launch a weekly newspaper, the *Rural World*, the first issue of which featured articles by Collings, Sir John Lubbock and 'the warm and old friend of the labourer, Mr Howard Evans.' For 1d, the reader was provided with 20 three-columned A5 pages with agricultural news, advice and advertisements. The only avowedly Unionist material was given in the editorial and the focus was clearly on the allotment holder with 'gardeners and allotment holders' news' and a series of seasonal recipes. The independence of this avowedly radical publication was clearly the cause of some nervousness among moderates: St. Loe Strachey welcomed it by blandly asserting that 'the paper should prove of great use,' and promptly never mentioned it again.[338] The Rural Labourers' League was adequately funded by the Party, as it had up to twenty-five travelling agents and 3,000 'local village volunteers.'[339] Collings felt that the Party

Image 26: A copy of Jesse Collings' *The Rural World*. 6 July 1895. Clifford 3 (2).

was making little use of his efforts, as he wrote to Wolmer in 1891 that 'it would be well if possible to waken up all the Unionist Party to see the necessity of increased work in this direction.'[340] William Morris was acidic in the scorn he poured on Collings and his 'poor foolish little scheme', mocking it ('how many rural labourers are in it, I wonder?') and describing those at the banquet to launch the League as 'the friends of the ejectors of the Irish, and the Scotch crofters.'[341] Derby unwittingly confirmed Morris's view in his diary when he described Collings as 'not an enemy to the rich as such.'[342] The organisation was obviously felt to be of value in the county seats, as, shortly before the 1892 election, it was granted £5,000 from Wolmer's secret electoral fund.[343] However, once the election was over, Collings found the Conservatives far less willing to engage in debates for further land distribution. Even attempts by Collings to influence the Royal Commission on Labour proved fruitless and he was reduced to issuing a number of independent recommendations.[344] Readman has identified the Tory opposition to compulsory purchase for the provision of allotments as both aristocratic and popular. With Chamberlain more concerned about the behaviour of the urban worker in his campaign for social reform after 1892, it is difficult not to find some validity in Morris' dismissal of the RLL.[345] The *Rural World* and the RLL continued until 1919 when it was dissolved after the achievement of the Land Settlement Act which benefited the returning servicemen.[346]

Funding

Such a large organisation, with a number of subsidiary bodies to support, which had been created largely from nothing in 1886, needed to be financed and per-haps the chief source of the Liberal Unionist Party's unexpected and unprec-edented longevity was its huge financial reserves.[347] As James confidently put it, 'we had within our small party many very rich men who contributed to our funds very generously.'[348] On 11 May 1886, *The Times* stated that the Duke of Bedford had sent the Liberal Unionist Committee a blank cheque.[349] Once the Liberal Union had been created on 22 May, it was reported that contribu-tions were flowing freely, many of them of £1,000.[350] Alfred Pease reported that a target figure of £100,000 had been set,[351] while Nathaniel Rothschild boasted that the Committee had 'unlimited funds.'[352] Despite the fact that no appeal for funding had yet been made, by 9 June it was reported that subscriptions had reached £30,000.[353] As a result, in those areas where the situation was monitored, such as Manchester, the amount of literature for the Unionist cause vastly exceeded that of the Home Rulers.[354] The *Birmingham Daily Post*, meanwhile, spoke of the Liberal Unionist Committee 'daily shak-ing its money bags in the face of the public' on 10 June.[355]

The clearest indication of the state of the Party finances comes from a report from Wolmer to Hartington in December 1888. He estimated income at between eight and nine thousand pounds per annum and anticipated that

it 'might predictably be increased to 10.'[356] The monies were soon spent. The
Liberal Unionist Association had six organising agents paid between £250
and £500 a year, but Wolmer wanted four more. There were the 'large staff of
lecturers' organised by the Liberal Union Club paid between a guinea a lecture
and £50 a month, with travelling expenses and organising agents 'a very heavy
item', and two offices in London – the Association's and the Metropolitan
Committee's. With publishing costs (including the *Liberal Unionist*), additional expenses included subsidies to 'weak-kneed' branch associations, registration expenses and an average of two contested by-elections a year, the
weight of this expense was clearly felt by a Party lacking in a large base of
popular support. In November 1890, T. E. Jacob, a self-confessed 'member of
the rank and file,' saw one of the main obstacles to efficient organisation as
'penury' and in the same month, the secretary of the newly found Yorkshire
Federation of the Party complained of 'want ... of money.'[357] The Party was
clearly well funded at its centre, due to the monies of the peers and landlords,
but, of the Liberal Unionist general committee, 'the majority of the members
contribute nothing to the funds.'[358] Lord Rothschild was asked by Hartington
to approach some of the wealthy peers for £60,000 to support the regional
Associations as the prospect of an election drew near. Rothschild gave £5,000
himself, but could only persuade Derby to pledge £2,000.[359]

At the annual meeting of the Women's LUA at Prince's Hall in Piccadilly
on 11 May the following year, having dwelt on the question of Ulster for the
bulk of his speech, Devonshire made an appeal for funds, commenting that
the Association operated on an 'extremely meagre income.'[360] In order to
raise funds for the forthcoming election, to supplement the remaining limited resources of the various Liberal Unionist Associations, Devonshire himself was reduced to sending personal letters of appeal to wealthy supporters
of the Party. The bulk of those who responded were businessmen, such as
bankers, tradesmen and brewers, and it is clear that they expected some
rewards from this trade. Four contributors, Henry Wiggin, John Jaffray,
Horace Farquhar and E. H. Carbutt all received baronetcies in Salisbury's
dissolution honours following the election. In total, Wolmer raised £131,785
'through [Devonshire's] letters in connection with and in preparation for,
the general election.'[361] £66,800 was spent in the months leading up to the
election. £27,000 was spent on the Liberal Unionist Association and £5,000
on Jesse Collings' Rural Labourers' League, in an attempt to minimise
the damage in the counties.[362] Even by 1895, £65,000 remained. Wolmer
reminded Devonshire, that 'I have still, as you may remember, some money
left over from the fund we raised for the General Election of 1892.'[363] By
then, however, he had acceded to his father's title and was more concerned

with maintaining the Defence Association. As James had commented a few months earlier: 'Wolmer appears to have dropped out almost entirely … you should ask Wolmer to take an active part in the collection of funds. He knows our wealthy men and has great tact.'[364] But James was more than happy with his replacement as Party manager, the radical Unionists' whip, Powell Williams. 'You know how highly I think of Powell Williams … the main responsibility of expenditure may well be left in Powell Williams' hands', even though he clearly felt less confident about Wolmer's replacement as Chief Whip:

> The more the management of our affairs is left in [Williams'] hands and the less in Anstruther's the better … Anstruther has not in any way whatever interfered in business matters − nor has he been near the office … If [the collection of funds] be left to Anstruther we shall soon find our funds very low … I do not wish to be unduly hard on Anstruther. He is very civil and zealous − but I do not think he is quite fitted to carry out the very delicate matters arising out of the collection or expenditure of a considerable political fund.[365]

Wolmer, either honestly or to avoid being pressed back into service at a time which no longer suited him, wrote to Devonshire to reassure him of Anstruther's abilities. 'I think you may be very much at your ease about [the finances],' as Anstruther had already collected £6,000 in excess of what was required to fight the election, and more funds were still arriving.[366] Chamberlain confirmed this positive picture in June, assuring James that 'there seem to be funds in hand enough to carry us on.'[367] The Liberals' financial difficulties in 1895 were effectively exploited in the election as the Liberal Unionists' organisation and funding resulted in a series of uncontested elections. Anstruther reported to Wolmer on the eve of the election that funds were 'prospering in my hands',[368] which he substantiated to Devonshire after the election in September:

> The state of the general election account stands at the 6 September:-
>
> Credit £41,846
>
> Debt £22,083
>
> = Ba. £19,763

> There are a few payments yet to be made; the result will shown roughly a balance of £20,000.[369]

The need for such large amounts of money is demonstrated by the balance sheet for the mid-Devon LUA for 1891. In this year, a professional secretary cost £30 p.a., registration expenses cost £15 and advertisements were £2/4/8.[370] Election years were even more costly and by the turn of the century with the development of new printing technologies, these could be prohibitive. The account book for the West Derbyshire LUA for 1906 survives and reveals that this single Association, in a seat that could be considered safely Unionist, spent £1,603/4/2 on the election, the costs being incurred from the employment of an agent and the expenses of canvassers, but mainly from the publication of materials. 20,435 placards were produced, 99,695 handbills, 43,050 cards and portraits of Victor Cavendish, 60,300 leaflets and pamphlets (most of which must have been purchased from the literature department in Great George Street) and 54,000 cartoons and picture leaflets.[371]

Of course, the production of such material, of other propaganda and indeed party organisation were not, in themselves, guarantees of electoral success, therefore the relationship of the Party with their electors needs to explored as a discrete issue. It must be credited that the Liberal Unionist Associations, their affiliated bodies and London headquarters were a significant demonstration of a Unionist culture that amounted to more than merely parliamentary whiggism and the demagoguery of Birmingham that most historians have been content to recognise. With substantial funding from both business and aristocratic sources and the influential support of so much of the national and provincial press, many Liberals clearly felt comfortable expressing their commitment to patriotic and constitutional principles through the Liberal Unionist Party. There is sufficient evidence to reject Lubenow's recent assertion that the Liberal Unionists 'withered away.'[372] Rather, they continued to raise funds and remained important and active participants in the political environment until at least 1903. There is, however, little evidence of the employment of local professional agents (outside certain regional and central organisations) which Kathryn Rix has identified as such a crucial feature in political success between 1883 and 1906.[373] In Bury, Henry James had to appoint his own amateur agent, a local solicitor named Butcher.[374] In this way, although the Liberal Unionists had managed to use their funding to guarantee short-term survival as the Liberals faltered, they had failed to establish the structures necessary for their growth in an age of mass democracy. Only in Glasgow and Birmingham was the Party sufficiently organised with professional agents that it could cope with the challenge of nationally divisive issues such as the reorganisation of state education in 1902 and tariff reform in 1903.

CHAPTER 5

LIBERAL UNIONISM AND THE ELECTORATE – 'A FARCE AND A FRAUD'?

The ability of the Liberal Unionist Party to fight and win so many seats as it did over the twenty-six years of its existence, in an age of mass politics, has traditionally been argued away by reference either to Chamberlain's unprincipled opportunism or to the 'jingo' factor – the ability of upper-class leaders to dupe working-class voters into supporting expensive and futile imperial ventures, most notoriously in 1900. The high-water mark in this failure to acknowledge any positive causes in the return of so many Liberal Unionists was at the height of enthusiasm for 'cliometrics' in 1977. Hugh Stephens of the University of Houston offered a structural explanation for the Liberal Unionist vote as being 'occasioned by the ... drastically altered constituency structure resulting from the reform acts' rather than by any actions on the part of the individual activists. With the aid of an impressive collection of statistics, he asserted that 'the Liberal Unionists .... were the beneficiaries of a lag in electoral mobilization which often happens after a large expansion of the franchise.'[1]

Unfortunately, this electoral sociology reduced the significance of the local MP and the specific issues of individual constituencies within the historical analysis, in much the same way that the 1884 Reform Act reduced their significance in the political structures of the country. If one wishes to engage with the creation and reception of the political discourse in the late nineteenth century, the historian must account for political behaviour at the grass-roots level. Unlike twentieth-century historians, those who study the late nineteenth century have no opinion polls or surveys to refer to. As

so few detailed results from canvasses survive, due to the low number of
Liberal Unionist Association records that have been preserved, the relationship between voters and organisers can only be tentatively analysed and some
inference has to be made from the methods of electioneering undertaken
(including the use of the provincial press) and the results in both by-elections
and general elections. Some of the relevant material on the effectiveness and
scale of party organisation at the association level has been dealt with in the
previous chapter, so this section of the book focuses on the outcomes of this
work and the particular problems the Party faced in enlisting the support of
the new, working-class electorate.

As the 1886 revolt was based primarily on the principles of, and the pres-
sures upon individual MPs as to which lobby to enter on 8 June 1886, there
was little cohesion to the location of most of the rebels' seats. In five areas
in 1886, the Liberal Unionists achieved more than ten seats. In some of
these cases, however, this was misleading as there was little coherence to the
areas represented. However, in two of these seats, the West Midlands and
the west of Scotland, strong initial party organisation was responsible for
pressure being brought to bear on the local Liberals to join the rebellion. In
the third, Cornwall, a largely accidental concentration of Liberal Unionists
was built upon in subsequent years and local circumstances were exploited
to create a third base of anti-Gladstonian Liberalism. As Dunbabin has
noted, there were 'significant electoral differences as between regions ...
often historically determined ... they proved surprisingly durable.'[2] Outside
these three areas, I believe, Liberal Unionism often became a feather on the
wind of the political temper, suffering from the national swing away from
Salisbury's Conservatives in 1892 and then benefitting from the failures
of the Rosebery administration in 1895 and the mood of patriotic fervour
in the 'khaki election' of 1900. Or it was dependent on the influence of
particular MPs in particular seats, with those who spent precious hours cultivating their constituencies (such as Henry Hobhouse in East Somerset or
Cuthbert Quilter in South Suffolk), exploiting the familial influence (such
as the Fitzwilliams in South Yorkshire, the Rothschilds at Aylesbury or
the Cavendishes in West Derbyshire), or relying on their particular appeal
to their constituents (such as the anthropologist and naturalist, Sir John
Lubbock, at London University), surviving while others found themselves
isolated and unloved.[3] These either swiftly re-joined the Liberal Party (as
seven MPs did between 1886 and 1892) or were removed in the 1892 cull as
the Liberal vote recovered.

The 1886 Election

The general election of 1886 demonstrated the extent to which various regional Associations had gained a foothold. In sixty-seven constituencies where the standing Liberal MP had voted for Home Rule, they were opposed by a Liberal Unionist.[4] In thirteen others, the sitting Liberal Unionist retired before the election, either because the local Conservatives would not support them and so they stood no chance of winning, or because they had been rejected by their caucuses.[5] E. A. Leatham, MP for Huddersfield, resigned and advised his constituents to vote for the Conservative candidate, while William Jacks, faced with the potential nomination of Gladstone in Leith Burghs, withdrew his candidature. 'What a fool Leatham has been,' wrote Chamberlain to Caine, 'to give his seat to Summers – he could have kept it easily. Jacks is the worst, however, the idea of bolting like a rabbit from a mere nomination of the G.O.M.'[6] One great advantage to the Liberal Unionists was the reluctance of the Eighty Club, which included so many Unionists, to take an active role against Liberal Unionists during the election.[7] Gell had spotted that the membership list should be scrutinised and those thought to be Unionist in their sympathies contacted and asked to help at Spring Gardens.[8]

Of the 102 Liberals who voted against the second reading of the Government of Ireland Bill or abstained, eighty stood for re-election in their original seats as Liberal Unionists and sixty-five of them were returned (twenty-eight unopposed). Where the Tories' chief agent, Richard Middleton, felt that Liberal Unionists stood a better chance of defeating the incumbent 'separatist' (as *The Times* dubbed the Gladstonians) only thirteen out of eighty-eight were successful in defeating a Home Ruler. Seventy-seven MPs who affiliated themselves with the newly formed Liberal Unionist Committee were returned in 1886. Forty-seven Liberal Unionists sat for county constituencies, thirty for borough seats (including two in London) and one for the University of London. Of the county returns, there were thirty-four in England, nine in Scotland, two in Wales and two in Ireland. The higher proportion of representatives of county constituencies had been noticed among Liberals who supported the Union before the election, but was more marked than before. The percentages of county representatives were: Liberal Unionists: 61%; Liberals: 53%; Conservatives: 40%. It has been suggested that in such areas, the persistence of deference allowed Liberal dissidents to take their working-class support into the Unionist camp with them as the prestige of the incumbent MP and the strength of his claim to consistency was often highly convincing.[9] Of the borough seats, twenty-one were in England, eight in Scotland, one in Wales and none in Ireland.

If one accepts Chamberlain's claim that forty-six of the ninety-three rebels of 8 June were radicals, it can be seen that the radical element were punished more harshly for their vote against Gladstone than the rest of the Liberal Unionists. Sixteen radicals either retired (usually in the face of impossible odds) or were defeated. Of the thirty who were returned, eight, according to Brand's conversation with Akers-Douglas, 'mean to rejoin Gladstone at once.'[10] Eighteen members of the NRU were returned, including D. H. Coghill and Walter Morrison, neither of whom had sat in the previous parliament. A week after polling began, Gladstone's chief whip, Arnold Morley, admitted to him that Chamberlain's influence in the Midlands was stronger than anticipated. According to Morley, one Gladstonian had changed to a Liberal Unionist at the last moment in order to avoid a contest.[11] Lewis Morris believed that Chamberlain's influence even extended into Wales, to his seat, Pembroke and Haverford West, where he had been defeated by Conservative.[12]

The south and the Midlands were where the 1886 election was won. The Gladstonians lost thirty-five county and twenty-eight borough seats in England, half of the latter in London. Middlesex, Surrey, Kent, Hertfordshire, Buckinghamshire, Berkshire, Hampshire, Huntingdonshire, Rutland, Worcestershire, Shropshire, Herefordshire and the city of Birmingham returned no Gladstonians at all. The Liberal Unionists also benefited from a large number of uncontested seats (more than a third of their parliamentary strength), which have usually been ascribed to lack of time for finding a Gladstonian candidate, or lack of funds as the rich Liberal donors flooded to Hartington's Committee.[13] However, William Harcourt did suggest that the policy may have been a deliberate one on the part of the Liberals, possibly with an eye to achieve reunion as soon as Gladstone could be persuaded to retire, 'we have hitherto been all of us able to avoid placing ourselves in individual conflict with our former colleagues of a recent date.'[14] In the 1885 election over four million had voted, but in 1886 only two and a half million had exercised the franchise (a fall in turnout from 84.4% to 74.1%).[15] These 1,639,010 fewer votes were partly due to the uncontested seats, but also due to Liberal voters' uncertainty towards the Home Rule issue. In such circumstances, with the future direction and leadership of the Party unclear, many voters appear to have given the incumbent the benefit of the doubt in most cases. Making allowance for the unopposed returns, it is possible to calculate that at least 800,000 voters must have abstained. Contemporary testimony suggests that the bulk of these were Liberals and Gladstone interpreted this to mean that many Liberals had not made up their minds about Home Rule.[16]

Liberal Unionist	Candidates	Elected
South-East England	23	14
South-West England	20	13
Midlands	26	18
Northern England	32	11
Wales	11	3
Ireland	7	2
East and North Scotland	32	9
West Scotland	14	8
Total	165	78
Total Vote	1885	1886
Liberals	2,157,612	1,244,683
Irish Nat.	299,784	97,905
Cons	1,934,450	1,036,649
LU		431,513
Uncontested		
seats	1885	1886
Liberals	13	40
Irish	17	66
Cons	10	91
LU		29[17]

Some Liberal Unionists may have also suffered from Conservative abstentions, as some Tories could not bring themselves to support those who had only recently been their adversaries. One Worcestershire Conservative farmer recorded that he could not vote for 'the black-coated, cotton-gloved gentry who, but yesterday, had been trying on the village greens, to prejudice the farm workers against their employers.'[18] Many other Conservatives found it difficult to support those who favoured church disestablishment, 'free schools' or restrictions to the liquor trade.[19] On the other hand, in some areas, the assistance of the Conservatives was crucial. In Grimsby, Heneage calculated 'that 2/5 of the Liberal Party voted for me (1,400) as against 3/5 (2,100), while 2/3 of Conservatives (1,582) voted for me.'[20] This dependence on the Conservatives was confirmed by the *Daily Telegraph* which pointed out that only twelve Liberal Unionist seats had been won entirely with Liberal votes.[21]

The most destructive impact on the Gladstonians was the sense of betrayal by the agricultural voters, especially farm workers, of whom, it was estimated, 400,000 had not voted. Their votes, won by the promise of 'three acres and a cow' in December, now deserted Gladstone, who, they felt, had become distracted by Home Rule and who had alienated their champions, Jesse Collings and Joseph Chamberlain.[22] Chamberlain's undoubted ability to appeal to the newly enfranchised agricultural labourers was sorely missed by his old Party in 1886. The self-proclaimed 'radical parson', William Tuckwell, considered that his absence from the hustings was 'an immeasurable disaster; his influence with the democracy had some for time past excelled Gladstone's; I found of late that if audiences cheered Gladstone's name for two minutes, they cheered Chamberlain's for five.'[23] Caine, facing his own caucus in Barrow, gave Chamberlain the credit for his victory, 'your visit added 500 to my score.'[24] The *Standard* wrote on 14 July that the Government's losses were not due to Unionist sentiment but to a reaction after the extravagant hopes of 1885 and the influence of Jesse Collings.[25] Henry Sidgwick also considered that Chamberlain's departure damaged the Liberals' electoral chances in the rural seats: 'There are various explanations of the swing-rounds of the agricultural labourer. Here [Essex], my Tory friends think he is partly disgusted at not having got his three acres and a cow, partly afraid of Irish competition in the labour market.'[26] Few sections of the community suffered more from cheap Irish labour than the farm workers. As well as making them unsympathetic to the Irish cause, this also made them susceptible to the claim that Home Rule would ruin Ireland and fill Britain with a swarm of starving Irish willing to work at almost any rate. C. R. Spencer, who stood in Mid-Northamptonshire, complained that the Unionists had flooded the division with pamphlets stating that the Gladstonian policy would swamp the labour market with Irishmen. He was also concerned that the timing of the election during the hay harvest had caused many to be away from home and thus unable to vote.[27]

The Gladstonians fared worse where the farm worker had most influence: in predominantly agricultural constituencies of large farms worked by paid labour. In Yorkshire, Durham and Northumberland, with large numbers of industrial workers and miners, the counties stayed loyal as the political interests of these workers were similar to those of the urban workers.[28] In Wales, where Gladstone held all his county seats, and in large areas of Scotland, a proportion of the constituencies were likewise ones in which miners and industrial workers predominated, but in the majority, the bulk of the voters were dependent on agriculture. In these constituencies, however, the largest number of voters were not farm workers, but tenant farmers with grievances similar to those of the Irish tenant farmers eager for the remedial legislation which they associated with the Liberal Party. This was especially true in the highlands and islands of Scotland.

The loss of so many Liberal landed families to the Unionists told heavily against the Gladstonians in the country, for as yet the Ballot Act had not seriously affected the influence of local landed families in politics. One contemporary observer noted that in those districts where the members of the great Whig families were still regarded as the natural leaders of the Party, the Gladstonians had suffered their worst defeats.[29] The promise of easier electoral victories may have played a role in explaining the decision of some county MPs to resist the temptation (and pressure from their activists) to return to the Gladstonian Party once the election was over and Home Rule had receded as an imminent threat. C. S. Roundell, in a letter to Spencer after the election, mentioned that in Skipton, West Yorkshire, the Devonshire, Ribblesdale, Tempest and Morrison influence had all been on the Unionist side and he had been the only person of any standing on the Liberal side.[30]

Urban workers and miners chose to support Gladstone, because only his Party seemed to offer a prospect of disestablishment, temperance, education, taxation and labour reforms. On the other hand, the issue of Home Rule made many abstain as they felt Gladstone was neglecting their interests. As Hammond wrote, 'no voter who wanted anything else [than Home Rule] had much reason for voting for him.'[31] Rev. Tuckwell noted that many workers felt that their devotion had been thrown away and their confidence abused.[32] The historian of the miners' unions of Northumberland and Durham recorded that when radical miners' agents began to advocate Home Rule with all the vigour which they previously expanded on social reform, there were protests, as not every miner could be convinced that Home Rule was a labour question.[33] Those who voted for Gladstone in 1885, but were unconvinced by the case for Home Rule, chose to abstain in 1886, not out of apathy, but due to a deep conflict in their loyalties. Chamberlain's radicals were more fully committed to these objects than the Gladstonian Party as a whole, but in most areas they had no candidates and no prospect of enforcing these policies on their erstwhile allies, the moderate Unionists and the Conservatives. Only in certain areas did urban voters support Unionists because they felt that do so would put pressure on Gladstone to abandon his new crusade and return to the true mission of Liberalism.

The Liberal Unionist Committee, now reconstituted as the Liberal Unionist Association, outlined this particular problem, which caused the defeat of nearly 50% of its candidates:

those seats were probably the most difficult to win from the Gladstonians as they were considered as safe Liberal seats when the Liberal Party was united under Mr Gladstone and consequently it was more difficult at short notice to induce the great bulk of the electorate to transfer their political allegiance from Mr Gladstone.[34]

One of the most significant defeats for the Liberal Unionists was Goschen's in Edinburgh East, which the *Scotsman* acknowledged as being the result of Gladstone's visit to the city during the campaign.[35] Other notable casualties included Trevelyan and Albert Grey.

The Liberal Unionist campaign was aided by the Irish speakers provided by the Irish Loyal and Patriotic Union, the Ulster Anti-Repeal Union and the Ulster Liberal Unionist Committee.[36] This was not surprising, given the improvised nature of the Liberal Unionist Party machinery, though Camperdown's letter to Cartwright in mid-Northampton confessing that 'we have no lecturers' is striking.[37] In some areas, a large number of Unionists resigned from the local Liberal Association, but in others, election committees and supporting workers had to be found almost entirely among those with no experience of electioneering. As many of the Liberal Unionist candidates were quite unknown, 'ticket-only' meetings were impractical, so in some cases no meetings were held and canvassing and election addresses were relied on instead.[38] The Liberal Unionists, as rebels against as popular a figure as Gladstone, were particular targets for trouble-makers and many meetings were broken up and candidates physically attacked. The 1886 election campaign proves O'Leary wrong for suggesting that 'riots and disturbances' had been replaced with 'the individual heckler' following the 1883 Corrupt Practices Act.[39] On 28 June 1886, *The Times* wrote that the election meetings in London had been the scenes of violence and disorder on a scale hitherto unknown and that a Unionist meeting in the south or east of the city was taken at once as the signal for a riot.[40] On 9 July, it stated that the election had been marked in many parts of the kingdom by unusual turbulence and that in London, where the political atmosphere had previously been cooler than elsewhere, there had been a large amount.[41] It hoped that the turbulence was temporary and this did not signal a return to what it termed the 'broken heads and drunken orgies' of elections in the past.[42] The *Daily Telegraph* wrote that many of the characteristics and incidents of the election had been honourable all round, but that like any other election, it had bred bad blood between many English gentlemen and had stimulated coarse appeals to the lower passions of the populace. It deplored the breaking up of meetings and the howling down of candidates.[43] The solidly Gladstonian *Daily News*, however, took quite a different view and claimed that violence in England and Ireland had been relatively limited, considering the passions aroused by Home Rule. It admitted that London had seen more disruption to meetings than elsewhere, but asserted that this was merely horse play.[44] As far it is possible to ascertain from the contemporary sources, the riots that broke out in Belfast on 3 June were independent of the general election, as were those that resulted from an Orange Order procession in County Tyrone on 12 July.[45]

It is clear that politics in the 1880s still afforded many the unusual opportunity to engage in partially licensed, physical 'ebullience', particularly in the capital.[46] Electoral violence continued to be aimed at Liberal Unionist meetings in London during the by-elections of the subsequent Parliament. In the 27 April 1887 issue of the *Liberal Unionist*, there is an account of a meeting at Kensington Town Hall at which H. O. Arnold-Forster spoke, was heckled and finally 'sticks were being wielded, some of [the] ornamental brasswork was broken and furnished weapons … after a few minutes of this terrible fighting a strong body of police arrived and quickly quelled the fray, making several arrests. Mr Hobhouse, MP was struck in the face with a fist and hit over the head with a brass bar.'[47] In reply, Strachey included an article on 11 May, entitled 'Hints to Home Rulers (which they do not need)', in which the following advice was offered: 'If you are short of an argument, a fist or a stick will do instead. If you cannot answer the reasoning of your adversary, it is advisable to break his head open.[48] Other Liberal Unionists struggled with the dilemma of how to reach out to a working-class audience in their constituencies, without putting themselves in physical danger. Heneage in Grimsby reluctantly had to hold ticketed meetings, in order to meet, as he put it, 'well conducted artisans and fishermen, but no roughs.'[49] In Bury, James was also forced to adopt a low profile:

> The hostility of the Irish clubs within the borough was so great that I was worried that personally it would not be safe for me to attend a public political meeting … the consequence was that whilst I was very assiduous in my attentions to the electors in private, I could hold no meeting in public, for it would have assuredly been broken up.[50]

Although there was little actual violence in Holmfirth and the surrounding area, the *Sheffield Telegraph* reported Liberal Unionist meetings as 'very disorderly.' In the constituency there was the first reported use of a common piece of political pantomime, as hostile audiences hoisted coats on poles, turned inside-out, reinforced with cries of 'turncoat.'[51] Such experiences persuaded one of those who had voted against the Home Rule Bill on 8 June, to recant. C. R. M. Talbot, the father of the House, was persuaded by Gladstone's offer of compromise and was adopted by the Glamorganshire Liberal Association as the official Liberal candidate for the 1886 election.[52]

In Glasgow, after a public appeal on 6 May, a Committee had been formed with 500 Liberals from the west of Scotland within a fortnight. As J. McCaffrey has ably explained, the Liberal Unionists carefully exploited 'long-standing social and economic prejudices against the Irish' and highlighted the impact of Irish separation on Scottish trade. Dr McGrigor, speaking to the Glasgow Chamber of Commerce noted the dependence of the Greenock sugar refining trade on exports to Ireland: 'At least three other sugar refineries would be added to the four now silent and smokeless.'[53] With the crucial support of the *Glasgow Herald* and the *Scotsman*, the Party was able to spread its message that the Home Rulers had surrendered to the Irish demands and that it was the duty of Scotsmen of character and determination to resist Parnell's dictation.[54] This message and the Liberal Unionists' organisation were clearly decisive. In the election, the Liberals lost seventeen seats to the Liberal Unionists, but only two to the Conservatives. This meant that Liberal Unionists held nearly a quarter of Scottish seats and these accounted for 20% of the Liberal Unionists' total parliamentary strength. Twelve of the Liberal Unionists seats were won in the west where the speed of the Liberal Unionist organisation was unmatched in any other region of the United Kingdom.[55] In Wigtownshire in 1886, the Liberal Unionists afforded the local Conservative, Sir Herbert Maxwell, 'the easiest [election] I had yet experienced.' Earl Stair assisted by 'throwing his great local influence in support of the Conservative Party'. The vote across the counties of west Scotland dropped by an average of 5.5%, but that in Wigtownshire fell by 15.7%. Maxwell, however, saw his vote increase by 200 votes from 1885. 'Thus loyally did the newly formed Liberal Unionist Party fulfil their pledge and rally in support of their former foes.'[56]

The east of Scotland presented a very different picture. Here, the local MPs appeared to be dependent on the work of a single electioneer, Rev. James Taylor D.D., and their source of literature was the Irish Loyal and Patriotic Union. Of the forty-three constituencies within the Committee's area of responsibility, thirty-five were contested (only three seats were fought by Conservatives).[57] The first LUA to be founded was the Dundee and District LUA, formed on 9 June, which found two candidates for the Dundee election: Brinsley Nixon, a London banker, and General Sir H. D. Daly. Both lost and Daly lost again in a by-election in February 1888. Recognising their position, they formed good relations with the local Conservatives.[58] The E&NSLUA failed to match the level of achievement of their colleagues in Glasgow and as early as January 1889, the honorary secretary, J. P. Grant (unsuccessful candidate for Ross and Cromarty in 1886), was warning that 'Scotland is the battlefield where the most disastrous blow to the Union can be struck,' as in three of the seventeen

Liberal Unionist seats in the country, the Liberal Unionist candidate held the constituency on a majority of less than one hundred. Grant warned that east Scotland was being targeted by the Liberals and that the Unionists were vulnerable 'for want of a constructive policy.'[59]

In Devon and Cornwall, the puzzle of the huge majorities for Liberal Unionists in 1886 and the relative success of the Party of the whole period, has not been effectively explained by Lubenow, Henry Pelling, Michael Dawson or even Patricia Lynch in her recent study of rural support for Liberalism in the period. In the Party newspaper it was noted in February 1890 that 'our Nonconformist supporters, who are especially numerous, are as devoted and hearty as can be desired,'[60] which does not correspond with Dawson's assertion that 'Unionism predominated in south and east Devon where nonconformity was weaker.'[61] There is a valid case for believing there was a genuine cultural basis to the support for Liberal Unionism here. As E. Jaggard has shown in his studies of Cornish politics before 1885, 'localism was too powerful a force to be ignored', as the independent minded population tended to prefer locally born and raised candidates, yet the appeal of Conservatism was limited.[62] Although it was admitted that 'the Liberal Unionist Party in west Somerset is scattered,' of the eleven rural seats west of Exeter, the Liberal Unionists represented seven of these after 1886.[63] What is more, they held all seven seats of these with majorities of over 1,000 each. F. B. Mildmay in Totnes won 80% of the vote and went on to hold his seat until 1922. In direct contradiction of Dawson's claim, the Liberal Unionists did particularly well in Devon and Cornwall where the Free Church movement was strongest and where the middle-class voters were most free of landlord influence.[64] It was acknowledged as 'the next strongest redoubt' of the Party after Birmingham.[65] Nonconformity in Devon and Cornwall was dominated by Wesleyan Methodism which, unlike Primitive Methodism, seemed particularly susceptible to fears for Irish Protestantism.[66] As early as the 1887 St Austell by-election, George Chubb, later president of the Nonconformist Unionist Association, could confidently assure Lord Salisbury of growing support for the Union among Wesleyans in Cornwall.[67]

On the issue of Home Rule here, the Liberals were deeply divided and the local Conservatives were reluctant to hand this opportunity to the Liberal Unionists. Hozier and Middleton were unable to settle the issue and Salisbury had to intervene.[68] Believing that in such a stronghold of nonconformity the Tories only stood a marginal chance of victory, he endorsed seven of the Liberal Unionists and called on the local Conservatives to support them. Salisbury had his limits though, and the radical MP, Lewis McIver, was not endorsed, following strong protests from the Conservatives of Torquay and a Conservative stood against him as well as a Gladstonian.[69] In Totnes, Mildmay refused to allow Conservatives to appear on his platforms, fearing the alienation of his Liberal supporters and the Conservatives sought, in vain, to run a candidate in protest. At Barnstaple, although the local Conservatives were instructed to support G. Pitt-Lewis, a meeting at Ilfracombe preferred to abstain rather than endorse his candidature, leaving him with no party workers. Pitt-Lewis was forced to attend Liberal meetings, where his voting record was criticised and he was reduced to invoking the name of General Gordon and to mitigate his vote on 8 June by condemning the meeting at Her Majesty's Opera House.[70] Conservative Central Office now had to come to his aid and send a letter from Lord Iddesleigh: 'As far as I can make out, Mr Pitt-Lewis is a fair example of the Liberal Unionists. He has gone very straight against Gladstone, and he is (I know) ready to pledge himself against the disestablishment of the Church in the next parliament.'[71] This clearly swung the Conservative vote behind him and Pitt-Lewis was returned with 59% of the vote.

Leonard Courtney, however, faced a serious rebellion in Bodmin from Liberals. As a supporter informed him, 'the general objection one meets with is "if Mr Courtney could not vote with Jesse Collins [sic], he might have been neutral; why need he go into the lobby with the Tories and against his own Party?"'[72] At a meeting of the central committee of the South East Cornwall Liberal Association, a vote to readopt him as the candidate for the division was defeated by fifty-nine to nine. He and his supporters had swiftly to form a new committee in order to nominate his candidature.[73] In Truro, William Bickford-Smith only just managed a majority of votes in his favour at a similar meeting.[74] Despite his fears that 'the working men are so thoroughly Gladstonian that the adverse poll will be fairly large', Courtney held Bodmin with a majority of 1,162.[75] The influence of an independent, thoroughly Liberal, locally popular candidate should not be underestimated in affecting the result in this part of the country. The Liberal Unionists also put up candidates in the Ashburton division of Devon and in Camborne in Cornwall that were, frankly, poor choices. R. B. Martin in Ashburton was a London banker and of little appeal to the fiercely independent voters and he suffered a torrid time on the stump. Arthur Strauss in Camborne was, in the words of the local newspaper, 'a German Jew', with such a considerable control of the local tin trade that he was detested by Conservatives and Liberals alike and had to withdrawn in favour of a local nonentity, J. D. Gay.[76]

The most marked feature of the voting in this strongly Liberal part of England was the decline in the overall poll, as many electors, unsure of how to respond to a sudden change in Gladstone's direction on Ireland and advised by many of Gladstone's former supporters, both in Parliament and the press, to abandon him, simply deferred their decision and stayed away. In her study of three rural constituencies in the period, Patricia Lynch found little enthusiasm for Home Rule among the Liberal electors.[77] The worst fall was in St Ives, where a decline of 21% of the total vote was recorded, and even in the best turn-out in the region in Torquay, it still fell by 6%. In St Ives, Sir John St Aubyn managed to secure the Liberal Party's endorsement and so the low turn out can be accounted for by confusion over the position of the two Liberal candidates and the unofficial Gladstonian received less than 1,000 votes. With the Conservatives backing him (albeit reluctantly) and such disarray among the Gladstonians, even Martin in Ashburton got over 3,000 votes.

The anti-Catholic attitudes of a nonconformist community, especially one on the western side of Britain, fearful of cheap Irish immigrant labour may seem to offer something of a solution to the regional variety of Liberal Unionist support, taking in Cornwall, Lancashire and the west of Scotland. However, one must not press this too far. The area of greatest Liberal Unionist defeat was also the strongest area of nonconformity in the British Isles, Wales, where the Primitive Methodist church, with its largely working-class congregation, remained loyal to the Gladstonian cause. The three Welsh seats won by Liberal Unionists in 1886 were not contested by the Liberals. Sir H. H. Vivian and C. R. M. Talbot both left the Liberal Unionists within a year and Colonel Cornwallis West managed less than half the votes of his rival when he stood for re-election in 1892.

The Welsh cause was clearly badly handled as Lloyd George's victory in the 1890 Carnarvon by-election result demonstrated. When Irish nonconformist and working-class speakers were brought in to bolster the Unionist cause, the meetings were held in Conservative clubs, not public halls, and no Welsh Liberal would enter such premises. The *Liverpool Post* believed that the 'Unionists had thus thrown away their trump card.' Lloyd George's campaign in which he played entirely on the theme of Welsh disestablishment, was well chosen to embarrass the Unionists, who were divided nationally on the issue.[78] In 1892, when all the Party's seats in Wales were lost, the Party suffered from its support for a government which had done nothing to address Welsh anger over the continued demands for tithe payments from the Church of Wales.[79] In the whole period of the Liberal Unionist Party's existence, only one Liberal Unionist ever won a seat in Wales. Sir J. Jenkins won Carmarthen District with a majority of fifty-two in 1895 (and failed to retain it in 1900). Kenneth Morgan, writing of the Liberal Unionists in Wales claims that 'Unionist efforts to whip up Nonconformist prejudice against the sinister menace of Irish popery ... failed completely.'[80]

The Pursuit of the Working-Class Vote

The Reform Act of 1884 had created a large number of working-class voters, as the electorate had increased from 3.04 million to 5.7 million in Great
Britain, particularly among the rural communities. While the impact of
this electorate on the rise of independent labour parties has been endlessly
examined since the 1960s, the appeal of Unionism to this new political class
has been explored only recently. There has been no published study examining the appeal of Liberal Unionism to this group. Only now, with Patrick
Joyce and James Vernon's analysis of how the contemporary language of
politics must be understood in order to explain the way the political elite
engaged in a discourse with the burgeoning electorate, has a methodology
developed which allows historians to explain how the Unionist Parties spoke
to the new voters.[81] In particular, Jon Lawrence has encouraged historians
to examine how activists attempted to create political identities among the
new electors by building on existing models of masculinity and freedom.[82]
In contrast to the perception of the Liberal Unionist Party as 'generals without an army', analysis of local campaigns proves that they were just as adept
at doing so as the other two Parties.

   The first person to identify the problem of persuading working-class men
to support Liberal Unionist candidates was A. V. Dicey, who revealed his
contempt for the mass electorate, believing that 'National Schoolmasters
would act as effective propagandists' and were 'more accessible than many
electors to argument.'[83] Courtney articulated Dicey's point more fully, when
he quoted a working man who disliked Home Rule, 'but Mr Gladstone has
been the friend of the working man and we must stand by him.'[84] As early
as June 1887, the energetic Robert Bird, secretary of the WSLUA, noted that
any attempt to appeal to working-class voters was bound to be difficult,
given the Unionist alliance and the traditional working-class distrust of the
Tories. He asserted that:

> the [Liberal Unionist] cause is growing in popularity and strength,
> and it has got a strong hold upon the middle and the mercantile classes
> ... Working men generally follow the lead of their employers; but in
> order to secure that following it is necessary that the working man
> should be got to see ... that the working man who also becomes a
> Liberal Unionist will not be called upon to renounce or in any way
> modify his Radical opinions.[85]

As a result, the WSLUA opened the first Liberal Unionist reading room in
the working-class constituency of St Rollox, where James Caldwell only had

a majority of 119.[86] The Party clearly had some way to go, however, as the by-election defeats at Ayr and Govan demonstrated.

When he visited the WSLUA in April 1890, Lord Wolmer emphasised future priorities:

> There are infinitely more Liberal Unionists among the working classes in any given constituency than any gentleman here has any idea of . . . They won't come to you . . . You must go to them . . . you must conduct a canvass, either by paid agents or by volunteers.[87]

The Party began to consider other ways in which working-class voters could be made aware of the Liberal Unionist message. In September 1888, it was suggested in the Party newspaper that literature might be distributed on workmen's trains in East End. It was also suggested, in order to reach the working man who was more likely to spend his evening in the pub or music hall, that there should be 'a distribution of literature during the dinner hour, at the gates of some of the large factories in West Ham and the Tower Hamlets.'[88]

In the Midlands, 'a Staffordshire Miner' agreed that 'what is wanted is to get among these men [miners] at the right time and in the right way.' He advised that traditional approaches to politics would yield paltry results, as 'the exchange of shots between the leaders of the opposing parties will not teach the lower orders of men the ins and outs of the Irish Question.' Instead he recommended political activity such as the Liberal Unionist van undertook as 'men will read a little work on the question, or listen on the road-side, who cannot be got to attend meetings a long distance from their homes.'[89] The choice of canvasser was crucial as well, as, within the complex hierarchies and identities of the world of skilled and complex manual labour, the Party recognised the need to promote the cause through those of similar trades and professions.[90]

In the north-west of England, already inclined towards Unionism due, so Peter Clarke believes, to its traditional fear of cheap Irish labour and working-class Anglicanism, there was a further pocket of Liberal Unionism with six MPs. In reality, seats such as Northwich in Cheshire, or Hartington himself in rural Rossendale, had little in common with urban seats such as that of Henry James in Bury, Peter Rylands in Burnley, or W. S. Caine in Barrow-in-Furness. There was little co-ordination and little active organisation in the north outside county Durham, which the Liberal Unionist chief whip and main party organiser after 1887, Lord Wolmer, believed to be the best organised district in the country. As a result, support for Liberal Unionism was not sustained in Lancastria; the first warning coming when George Goschen failed to win the securest Unionist seat in Liverpool, Exchange, by seven votes in February 1887.

The experience of Heneage in Grimsby could give an indication of why the Liberal Unionists failed in the north. Although he could count on the sympathy of the many Wesleyan Methodists of Lincolnshire, Heneage's attitude towards the organisation of his local party remained largely aloof. He remained close to his agent, James Wintringham, but failed to perceive that Wintringham's commitment to Home Rule might have made him less enthusiastic for Heneage's re-election than he might have been. Although he informed Wintringham that he was being told that 'my interests are being neglected' and complained, 'I do not know what you are and Reed are doing' in February 1892, he continued to use Wintringham as his agent.[91] A local supporter, Ben Coulbeck, wrote to Heneage in despair: 'I am amazed at the apathy shewed by ... our leading people in the Unionist cause.' He warned that 'we have a formidable rival ... unless something is done quickly we shall ... "be caught napping."'[92] Wolmer himself became concerned and in March demanded that Heneage investigate the state of Party activity. Heneage was dismissive, however: 'I do not see that he can do any good myself and might do harm,' and expressed continued confidence in Wintringham, informing Boraston of the situation.[93] Instead, Heneage chose to use personal attacks on the Liberal candidate, Josse, who had been encouraged to stand by Edward Watkin, denouncing him as a former lunatic, Frenchman, Republican and Roman Catholic.[94] Additional problems were the on-going poor relations with the Conservatives caused by their refusal to endorse Heneage as chairman for Lindsey County Council.[95] Heneage was also in poor health, retreating to Eastbourne for ten days in April 1892.[96] He faced the opposition of the local paper, the *Grimsby News*, who accused him of being a 'deserter' and throwing himself into Tory arms.[97] Eventually, Heneage realised that his position was serious and dismissed Wintringham and began to seek the support of Lord Cross and the M.S. & L. Railway Company.[98] By then it was too late and Heneage lost the 1892 election by the substantial majority of 636 votes.

Manchester and Lancashire, despite the enclaves of support for Derby, Westminster and Hartington, remained largely loyal to Gladstone in 1886. Only in fifty-three seats across the country did the Gladstonian vote increase in 1886 and ten of these were in Lancashire.[99] There were far fewer Liberal abstainers here than elsewhere. The Liberal Unionists failed to find a candidate in 1886 for the one seat that the Conservatives were willing to allow them to contest, South Manchester. Despite an opportunist letter to Leonard

Courtney inviting him to stand from T. C. Rayner, secretary of the Manchester Branch of the Liberal Unionist Committee, who had heard of Courtney's problems in Bodmin, 'they were unfortunately not attended with success.'[100] In 1892, Hopkinson was invited by the Conservative Association to contest Manchester South West. Seats were also contested in Lancaster, Clitheroe and Heywood, Rossendale, Liverpool Exchange and Bury. All were lost except Bury. Moore suggests that 'support for Home Rule united [Manchester's] large Irish population behind the Liberal Party – a move which compensated for the loss of the Liberal Unionists.'[101]

Rebels against an admired leader knew they faced difficulties in getting re-elected, especially in Gladstone's heartland in the north of England. Henry James informed his electors in Bury that 'I am going to take up my abode in no cave. The climate of a cave would not suit me.'[102] He was right to do so, for once he became a leading figure in the Liberal Unionist Party, his local caucus disowned him and attacked him. James had some sympathy with their position, though. After all, 'they had won the seat in 1885 for me, and now a year afterwards they saw me holding it for those we had defeated.'[103] As Hartington wrote to his father on 9 July:

> A great many of my old supporters seem to be very angry and are working as hard as they can against me. Both the Manchester Liberal papers [the *Guardian* and the *Evening News*] are strong against me and we are certainly on the unpopular side with the mob this time.[104]

By contrast, in Bury, the relatively small numbers of Irish-born residents and the undeniably Liberal profile of the MP, Henry James, helped to secure this constituency for the next nine years. Despite Jeremy Smith's assertion that dislike of local Irish communities motivated working men to vote Unionist, the only seat in Lancashire which the Liberal Unionists held for longer than the first parliament after 1886 was that with the smallest Irish population.[105]

Even after the 1895 electoral victories, the Liberal Unionists never recovered in the north, with the veteran radical Unionist, Sir Savile Crossley, losing heavily in the Halifax by-election in March 1897. Those seats that they did win in the area were largely safe, affluent seats, such as Central Bradford, Skipton and South Manchester, the gift of local Conservatives, encouraged by Balfour and Salisbury to keep the Liberal Unionist leaders happy and, as a consequence, to urge their supporters in marginal seats elsewhere to vote Conservative, despite their scruples (as solidly Liberal figures such as Henry Sidgwick did in Cambridge).[106]

As has been noted above, there was an attempt to create leisure facilities for working men in Lancashire, with reading rooms and clubs set up in 1889. The Devon and Cornwall Association had already established one in Plymouth and Caine's Metropolitan Committee had done so in South St. Pancras. This was applauded by Walter Thorburn, MP for Peebles and Selkirk, who called for more such clubs Jonathan. Backhouse, who represented an area which was struggling to recruit, was also keen, but he was aware that the initial expense was considerable and suggested that in many places these clubs would have to be subsidised by the local leaders of the Party. Heneage, on the other hand, stated that under proper management they paid very well and the Organising Council refused to commit themselves to subsidies, choosing instead merely to recommend 'that clubs available for working men be established wherever practicable in towns and populous places.'[107]

However, in October, at the Liberal Unionist Council meeting, Wolmer had to defend the very notion of working men's clubs from radical pro-temperance Unionists such as E. C. Baily, secretary of the Bradford Association, who claimed that his experience of political clubs in Birmingham had taught him 'that there was a strong tendency for the political element to become subordinate to the social element … frequently the clubs became more drinking shops and card-playing places.'[108] In Wolmer's view, the fact remained that 'clubs had a great attraction for young men particularly.'[109] When the Party paper printed an encouragement to establish such clubs in working-class areas, it did so in a fashion that would have made most local activists blanch, as the need to be affordable and need for efficient management made it clear that no help from headquarters would be forthcoming.[110] Thus, only in areas of wide-spread Liberal Unionist support such as Birmingham or areas where rich Unionist leaders were prepared to subsidise the establishment of such facilities, such as Bristol and Durham, were such vital sources of influence and social centres established.

The Women's LUA were a major source of canvassing, although the efforts of the upper middle-class women of the Association sometimes demonstrated a complete lack of understanding of the demands of working-class life. In 1894 the Oxford WLUA organised a meeting in a rural constituency, but 'the time was unfortunately chosen and all the people were busy haymaking.'[111] Getting suitable workers was hard as well, as Mrs Sinclair complained in May and again in June, when she noted that 'the privates and recruits are conspicuously absent in the organisation.'[112] Those that could be persuaded to go house to house were reluctant to enter working-class areas; as another organiser reported to Mrs Gell in June, 'others said they would not go into the courts and alleys [of Witney]. So it ended in my employing a lame man to distribute some [leaflets].'[113]

The Oxford WLUA records also reveal the problems of persuading Liberal Unionists to vote for Conservative candidates. As Mrs Sinclair, one of Mrs Gell's most active workers, found when she visited the local villages, there were 'Gladstonians who might become Liberal Unionists', but only 'if they had a Liberal leader. I do not think they would vote Tory unless associated to strengthen each other and well led.' She quoted verbatim the attitudes of several Liberals. One, John Adams, an 'old labourer', voted Liberal even though 'he could never see that Home Rule was right.' Another had 'doubts about Home Rule but G.O.M. is always right so "lumps it."' This sentimental attachment to Gladstone's reputation as the friend of the working man was a challenge that the Liberal Unionists had to struggle with, even after the Liberal leader's retirement. As early as April 1886, Boraston noted that 'the very name of Gladstone is a most potent instrument to conquer with. The creed of the majority seems to be "if you cannot see eye to eye with Mr Gladstone in this Irish matter, you are no Liberal."'[114] Another common attitude among rural workers, which was a major stumbling block, was that the labourer 'hates the farmers' and 'fears the Tories are against free trade.' Mrs Sinclair was convinced that many wives were Unionists but their husbands remained Liberals by default.[115] In many cases, in rural England, the constitutional implications of Home Rule seemed far removed from the lives of most labourers, as Mrs Sinclair complained, 'it is very difficult to get the country people I meet, even our own lads, to take any interest in the Irish Question.'[116]

Even before the 1892 election, an official of the WLUA asked pointedly in 1889: 'Have we made the way that we should with the working classes?' She contrasted the experience between the regions of the country: 'Why should there be a large number of Liberal Unionist working men in Birmingham and a good many in Cornwall, and not in other constituencies?' The writer, in common with other activists, questioned the value of 'large meetings and set speeches ... however good these may be, it is probable that the country is growing a little tired of them.' The solution had been found in areas were volunteers were plentiful and the WLUA was keen to offer the same services: 'What is wanted is more work among individuals in each constituency, more careful finding out and bringing together of those, who, whether rich or poor, whether men or women, would have some influence over their neighbours when the time for action comes.'[117]

By November 1889, Wolmer was almost in despair as shown by his candid comments at the Liberal Unionist conference in Leeds. In his view, the focus on traditional political methods meant that 'they had quietly allowed the Gladstonians and the Conservatives to monopolise the working men.' Wolmer concluded that 'if no attempt was made to get at the working men, all the organisation would be of very little avail.'[118] In London, the WLUA kept up its efforts to reach working-class men at times which suited them, rather than the Party. Bompas, Leedham White, Robert Purvis and Thomas Richardson all addressed meetings in the mess rooms of the locomotive sheds at St Pancras organised by the N. St Pancras WLUA.[119] It is possible to presume that even the title 'Unionist' had become tainted with 'Toryism' among working-class voters by the early 1890s, as a 'Constitutional Open Air League' had begun holding meetings every Sunday at St Pancras Arches, Mile End Waste, Regent's Park, Victoria Park and Wormwood Scrubs, in opposition to similar Socialist meetings. As it was proposing opening reading rooms in working-class districts in winter, it was clear that it was being funded from a deeper pocket than that of its organiser, John Byland, who lived in Hammersmith. The source was mostly likely the Constitutional Club itself, which had already learnt the art of keeping its name free of Conservative associations since 1883.[120]

Finally, in mid-1891, the central Party responded with a leaflet, *What the Unionist Government has done for the Working Man,* which included twenty-one measures passed by the Conservatives which would be of benefit to lower class voters. As a piece of sophisticated political persuasion it was not highly convincing. Important measures such as free education and local government were hidden beneath such trivial issues as the 'Margarine Act', whilst the attempt to claim that 'the reduction of National Debt' was worthy of inclusion smacked of a desperate attempt to produce as long a list as possible, especially when it was accompanied by the limp hope that 'much of that ... will go to the working man.' Finally, the exhortation that 'is it not his duty and his interest to support the men who have done these things and who are ready to do more in the same direction?' implied an ability to command and expect deference from the lower orders that surely belonged to the paternalistic politics of pre-1867 Britain, not the age of militant trade unionism and the year of the founding of the Social Democratic Federation.[121] Argyll suggested that Bright should be politically disinterred and his writings on the Irish Question widely distributed as '*nothing* so useful has been written because of the writer's influence and authority with the working classes', thus demonstrating an attitude towards the working classes that was, at best, twenty years out of date.[122]

As the by-election defeats continued and the Liberal Unionists' rather ham-fisted propaganda and organisation failed to halt the tide, despite the money thrown at Union Jack vans, leaflets, Association meetings and agents' fees, the attitude towards the electorate became quite bitter. The Birmingham WLUA held a meeting in April 1892 with the revealing title: 'How best to deal with the ignorance and apathy of the voters.'[123] The Party did try to overcome its limited appeal to the mass electorate in 1892 by targeting key working-class groups. As well as the work of the Rural Labourers League, Chamberlain had been cultivating the assistance of the sailors' champion, Samuel Plimsoll. In July 1892, Plimsoll wrote to the *Liberal Unionist*, contrasting the lack of pertinent reform proposals from the Liberals with the 'warm and decided part' taken by Chamberlain and urging those 'who think sailors' lives are of more importance than party politics ... to support those candidates who will aid to keep the present Government in power.'[124]

By-election performance

As T. G. Otte has noted, historians have paid little attention to by-elections before 1918, yet these are, arguably, the most useful indication of the Liberal Unionist Party's success in establishing a separate position in the political spectrum of late Victorian Britain (see Appendix 7).[125] The returns from the initial by-elections in 1887 clearly worried the Liberal Unionist organisers, in particular, W. S. Caine, the radical Unionists' whip. He wrote in the initial issue of the *Liberal Unionist*:

> The by-elections ... teach a lesson to LUs. In every instance we should have done better had our party been organised and educated ... it is very clear that those Liberals in Ilkeston who refused to bow the knee to Baal could not bring themselves to vote for a Conservative candidate and abstained altogether, to the number of nearly 1,200.

> The increased Parnellite majority in Ilkeston was made up of LUs, who are Unionists still, but who, for want of mutual support and encouragement, have been persuaded by an unusually clever candidate to support him on other grounds than the Irish question, such as Local Option, Disestablishment and what not.[126]

Due to an unfortunate piece of editing, the same issue of the paper revealed the current, clearly inadequate, Liberal Unionist electoral tactic: 'Mr O. T. Duke and Mr J. Parker Smith have been canvassing the Liberal Unionists in Ilkeston [sic].' As both these figures were (at this stage) minor figures in the

LUA, perhaps it is not surprising that the Liberal electorate was less than impressed.[127]

A letter from 'Unionist' in Lewisham in the 13 April edition of the Party journal made it clear what the fundamental problem was for the average Liberal Unionist:

> 'Vote for a Tory Unionist!' Hundreds, ay and thousands of them will not, talk as you will. Burnley and Liverpool were lost in this way. At Ilkeston the majority of the Gladstonians might and would, I feel confident, have been still further reduced [by the presence of a Liberal Unionist candidate].[128]

In the heartland of Liberal Unionism in the south-west of England, the Party had already learnt this lesson. As the Party newspaper reported after the St Austell by-election, despite the majority of the Gladstonian candidate exceeding 2,000 in 1886, the Liberal Unionists, given their success elsewhere in Cornwall, 'resolved to bring forward a LU candidate to contest the division.' The reduction of the Gladstonian majority from 2,281 to 211 was reported to have 'far exceeded the expectations of the local Unionists.' Revealing the reason for this relative success, the paper gave credit to Willyams, the Liberal Unionist candidate, attributing this in part to his religion, as being a Methodist he could appeal to the sectarian interests of the '¾ of the constituency [that] are followers of Wesley.' No doubt determined to counter the pessimism that appeared to be infecting the Party, St. Loe Strachey opined that 'the St Austell election must be reckoned as by far the most significant political event since the general election.'[129] In doing so, however, he confirmed that there was much truth in both 'Unionist's' and Chamberlain's assertions that many Liberal Unionists would only vote for a Liberal candidate and that the choice of candidate to suit the profile of constituency was crucial. An Irish correspondent commented similarly following the Spalding by-election in July, noting that, with the Home Rule Bill now safely consigned to history, 'the average Liberal or Radical Unionist will ... rather vote for the candidate with whom he disagrees on one question only, than for the candidate with whom he agrees on one question only,' with the consequence that Gladstonians will probably win 'every bye-election [sic].' The anonymous commentator suggested that a Liberal Unionist candidate should be found for every seat and should fight, even if the Conservatives put up a candidate.[130] In reality, of course, the Party could not pursue such a policy with Middleton's eye upon every constituency and had to put their efforts into campaigning for each Unionist candidate, regardless of his party orientation, with limited results.

In the campaign to retain West Edinburgh for the Liberal Unionists in the wake of Buchanan's defection, Henry James visited, after being told by Hartington that the election was 'very important.'[131] Caine reported after the defeats of February 1888, that the Gladstonian candidates had succeeded as 'many Liberal Unionists were induced by the large concessions now made by every Gladstonian candidate to Liberal Unionist sentiment to vote for men whose professed views are not the views of their great leader.'[132] The Liberals had also turned Salisbury's typically unguarded words, 'it is only to the judgement of Conservatives that I attach any importance,' spoken at a Conservative meeting in Liverpool on 13 January, to their advantage. As they pointedly asked of Salisbury's supposed allies: 'Liberal Unionists – will you be insulted in this fashion? If not, do all you can to inflict a crushing defeat on these Tory insultors [sic].'[133] The quality of the candidate was not necessarily a cause of defeat either. The prominent Liberal journalist, H. O. Arnold-Forster, adopted son of W. E. Forster, stood for the Party in Dewsbury in November 1888 and lost by over 2,000 votes in a Yorkshire that seemed to have become an impregnable Gladstonian fortress. The Party was left clutching at increasingly insignificant straws, claiming that, 'Arnold-Forster succeeded in materially diminishing the Gladstonian majority' (when he had only reduced it by 250 votes) and that his achievement of 40% of the vote was considerable as, according to Arnold-Forster's agent, 'no one could have named a score of Liberal Unionists in the parliamentary borough,' which says little for the local Association's activity in the preceding two and half years.[134]

Even in Scotland, the tide of defeat could not be stemmed. The first warning came in Glasgow Bridgeton in August 1887, when Evelyn Ashley was defeated by nearly 10% of the vote in an area thought to be the heartland of Scottish Liberal Unionism. Milner, writing to Gell, was cutting in his assessment of the Liberal Unionist electoral efforts:

> We are a lot of miserable, well meaning amateurs and we share the fate of patriotic volunteers fighting against mercenaries; of amateur actors figuring in a London company; of laymen pleading against professional lawyers ... don't let your people massacre any more innocents.[135]

In Ayr Burghs the following June, Ashley stood and lost again (albeit by the tiny majority of fifty-three votes), eliciting the criticism of 'a Scotchman' who blamed the defeat on 'Unionists not exerting ... in getting a sufficient

number of volunteer canvassers' and who revealed the parochial nature of
Scottish politics, exhorting the leadership to 'secure, wherever it is possible, candidates with local influence.'[136] This opinion was echoed by John
Borland's comment at the AGM of the WSLUA in December 1888, when he
opined that the 'election in Ayr was lost through over-confidence on the part

Image 27: *The Owl* revels in the string of Liberal Unionist by-election defeats. *The
Owl*, 20 September 1889.

of the Unionist Party – and through their organisation not being in proper order.'[137] The concern about poor organisation was also expressed following Sir John Pender's heavier defeat at Govan in January 1889. John McCulloch, radical MP for St. Rollox between 1885 and 1886 (who had voted for the Home Rule Bill in June 1886 but had retired in favour of Caldwell in 1886), believed that neither Ashley nor Pender had been chosen by the electors, going so far as to say that 'he did not see why it should be that a certain coterie or number of gentlemen should choose a candidate for a district without taking the constituency into its confidence.'[138] McCulloch commented on Pender's defeat that 'if Sir John had been able to adopt certain planks of the Liberal policy, which he did not do, he would have carried with him a third more of the constituency.'[139] The *North British Daily Mail* asserted that Pender had attempted to improve his reputation as a friend of the workers by bringing in Orangemen from Belfast to bolster the attendance at his meetings in the poorer areas.[140] When this was reported, it must surely have disheartened some Liberal voters who, like T. W. Russell, saw co-operation with the Orange order as a betrayal of Liberal principles. 'Another Scottish Radical' was so provoked by Pender's behaviour that he suggested that 'if our candidates do not come up to the mark, we must stand aside and the Unionist cause will lose votes and work which it can ill spare.'[141] For the secretary of the Party Association responsible for both these defeats, however, the problem was larger than organisation or temperance. Robert Bird commented in March that 'what is dealing disaster among the Scotch constituencies is our identification with Conservatism brought about by our negative attitude.' The majority of Scots had rejected the principles of Conservatism for so long that, as the organiser of an Association of genuine Liberals, he felt that 'the cure for this lies in a forward Liberal programme, not urged to excess, but advocated with earnest freedom' and he called upon the Conservatives to show a greater flexibility in their attitude to reform.[142]

The returns from the by-elections did not improve and Chamberlain concurred with Bird's conclusions in dispirited fashion in October 1889, following the loss of Peterborough: 'The bye-elections are most discouraging. I am afraid the Liberal cry is too strong for us, and that it is true, as Harcourt says, that the Liberal Unionists of 1886 have largely become Gladstonian since then.'[143] The *Liberal Unionist* did its best to find crumbs of comfort in the defeat of Robert Purvis, by asserting that voters of Peterborough had fallen 'prey to separatist misrepresentations.'[144] The truth was that Purvis had been a second choice candidate, largely as the dominant gentry family in the area, the Wentworth-Fitzwilliams, refused to put up a candidate despite Hartington's entreaties.[145] The defeat of C. B. Logan in Elgin and Nairn in the same month was attributed to an ungentlemanly and unwise campaign: 'The Unionists ... probably lost some votes – they certainly deserved to lose some votes – by an indiscreet and abortive attempt to rake up an old charge against Mr Seymour Keay.'[146] Hartington's only comment confirmed his lack of understanding of the electoral mood, as all he could write to Wolmer was that 'Peterborough and Elgin are very depressing.'[147] Only the Ulster LUA seemed capable of some decisive effort. Conscious of the damage that Nationalist accusations of government oppression and landlord exploitation were doing to the Unionist cause, a group of seventeen 'good men – Methodists ... and working men' were selected 'to assist at the by-elections ... to help to stem the torrent of Nationalist misstatements.'[148]

The trend of defeats was finally reversed with the election of James Parker Smith, one of the original members of the Liberal Unionist Committee, to the seat vacated by Craig Sellar in Partick. The quality of his campaign and the high level of organisation in the constituency Association is evident in the Parker Smith papers at the Mitchell Library in Glasgow, which include a highly detailed canvass of the constituency, with pledges of support outnumbering those for the Gladstonian Liberal in every ward.[149] Parker Smith made considerable efforts to maximise his support, appealing to the Conservative electorate by agreeing to abstain on the issue of Scottish disestablishment and emphasising his principles as a prohibitionist for the Liberal voters. As a result, the seat was retained despite a 5% swing away from the Liberal Unionists. Although the Liberal vote had increased since 1886 by 644, enough Liberals had abstained (the *Glasgow Herald* estimated that '1,350 voters ... refrained from polling') or voted for Parker Smith, that, together with the Conservative vote he had secured, he had improved on Craig Sellar's poll of 1886 by 422, giving him a majority of 219. The relief was palpable. 'I hope it marks a turn in popular feeling,' wrote one Liberal Unionist. 'Your success has been a pleasure to all Liberal Unionists' added St. Loe Strachey.[150]

Sadly, Parker Smith's success in Partick proved the exception rather than the rule and one of the few seats in the north of England was lost in January 1891, when the railway director, Sir William Gray, was defeated in Hartlepool, in what even the Party newspaper admitted was 'unquestionably a serious blow.'[151] In these circumstances, perhaps it was inevitable that Chamberlain would be tempted to announce a policy innovation without consulting the Party's leaders. Although his declaration of support for old age pensions was given in support of a Conservative candidate, Chamberlain's priority was to avoid any impression of Unionist weakness in Birmingham. This he achieved spectacularly, with a four-fold increase in the Conservatives' majority in the 1891 Aston by-election that was a striking contrast to the

Liberal Unionist experience in the two subsequent by-elections in their other strongholds of Devon and Cornwall and Lancashire.

South Molton was in the Liberal Unionist heartland of west Devon and Cornwall and there appears to have been a sense of local confidence but a fatal lack of organisation. As late as October 1891, Hartington was having to ask Wolmer, 'what is doing about South Molton?' Clearly no local candidate had been brought forward, as Hartington went on, wearily, 'I suppose we ought to contest it.'[152] A. V. Dicey, visiting the constituency, warned Wolmer that the situation looked bleak: 'From what I hear, I fear that we shall be defeated in Devonshire.'[153] In a seat with a Liberal Unionist majority of 1,689 in 1886, the Liberal candidate managed a spectacular swing of 21% and took the seat with a majority of over 1,000 in what Chamberlain described as a 'smash.'[154] Although the hostile *Bristol Mercury* asserted that the seat was lost because of the unpopularity of 'Whiggism' with the working man, the leader writer of the Liberal Unionist *Exeter Flying Post* put the blame on more prosaic failures by the local Party:

> The Unionist registration has been scarcely worthy of that name, and to sum up the whole matter we say that until the recent election was forced upon the constituency the Unionist Party went to sleep.[155]

Emerson Dawson, writing in the *Liberal Unionist*, commented that the South Molton election came as 'a surprise upon everyone.' Like many Unionists, he had relied on the attitude of the Methodists of Devon, as 'dissent is a great power in the constituency', but noted that the electoral effect of this had been mitigated by the work of the 'protestant Home Rule Association', who had 'quite imposed their views on the Nonconformist ministers – a very influential body in the constituency.' Clearly, they had made a sophisticated appeal to the charity of such influential local figures and 'succeed[ed] in persuading the South Molton ministers that the protests made against the really monstrous interference of the priests with Irish electors was merely 'the old "No Popery" cry slightly disguised.'[156] Although the Party paper concluded that 'Unionism seems to have for the time being lost its charm to the average voter', the truth was that the Party had failed to counter the effective Gladstonian canvassing in the constituency. 'A Local Liberal Unionist Secretary' acidly complained of a fundamental failure in a letter that is worth reproducing in detail:

> What is the use of appointing Liberal Unionist Agents or Conservative Agents to work divisions up, when, as I know, a few weeks after

their appointment, country parsons and squires (in whose hamlets a Radical lecturer has been speaking more than once) come down to the office to tell the agent not to disturb their little corner with lectures, or even canvassing or formation of committees; but to leave it all to them. They know all and will see to it themselves when the election comes. Come it does with results like South Molton and Market Harborough and then the agent is blamed by the very country squires and parsons who would not allow him to work on modern lines with modern methods and weapons ... They must work themselves with the committee and help heartily instead of hindering the working agent or secretary, coming more often into more direct and personal contact with him, instead of trusting to honorary and ornamental secretaries of their own class, who know nothing of the working classes and their wants.[157]

Then, in January 1892, Hartington's own seat at Rossendale was lost after his accession to his father's dukedom. Wolmer hoped that a low turn-out might save the seat, writing to Salisbury, 'on a poll of 85 per cent we should pull it off by about 150.'[158] Unfortunately, the local Liberal Association brought out the urban working-class voters by carefully stressing those elements of the 'Newcastle Programme' that would appeal to the constituency (in particular the proposal for a eight-hour working day) and the seat was lost on a 92% turn-out, despite the appalling weather on polling day.[159] Although the loss was merely described as 'unfortunate' by the Party organ, there was an admission of how little progress the Party had made in establishing itself in Lancashire: 'It was felt in 1886 by all well-informed persons that Lord Hartington owed his election to his great popularity with all classes in the constituency. It was not a seat then which any other Unionist could have carried.'[160] Hartington was less sanguine in private, describing the prospect of defeat to Wolmer as 'simply disastrous' and one which would 'affect the thinking of all possible and impossible candidates.'[161] Even Chamberlain was taken aback, writing to Wolmer on 25 January: 'Rossendale is a great blow. I am afraid it will seriously affect the business of the Session. How the voters must have lied. I confess the result altogether surprises me.'[162] The culprit responsible for the disaster, was not difficult to find. Despite the death of the Duke having been long anticipated, Hartington appears to have done almost nothing to prepare for a by-election until December 1891, when he wrote in desperation to Wolmer whether a candidate could be found: 'Is there anybody in Manchester or could the Birmingham people find us anybody?' Hartington hoped to persuade Sir Thomas Lea to move seats from South

Londonderry but the Irishman had too much sense to abandon a safe seat for
the unhealthy climes (for Liberal Unionists) of Lancashire.[163]

Electioneering and 1892

Jon Lawrence has recently explored how the coming of a mass electorate
led to a 'late Victorian explosion of outdoor speaking'[164] and Katherine Rix
has explored the importance of a new class of professional political opera-
tive in reaching out to the newly enfranchised rural labourer.[165] In 1888,
the Liberal Unionist Club took the decisive step to improve their canvassing and electioneering in the crucial rural seats by imitating one of the
Liberals' most effective forms of propaganda, the 'anti-coercion van.'[166] They
unveiled the Liberal Unionist van, part of 'a flying column consisting of a
van and one or two tricycles, to traverse some of the more remote parts of
the country.' The van contained posters of Irish brutalities and sometimes
had a limelight projector with slides.[167] There was clearly no problem in
meeting the 'necessarily heavy' expense since 'it will carry with it the dissolving view apparatus belonging to the club, ... and it will be attended
by one or more assistants on tricycles, who will visit all villages adjacent
to the line of march, distribute literature, and call attention to the van and
its movements.'[168] This first van cost the considerable sum of £400 a year
to run, but, such was the sense of crisis engendered by the continued by-
election defeats, that in May 1889 it was announced that a second van would
be started by the Club.[169] The leadership clearly took some persuading, as
in August Duke was still pressing for a second or even a third van, since
Wolmer was convinced that it was absolutely necessary to reach the rural
communities.[170] The second van, specifically designed to cover the north
of England, was run by James Dingle from March 1890, although local
activists still felt more were needed.[171] By November 1890, a third van was
operating,[172] and, after a financial appeal by the Liberal Union Club, two
more were launched in Spring 1892, in two of the most vulnerable areas of
Liberal Unionism, the east of Scotland and East Anglia.[173] On occasions, the
vans clearly did much good, as the following, unique report of the visit of a
van to Wellow parish in Somerset reveals:

> The Union Jack Van, belonging to the Liberal Union Club, visited
> Wellow and created a sensation ... The van was illuminated, in a novel
> way, by some ten or twelve youngsters sitting on the tailboard holding
> candles, the effect was decidedly good and the inhabitants turned out
> en masse to witness the procession ... At Mr Willis's wagon-house the

lecturer, Mr Foster Boggis, spoke at some length on the Irish question, giving some very cogent reasons why Home Rule should not be granted to Ireland … After the address some magnificent lantern views were exhibited with the brilliant lime light. The views were

Image 28: A typical lime-light slide shown in the Union Jack vans. This image shows a Fenian mob attacking the cottage of an injured policeman, while the victim's wife and children cower inside. 'Land League Cruelty' in G. Lucy (ed.), *The Ulster Covenant: A Pictorial History of the 1912 Home Rule Crisis* Belfast: The Ulster Society, 1989, p.4.

unusually fine and were much appreciated by the audience ... The meeting altogether was a good one ... and ended with the singing of the National Anthem, it will long be remembered by the people.[174]

However, five vans covering the country could only do so much in rural Britain and in East Perthshire the secretary of the combined Unionist Associations organised a 'Unionist Cycling Corps' to spread the message, 'firstly to the smithies and secondly to the bothies of the constituency.'[175]

Despite this innovation, the Liberal Unionists, as the by-election results suggested, were in a particularly vulnerable position, which the 'Newcastle Programme' sought to worsen. Somehow, despite their personal commitment to many of the issues contained in the Programme, the Liberal Unionists had to oppose it as a whole and yet offer alternative constructive policies in order to retain their claims to be Liberal. Robert Bird, WSLUA agent, warned that a purely Conservative domestic programme would not satisfy the voters and called for a return to the 'unauthorised' programme of 1885.[176] Even the normally moderate WLUA recognised the centrality of social questions in the forthcoming election.[177] Chamberlain did his best in the time he had, considering the constraints that both Conservative and moderate Liberal allies placed upon him. He re-stated his personal commitment to old age pensions and industrial accident insurance, industrial arbitration courts, shorter working hours and aid for home improvements and house purchase, but he was forced to tone down his proposals. At the Liberal Unionist Club on 8 March, he talked of 'a simple moderate programme',[178] and at the annual meeting of the Grand Council of the Birmingham Liberal Unionist Association on 29 April, he used that classic phrase of inaction, 'we are not going to build Rome in a day' when referring to old age pensions.[179] He did support the second reading of the doomed Miners' Eight Hours Bill at Westminster, on a matter of principle chiefly, but also to counter the appeal of the 'new' unionism that had been behind much of the industrial unrest since the successful London dock strike of 1889. As he noted in his political memoir, 'legislation was a more convenient way of securing the result than strikes.'[180] Yet he risked provoking the ire of Conservative industrialists like George Wyndham and moderate financiers such as the Chancellor of the Exchequer, George Goschen, who feared the increase in costs that such a bill would bring in a period of intense foreign competition.[181] Chamberlain's influence, along with Salisbury's concerns over the voting intentions of agricultural labourers, also lay behind the Small Holdings Bill finally introduced in 1892, but this was not enthusiastically supported by the Conservatives. Chamberlain approached the 1892 election without a clearly defined political role and tied to an exhausted Conservative ministry on the one hand and passive and unambitious moderate allies on the other.

Unsurprisingly, in these circumstances, the leadership chose to warn of an imminent rebellion in Ulster and encouraged the holding of anti-Home Rule demonstrations in and around Belfast. This culminated in the Ulster Convention of 17 June, held in a specially erected building. This was reported by the *Tory* as having included 12,330 Ulstermen from all classes, amongst whom there were 730 clergymen, 443 magistrates and 915 professionals.[182] As J. Bardon comments, this was a carefully choreographed demonstration of respectable resistance, 'Unionist leaders were determined to erase the memory of the vicious rioting that had so besmirched the opposition to Home Rule in 1886.'[183] Chamberlain was quite prepared to clutch at this straw, noting in his diary that the general election should be postponed as long as possible as 'the Ulster Convention would have great influence and its effect would increase during the next few months.'[184] Chamberlain also attempted, once again, to use his personal identification with nonconformist politics to influence traditional Liberal voters. On 30 March, at a meeting of the Nonconformist Unionist Association, Chamberlain resorted to outspoken sectarian language, referring to 'the extraordinary and baneful influence on political movements by the Catholic priests of Ireland',[185] which he again employed at the Birmingham Liberal Unionist Association meeting of 29 April:

> Our fellow subjects in Ulster, the strongest race in Ireland, the most determined, the men who have made whatever prosperity that exists in Ireland, would never submit to the dominion of a parliament, a great majority of whose members were to be elected at the dictation of the Roman Catholic priests.[186]

Having made his name as the founder of the political caucus in Birmingham, Chamberlain was also alarmed by the lack of effective structures among the Liberal Unionist Party at a provincial level outside the West Midlands. In Leicester, the most influential Liberal Unionist, Thomas Wright, not only refused to stand as a Liberal Unionist candidate, but shortly afterwards rejoined the Gladstonian Party. The incumbent Liberal MP was returned and the Liberal Unionist Association was wound up in the city.[187] Even in Stratford-upon-Avon, just outside Chamberlain's sphere of influence, it was April 1892 before local Conservatives were able to report that 'considerable progress has been made in the formation of a Liberal Unionist Association.'[188] As Chamberlain baldly warned the Party, 'What is necessary in order that our side might win at the election? Of course, organisation.'[189] He went on

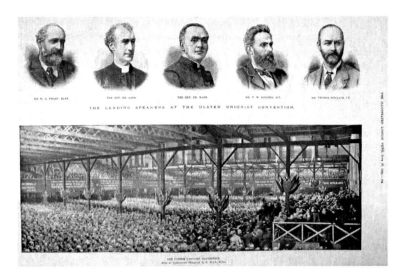

Image 29: The *Illustrated London News* emphasises the range of denominations, the scale of support and the orderly behaviour at the Ulster Unionist Convention, 17 June 1892. *Illustrated London News*, 23 June 1892.

to draw the lesson from the failure of the 'Moderates' (the Unionists) in the London County Council elections of the previous week, who were beaten 'in the first place because their organisation was less effective than that of their opponents, and above all, because they had no policy, except a policy of negation.'[190]

Given these problems, it is not surprising that Chamberlain wanted to wait as long as possible before fighting an election, to give time for his new programme to be fully publicised and for the revitalised Liberal Unionist Association to start making progress. In a symbolic reminder of the continued divisions between the radical and moderate Liberal Unionists on even procedural matters, he found himself in a minority of one when the date for the dissolution was decided at Devonshire House on 25 May 1892. Chamberlain tried to argue for an election in the autumn, believing, as he had written to the Metropolitan Liberal Unionist Federation only two days previously, 'it appears to me that the "flowing tide" is with us.'[191] But both Captain Middleton, the Conservative chief agent, and Lord Wolmer, the Liberal Unionist chief whip, believed that the Unionists might benefit from the bitter splits among the Liberals and Irish Nationalists over the post-Parnell strategy for Ireland and suggested an immediate election. Balfour and Devonshire agreed and Salisbury called the election next day.[192]

In 1892, Chamberlain faced Liberal opposition in every one of his Party's Birmingham seats except Edgbaston. In the circumstances, he made his priority the defence of these seats and those of the three county 'duchy' he had been allocated in 1889,[193] perhaps with the cynical reasoning that they were held by loyal 'radical' Unionists, unlike most of the rest of the Party's seats which were held by moderates, who had distrusted his intentions since 1880. He opened his campaign a month before the polls in Smethwick and spoke in every constituency in the city and in most of the surrounding counties of Warwickshire, Staffordshire and Worcestershire, only venturing out of his electoral 'duchy' to Manchester after Birmingham had voted. In his immediate objective, he succeeded spectacularly. The six Birmingham seats and four surrounding seats (Aston, Handsworth, Lichfield and East Worcestershire) returned Liberal Unionists with increased majorities. Chamberlain's support for the Miners' Eight Hours Bill not only helped Hamar Bass to be re-elected with a considerable majority in West Staffordshire,[194] but it also allowed him to take credit for extending the Liberal Unionist Party's influence further into the Nottinghamshire coalfields, where Charles Seely, a Liberal Unionist mineowner, defeated Henry Broadhurst, an opponent of the Bill, in Nottingham West, when the miners' local agent called on his branch members to vote against their MP.[195] Chamberlain's comments to Wolmer at the time reveal him to be entirely concerned with the results in the Midlands.[196]

It is clear from the details of the 'special fund' raised by Wolmer to fight the election, that one factor in the outstanding results in the West Midlands was the support of the press in the area. John Jaffray, the owner of the *Birmingham Daily Post* and the *Birmingham Mail* was felt to deserve a reward from the honours systems, as Powell Williams revealed in a letter to Chamberlain:

> Here then are the brilliant results in the Midlands and the claims of a man who, through the press which he owns – and especially through the *Mail* – has contributed not a little towards them. I think that even the reward which he seeks wd. be universally deemed appropriate, for in the range of no other Unionist paper can similar results be found.[197]

Wolmer himself had reason to feel satisfied, regaining Edinburgh West for his Party. But these successes went against the national swing of the electorate. For the Liberal Unionists as a separate political force, the election was a major setback. Chamberlain had anticipated problems when he wrote to Provost Watson on 24 February, warning that 'we shall lose some seats in the agricultural districts of England', but he expressed the hope that in Scotland and Ireland, where Home Rule remained a major issue of concern, 'we hope to make amends.'[198] This rather hopelessly optimistic attitude was shared by James and Devonshire.[199] Wolmer's prediction for the 1892 election, still preserved in its original notebook in the Bodleian Library, was far more pessimistic but ultimately accurate in its overall figures. He predicted the loss of ten Liberal Unionist seats, which he noted was 'the <u>worst</u> which can befall us on our present available data – we shall probably do appreciably better.'[200] In fact, apart from the West Midlands, the Liberal Unionists lost seats from all areas. In Scotland, Roxburghshire, South Ayrshire, Falkirk Burghs, Inverness Burghs, Invernesshire and even St Rollox in the Unionist stronghold of Glasgow were all lost. The one remaining Liberal Unionist seat in Glasgow, Tradeston, and the one captured by Alexander Cross, Camlachie, were only secured with majorities of less than 200 each. In complete contrast to its leaders' predictions, the Party was very lucky to lose only six seats, as no single Liberal Unionist managed to win with a majority of over 1,000 votes. As the East and North of Scotland Liberal Unionist Association had received £4,000 thanks to Devonshire's fund-raising, one can only wonder at the possible scale of the Liberal Unionist losses in Scotland had this money not been provided for the publication and distribution of electoral material.[201] Charles Cooper revealed that there had been much complacency among the Scottish Liberal Unionists and despite his position as editor of the *Scotsman,* 'I did not expect we should be beaten by so many.'[202] The Conservatives had not provided a major source of support as, before the election Salisbury had written to Balfour, 'we have so little to lose (or gain) in Scotland at present,' that he did not regard the prospect of electoral defeat in 'that country … as important.'[203]

In Wales, Chamberlain had taken his new wife to Camarthenshire during an ill-fated expedition marked by low turn-outs, gales and local derision. The Liberal *South Wales Daily News* had cut through his rhetoric and exposed Chamberlain's weakest point when it contrasted the content of his speech with the denominational make-up of his political allies:

> Mr Chamberlain, as strongly convinced as ever of the need for disestablishment and of the justice of Welshmen's demand to be set free from the insulting dominance of an alien sect, is at Llanbyther hobnobbing with pillars of the Church and using the desire for Disestablishment as an instrument for breaking in pieces the Radical Party.[204]

In 1892, five out of seven Welsh Liberal Unionist candidates were heavily defeated with the added humiliation of seeing the Liberal Unionist candidate in East Carmarthenshire, Captain Davies, rejected by over 3,000 votes.[205] The problem, so Chamberlain thought, was Salisbury's refusal to countenance any prospect of disendowment for the churches in Scotland or Wales. 'We will do nothing in Wales without disestablishment,' he wrote to Balfour after the election, adding that supporters of the established church in Scotland, such as Argyll, had failed to make any impression on the election outcome there.[206] Matthew Cragoe concludes that Liberal Unionism, like Conservatism before it, failed in Wales where 'the primary commitment of Liberals remained the support of William Gladstone.'[207]

In the south and west, North Bristol, Portsmouth, Tavistock, Biggleswade, Cricklade and Barnstaple were lost. Most revealing of the persistence of personal influence and political patronage in the region, was the comment on Tavistock:

> Much interest attaches as to the attitude which the Duke of Bedford, may adopt; for in the town and vicinity of Tavistock, the Russell influence is still powerful ... If, before the election, the Duke of Bedford, openly espouses the cause of the Unionists, the result will be a foregone conclusion.[208]

Judging from the result, a personally popular candidate, a strong religious identity, effective, centralised organisation and cross-party co-operation made a difference in some seats, but could not compensate when a powerful landowner chose not to favour the Party. Tavistock was lost in a 10% swing against the Liberal Unionist candidate.[209] In other cases elsewhere in the country, the importance of aristocratic support was declining in comparison with modern political organising. When Robert Purvis, an able and capable candidate contested Peterborough at the 1889 by-election, he had on his side, 'the support of the Fitzwilliam influence' yet was still defeated by over 250 votes.[210] The defeat may have been due to the fact that a Liberal Unionist Association was not founded until May 1890.[211] The belief in the influence of the 'leading and influential men' persisted, however, among important Party men such as Harry Anstruther, who claimed that 'a Fitzwilliam for Peterborough, a Doulton for Kennington, a Pearce for Lanark, a Verdin for Northwich, etc and possibly all these seats might have been saved.'[212]

In East Anglia, Mid-Norfolk fell. The attempt to win seats in the north of England completely failed, as working-class loyalty to Gladstone held fast, although the Party only missed taking Liverpool Exchange and Darlington and failed to hold Skipton and Hartlepool by less than a hundred votes in each case. However, South East Durham, Doncaster, Great Grimsby, Chesterfield and Colne Valley were lost more emphatically. Perhaps most disappointing for Chamberlain personally was the heavy defeat of Richard Chamberlain in Islington, which was accompanied by a major Liberal revival in London. Of

course, there were now four Liberal Unionists in Ireland, but some such as
H. O. Arnold-Foster in West Belfast, owed their survival to appeals to the
sectarian politics of Ireland, rather than to the more unequivocally Liberal
approach of T. W. Russell. Devonshire was reduced to pleading to Salisbury
for a baronetcy for South Londonderry's MP, Thomas Lea, in an attempt to
maintain the influence of the Party in the country.[213]

Effectively, the Party was reduced to two main pockets: in central Scotland
(mainly in and around Glasgow); and Chamberlain's fiefdom in the West
Midlands. The other seats were mostly isolated in Liberal areas and often
held due to the personal influence and patronage of prominent Whig landlords. The attempts to increase the Party's spheres of influence had failed,
having fought to win seventy-four new seats across the country and having
lost in seventy of these. The Party also had to bear the financial costs of fighting 139 elections on its own, yet having lost nearly a third of its MPs. Edward
Heneage was one of the principal casualties as his Grimby seat, exposed amid
the sea of Liberal Lincolnshire, was lost. In a consoling letter, Chamberlain
revealed the level of his concern for the Party:

> I was extremely disappointed to see the return from Grimsby ... Besides
> my personal feeling in the matter, it is undoubtedly serious that the Liberal
> Unionist Party should suffer such heavy reverses. Up to the present time
> we have not gained in a single contest except that in Nottingham where
> there was a division owing to the Eight Hours Bill.[214]

Among the Liberal Unionist Party managers, there was an attempt to write
off the 1892 slump as inevitable, given the peculiar, cross-party battles of
1886. In his report to the Liberal Unionist Association at the end of the year,
Boraston, the recently-appointed Association secretary, claimed that defeats
were due to 'Liberal voters, tired of a Conservative government, [who] ultimately returned to their allegiance to Mr Gladstone as a matter of blind
faith rather than of reason.' The defeat was due, he claimed, to 'wholesale
falsehoods and misrepresentations which were disseminated', rather than
any failings on the part of the Party organisation.[215] This view was not
shared by many other leading Liberal Unionist MPs. In his post-mortem,
James lamented the weakness of the Party's organisation: 'Outside the House,
there is a very wide field for improvement. We have been sadly out-generalled
in the last five years and it must not occur again.'[216] In his 'political memoir',
completed in 1892, Chamberlain agreed with James' analysis, writing that
'they were without efficient organisation.'[217] Others close to the Party agreed.
A member of the Liberal Union Club, Ebenezer Le Riche, wrote a letter which

was printed in the final edition of the *Liberal Unionist*, in which he asserted that 'our defeat has been rather due to our own mistakes than to the conduct of our opponents.' In particular, given the string of by-election defeats and the confident predictions that the Liberal Unionists would be 'wiped out' as William Harcourt claimed, Le Riche believed that many Liberal Unionists had lost heart and so 'they did not work as they should have done.' Tellingly, despite the apparent success of the LUA claimed by Boraston, Le Riche asserted that 'deficiency in organisation' had proved costly. In Le Riche's final comments that it would be 'desirable' to dismiss candidates and agents who had failed, there was a suggestion that the Party's new leadership wished to sweep away the kinship and friendship influences that had dominated the Party's local organisation: 'These are not times to be guided by personal likings or private interests; failure is frequently a sign of unsuitability.' [218]

It is clear that the Liberal Unionists lacked an effective electoral organisation at grass-roots level (at least outside the West Midlands, the west of Scotland and Cornwall), prior to Chamberlain's accession to the Party leadership. The Party had been, for the previous six years, largely an aristocratic club, which had taken a 'compact' agreed at the level of the Party leadership to apply to the rank and file of the Conservative Party. By 1892, however, the relationship was beginning to be strained by such assumptions and Primrose League dames, local party agents and Association members failed to bestir themselves quite so actively on behalf of their Liberal and radical allies as they had done in 1886.[219] With little effective organisation of their own to fall back on and facing a Liberal Party re-invigorated by the 'Newcastle Programme', the Liberal Unionists were forced to appeal to nationalist zeal, with reminders of the threat posed by Home Rule to the Empire, to traditional Protestant fears of 'popery', with the campaign to mobilise the nonconformist vote, and to prejudice against the Irish, with the revival of the cause of Ulster.[220]

That this campaign was of only limited effectiveness may be due to the reluctance of many Liberals to lower themselves to engage in such populist rabble-rousing, but is more likely due to the failure of any such negative policy as this to succeed, when it lacked an effective political structure to hammer it home. Chamberlain himself had realised this when he had confronted the Liberal Unionist Club with his harsh diagnosis of the Party's position in March:

> In municipal as well as in national politics, a policy of negation is no good in a democratic representative system ... I believe they [the voters] would rather vote for half a loaf from those who are in a position to give it to them than for a whole loaf from those who are not in a position to give it to them.[221]

Once the dust had settled, the Party's leaders went into conclave, with a meeting on 'the prospects of the Party' closed to all press, even their own Party paper. The membership of the meeting was a fair indication of the growing influence of the more radical wing, as of the twelve MPs, four were from West Midlands seats,[222] and three others could be described as radicals.[223] Despite Asquith's claim that the reduction in Liberal Unionist seats sealed the fate of 'a small and dwindling band of deserters from the Liberal camp ... which was born the day before yesterday' and that they would as a consequence 'be forgotten the day after tomorrow', the Party was determined to move forward.[224]

Reinvigoration 1892–1895

With Chamberlain as the new leader, who was far more comfortable with the new methods of electioneering, the Liberal Unionists became much more adept at using modern media after 1892. This included the lure of celebrity, as when H. M. Stanley agreed to stand as a Liberal Unionist candidate.[225] At first they appeared becalmed; only managing to win one of the by-elections held between the general election and the elections consequent on the appointment of Rosebery's Cabinet in March 1894,[226] but as the 1895 election approached, if one ignores the crisis of the alliance which was emerging in Warwick and Leamington and at Hythe, the electoral prospects looked highly positive. The failure of the Liberal government to achieve any significant reforms and its consequent attacks on the Lords, the on-going bitter divisions within the Nationalist Party and, most importantly perhaps, the retirement of Gladstone himself, had left the Liberals looking weak and rudderless. In April 1895, the Liberal Unionist Party managed its first electoral gain in East Anglia since 1886. Despite his own difficulties at the time, Chamberlain saw the victory of R.T. Gurdon in Mid-Norfolk as a herald of greater success: 'If we could only get the Tories in the constituencies to a take a long view of this situation, there must be a sweeping victory at the next election.'[227] Even with the enmity of the local Conservative leadership, Alfred Lyttelton managed a comfortable victory in Warwick and Leamington and Lewis McIver finally managed to win a seat as a Unionist, when he won West Edinburgh with the healthy majority of 508 in May 1895. In Scotland, the *Glasgow Herald* reported the local Association as ready for the coming campaign as early as autumn 1893:

> The war chest replenished, active canvassing is being carried out, and due attention has been paid to registration, with excellent results. We look forward with confidence to the results of these labours, which will appear at the coming general election.[228]

Image 30: A highly attractive four-colour poster, issued by the Liberal
Unionist Association in 1893. Clifford Papers 3(2),
Ugbrooke House, Devon.

The central Association had already signalled a greater willingness to engage
with a less top-down model of political engagement. Boraston had distributed
copies of a 'draft petition to parliament against the passing of the Home Rule
Bill' in 1893 for LUAs to copy and collect signatures.[229] Some LUAs such as Mid-

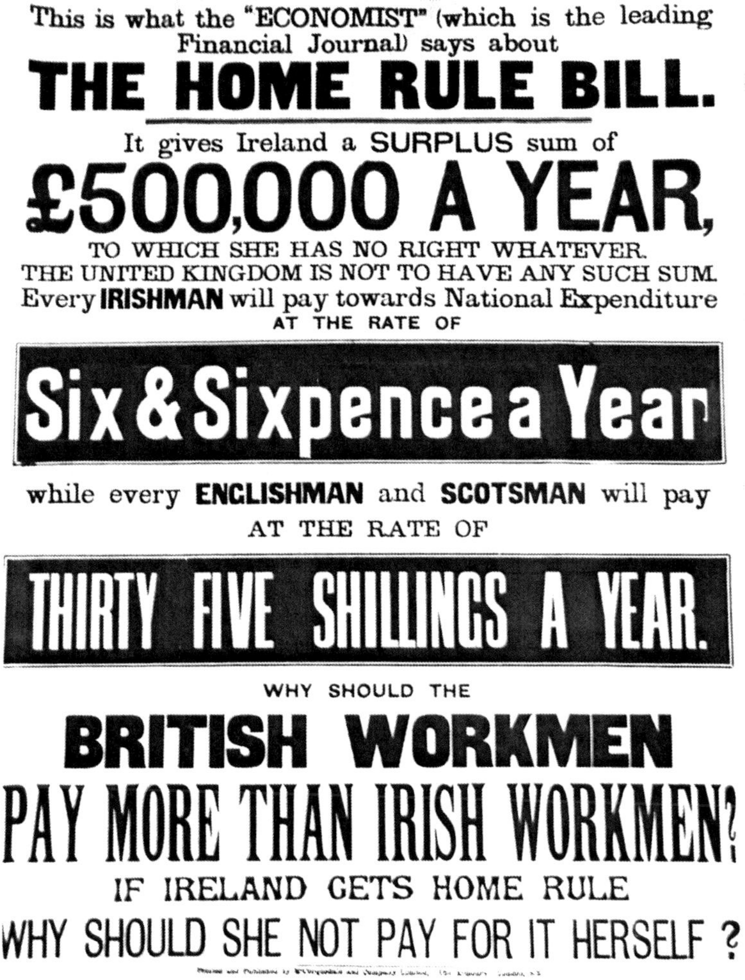

This is what the "ECONOMIST" (which is the leading Financial Journal) says about

THE HOME RULE BILL.

It gives Ireland a SURPLUS sum of

£500,000 A YEAR,

TO WHICH SHE HAS NO RIGHT WHATEVER.
THE UNITED KINGDOM IS NOT TO HAVE ANY SUCH SUM.
Every **IRISHMAN** will pay towards National Expenditure
AT THE RATE OF

Six & Sixpence a Year

while every **ENGLISHMAN** and **SCOTSMAN** will pay
AT THE RATE OF

THIRTY FIVE SHILLINGS A YEAR.

WHY SHOULD THE

BRITISH WORKMEN
PAY MORE THAN IRISH WORKMEN?

IF IRELAND GETS HOME RULE

WHY SHOULD SHE NOT PAY FOR IT HERSELF ?

Image 31: Two colour poster issued by the Liberal Unionist
Association in 1893. Clifford 3 (2).

Devon sent pre-printed circulars calling on local Liberal Unionists to fill in their names and return, 'no subscription whatever is necessary.' [230] But the crucial new initiatives were in the use of visual propaganda and populist slogans. As James Thompson has noted, 'discussion of late Victorian political culture hitherto has paid little attention to its visual dynamics' and these were a vital element of the revived electioneering approach under Boraston. [231] Lengthy, excessively pedantic

BRITONS
DON'T BE CHEATED.

➥ **THIS BAG SHOWS WHAT**
IRELAND OUGHT TO PAY
**EVERY YEAR TOWARDS NATIONAL
EXPENSES ACCORDING TO HER
POPULATION.**

Seven Million Seven Hundred Thousand Pounds.

✎ **THIS BAG SHOWS WHAT**
IRELAND OUGHT TO PAY
**EVERY YEAR TOWARDS NATIONAL EXPENSES ACCORDING
TO HER WEALTH, AS SHOWN BY THE DEATH
DUTIES, WHICH MR. GLADSTONE SAID IN 1886 WERE
THE BEST POSSIBLE TEST.**

Three Million Seven Hundred Thousand Pounds.

THIS BAG SHOWS WHAT
IRELAND WOULD PAY
EVERY YEAR TOWARDS NATIONAL EXPENSES UNDER THE
HOME RULE BILL.

One Million Five Hundred and Fifty Thousand Pounds.

THE DIFFERENCE MUST COME OUT OF THE POCKETS OF THE BRITISH PEOPLE.

BRITISH ELECTORS
REFUSE YOUR CONSENT TO SUCH AN UNFAIR BARGAIN.

PRINTED AND PUBLISHED BY M'CORQUODALE & CO. LIMITED, "THE ARMOURY." LONDON, S.E.

Image 32: Two colour poster issued by the Liberal Unionist
Association in 1893. Clifford 3 (2).

and intellectually taxing print propaganda such as *The Speaker's Hand-book on the
Irish Question* and *Think It Out*, a forty-page lecture, was abandoned.[232] Even
A. V. Dicey replaced his legalistic *England's Case Against Home Rule* with the
more readable *A Leap in the Dark*.[233] Money was no longer being wasted on a
weekly newspaper, but was instead focused on the new colour printing technologies, producing attractive campaign material. Perhaps the most innovative piece
of election literature was a small card entitled 'the Union Jack' which unfolded
to reveal flags of St George, St David and St Patrick which could be taken

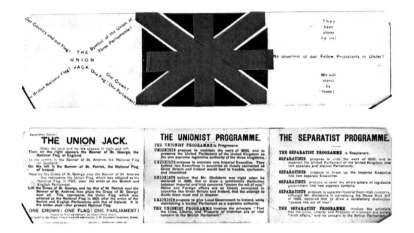

Image 33: Front and reverse of election material distributed in the 1895 election. The item is approximately 31cm long when opened, but folds to a pocket-sized 10cm. Clifford 3 (2).

out and then reassembled to form the Union flag, 'our present National Flag', with the exhortation, 'No desertion of our Fellow Protestants in Ulster.' On the reverse were printed 'the Separatist Programme' (with a red title) which was claimed to be 'Reactionary' and 'the Unionist programme' which was stated as being 'Progressive' (though no mention of social reform was included).[234] One can imagine the tactile nature of such material appealing to children of all classes and it was a highly effective means of spreading the Unionist message beyond the politically engaged. Posters, in particular, were given great emphasis by the Association, as can be seen in the report of the Somerset Liberal Unionist Association of 1894, which reported that an agent, Mr J. M. Trotter, was engaged to ensure the posting of bills in 'protected country stations' so that it could be guaranteed that 'something has been done to bring every phase of the Home Rule question home to the voter.' The four colour poster 'Mr Gladstone's patent process' of 1893 and the two sheet 'Britons Don't Be Cheated' for the 1895 campaign were perhaps the best examples of the increasingly sophisticated visual resources employed by the Party.[235] Over 25,000 leaflets were distributed in one year in Bath alone. These were carefully composed to appeal to working-class voters and included examples of efficient rebuttal of Liberal accusations, highlighting of the Unionist programme and attacks on 'unpatriotic' behaviour of the Rosebery government towards the Navy (presaging the naval campaigns waged by Unionist groups after 1906).[236]

In his notes for the 1895 election, Chamberlain clearly saw that the work-ing class electorate must be appealed to:

Policy	Constitutional	Nil	
	Army & Navy	Army Reform	Navy Extension
	Colonies	Develop	
	Foreign	Por – Russia, Egypt – Siam	
	Social	Old Age Pension	
		H. Purchase	
		Art. Dwellings	Courts, Arbitration
		E. Liability	
		8 Hours	
		Ship.	Labourer's Disputes
		Alien Immigration	Temperance Reform
		Railway Rates	
		Light Railways.[237]	

He wrote to Henry James: 'I find a general disposition to accept warmly my general policy of putting forward Social Reform as an alternative to Constitutional changes.'[238] The programme was clearly laid out in 'Mr Chamberlain's Labour Programme', perhaps the most widely distributed Liberal Unionist leaflet of 1895, which included:

1. Limitation by Law of the Hours of Labour
   a) Miners
   b) Railways servants
   c) Shop assistants
2. Arbitration
3. Labour bureaus of exchange
4. Compensation for industrial injuries
5. Old age pensions 'guaranteed by the state'
6. The regulation of alien immigration
7. Better housing of the working classes
8. Purchase of housing for working classes

The leaflet reminded the reader that Chamberlain was 'the chief advocate of Free Education' and assured that 'the Unionist Party is prepared to deal at once with the Social Questions and the interests of Englishmen'. The leaflet very cleverly concluded by quoting Keir Hardie from 1892: 'The sufferings of the people of this country are a thousand million times greater than those of the Irish.'[239] The message was reinforced with a striking double sheet, two colour poster, 'Mr Chamberlain's Programme', which the Liberal press satirised with some prescience.[240]

Certainly, there is abundant evidence of Liberal Unionists, and some Conservatives, using this platform to appeal to the working class electorate. As well as in the West Midlands, the Scottish Unionists endorsed many of the proposals publicly, despite the lack of a clear party policy, most notably in Falkirk, where the Conservative candidate for the county and the Liberal

Image 34: The *Westminster Gazette* pours scorn on Chamberlain's social programme. *Westminster Gazette*, 9 July 1895.

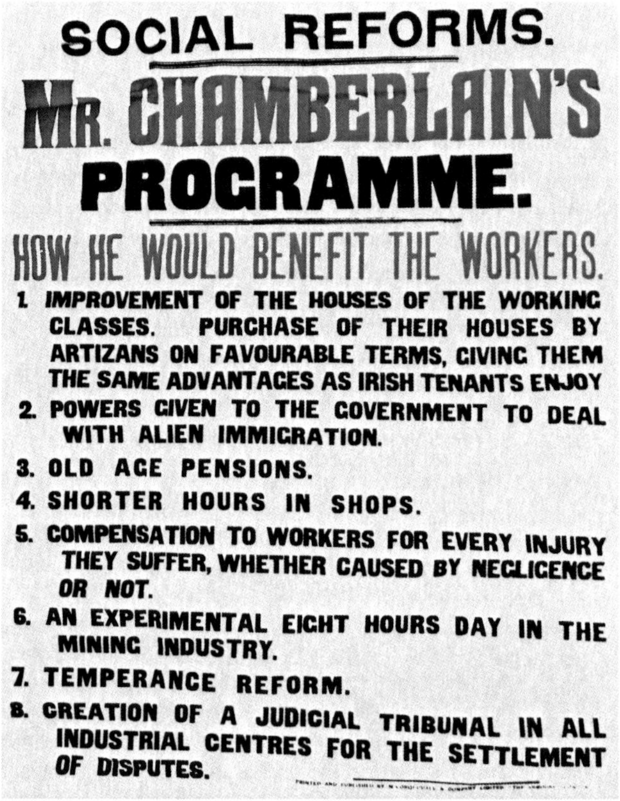

SOCIAL REFORMS.
Mr. CHAMBERLAIN'S PROGRAMME.
HOW HE WOULD BENEFIT THE WORKERS.

1. IMPROVEMENT OF THE HOUSES OF THE WORKING CLASSES. PURCHASE OF THEIR HOUSES BY ARTIZANS ON FAVOURABLE TERMS, GIVING THEM THE SAME ADVANTAGES AS IRISH TENANTS ENJOY
2. POWERS GIVEN TO THE GOVERNMENT TO DEAL WITH ALIEN IMMIGRATION.
3. OLD AGE PENSIONS.
4. SHORTER HOURS IN SHOPS.
5. COMPENSATION TO WORKERS FOR EVERY INJURY THEY SUFFER, WHETHER CAUSED BY NEGLIGENCE OR NOT.
6. AN EXPERIMENTAL EIGHT HOURS DAY IN THE MINING INDUSTRY.
7. TEMPERANCE REFORM.
8. CREATION OF A JUDICIAL TRIBUNAL IN ALL INDUSTRIAL CENTRES FOR THE SETTLEMENT OF DISPUTES.

Image 35: Chamberlain's 'social programme' is explicitly laid out in this widely distributed poster from the 1895 election campaign. Clifford 3 (2).

Unionist candidate for the Burghs supported the social reform programme on a joint platform.[241] There is also evidence of similar cross-party support for 'constructive Unionism' in the north of England, most notably in Bradford and Liverpool.[242] The *Rural World* continued to champion the Unionist cause among working-class voters in rural constituencies, with an editorial on 6 July which announced 'joy among farmers and others associated with land at the change of Ministry.'[243] It is therefore incorrect of David Steele to claim that 'the 71 Liberal Unionists in the Commons [elected in 1895] were there, most of them, thanks to Tory organization and Tory votes.'[244]

When the Liberal Party was finally defeated over a minor item in the army estimates in 1895, this was a perfect opportunity to contrast the 'little Englander' attitudes of the Liberals with the imperialist sentiments of the Unionists. Although the tensions of the Unionist alliance had forced Chamberlain to muzzle his support for social reform, the public were presented with the image of a strong united Unionist leadership, which contrasted effectively with the Liberal dissensions.[245] Chamberlain carefully altered his rhetoric to avoid all accusation of 'ransom', preferring instead to pour scorn on Rosebery's Liberals for attempting 'to show that the interests of landlords, farmers and agricultural labourers were divided. That was an absurdity.'[246] Although left-leaning historians have tended to swallow J. Cornford's analysis of the Unionist victory as based on Conservative organisational strength,[247] Paul Readman has shown that there was a vitality of local issues which Unionist candidates were especially adept at exploiting. That they could contrast their concern for the 'bread and butter' economic issues of working-class daily life (on both a constituency and national level) with the 'faddist' Liberal concerns with temperance, Welsh disestablishment and Irish Home Rule, was due to their growing expertise in political presentation.[248] In particular, of course, they could highlight their own support for the freedom of the working man to enjoy his leisure time in a public house or at a race-course, in contrast to the puritan interference of the Liberals, who had attempted to pass a Local Veto bill in the previous parliament. As John Davis has shown, the newly enfranchised were still receptive to 'apparently undemocratic causes' such as the nuanced voluntaryism of the Liberal Unionist social reform programme and the defence of the Union.[249] In 1895, as in 1886, it was the *Liberal* Unionist agenda that convinced the mass electorate, not propertied defensiveness nor an Anglican revival (as in 1874). The shadow of the 'khaki' election of 1900 has too often been allowed to extend to 1895, yet this was an election fought largely on a choice of *Liberal* programmes, between the official Liberal Party and those who claimed to be the true heirs of mid-Victorian Liberalism. Even an apparently 'imperial' figure, such as H. M. Stanley, owed his success in North Lambeth to his support for Chamberlain's social programme and his identification with the experience of the working class man.[250] For this reason, the Party made an effort to run former MPs who had been defeated in 1892 in their old seats, with the implication that the electorate had made a mistake in unseating their Unionist representative thee years earlier and was now offered an opportunity to correct their error.[251]

Examples of imperialism 'tub-thumping' and xenophobia were distinctly lacking in the extensive propaganda for 1895 collected by Whiteway-Wilkinson, the secretary of the Mid-Devon LUA.[252] The only example of anti-Catholic rhetoric, the expensive poster, 'Ulster refuses Home Rule', was expressed on strictly liberal grounds, contrasting the cross-community convention at Belfast in 1893 with the (alleged) interference of the Catholic episcopacy in the South Meath election campaign and the poverty of contemporary Tipperary with the poverty of Belfast under Home Rule.[253] Boraston was tireless in sending letters to the secretaries of LUAs recommending how to combat Liberal tactics in their constituencies and advising on how to 'ensure the fullest possible representation of the Unionist Party' in the forthcoming registration with details of the latest legislation affecting organisers and agents.[254] As Readman has shown, despite Chamberlain's 'muzzling', in the 1895 campaign, 52% of all election addresses by Liberal Unionists *and* Conservatives mentioned old age pensions, with a further third mentioning workers' compensation and working-class house purchase.[255] In the different circumstances of Ireland, revitalised organisation and a carefully chosen campaign based on local government reform and land purchase led to the spectacular victory of the Catholic Unionist, William Kenny, in Dublin St. Stephen's Green, despite the invective heaped upon him by the *Freeman's Journal* and the *Irish Daily Independent*.[256]

Of course, the divisions that bedevilled the Liberals after Gladstone's resignation and their shortage of funds also told, as Liberals struggled to run candidates in many seats, and seventeen Liberal Unionists were returned unopposed, as the Party continued to benefit from Wolmer's energetic fund-raising.[257] Unlike in 1892, canvassing had sufficiently improved for the Liberal Unionists not to waste as much time, money and effort on hopeless seats and only thirty contests were

Image 36: 3 colour election poster issued by the Liberal Unionist Association in
1895. Clifford 3 (2).

Image 37: 2 colour election poster issued by the Liberal Unionist Association in 1895. Clifford 3 (2).

Image 38: This poster, produced by the Liberal Unionist Association at the height of the 1893 Home Rule debate, provides a good visual summary of the Liberal Unionists' fears of the consequences of Nationalist rule in Ireland: Catholic interference in politics and economic collapse. Clifford 3 (2).

BRITONS, ARE YOU WILLING TO BE GOVERNED BY THE IRISH?

80 IRISH MEMBERS AT WESTMINSTER BUT *NO* BRITISH MEMBERS AT DUBLIN.

John Bull: *Don't you think you ought to be satisfied with a seat all to yourself, and not to occupy my chair also?*
Pat: *Shure you can sit down there, and I'll make a bit of room for you; but you mustn't be after expecting a chair to yourself.*

Under **HOME RULE** Ireland would have a Parliament to itself, but England would not.

VOTE FOR ONE PARLIAMENT FOR THE WHOLE KINGDOM. VOTE FOR THE UNIONIST CANDIDATE!

PRINTED AND PUBLISHED BY M°CORQUODALE AND COMPANY LIMITED. THE ARMOURY. LONDON S.E.

Image 39: An example of an entirely negative campaign poster produced by the
Liberal Unionist Association in 1895. Clifford 3 (2).

lost. That said, the Party still suffered some unexpected defeats, demonstrating
their dependence on both Conservative and Liberal support outside their stronghold areas. Heneage was defeated yet again at Grimsby, Dumfriesshire was lost

Image 40: A campaign poster from 1895 that could be easily printed with the Unionist candidate's name. Clifford 3 (2).

Image 41: Such was the popularity of Unionism in the 1890s that products were marketed using the imagery of the alliance, adapted from political posters.

by a whisker in Scotland and Gurdon's April triumph in Mid-Norfolk was short-lived. Despite these setbacks, the Party had managed to win seventy-one seats, exceeding the number of MPs that had sat at the end of the 1892 parliament, and could justifiably boast that it enjoyed genuine cross-class and cross-party support. It is completely untenable, in light of the electoral evidence of 1895, for the two most recent commentators to claim either that the Party was 'electorally squeezed out of the political arena,'[258] or that 'their numbers always eroded.'[259]

For those, such as James Vernon and Lawrence Goldman, who see a rapid decline in the traditional, locally-based political culture based on the 'character' of the candidate after 1883 and its replacement by a national, class-based politics, the existence of the Liberal Unionists and their survival as a separate political force for twenty-six years has proved a difficult issue to reconcile with their argument and has consequently been largely ignored.[260] With the recent work of James Thompson, Katherine Rix and Jon Lawrence, it is possible to see the thirty years before the First World War as a period of transition, in which localism, 'deference' and 'character' all retained their electoral resonance at the public meetings which still remained the crucible of political reputation, as I have shown was the case in Leamington in 1895 for George Peel.[261] There was, as Thompson has shown, a dramatic increase in the use of visual, musical and print propaganda, which the Liberal Unionists were at the forefront of exploiting, but in addition, they proved themselves successful pioneers of the use of women canvassers, quasi-independent organisations and travelling political propagandists.[262]

For the Liberal Unionists, local political identity was far more significant than either class or ideology and this allowed the Party to prosper as an independent faction at least until 1895. From the advent of Lord Wolmer as chief organiser in 1888, the Party had begun to accept, as Vernon suggests, that the instinctive popular support for a Liberal and Unionist position had to be 'disciplined' by the strictures of a modern political party.[263] In contrast to the views espoused by Biagini, Cornford and Stephens, one must explain the Liberal Unionist successes between 1886 and 1895 as the result of effective campaigning on a local level, which highlighted the discrete identity of the Party's MPs, married to good organisation. The Party's survival was thus assured into the twentieth century, but eventual fusion with the Conservatives could only be avoided with the active cultivation of the local Party's separate identity by the leadership, even as they entered a Unionist coalition cabinet. That this support was not forthcoming is clear from the Party records after 1895, which show little opposition to Middleton's appropriation of former Liberal Unionist constituencies, at least outside the area controlled by the WSLUA. According to a 1903 article in the *Nineteenth Century and After*, the Party was badly and, as I will argue in the next chapter, deliberately neglected for eight years.[264] The Party may have been 'officers without an army' at first, but by the mid-1890s, in certain areas, and for differing reasons, a genuine Liberal Unionist identity had emerged, which had a long term impact on the politics of certain regions, as well as on the Conservative Party nationally.

CHAPTER 6

'STRANGLED BY ITS OWN PARENT': THE STRANGE DEATH OF LIBERAL UNIONISM

Once one accepts that Liberal Unionism remained a distinct and independent partner in the Unionist alliance between 1886 and 1895, the question of the Party's role in an age of 'tub-thumping' jingoism after 1895 comes into sharp focus. Although there is limited research to support the assertion, it is possible to regard the 1897 Diamond Jubilee as an attempt to create a cultural event around which the Unionist alliance could coalesce and find a new trope of imperial discourse with which to engage an electorate, now that the spectre of Home Rule had receded.[1] The crucial issue, which has been long-debated, is how the Unionist alliance managed to successfully pose as the 'patriotic party' and the defender of the constitution between 1895 and 1902, but quickly lost that status (and its own internal coherence) until the disruption of modern British politics during the Great War.

This chapter aims to illustrate how the Party leadership of the Liberal Unionists either enthusiastically championed or morosely accepted an attempt to create a national Unionist identity after 1895 and how certain elements of the Party's activists actively resisted this attempt to recast their political orientation. If one accepts that political history has benefited from an understanding of the semi-autonomous nature of the various spheres of political activity, it is possible to interpret the Unionist alliance as a battle-ground between central and regional elites, each of whom believed that they possessed the strategic solution to appeal to a mass electorate in the years after 1895.

After the election of 1895 gave the Liberal Unionists numerical security and confirmed their position in Salisbury's third government, the organisation, previously controlled by the National Liberal Unionist Association in Birmingham, appears to have reverted back to the Liberal Unionist officers, principally Boraston.[2] The Party manager from 1892 to 1895 and Chamberlain's chief organiser in the NLUA, Powell Williams, became a junior minister at the War Office and there appears to have been no overall 'manager' of the Party for the next five years, suggesting that the Liberal Unionist leadership became swiftly disinterested in the organisation once they entered government. As *The Times* announced on 3 August 1895, Chamberlain now decided not to bother with a separate whip for the Liberal Unionists, allowing Anstruther to be nominated and accepted as a 'ministerial whip', together with T. H. Cochrane, with both of them subordinate to the Conservatives' new chief whip, Sir William Walrond.[3] In this way the Party's organisation was allowed to gradually subside, with only committed activists in areas such as Glasgow and London demonstrating any activity in the following months.

After the 1895 election, Henry James urged on Devonshire the necessity for making the position of the Party clearer to constituency workers now that the Liberal Unionists had entered into government with the Conservatives. There was, of course, a danger that having accepted subordinate office under a Conservative Prime Minister, the Party would finally lose any authentic Liberal identity in the eyes of the electorate and even its own activists. Devonshire received a letter during the campaign from such a worker who identified this on-going problem: 'The fear of being labelled "Tories" with any semblance of justification is already leading many Liberal Unionists to abstain from active work in the constituencies and even driving some of them to support Gladstonian candidates.'[4] In August 1895, Devonshire wrote to Chamberlain urging the maintenance of an organisation separate from the Tories where a flourishing Association already existed. On the other hand, he accepted that it would 'no longer be necessary' to maintain separate organisations in every constituency. Without a party organisation, the Duke argued, the Liberal Unionist ministers and MPs would become dependent on Conservative charity: 'This is the only way to keep our power.' As the Conservatives were in a majority, there was little chance of the Liberal Unionist Party growing through Tory defections, so the only way 'to make converts' was 'from the Gladstonians.'[5]

Surprisingly, given his strong defence of Liberal Unionist independence since 1886, Chamberlain was even less sure that the maintenance of a separate Liberal Unionist organisation was necessary. He wrote to James in August 1895, stating that he felt it 'best to let things take their course in the localities without attempting to give instruction from headquarters.' He was aware that this would lead to 'the weaker organisations' dying out but his priorities had now clearly changed. If the leadership continued to urge the Associations to bestir themselves, 'we shall give offence to our allies:'[6] James, confused by this dramatic volte-face on the part of his leader, wrote to Devonshire in puzzlement:

> From numerous representations I have received I am quite sure that it is absolutely necessary some authoritative statement should be made by you – or by you and Chamberlain as to the necessity of maintaining the Liberal Unionist organisations throughout the country. In the absence of some such 'lead' in many places the organisation will be broken up with the result that the Liberal Unionists will be divided – half joining the Conservatives and the remainder returning to the Radicals.
>
> Last night I had to address the Metropolitan LU Federation. Everyone was asking What of the future?' Fortunately no reporters were present so I refused to give my reply but told them I had no doubt that an authoritative statement would be made by our leadership at an early date.[7]

Wolmer (now Lord Selborne) was directed by Devonshire to meet with Powell Williams to decide what actions should be taken. He reported back to the Duke and to Chamberlain on 6 December that it was agreed that if 'an amalgamation of the Liberal Unionist and Conservative organisations is desired by local people ... [it] should not be discouraged', but that 'in most constituencies it is absolutely necessary to maintain separate Liberal Unionist organisations.' There should be relations between Great George Street and Carlton Square 'of a much more frequent and co-operative nature', but Powell Williams was keen to avoid any talk of amalgamation of the Unionist Parties. Selborne was far more willing to make preparations 'for future amalgamation,' as 'the final goal,' but only 'if and when the psychological moment occurs.' Both men agreed with James and demanded that Devonshire issue 'an authoritative statement of the necessity for the distinct and separate Liberal Unionist organisation to be kept up,' but one that would not damage relations with the Conservatives.[8]

Devonshire therefore sent a letter to James and on 23 January 1896 James met the MLUF again. However, before reading Devonshire's letter, he attempted to bolster the Federation by emphasising their contribution to the recent Unionist landslide:

> Liberal Unionism has never been so paramount as during the election of 1895. Our numerical and moral forces exercised upon the elections

a more powerful effect than had ever been seen during the whole time of our existence. Is this to be thrown away?

James then read the less than rousing letter from Devonshire, in which the Duke explained that he had consulted with Chamberlain on the question of the Liberal Unionist organisation:

> Having regard to the excellent relations existing between the Conservatives and ourselves, I do not think that any of us, either in the government or in Parliament, consider that a distinctive name or organisation is necessary to us for the purpose of asserting our principles.

Where amalgamations of Conservative and Liberal Associations were proposed, 'nothing should be done to discourage such a proceeding,' but Devonshire admitted that 'it would be a misfortune if, by the premature relinquishment of the name and organisation … any of our friends should feel compelled to make a choice between the Liberal name and principles … and … Unionism.' He concluded that, rather than for any commitment to Liberal principles and policies but rather 'for these reasons, I think our Liberal Unionist organisation should … be maintained.'[9] *The Times*, in reporting the meeting, noted that this meant that 'the Liberal Unionist chiefs have resolved to make the maintenance of a separate organisation, practically a matter for "local option."'[10] This was hardly 'the authoritative statement' that Selborne and Powell Williams had asked for.

Despite this public statement, Devonshire's commitment to the Liberal Unionist Party apparatus, never strong, had evaporated once the Liberal Unionists had entered the coalition. He wrote to James after the MLUF meeting, admitting that 'I do not see how the L.U. organisation is to be kept up locally, now that there is no particular danger to the Union.' Boraston's Association should be limited to fund-raising and the Party should gracefully decline. Even Party conferences were best avoided in the Duke's eyes, as:

> If they are invited to discuss Education or anything else from a L.U. point of view, they may probably indicate some considerable difference of opinion with the Conservatives which may make matters worse instead of better.[11]

Like Chamberlain, Devonshire seemed more concerned with the feelings of the Conservatives than those of his own Party and he continued to make his priorities clear. Later in 1896, he addressed a meeting of the British Empire League, which he had helped to found at Lubbock's request, rather than his own Party.[12]

Chamberlain clearly wished to draw closer to the Conservative leadership and assuage any lingering fears as to his radical past. As Henry James wrote in 1895, 'especially he seems desirous to show his accord with Arthur Balfour ... they sat and acted together in the House of Commons.'[13] In 1896, he yielded his opinion on a crucial issue for his nonconformist powerbase and permitted an Education Bill to proceed which would have benefitted denominational schools.[14] In April, he defended the government in the face of criticism of the proposed Bill from W. Ansell, a member of the Birmingham school board, in the pages of the Party newsletter.[15] That he chose to do so can be seen to mark a crucial point at which his manifesto became one of calculated appeal to the Conservatives and an increased distance from the Liberal Unionists. Later that month, he spoke at a Constitutional Club for the first time, emphasising his commitment to the government's foreign and imperial policy, while he told the Birmingham Liberal Unionist Association that he had 'changed his mind since 1870' on the issue of voluntary schools.[16] Chamberlain's changed priorities were best summarised by Selborne who wrote in his unpublished reminiscences, 'he [Chamberlain] told me that he meant to make the [Colonial] Office he held to be reckoned as highly as the Foreign Office.'[17]

Leonard Courtney, who had made a point of standing as an 'independent Liberal Unionist' in 1895, unsurprisingly disagreed with this approach. Speaking at Liskeard on 6 January 1897, he averred that 'the existence of the Liberal Unionists as a distinct organisation had been proved to be a guarantee of stability' and he declared that 'he rejoiced in their vitality.'[18] Outside Cornwall, however, the leadership did their best to avoid attending Liberal Unionist functions. Between May 1897 and May 1898 when he spoke at the Birmingham Liberal Unionist Association annual meetings, Chamberlain was not present at a single Liberal Unionist event. In addition to a speech to the Conservative Club at Glasgow University on 4 November 1897, he spoke at the Chamber of Commerce in Liverpool on 18 January 1898 and to the Jewellers' Association in Birmingham on 29 January 1898. Chamberlain also did nothing to oppose the selection of a Conservative, F. W. Lowe, for George Dixon's old seat at Edgbaston in January 1898, which contrasted with his actions in 1889, 1892 and 1895 in defending the Liberal Unionists' right to contest Central Birmingham, East Worcestershire and Central Birmingham again.[19] Other Liberal Unionist leaders shared this studied neglect of their Party, as in Edinburgh, where Lord Lansdowne addressed the Primrose League, which the Liberal Unionists had shunned hitherto, rather than his own Party.[20]

From the West of Scotland Association records more direct evidence emerges that Chamberlain deliberately avoided being seen on Liberal Unionist platforms. The WSLUA had, uniquely among Liberal Unionist Associations,

I.—THE EDUCATION CHAMELEON.

"The thin chameleon, fed with air, receives,
The colour of the thing to which he cleaves."
DRYDEN.

Image 42: Carruthers Gould identifies the bitterness with which Chamberlain's
support for the Education Bill of 1896 was received by his nonconformist
supporters. *Westminster Gazette*, 4 May 1896.

attempted to define its own position towards the Conservatives once the coalition government of Unionists had won the 1895 election. The WSLUA had
decided unanimously to continue with separate Liberal Unionist organisations and opposed the creation of joint Liberal and Conservative Unionist
Associations. Joint committees would be established but clearly there was no
desire in the region to amalgamate. In fact, the number of Liberal Unionist
Associations continued to increase, as Bird reported at the Association AGM,
reaching 131 by the end of the year.[21] The President, Lord Kelvin, declared that
although the threat of Home Rule had retreated for the foreseeable future, the
Association should regard the current situation as merely 'an armed truce.'[22]
In his report at the 1896 Association AGM, Bird developed this theme, commenting that 'so long as the Liberal Party maintain and assert their adherence
to Home Rule, so long the Liberal Unionists are bound to keep up their various
organisations.' The Party was clearly restive about the efforts it had put in to
promote the social programme urged by Chamberlain and Powell Williams,
however. At the Association's AGM in November 1896, Alexander Cross, who
had come within seventy-one votes of losing his seat at Glasgow Camlachie in

1895, proposed the motion that 'the paramount duty of the Government was to promote measures of social reform.'[23] The following year, although Corbett welcomed the introduction of the Employers' Liability Act, he articulated the second demand of the more radical wing of the Party, 'an extended measure of local government for Ireland.'[24] There was evidence that the electoral success and the government's concentration on foreign and imperial affairs had led to a falling away of active support. The organisation of the North Ayrshire Liberal Unionist Association was found to be 'defective' and, by May 1897, the total amount subscribed to the WSLUA was a mere £27.[25] Chamberlain was thus invited to speak in Glasgow, no doubt in the hope that he would reanimate his social reform campaign when faced with such a receptive audience. To the Association's obvious amazement, the man who had previously insisted on speaking only to radical meetings organised through or at least co-chaired by the NRU or NLU, now insisted that he would only speak to a joint Unionist meeting, with Conservatives given equal precedence.[26] The local Liberal Unionists angrily refused, largely because the WSLUA, as the oldest provincial Party organisation, had always prided itself on its Liberalism. The visit, when it took place, involved no mass meeting under the WSLUA banner and, at the joint Unionist meeting, the attitude of the WSLUA towards the Conservatives was 'freely criticised'.[27] The Association replied to this snub by inviting Devonshire to speak instead.[28] Kelvin made it clear that 'I am decidedly of the opinion that it should be under the Liberal Unionists' auspices.'[29]

In 1897, Chamberlain seized the opportunity to use Victoria's Diamond Jubilee to assert the primacy of the British imperial mission and thus unite the bulk of the Unionists behind the figurehead of the Queen. As the cynical *Western Mail* noted the day before the thanksgiving service at St Paul's, 'the Liberal Unionist section of the Cabinet have resolved to play Imperialism as their trump card.'[30] With doubts about the consequences of coalition spreading among the radical and moderate Liberal Unionists, now that Home Rule was in abeyance, it was a timely distraction and one in which Chamberlain invested much time and effort.[31] As Hammerton and Cannadine suggest, the Diamond Jubilee was carefully choreographed to provide different groups with different reasons for celebration, ranging from the elite's pleasure in the reaffirmation of hierarchy to the working classes' enjoyment of an extra day's holiday.[32] Thompson suggests that the Diamond Jubilee (and, less convincingly, the tariff reform campaign) was an attempt 'to foster a more general attachment to empire among ordinary working people by making them feel proud of it', but to do so through popular movements and activities that, just like the Primrose League, incorporated working-class and lower-middle-class patterns of behaviour, rather than challenging them.[33] Chamberlain, always willing to resort to 'tub-thumping' rhetoric when it suited his needs, became far more extravagant in his claims for the 'imperial mission' at this point:

> This great Empire of ours, powerful as it is, is nothing to what it will become in the course of ages when it will be in permanence a guarantee for the peace and civilisation of the world.[34]

He was now building larger and more lasting alliances for his own benefit, rather than for the benefit of the Party of which he was leader. In the by-elections in 1898, T. G. Otte has highlighted how the Coalition emphasised foreign and imperial matters and almost totally avoided any mention of the Employer Liability legislation of the previous year.[35] For Chamberlain, 'the game of politics' had now entered a different phase.

A pattern thus began to emerge among the Liberal Unionists. For isolated Liberal Unionists, dependent upon Conservative aid, such as Stanley in North Lambeth, Victor Cavendish in West Derbyshire or Walter Morrison in Skipton, there was little alternative but to find those areas of policy (mainly foreign and colonial) where the two Parties touched hands and to avoid issues such as disestablishment, social reform and protectionism. In those areas where a strong tradition of Liberal and/or radical Unionism had been established in 1886, there was a marked reluctance to follow the Party leaders and draw ever closer to the Conservatives. Despite the lukewarm attitude of Campbell-Bannerman towards Home Rule, *LUAM* constantly warned that the Liberal leadership had not changed its attitude. In November 1897, an article appeared entitled 'Is Home Rule dead?' and reproduced recent quotations from Morley, Asquith and others to refute the claim.[36] This was clearly not having the desired effect, as Henry Sidgwick revealed after the Liberal Unionist Council meeting in February 1898:

> I have just come from a meeting at which – with the help of the Duke [of Devonshire] – we managed to be cheerful enough as long as the reporters were there: but when the reporters were gone, 'leakage' and how to stop leakage was the only topic. The humiliating thing is that we pose as a specially intelligent part of the community, and yet have to confess that 'leakage' means that many of us are so irredeemably stupid as to believe the Home Rule question dead.[37]

As a result, a further series of speeches and articles were undertaken with the theme 'Home Rule is not dead', starting with Chamberlain speaking to the Birmingham Liberal Unionist Association on 13 May 1898,[38] followed by an letter by A. V. Dicey to the *Spectator* on 17 September.[39] The initial decision to allow the Liberal Unionist organisation to merge gradually into Unionist bodies also appeared to have been reversed, if Devonshire's and Chamberlain's letters to the Yorkshire Liberal Unionist Federation of June 1898 are to be taken at face value. Devonshire wrote that 'I am glad of the opportunity of urging on the [YLUF] the importance of not relaxing their efforts', while Chamberlain opined that 'wherever there is already a fair number of Liberal Unionists, the organisation of the party should be maintained in full efficiency.' On the other hand, neither leader showed much commitment in one of the vital areas for Liberal Unionist growth, as they both pleaded prior engagements and did not attend the meeting.[40] However, such was the dissension among the Liberals that, in purely electoral terms, there seemed to be no need for exertion. The Liberal Unionists won six by-elections between November 1897 and September 1898, including four seats in the hitherto difficult north of England.[41] Unusually for a government Party in the mid-term, they only lost three by-elections in the same period, although two of these had been Liberal Unionist seats in 1895.[42]

The first full Liberal Unionist conference to take place since the 1895 election was only organised for 15 November 1898. A very optimistic view of the Party's progress was presented in Sir John Lubbock's presidential address. He reported that 'the Liberal Unionist party was growing in strength and that there were 1,000s throughout the country who were really Liberal Unionists though they had not joined any Liberal Unionist Association.' Despite such a conclusion, reached in spite of any evidence, the true dilemma for the Party was made clear by the resolution proposed by Jonathan Backhouse, in which he warned the Liberal Unionists against 'becoming mere agents in the Conservative Party' and declared that Liberal Unionist organisation should be kept entirely separate, in spite of the attitude displayed by Chamberlain and Devonshire in 1896 and 1897. The resolution was unanimously passed, with Arthur Conan Doyle, future Liberal Unionist candidate for Central Edinburgh, speaking in favour of it. Chamberlain perceived that he had tried to abandon the Party of which he was leader a little too hastily, as he spoke at the Free Trade Hall and declared that 'it is our bounden duty in every district to maintain our organisation.'[43] Despite Chamberlain's oratory, the main attempt to maintain the operation of the LUA was led by Leonard Courtney, still smarting from the snub he had received from his leaders and the Tories over the speakership in 1895. Demonstrating regional independence that matched that of the west of Scotland, the Devon and Cornwall Liberal Unionist Federation held its own conference, independent of the national conference in Manchester, two days later. Here Courtney made his defiance clear:

> The Liberal Unionists could not dream of deserting the position they occupied ... He [Courtney] desired above all things, to encourage in

them, that spirit out of which as a party they were born – that spirit of indefatigable loyalty to the associates with whom they were working, but at the same time, of freedom in that association and co-operation.[44]

Even in Birmingham, the annual reports of the All Saints Ward LUA for 1897 and 1898 reveal a determination to preserve and celebrate Liberal identity, despite the absence of 'the advancement of those principles for which we have fought and still hold so dear' in the priorities and many of the policies of the Unionist government.[45] For those Liberals who remained suspicious of the Conservative attitude towards reform, this was a deeply disappointing period. Once Chamberlain's close ally, Edward (now Baron) Heneage, chairman of the Liberal Unionist Council, condemned the Unionist government in private to his agent, Ernest Grange.[46] After his election, he worked closely with Courtney as their dissatisfaction grew. Heneage wrote to his agent in 1899: 'I am a strong supporter of Lord Salisbury personally and his foreign policy, but I am not a supporter of Her Majesty's Government, which is one of the most unpopular and inefficient governments I have ever known in 30 years.'[47]

Leonard Courtney became an increasing irritant to Chamberlain in the Commons, frequently attacking the coalition government's foreign and colonial policy. His criticism culminated in his famous intervention in the debate on the 1899 Clerical Tithes Bill, when he stood and asked 'why are the Liberal Unionists here?' His speech is worth quoting at length, as he ably contrasted the position of the Liberal Unionists after 1886 with their role since 1895:

> Some of us, even before 1886, were returned as Liberals and we represented constituencies which, presumably, from that circumstance, apart from Home Rule, were Liberal constituencies. But we ourselves were opposed to Home Rule and we were supported – those of us who survived – in these constituencies by a section of Liberals like ourselves, opposed to Home Rule, but not otherwise changed in their opinions, and who came to join a minority of Conservatives in those constituencies, and so secured a majority. The Liberal Unionists, representing old constituencies of this character, sit here to make what was a Conservative minority into a Unionist majority. And then, consider these Hon. Members who have come in since. Why do the astute managers of party conflict who select candidates to go here and there, choose or select men who are Liberal Unionists instead of men called Conservatives to go to one constituency rather than another? [opposition cheers and laughter]. They don't do it if they can help it, perhaps [laughter], but that only enforces the argument. The Liberal Unionists are necessary evils. [Renewed laughter]. That is the point which I am endeavouring to drive

XVIII.—THE CUPBOARD WHICH WAS BARE.

The Old Age Pensions Commission in their Report did not recommend any specific plan.   The consequence is that the Commission has had no positive result whatever.

Old Mother Hubbard went to the cupboard [a]
To fetch her poor dog a bone ; [†]
But when she got there, the cupboard was bare, [‡]
And so the poor dog had none. [§]

[a] The Aged Poor Pension Commission.   [†] Pensions for Aged Poor.   [‡] Nothing specific.   [§] Just what he might have expected.

[WESTMINSTER GAZETTE, January, 7, 1898.]

Image 43: The *Westminster Gazette* comments on the lack of substantial progress on Old Age Pensions in 1898, despite Chamberlain's earlier promises. *Westminster Gazette*, 7 January 1898.

home. They are selected because they can appeal to a certain number of electors who can turn the scale and elect them.[48]

As Courtney's opposition to the Tithes Bill demonstrated, many Liberal Unionists found it difficult to reconcile their hostility to legislation designed, ultimately, to benefit the established Church. This explains why, between 1895 and 1900, despite the divisions within the Liberal Party, there was no second defection from official Liberalism, led by Lord Rosebery. As Robert Perks, MP for Louth, made it clear, a Liberal might abandon his commitment to Home Rule, but should never join with the Conservatives as he would have to vote against disestablishment and disendowment of the established churches, he would have to support the maintenance of denominational elementary schools, he would have to relinquish his support for the temperance movement, for proportional representation and the reform of the House of Lords.[49] Notwithstanding the Employers' Liability Act of 1897, the bargain that Chamberlain had made with the Conservatives clearly did not attract many Liberals. Even amid the jingoism of the outbreak of war in December 1899, a few voices at the Leicester Liberal Unionist conference, such as Fortescue Flannery, were still calling for 'pensions for the old and deserving workpeople.'[50]

As the 1900 election drew closer and the Party organisation appeared, at least outside the west of Scotland, to be in a state of torpor, the recently returned Governor-General of Canada, Lord Lansdowne, asked, 'are we raising a Liberal Unionist fund for the election? I have not been approached on the subject.'[51] Although accurate figures do not survive, from a later letter from Anstruther it is clear that an election fund was raised by the Party whip 'on instructions given by you [Devonshire] in 1900.' The balance from the fund survived with £10,980 invested in Selborne and Anstruther's names (which was surely the remainder of the £15,000 invested in 1895) and £5,000 in Cavendish and Anstruther's, with an additional £300 in cash.[52] Chamberlain and Devonshire now appeared far more enthusiastic about the need for Liberal Unionist organisation, telling the WLUA in June that 'it is extremely creditable to the members, and especially to the committee, of this association, that it should up to the present time have retained its organisation in full force and vigour.'[53]

By the time of the election, not only did the Second Boer War offend those such as Professor Caird, Master of Balliol, and Leonard Courtney who were committed to a peaceful foreign policy, but the Party's manifesto even drove two peers back to the Liberals, such was its lack of reform. The Earl of Durham, whose generosity had largely kept the Party afloat in the north-east of England, rejoined the Liberals in September 1900 and wrote to the Newcastle Liberal Club that:

> I cannot recall a single instance during the existence of this Parliament in which the Liberal Unionists have asserted their independence or

what ought to be their convictions. They have allowed themselves to become the slaves of the Tory leaders.[54]

Lord Portsmouth, an outspoken critic of the established church, published a highly embarrassing letter to Boraston in *The Times*, in which he commented of his own leaders that 'I am no longer able to share their political views or to understand their public position ... not a single Liberal reform is mentioned or alluded to.' He reached the same conclusion as Courtney: 'Liberal Unionism – having exercised no Liberal influence on the Government or party – has degenerated into a mere device for obtaining Liberal votes for Conservative uses.'[55] Chamberlain struck back in Birmingham, defending the Unionists' record on social reform. He could only give two examples, however. The first, free education, was now nine years in the past, while the other, employer liability, provoked a heckler to shout 'what about contracting out?' Chamberlain did return, once again, to old age pensions, vowing that 'we have not done with old age pensions. I am not dead yet', but he was unable to do more than criticise a Liberal candidate's promise of universal pensions funded by taxation and he even announced that 'I do not very much like' the phrase 'old age pensions.'[56] In private he wrote dismissively, 'if the working classes do not want and will not pay for them [old age pensions], then they must go without'.[57] His election address for the 1900 general election contained no mention of any social reform and, with the election safely won, in May 1901 he declared in Birmingham that 'we should hear no more of a universal old-age pension.'[58]

As a result of this attitude, together with the acquiescence of Devonshire and the relative passivity of the LUA, the decision to fight the 1900 election on the issue of the Boer War was heartily endorsed by the Party.[59] However, the result was perhaps confirmation of the growing irrelevance of the Liberal Unionists. The Party's MPs were reduced to sixty-four (which included 'independents' such as T. W. Russell) and it seems that many Liberal voters turned away from the Party at last, unable to sacrifice their long-held commitment to the 'moral' foreign policy advocated by Gladstone and John Bright. The limited social reforms of the Salisbury administration, despite the pledges of the 1895 campaign, also harmed many Liberal Unionists. Those Liberal Unionists who were returned had reduced majorities in nine cases whereas the Conservatives who retained their seats did so with substantially increased shares of the vote. Had not the Liberals been so badly divided between 'Limps' and 'pro-Boers' and failed to oppose twenty-seven Liberal Unionist candidates, it is possible that the Party might have performed even worse.[60] In many areas, it was difficult to find men to stand as Liberal Unionists and in seats such as North Lambeth and Cheltenham, Middleton was finally able to achieve through default what he had previously had attempted through subterfuge and these were contested and won by Conservative candidates.

In the east of Scotland, the Conservatives gradually superseded the Liberal Unionists, contesting more seats in 1900 than their allies, including six which the E&NSLUA had previously identified as 'key seats.' In May 1899, the secretary had to investigate whether the organising secretary of the Association in Dumfriesshire was still active.[61] In Edinburgh, the E&NSLUA shrank into relative inactivity, as can be seen from Conan Doyle's experience when he contested Central Edinburgh in 1900. As far as it is possible to detect, the author appeared to have no correspondence with the local Association, negotiating his eventually unsuccessful candidature entirely through Boraston in London.[62] The WSLUA refused to quietly dissolve or to be sidelined by their own leadership, however. A thorough canvass of all its divisions was carried out and 'defunct' Associations were revived.[63] The canvass results throw an interesting light on the relative strengths of the Parties in a working-class area of industrial Scotland following the Liberal defeat in 1895:

Gladstonians	250
Liberal Unionists	220
Conservatives	140
Doubtful	60
Non-contacts	330[64]

Although the canvass suggested that Unionists were in a majority in the district, the continuing poor relations between the two Parties and the large number of non-contacts actually gave greater significance to the fact that the Gladstonians were still the largest party in the area. These figures seem consistent with the Liberal Unionist canvasses carried out later in 1899 throughout the region, from which it appeared that the Liberal Unionists were the smallest Party in all areas, with the exception of Govanhill (where they were the largest) and Possilpark (where they outnumbered the Tories).[65]

The task of reversing this decline proved difficult, as the district organisation was dependent on the support of a few prominent and wealthy men. J. A. Marshall, the honorary secretary of the Partick Liberal Unionist Council admitted to Sir Andrew Maclean, the new president, that money was short in Maryhill, as 'at present the funds are, if not wholly, very nearly, exhausted.'[66] Initial plans for a series of social meetings to appeal to working men were abandoned and Marshall promptly resigned as Council secretary and Maclean began to realise what a challenge he had taken on, especially as the election drew near: 'Sir Andrew Maclean and other members of the Council from Partick were alarmed at the backward state of the Party organisation in Partick.'[67] The new Council secretary, Fleming, tried his best, but by the time of the next election, Fleming was acting as Council secretary, chief registration agent and treasurer.[68] As the regional Association noted, there were fears for the long-term survival of the organisation:

> In almost all the branches there are vacancies in the principal offices, and it is very difficult to induce anyone to take up the work. Death and other causes have removed many of our best men … there are no evidences of accessions to our ranks from the Gladstonians, such as took place prior to the last election. The result is to make the work of Liberal Unionist organisation increasingly difficult.[69]

The WSLUA also attempted to assert its autonomy, as it openly supported T. W. Russell's successful campaign for local government reform in Ireland, reminding their leadership when it was granted that 'it was the chief reform to which they pledged themselves at the time of the split in the Liberal Party.'[70] When the election came in 1900, all the existing Scottish Liberal Unionists faced opposition, but the WSLUA was able to offer a strong response. A fund raising campaign had been begun in May 1899.[71] The series of lantern lectures was stepped up, as the following table demonstrates:

Season	No of lectures	Total attendance	Average attendance
1895/6	49	9,353	191
1896/7	40	7,315	183
1897/8	72	15,710	218
1898/9	91	24,045	264
1899/1900	104	30,440	292[72]

Most candidates were in the field by January 1900 and Associations prepared.[73] As late as September 1900, however, two seats (N. W. Lanark and N. E. Lanark) were still without candidates and the candidate in the former had to be funded from Boraston's London Association, while that in the latter had to contest the seat at his own expense. Unsurprisingly, neither prevailed, but the Scottish Conservatives expressed gratitude that the seats had been fought.[74] Overall, seven seats were won in the west, giving Scotland a total of eighteen Liberal Unionist MPs, the same as the Midlands, where eleven Liberal Unionists had not faced a contest.

The WSLUA finally began to struggle after the 1900 election. Funding continued to prove difficult and the balance of the Association gradually declined.[75] The Party became almost entirely dependent on McCulloch's lecture series, but refused to fund them more generously until his talks contained 'fewer trees and more faces in the pictures, and more anecdotes in the byographical [sic] matter.'[76] The Association was, perhaps surprisingly, not disrupted by the disputes over the 1902 Education Bill, but certainly was by the sudden resignation of Chamberlain in 1903. When the business committee met in October, out of eleven members, only five voted in favour of the habitual resolution expressing confidence in Balfour's government, three voted against and the final three abstained.[77] As Bird commented in his report at the AGM of the Association in December, 'Liberal Unionists are passing out of trade winds into troubled waters.'[78]

As the weakness of the Party's apparatus was revealed, Powell Williams was persuaded to retire from public office by Chamberlain and, as James put it, 'it was arranged that he should take the principal charge of the LU Central Office.' Powell Williams was clearly struggling with the illness which would kill him in 1904, as 'a committee was formed consisting of Mr Williams, Mr H. T. Anstruther and [James] for the purpose of controlling the organisation of the party,' which met weekly.[79] The WLUA appeared to revive one element of its activity after the 1900 election, working, as Fawcett

Image 44: The *Westminster Gazette* highlights the growing irrelevance of the Liberal Unionist Party. *Westminster Gazette*, 15 March 1901.

wrote, 'at the distribution in foreign countries of literature setting forth the causes of the war in South Africa and vindicating the conduct of it.'[80] On the other hand, most of the leading figures of the WLUA became distracted by the cause of the Liberal imperialist Victoria League,[81] and as a result, Lady Frances Balfour considered in October 1903, when tariff reform divided the WLUA, 'we were a decaying industry, before this happened'.[82]

Although it appears to have escaped the attention of most historians, there was a further attempt to move the Unionist Parties towards 'fusion' in the years between the khaki election and the launch of the tariff reform campaign. The secretary of the Partick Liberal Unionist Council, W. Fleming, revealed in a letter to the president of the Council, J. M. Taylor, that the impetus came from the Party managers:

> I have managed to see Mr Russell and have had a long talk with him. He informs me that the proposed fusion of parties is at the instance of the two British associations and that Mr Parker Smith has expressed his approval of the proposal.[83]

That the proposed fusion had the support of the Conservative managers, given their record of protecting Conservative interests, often at the cost of the Liberal Unionists, should give pause for thought. Parker Smith's benediction on the arrangement leads one to consider whether Chamberlain was behind this move. His closest lieutenant, Powell Williams, was the chief organiser of the Liberal Unionist Association at this time and clearly the prime mover on the Liberal side of the alliance in this strategy. Was Chamberlain seeking fusion in preparation for a bid for the leadership of the united Party, now that Salisbury's premiership was clearly in its last months? If he was, he was to be disappointed in the outcome, for clearly Powell Williams and Parker Smith had taken little account of how such a dramatic move was to be achieved, as Fleming reported on 25 February:

> The meeting today ended in a fiasco. Everyone seemed amazed at the irregularity of the proceedings and refused to consider the proposed 'fusion of parties.' We therefore, after a little angry discussion broke up. I do not think anything further will be done towards 'fusion'!![84]

Fleming, with a certain degree of satisfaction, informed Russell that 'the more I think over this matter, the more I am inclined to think that you should let the matter drop entirely ... to do more would just ... emphasise the feeling of triumph of the opponents of the scheme.'[85]

Chamberlain's adoption of protectionism was, in Brooks' opinion, prompted by the difficulties he had faced in his heartland over the 1902 Education Act.[86] He had been opposed to those clauses that provided ratepayer funding for the National, denominational schools, but had been forced to defend the Cabinet's decision in a series of ill-tempered meetings in Birmingham.[87] Chamberlain's great achievement between 1886 and 1902 had been in securing the affection of a substantial body of nonconformist Liberals though the agency of bodies such as the Nonconformist Unionist Association, Now, as he wrote to Devonshire, 'our best friends are leaving us by scores and hundreds never to return.'[88] This spread nationally until a major protest meeting was held at Queen's Hall, London on 10 June, where Nonconformist Unionists were described as those 'who gave their votes to the betrayal of their co-religionists'.[89] Paul Readman has suggested that the Bill was valuable ammunition in the Liberal Party's post-war attempt to regain ownership of liberal, patriotic constitutionalism, in the face of the (allegedly) denominational, sectarian and anti-democratic Bill.[90] At the time, Edward Porritt considered that 'much of the disappearance of Liberal Unionism is traceable to the Education Act of 1902.'[91] It is also possible to conjecture that Chamberlain had little choice in supporting the Bill. After the 1900 election that confirmed the Tory majority, the Conservatives appear to have become even less willing to pander to the Liberal consciences of their junior partners. James became aware of the increasingly dictatorial attitude of the Conservatives towards their junior partners immediately after the election when Devonshire mentioned that it would suit Salisbury if all the Liberal Unionists resigned their positions in government and were then reappointed by the Prime Minister. James refused to co-operate with this blatant demonstration of Tory power and he later learnt that 'the Duke was *requested* to make this communication to me.'[92]

Chamberlain was therefore desperate to reassert his radical credentials and to prevent the Tories forcing the remaining Liberal Unionists to choose between amalgamation on their terms or a return to the opposition benches. The tariff reform campaign, with its initial promises of social reform combined with its overtly imperial message, allowed him to consolidate his support in Birmingham and reach out to the more radical elements among the Conservatives (particularly the young).[93] To take a more sympathetic view, the new policy can be seen as consistent with all Chamberlain's actions since 1886. Tariff reform was another attempt to promote the interests of the nation above those of particular classes or national groups, just like the defence of the Union in 1886 and 1893, and the promotion of 'constructive Unionism' in his social programme of 1892–1895. The attempt to fuse patriotism with an attack on 'the condition of England' had motivated his negotiations with

Lord Randolph Churchill in the mid-1880s and his wooing of Balfour after 1891 and helps to explain his enormous popularity in the Midlands.[94] It also provided an ideological glue to bind the two Unionist Parties together as the Conservative Party had a long-standing protectionist instinct that even Salisbury had occasionally indulged. After Chamberlain's famous speech at Birmingham on 15 May 1903, in which he publicly announced his support for colonial preference, Powell Williams arranged for copies of the speech to be provided to LUAs free of charge, much to Henry James' horror.

To Liberals like Elliot, James and Lubbock (now Lord Avebury), the abandonment of the principle of free trade and the legacy of Cobden and Bright, was one pill they would not swallow under any circumstances. While there was some sympathy for imperial preference among the free traders there was complete opposition for the policy of retaliation, which, as Avebury pointed out to Lansdowne in the Lords, had caused tariff wars between France, Switzerland and Italy in recent years.[95] With the free traders having alerted Devonshire to the threat, the Organising Council of the LUA (Powell Williams, James and Anstruther) met with Chamberlain and Devonshire on 20 June. As James reported, Chamberlain now appeared to regard his former allies as his chief opponents and behaved in a fashion that convinced James that he was 'somewhat unsteady mentally'.[96] James now began correspondence with Campbell-Bannerman and Asquith via Harcourt to try to rally cross-party defense of free trade.[97]

Despite the formal agreement that the LUA should remain neutral on the fiscal issue,[98] the conversion of Lord Lansdowne to the tariff reform cause led James to organise a free trade group, the Unionist Free Food League, with Goschen and Northbrook, which began to issue free trade literature in collaboration with the LUA's original publications manager, Henry Hobhouse.[99] At first, Devonshire was relaxed about the threat to the LUA,[100] but after Chamberlain's resignation from the government in 1903, he immediately contacted Anstruther who compiled a list of Liberal Unionist MPs 'with such notes as I have in hand of their attitude on the fiscal question.'[101] After the formal foundation of the Tariff Reform League, there began a battle between Chamberlain and Devonshire for control of the Liberal Unionist Association. Devonshire was able to call on the support of those who had backed his position in 1886, namely James, Elliot, St. Loe Strachey and Goschen. Chamberlain had the backing of his Birmingham 'duchy' (the only challengers to his preeminence in the city, Bright and Dixon, were both long dead) and enthusiastic imperialist radicals such as J. L. Garvin, H. O. Arnold-Forster and Lord Selborne (now First Lord of the Admiralty). In October 1903, Chamberlain began to assault regional LUAs, beginning with Durham and North Riding.

A resolution was passed in favour of fiscal reform and a number of free-traders resigned in protest.[102] Devonshire continued to propose that the Association should remain neutral as Boraston was 'receiving many enquiries' on the issue,[103] but James was becoming suspicious that Powell Williams was siphoning off the Association's still considerable funds to fund tariff reformers in regional Associations and Collings' *Rural World,* which was inevitably loyal to Chamberlain's crusade.[104] In the end, news of more local LUA resolutions in favour of tariff reform and a letter from Powell Williams to James threatening the demise of the Party if protection was not adopted, proved too much for the Duke.[105] Having written to the electors of Lewisham in December 1903 advising them to vote against supporters of the Tariff Reform League and agreeing to address the Liverpool branch of the Unionist Free Food League,[106] he and James were subject to an extraordinary series of attacks from his own Party in the pages of *The Times.* These included one from J. L. Wanklyn, MP for Central Bradford, which criticised Devonshire for paying too much heed to 'the "evil genius" of the Liberal Unionist party,' warning that 'disappointed lawyers are not safe friends for dukes in difficulty.'[107] The bulk of the letters were written by Liberal Unionists in the north of England, including Albert (now Earl) Grey who announced that 'the overwhelming majority of Liberal Unionists in the north' supported Chamberlain's policy.[108] Devonshire wrote angrily to Chamberlain in January 1904 that he wished 'to prevent the Association of which I am president from becoming actively identified with the support of a policy disapproved of by me.' In the circumstances of the split in the Party, he concluded that 'the continuance of the existing Liberal Unionist organisation ... is no longer necessary and [it] should be dissolved with as little recrimination or bitterness as may be possible.' If the Association did have a policy of fiscal reform forced onto it, 'I should have no other alternative than to resign.'[109] Chamberlain, confident of his popular support, attempted to call a general meeting of the Association. Devonshire obviously turned down this loaded invitation, for Lord Durham congratulated him on having 'declined Chamberlain's courteous (!) attempt to draw you into a trial of strength at a Liberal Unionist conference'. He also revealed that, although many suspicions of Chamberlain's behaviour in light of his record before 1886 had been repressed (particularly since he became leader in the Commons), they had not been forgotten, as he condemned 'Chamberlain's ambitious and unscrupulous campaign.'[110]

Chamberlain proposed instead that there should be a meeting of the Liberal Unionist Council, which duly endorsed the protectionist cause on 3 February 1904.[111] When C. H. Seely, MP for Lincoln, supported John Morley's free trade amendment on 15 February, he was promptly de-selected by his constituency Association.[112] Finally, Devonshire compromised and agreed that the Liberal

Image 45: The conflict between Devonshire and Chamberlain over the position of the Liberal Unionist Association on the tariff reform question is publicly revealed in *The Times*, 11 January 1904.

Unionist Association should adopt a 'semi-dormant state, taking no part in the fiscal controversy.' Under these terms, no LUA would be allowed to act either for Chamberlain's Tariff Reform League or the Free Food League.[113] To prevent the Association being hi-jacked by either faction, a committee was to be established, with two of Devonshire's supporters and two of Chamberlain's, to manage the Association.[114] Devonshire reassured James that Chamberlain's policies had not been accepted by the Liberal Unionist Association.[115] He had reckoned without the tariff reformers' determination. Anstruther retired as Party whip in March and Chamberlain arranged for H. Pike Pease, MP for Darlington and one of those who had attacked Devonshire at the beginning of the year, to fill the post.[116] Austen Chamberlain was deputised to pass a tariff reform resolution at the near-dormant Liberal Unionist Club, which he achieved on 23 March.[117] Joseph Chamberlain now chose to propose a reorganisation of the party machinery, a fusion of the Organising Council and the Association into the 'Liberal Unionist Central Council.' He achieved this on 18 May 1904 and Devonshire promptly resigned as president of the old Association.[118] The leading free-trade Unionists, Elliot and Strachey, waited until the meeting of the Liberal Union Club on 29 June, where a resolution was proposed in favour of Chamberlain's reorganisation, to which Elliot proposed a negative amendment. It was defeated by 108 to 64 and Elliot prompted walked out with Devonshire's supporters and set up a rival Unionist Free Trade Club.[119] Chamberlain then called a meeting of the new Council on 14 July, at which he was elected president with Lords Lansdowne and Selborne as vice-presidents, although some regional Liberal Unionist Associations such as the WSLUA and the Nottinghamshire LUA refused to recognise the authority of the new body.[120] Devonshire's and James's positions as president and vice-president of the LU Club were taken by Lord Lansdowne and Lord Selborne respectively. A public meeting was held at the Albert Hall in the evening at which the Party formally announced that 'that day they had elected Mr Chamberlain as their great general to lead the Liberal Unionist Party.'[121] In protest, Elliot, F. W. Lambton, Hain, J. Simeon, Cameron Corbett and H. C. Smith wrote to *The Times* attacking 'the persistent efforts recently made to alter the character of the old organizations and to turn them into a "machine" for promoting the old Birmingham doctrine of preference and protection.'[122] The unsympathetic WSLUA complained that the new Central Council was 'more of a chorus than a Council.'[123]

The free-fooders were hopelessly divided on tactics, however, with some such as Hain crossing the floor, others choosing to support the opposition in debates on fiscal policies, others abstaining and some remaining loyal in the hope of influencing Balfour to stand firm against Chamberlain's onslaught. The Free Food League could not survive these divisions and so Devonshire disbanded the organisation in January 1905.[124] For those such as James, Corbett and Mildmay, who could remember the events of eighteen years before, this period must have been a dreadful re-enactment of the awful choice they had faced in May 1886, as once again they struggled with their consciences as to whether to endorse policies of their political rivals in the forthcoming election.[125] For Elliot, Chamberlain's resort to vulgar materialism required a repeat of the self-sacrifice that the Liberal Unionists had performed in 1886 to obstruct Gladstone's sentimental nationalism, in order to maintain the 'purity of politics.'[126] For him, free trade was of greater significance than even the Union and so he resigned from the Liberal Unionist Party on 3 February 1905, ensuring that the *Edinburgh Review* continued to hold to the traditional Liberal Unionist line. He stood unsuccessfully for his old seat in Durham in the 1906 election as a 'Free Trade candidate,' supported by the Liberal Association.[127]

The divisions in the Party spread to the Women's LUA. Millicent Fawcett, whose enthusiasm for the cause had waned throughout the 1890s, was against the new policy and she was clearly not alone, as she noted that 'the Ex Com of the [WLUA] and the Society itself is hopelessly divided.'[128] Lady Frances Balfour clearly shared Fawcett's concerns, writing to her friend, 'where are you, what are you thinking about? Damming Joe I trust!!' Lady Balfour also

OUR BIRMINGHAM METHOD.

As the result of pushful enterprise our artist has succeeded in sketching a meeting of the Tariff Committee of the Birmingham Liberal Unionist Association. All its members were said to have been present.

Image 46: A postcard reproduction of a *Westminster Gazette* cartoon, implying Chamberlain's dominance of the Birmingham Liberal Unionist Association after the tariff reform split. Uncatalogued item, Cadbury Research Room, University of Birmingham.

resigned from the West of Scotland WLUA, in protest against Mrs Parker Smith's decision that 'it will be worked in Joe's interest.'[129] To Mrs Fawcett's eyes, there was only one course for the WLUA, 'I strongly favour the dissolving of the Association.'[130] Eventually, however, with a Chamberlainite majority on the executive committee, Balfour, Stevenson and Fawcett had to resign, with Fawcett writing to the President of the WLUA on behalf of her supporters, 'we believe we differ fundamentally from the majority of our colleagues.'[131] By 1906, the WLUA had ceased to exist, absorbed into the Women's Association of the Tariff Reform League and its leading members had re-joined Campbell-Bannerman's Liberals.[132]

LUAs were invited to affiliate to the new Council and were sent a set of policy heads to endorse, including 'closer union to the Colonies on the basis of Preferential Tariffs' and retaliatory tariffs against competitor nations.[133] Judging from the reports in *LUAM* and the records of the West Derbyshire and Mid-Devon LUAs, most seemed to do so enthusiastically. The Mid-Devon Association declared itself 'definitely in favour of Mr Chamberlain and his fiscal views.'[134] In the second Liberal Unionist heartland of Glasgow, however, the effect of tariff reform was disastrous. Typically, Chamberlain had no recall of the ill-will that he had generated by his behaviour towards the local Party in 1897.[135] In early October 1903, Balfour of Burleigh reported to James that only J. Wilson of all the west of Scotland MPs was even planning to attend Chamberlain's meetings.[136] This antipathy was shared by the activists, as the Partick Liberal Unionist Council refused to send any representatives to the newly reconstituted Liberal Unionist Council in 1904.[137] Lord Kelvin, despite his personal support for Chamberlain's policy, spent the next three years carefully ensuring that the WSLUA avoided an outright split at its AGMs, but the hostility was clear.[138] Only Parker Smith, Chamberlain's private secretary, endorsed the tariff reform case enthusiastically. Although Charles Cooper of the *Scotsman* trumpeted the protectionist cause (Chamberlain consequently described him as 'a brick'[139]), the *Glasgow Herald* turned against Chamberlain and he was forced to suggest starting a rival paper.[140] Given the huge benefits that would accrue to Glasgow with its dependence on Imperial trade, it demonstrates the lack of trust that many in the WSLUA felt towards Chamberlain.[141] As a result of the tariff reform campaign, many Scottish Liberals who had embraced Unionism were now driven to return to Campbell-Bannerman's Party. Both Corbett and Cross retained their seats in 1906, but only by standing as 'Liberal Unionist free traders.'[142] Between 1903 and 1906, six Liberal Unionist free-trade MPs had left the Party and rejoined the Liberals.[143] James, in common with the remaining Liberal Unionist free traders, refused to campaign for Balfour and Chamberlain:

We see the Unionist flag held aloft, but beneath it Protectionist forces are gathered. We free traders have a right to say these are not our friends, we will not fight on their side.[144]

As the former governor of Ceylon, West Ridgeway, noted in the article in which he claimed that the Party had been 'strangled by its own parent', 'the Liberal Unionist free traders are the only faithful survivors of the party which saved the Union.'[145]

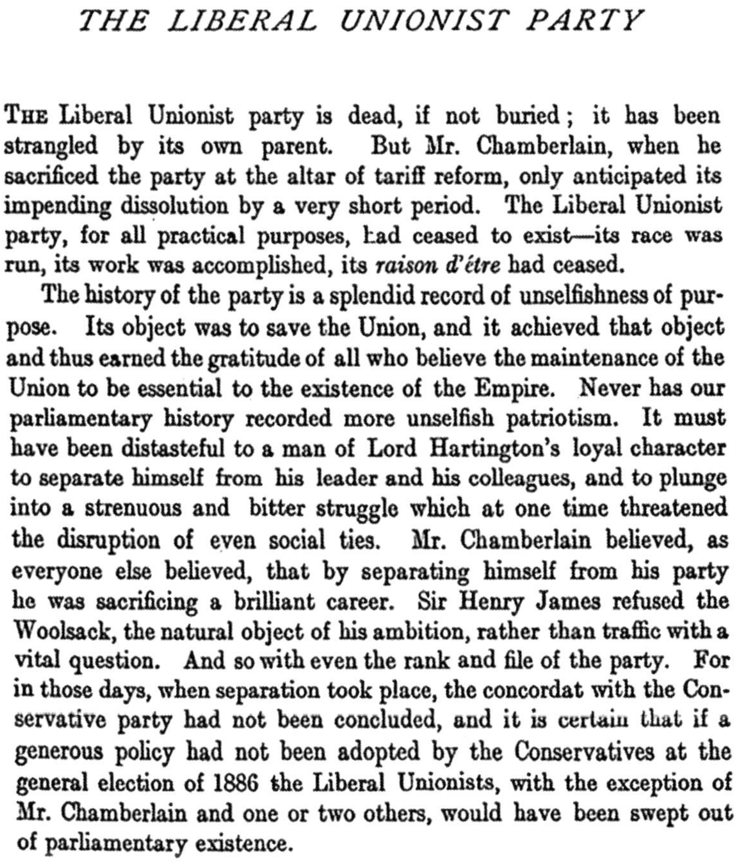

THE LIBERAL UNIONIST PARTY

THE Liberal Unionist party is dead, if not buried; it has been strangled by its own parent. But Mr. Chamberlain, when he sacrificed the party at the altar of tariff reform, only anticipated its impending dissolution by a very short period. The Liberal Unionist party, for all practical purposes, had ceased to exist—its race was run, its work was accomplished, its *raison d'être* had ceased.

   The history of the party is a splendid record of unselfishness of purpose. Its object was to save the Union, and it achieved that object and thus earned the gratitude of all who believe the maintenance of the Union to be essential to the existence of the Empire. Never has our parliamentary history recorded more unselfish patriotism. It must have been distasteful to a man of Lord Hartington's loyal character to separate himself from his leader and his colleagues, and to plunge into a strenuous and bitter struggle which at one time threatened the disruption of even social ties. Mr. Chamberlain believed, as everyone else believed, that by separating himself from his party he was sacrificing a brilliant career. Sir Henry James refused the Woolsack, the natural object of his ambition, rather than traffic with a vital question. And so with even the rank and file of the party. For in those days, when separation took place, the concordat with the Conservative party had not been concluded, and it is certain that if a generous policy had not been adopted by the Conservatives at the general election of 1886 the Liberal Unionists, with the exception of Mr. Chamberlain and one or two others, would have been swept out of parliamentary existence.

Image 47: J. West Ridgeway's article announcing, prematurely, the death of the Liberal Unionist Party as a result of the tariff reform split. J. W. Ridgeway, 'The Liberal Unionist Party', *Nineteenth Century and After*, 342 (August 1905), p. 182.

Although the causes of the Unionist defeat in 1906 extend far beyond the position of the Liberal Unionists, Phillip Williamson is surely right to identity that Chamberlain's folly was in 'disregarding the established Unionist identity and the bases of a successful electoral combination.'[146] The defeats in the electoral landslide reduced the Liberal Unionists to twenty-six. Despite Joseph Chamberlain's stroke on 13 June 1906 and his subsequent retirement from active politics, there was no sign of a rapprochement between the two wings of the Liberal Unionists.[147] Twenty-two of the Liberal Unionists were fiscal reformers (mainly in the West Midlands) and only four were free fooders (Corbett, Cross, Lambton and Mildmay).[148]

At this point, with both Liberal and Conservative Unionists belonging to rival Clubs and Associations over the tariff issue, it becomes impossible to speak of a Liberal Unionist Party in any meaningful sense.[149] Its continuance until 1912 was largely to suit individual MPs, not least Austen Chamberlain, who used the label to appeal to their local electorates, and the Council and Club both waned in these years.[150] The radical Unionists, both Liberal and Conservative, who had followed Chamberlain in 1903, now strove to take control of their local Party organisations and in the struggle between the local Tory elites and this younger generation of male and female activists, the distinction between Liberal Unionist and Conservative became increasingly unimportant.[151] Many Associations seem to have acted pragmatically, as Mid-Devon did, after the 1906 defeat. By 20 July 1906 the Association had been amalgamated with the Conservatives to form the Mid-Devon Unionist Association and no further subscriptions to the LUA are recorded.[152] Clifford reluctantly agreed to this, seeking assurances that they would not have to give up 'their position as Liberals.'[153]

Devonshire ultimately resisted those siren voices who attempted to persuade him to form an 'Independent Unionist Party', believing the threat of Labour too serious to risk dividing the Unionists further.[154] By the time of the elections of 1910, candidates were, for the first time, identified in *The Times* merely as 'Unionist,' with no prefix.[155] With Devonshire dead and Joseph Chamberlain incapacitated, the battle over the Lords and the challenge of Labour was sufficient to bring the fractured Parties together again.[156] When the threat of Home Rule was raised once again in the aftermath of the Parliament Act of 1911, the decision was taken by the new Conservative leader, Bonar Law, and Austen Chamberlain, to finally achieve Joseph Chamberlain's ambition from the later 1880s and to 'fuse' the two wings of Unionism at last.[157] In October 1911, Lord Selborne was the first Liberal Unionist to be elected to the Carlton Club since Goschen and then Austen Chamberlain was admitted to the Carlton in February 1912.[158] On 21

Image 48: By the 1906 election, Chamberlain had ensured that the troubled position of Liberal Unionism had been firmly replaced by the question of 'fair trade vs free trade.' Postcard, uncatalogued item, Cadbury Research Room, University of Birmingham.

March, it was announced in *The Times* that 'the expediency of amalgamating the headquarters organization of the Conservative and Liberal Unionist parties is again under consideration,' though in reality, no Liberal Unionist MP opposed the proposal. Under the contemplated 'fusion,' the Liberal Unionist Associations across the country 'would become affiliated with the Central Conservative Association.'[159] The following month, *The Times* revealed that 'in a number of places fusion [of local Associations] has already taken place.'[160] The only resistance to fusion was voiced, perhaps unsurprisingly, in Birmingham, where C. A. Vince still harboured resentment over the actions

Daily News and Leader.]

THE CAT : " I've eaten the canary."

(The " Liberal Unionist Party" has been " fused " into the Conservative Party under the title of " The National Unionist Association of Conservative and Liberal Unionist Organisations." Quite a mouthful.)

Image 49: The Liberal *Daily News and Leader* reports the fusion of the two Unionist Parties. *Daily News and Leader*, 10 May 1912.

of the city's Conservative Association in the 1890s. A resolution was tabled at the Association's meeting on 22 April to discuss the proposed amalgamation that 'it is most desirable in the common interests of the Unionist Party that … the separate organizations of the Liberal Unionists shall be maintained.'[161] As a result, perhaps to spare Chamberlain and Steel-Maitland's blushes, complete amalgamation was postponed for an 'interim period' (of an unspecified duration) during which constituencies were allowed to maintain 'separate organizations.'[162] On 9 May therefore, two 'special' conferences of the National Conservative Union and the Liberal Unionist Council were held and the resolutions were carefully phrased to limit the proposed fusion to 'the amalgamation of the *central* organizations of the two wings of the Unionist Party.'[163] The achievement of 'fusion' was therefore the combination of the National Conservative Association and the LUA into the National Unionist Association of Conservative and Liberal Unionist Organisations (NUACLUO).[164] The *Daily News* provided a cartoon showing a Conservative cat, licking its lips, next to an empty birdcage.[165]

An Executive Council of the new organisation was formed in June 1912, with the veteran Savile Crossley and Lord Selborne representing the Liberal Unionists, but the chairmanship of the Council was given to the NCA chairman, William Crump. John Boraston's long and difficult period as secretary of the Liberal Unionist Association was finally rewarded, with his appointment as principal agent of the unified Party.[166] A celebratory dinner took place on 27 June at the Hotel Cecil, at which Walter Long acknowledged that 'there had been since 1886 a real fusion among those who belonged to the two parts of that party.'[167] Unfortunately, without a leader such as Chamberlain, capable of reaching beyond the core middle-class Unionists and with a derelict organisational structure, divided, undermined and then abandoned in the struggle between free fooders and protectionists, the Party failed to break out of its association with reaction, landlord interest and sectarian Ulster patriotism in the years immediately before August 1914. Once the First World War had finally rendered the Union unsustainable, the triumph of democracy irreversible and the role of the state supreme, the Unionist Party reconfigured itself (after its flirtation with Lloyd George) as a centrist, patriotic party of moderate reform and fiscal probity.[168] This would allow it to pose as the 'National Party' from 1918 until 1929 and then as the bastion of the patriotic alliance from 1931 to 1939. That Neville Chamberlain was Chancellor and then Prime Minister of the 'National' government, was, for him, as for many former Liberal Unionists, proof that all their compromises had ultimately been worthwhile.

CONCLUSION – WHO WERE THE LIBERAL UNIONISTS?

For a hundred years, historians described the Liberal Unionists as composed of two distinct groups, the Whigs and Chamberlain's radical Unionists.[1] Perhaps this was an unsurprising conclusion, given Henry James' description in his memoir:

> There were, in fact, two sections of the Party. The majority were Whigs or moderate Liberals, who always regarded Lord Hartington as their leader; the minority were Radicals, who, for instance, were in favour of the disestablishment of the Church, and they followed Mr Chamberlain. Of the whole Party, however, Lord Hartington both in the House of Commons and generally was the leader, and to him Mr Chamberlain gave a most loyal support. No differences of opinion were ever made apparent.[2]

Twenty years ago, in *Parliamentary Politics and the Home Rule Crisis,* W. C. Lubenow exploded the myth that there was a clear religious, political or even occupational pattern to the division of the Liberal Party in 1886. This analysis suggested for the first time that the motivation for belonging to the Liberal Unionists was more nuanced than had previously suggested. If one relies on a contemporary view of the Party from an outsider (the Liberal MP, Alfred Pease), a more complex pattern of Liberal Unionist identity emerges:

> Some were merely Liberals in name, others were Whigs, some were Liberals apart from the Irish question, others were Radicals, others tee-total fanatics, and a small body was whatever Chamberlain was.[3]

In September 1887, the *Pall Mall Gazette* published an article entitled 'the Black Book' in which it attempted to delineate between the different factions that composed Liberal Unionism. As an apostate Unionist, Stead listed 'the converted', then 'the Chamberlainites', on the grounds that they were 'nearest to salvation.' The 'T. W. Russellites' were listed next ('soon told for they are a party of two') and then, before the 'out-and-out Coercionist, Landlordist, anti-Gladstonian, no-surrender "Liberals"', which on previous occasions the *Pall Mall Gazette* had described as 'Hartingtonians', there was an intriguing list of 'Independent Dissentient Liberals.' Although Stead is not specific on the grounds that separate the 'Independents' from the 'Coercionist – Landlordists', the names on the list suggest that this group comprised not only those who objected to the dictatorial tendencies of the whips and the caucuses (such as Heneage, Quilter and the venerable C. P. Villiers of Wolverhampton), but also of those with particularly strong Liberal principles (such as George Dixon and Leonard Courtney, including some, like James Caldwell, whose principles would lead him to stand as a Gladstonian in 1892).[4] Although one cannot read too much into Stead's precise classifications of the individual MPs (W. S. Caine is listed, rather unconvincingly, in the 'Coercionist – Landlordist' group and Wolmer's name is misspelled), based as it is on an analysis of only eight Commons divisions between February and August 1887, it indicates the fragmented nature of the Liberal Unionists, beyond mere Whig-radical categories. It illustrates the problem for any modern political party, in organising its forces and presenting its case, with such a spectrum of opinion and attitude.

As John Vincent wrote in his introduction to *The Later Derby Diaries*, 'there were many types of Liberal Unionist. There were those who wanted a split and those who feared one; those who were mainly interested in Ireland and those who were not.'[5] In fact the only true definition of a Liberal Unionist was one who rejected Gladstone's policy on Ireland and looked back to 'the party of 1885' as the true embodiment of orthodox Liberal principles before these were abandoned by their own leader. Steven Fielding has recently commented that political historians 'need to address issues that transcend conventional notions of party politics.'[6] In an age when the modern party organisation was being re-forged in the furnace of mass political involvement, the Liberal Unionists attempted to restore much of the moral imperative of mid-Victorian politics, while building a more democratic structure in order to convey their principles to the electorate. With such a challenge, it is not surprising that many fissures existed as to the Party's philosophy, priorities and methodology.

Moving beyond the parliamentary Party, Cooke and Vincent are far from flattering in their analysis of the Liberal Unionists, dismissing them as 'underemployed journalists, academics and members of the upper classes

We may now proceed to dissolve the united Liberal Unionist party into its elements. First comes the list of the Converted. These are :—

Buchanan, T. R.	Hingley, B.	Talbot, C. R. M.	Vivian, Sir Hussey
	Winterbotham, E. B.		

Nearest to salvation amongst the remainder are, we suppose, the Chamberlainites. Here is this little family party :—

Chamberlain, Right Hon. J.	Chamberlain, R. Kenrick, W.	Collings, Jesse Williams, J, Powell

Next is a smaller, but not less influential, section—the T.-W.-Russellites. They are soon told, for they are a party of two :—

Lea, T.	Russell, T. W.

Fourthly, come the "Independent Dissentient Liberals." These are :—

Barclay, J. W.	Courtney, L. H.	Heneage, Rt. Hon. E.	Pitt-Lewis, G.
Brown, A. H.	Dixon, George	Jardine, Sir R.	Quilter, W. C.
Caldwell, James	Goldsmid, Sir J.	Lymington, Viscount	Villiers, Right Hon.
Corbett, A. C.	Gurdon, R. T.	Mackintosh, C. F.	C. P.

Lastly come the entirely lost—the out-and-out Coercionist, Landlordist, anti-Gladstonian, no-surrender "Liberals." These are as follows :—

Anstruther, H. T.	Crossley, Sir S. B.	Hartington, Marquis	Richardson, T.
Baring, Viscount	Crossman, Sir W.	Hastings, G. W.	Rothschild, Baron H.
Barnes, Alfred	Currie, Sir D.	Havelock-Allan, Sir H.	Sellar, A. C.
Bass, Hamar	Ebrington, Viscount		Sinclair, W. P.
Beaumont, H. F.	Elliot, Hon. A. R. D.	Hobhouse, H.	Sutherland, T.
Bickford-Smith, W.	Elliot, Hon. H. F.	James, Rt. Hn. Sir H.	Taylor, F.
Biddulph, M.	Finlay, R. B.	Lubbock, Sir J.	Thorburn, W.
Bolitho, T. B.	Fitzwilliam, Hon. W. J. W.	Maclean, F. W.	Vernon, Hon. G. R.
Bright, Rt. Hon. J.		Maskelyne, M. H.	Watkin, Sir E.
Caine, W. S.	Fry, Lewis	Story	West, W. Cornwallis
Campbell, R. F. F.	Goschen, Right. Hon, G. J.	Mildmay, F. B.	Wiggin, H.
Cavendish, Lord E.		More, R. J.	Wodehouse, E. R.
Coghill, D. H.	Grove, Sir T. F.	Morrison	Woolmer, Viscount
Corbett, John			

It may be convenient lastly to put in tabular form the position of parties at the end of the Session :—

Conservatives	313	Liberals	199
" Unionists "—		Parnellites	86
Coercionist-Landlordists	49		
Independents	15		
Russellites	2		
Chamberlainites	5		
	— 71		— 285
	384		384
		Speaker	1
			— 670

Image 50: W. T. Stead's *Pall Mall Gazette* attempts to distinguish between the different branches of Liberal Unionism. 'The Black Book', *Pall Mall Gazette*, 14 September 1887.

whom for one reason or another life had excluded from a political role.'[7] They regard the Liberal Unionists as relying on a 'moribund tactical tradition' of 'disorientated activism among the unoccupied;' what Mrs Fawcett described as 'grand formal receptions and garden parties, long business gatherings, stirring propaganda meetings, demonstrations, publications, protests, election campaigns and all the rest.'[8] Despite his criticism of Cooke and Vincent's approach, Harvie largely agrees, describing the Liberal Unionists as 'a political party run by intellectuals for intellectuals: all officers and no awkward rank and file.'[9] They offer no explanation as to why, if this was the case, the Liberal Unionists managed such unexpected longevity and maintained a distinct position nationally until 1895 and, in certain regions, until well after that.

The only detailed analysis of the occupational basis of Liberal Unionism on a constituency level has been carried out by Victoria Barbery, based on the unique directory of Liberal Unionist activists held by the Bury Archive Service. By cross-referencing this data with the 1891 census returns, she has produced an insight into the composition of the Party on a local level that is highly illuminating. In contrast to the interpretation that the Liberal Unionist Party was a middle-class revolt against the growing radicalism of the Liberals, the data reveals that only 42.6% of the Party activists were middle class, with, consequently, 57% of the canvassers, fund-raisers and organisers of the Liberal Unionist Party belonging to the working class.[10] In the age of the secret ballot and the crack-down on corrupt practices that so concerned the WLUA, the worker was not obliged to vote as his employer wished. In fact, while nearly 40% of the Bury Liberal Unionist factory owners controlled dyeing, bleaching or printing works, only 5.6% of the working-class Liberal Unionists worked in these trades, suggesting that the owners' politics had a negative impact in larger trades. Given the fear of cheap Irish labour undermining their privileged position among the working classes, perhaps it was not surprising that the skilled artisans made up a third of the working-class Unionist activists in Bury. Barbery concludes that 'the LUA activists ... tended to be drawn from the most independent groups.'[11] The largest group among the Liberal Unionist cotton workers, for example, were the spinners. This seems to confirm the impression of Liberal Unionist support in all the areas of consistent Liberal Unionist strength (Cornwall, the West Midlands, Glasgow and its environs), that there was, in fact, no clear difference in social structure between the Gladstonian Liberals and the Liberal Unionists; they both represented all the classes in late Victorian society.[12] The Liberal Unionist victories in the Glasgow working-class seats of Camlachie and Tradeston in 1892 and 1895 provoked an ironic comment from John Wilson, MP for Falkirk, at the 10th AGM of the WSLUA:

Did the classes reside in Camlachie? (laughter) They did not usually
look for Belgravia and Mayfair in the district Mr Cross represented . . .
he thought the Falkirk burghs and Kilmarnock burghs did not exactly
represent the homes of the aristocracy.[13]

Fundamentally, in an age when most people divided their friends, their
guests and their business dealings into Liberal and Conservative, and had
done so since the defeat of Peel's government in 1846, it was hard for many
to change their habits, especially as the threat to the Union was swiftly disposed of on the two occasions before 1900 when it appeared to threaten. This
is what Wilde meant in his aphorism – Conservatives like Lady Bracknell
might tolerate Liberal Unionists, but they remained Liberals, so would not
be invited to dinner. In these circumstances, as Henry Sidgwick observed in
December 1886, 'I think party organisation is too rigid a thing to be broken
up and that Liberal Unionism will be broken against it at the next election.'[14]
Chamberlain felt the same, telling Austen in 1895 that 'no one who has
not worked among the electors can be aware how strong are the old prejudices in connection with party names and colours and badges.'[15] That Liberal
Unionism survived for as long as it did, in spite of the growing tendencies
of political dichotomy, speaks volumes for the commitment and hard-work
of the Party organisers, the actions of certain key leaders and the success of
the Party in fashioning an appeal to a broad range of voters with different
religious, regional, political and class identities. It is also a very important
indicator of the survival of a traditional political culture of localism, deference and patronage that supports Jon Lawrence's argument that a 'national
politics' (in which individuals defined themselves by party labels) only truly
emerged during the First World War.[16] If one takes the examples of Ireland,
the west of Scotland, Cornwall and Birmingham, as well as isolated seats such
as Bury, East Somerset, Ross-on-Wye and Sudbury, in contrast to the views
of Cooke and Vincent and Harvie, it seems more likely to suggest that more
than just a small body of Liberals supported Hartington and Chamberlain
and that many, entirely new to politics, were inspired to take up their first
political activity for the Liberal Unionist Party. These examples also suggest
a close and effective relationship between MPs and their Associations and one
which, in the case of the Irish Liberal Unionists at least, acted a successful
lobby group on the Unionist government.

In 1886, the majority of Liberal Unionists looked to Hartington as their
leader, rather than Chamberlain, despite Biagini's claims.[17] 'Chamberlain
is sometimes referred to as the leader of the Liberal Unionist Party', wrote
Alfred Hopkinson; 'this was not so. The real leader from the beginning

was Lord Hartington.'[18] Dicey confirmed this judgement in December
1886, when he wrote to Hartington, urging him to take the premiership
in the wake of Randolph Churchill's resignation: 'You are the only leader in
whose honesty, common-sense & patriotism, men of the most different parties absolutely confide.'[19] As these quotes suggest, many Liberal Unionists
and their supporters saw the issue as one of character, rather than ideology
and this reveals much of Victorian attitudes towards public behaviour. In a
speech to the Lords on 12 July 1886, Argyll praised the 'masculine honesty'
of both John Bright and Lord Hartington.[20] This was in marked contrast
to the behaviour of Gladstone, who, as Argyll put it in a letter to Granville,
was guilty of 'a violence of language ... a contemptuous treatment of all
who could not follow him ... perversions of historical fact ... the free use of
all the Irish revolutionary cant – which constitute together an unparalleled
series of provocations.'[21] As Argyll claimed in Edinburgh, shortly before
the election in 1892, the Liberal Unionists stood for the authority of the
crown, the power of parliament and the integrity of Empire, 'but we fight
for something better.' Far more important for Argyll and those moderate
Liberal Unionists around him was 'honour and truthfulness and openness
and candour among public men.'[22] As Jonathan Parry has demonstrated,
such language was a deliberate attempt to re-animate the discourse of 'character' which had dominated much of mid-Victorian political culture until
1867.[23] To most Victorians, 'character' implied the civic virtues of public-
spiritedness, restraint, independence of conscience, strict personal morality
and 'manliness' and this had a distinguished pedigree among the Liberals.[24]
John Stuart Mill had considered that 'the problem of character is the determining issue in the question of government'[25] and Herbert Spencer, who
publicly endorsed the Liberal Unionists in 1886, wrote in *The Principles
of Ethics* that 'the end which the statesman should keep in view as higher
than all others is the formation of character.'[26] The remarkable victories of
William Kenny, a Catholic Liberal Unionist MP in Dublin, were credited
by the sympathetic *Irish Times* to his 'utmost pluck and determination ...
sheer force of personality ... his marked abilities, strength of character and
modesty of bearing.'[27]
    Milner shared the distrust of the new politics that had emerged and he
exulted when the Liberal Unionists left the Eighty Club en masse, in protest
against the confrontational politics of ideological conflict that were creeping
into all aspects of the cultural fabric of political life:

It is a triumph of character agreeable to witness and how wholesome
in an age apparently given over wholly to political dodgery ... what a

few men can do even in our vast democratic whirlpool if they have the courage to stick to the opinions of their own.[28]

Henry James held his seat in Bury until 1895, while Liberal Unionists elsewhere in Lancastria went down to defeat, largely due to the high local regard for his character and integrity. As Barbery notes, James' success was based on 'his reputation for those attributes valued most by Bury Liberals – political integrity and independence.'[29] He was seen to have opposed Redmond's attempts to persuade Lancashire Irish voters to support the Conservatives in 1885, as he felt such interference in a voter's freedom to choose went against the Liberal principles which he had attempted to uphold by his work on the Corrupt Practices Act of 1883. When he refused to join Gladstone's Cabinet in February 1886 and then voted against the Home Rule Bill, his supporters could argue that, in contrast to Gladstone, who had denounced boycotting in 1882 as 'combined intimidation ... for the purpose of destroying private liberty', James had 'been true as steel to the ticket he ran upon at the last election.'[30] The victory of Liberal Unionists in Bury, as in Birmingham, Cornwall and Scotland, owed everything to their commitment to unbending Liberal principles and absolutely nothing to the alliance with the Conservatives.

Respect for an individual MP's determination to stick to his stated principles in the face of the pressure from party 'wire-pullers' was, in this period, often characterised by reference to what Lawrence describes as the 'near-ubiquitous rhetoric celebrating candidates' supposed "manly independence."'[31] John Tosh has recently identified manliness as 'the most clearly articulated indicator of men's gender in the nineteenth century.'[32] Manliness was a positive judgement of a politician's character and actions and, in the first age of mass electorates and increasingly sophisticated political organisation, the refusal of Liberal Unionists to bow, either to the local party caucus, or to the diktat of the party leadership, was 'manly', in that it demonstrated the courage, steadfastness and independence so admired by mid-Victorian commentators such as Samuel Smiles, Thomas Carlyle and Charles Kingsley. In local political discourse, the refusal to follow the dictates of the central party could pay electoral dividends, especially in the north and west of England where such behaviour was particularly admired.[33] It was not merely in public that 'manliness' could affect political loyalty, however. When Powell Williams agreed to follow Chamberlain in opposing the first Bill in 1886, he did so due to his admiration of Chamberlain's 'manly course.'[34] James Dingle, the sole martyr to the Liberal Unionist cause, similarly praised Leonard Courtney's decision to vote against Jesse Collings' amendment of January 1886, as the product of 'a manly sentiment.'[35] Scientists such as Lubbock, Tyndall and Huxley favoured a politics founded on reason, rational argument and manly self-control.[36] Such an approach was to be contrasted with Gladstone's emotional, sentimental and, therefore, essentially feminine attitude towards the sufferings of Ireland, which he seemed to confirm with his use of the distinctly effete term, 'a union of hearts', to describe his proposed alternative to the dominance of Westminster.[37] It also served to highlight the shortcomings of Parnell's character, who was perceived by Unionists as a liar and dissembler, who either advocated political murder, or did nothing to prevent it and who was finally revealed as an adulterer, much to the discomfort of the Nationalists' allies. Finally, it condemned those Liberals such as Rosebery and Spencer, who had no enthusiasm for Home Rule, but who had abandoned their principles out of unmanly panic, as a result of the 1885 election results. The Catholic poet, Aubrey de Vere, praised 'the Liberal Unionists of 1887' in language which reveals much of the political culture to which their position appealed:

Ye, who, to Virtue and your Country vowed,
Reject, denounce dishonoured party ties
And side by side with ancient enemies
Confront the Jacobin onset blind and loud
Nor snared by sophist tongue nor clamour-cowed ...
Firm as a flint your face 'gainst such is set:
Old friends change faith: to old convictions true
Ye change but place. Changelings are they not you.[38]

From a reading of Unionist literature, it can be demonstrated that the character of the Irish Catholic was felt to be more childish (in the sense that they failed to mediate their selfish and often brutal instincts), compared to that of the English Protestant, Scottish Presbyterian, Ulster Nonconformist or Cornish Wesleyan.[39] The Irish needed to be restrained in order to avoid recourse to violence, while being encouraged towards the responsible exercise of self-government. There is an argument to be made that those who attempt to read 'racist' attitudes into the behaviour of the Liberal Unionists are using ahistoric paradigms, while concepts of 'national character' were much more subtle and nuanced in their application in this period.[40] That said, attempts to define the British character, which would later become a fetish under Baldwin's leadership, began as a response to the challenge of Irish nationalism.[41] It was a character that had widespread appeal to the new electorate, but one that was based on traditional identities of religion, public behaviour, gender and locality rather than class or a consistent ideology. Where these identities were strongly associated with Gladstonian Liberalism, as in Wales, Liberal Unionism failed to establish itself. In the north of England, where class politics were beginning to take root in the 1890s, Liberal Unionism found it difficult to find an electorate. Despite this, in a number of northern constituencies, the apolitical, selfless commitment to the perceived benefits of the Union, allied to a stronger nonconformist tradition, won the Liberal Unionists support that would not have been forthcoming for a Conservative candidate. When the Liberal Unionists took eleven seats in northern England from the Liberals in 1895, they did not do so on a manifesto of Empire, or anti-Irish bigotry; rather they demonstrated what Patricia Lynch has described as 'the enduring popularity of supposedly outdated political traditions' and won as consistent Liberals, who put the needs of the whole community above those of any one ethnic, religious or class faction.[42]

Lubenow argued that, in 1886, 'political conflict became social only when parties and the parliamentary system failed to accommodate the diverse forces at work in the House of Commons.'[43] Between 1886 and 1895, the political structures of Britain were tested, not only by the constitutional challenge of the Irish Nationalists, but also by the rejection of the new political methodology by a group of politicians whose Liberalism compelled them to resist the dictatorial demands of their leader, their party whips and their activists. That the issue on which they divided was one of patriotism was largely immaterial at first and they proceeded to exercise an influence on government that has been unmatched by any small party in British political history. Had Gladstone not felt obliged by his overwhelming belief in his divine mission in Ireland to remain leader, it is likely that Hartington could have become leader of a re-united Liberal Party, which would have passed some measure of land purchase and local government in Ireland, after the initial imposition of mild coercion. The moderate Liberals would not have been able to resist the influence of Chamberlain, the Glaswegian radicals and T. W. Russell's faction. In reality, the pressing demands of an increasingly democratic and demanding electorate drove the Liberal Unionist Party to embrace a less high-minded nationalism in 1892, which provided common ground with their Conservative allies, while the advent of Chamberlain's leadership led to a renewed drive for constructive reform. That Salisbury and his lieutenants successfully resisted these demands and managed to exploit the fundamental divisions among the Liberal Unionists in 1895, was a crucial turning point for the Party. All that survived of the Liberal Unionists' principles, beyond the maintenance of the Union, was a commitment to the concept of a Liberal

empire which, in an age of aggressive imperialism, was insufficient to prevent the gradual defection of the independent nonconformist Unionists in a
series of crises after 1895.[44]

Once the Party leadership accepted the junior governmental positions
offered by the Conservatives and, perhaps most decisively, once the Tories won
a majority in 1895, the existence of the Party became an increased irrelevance.
Spurned by their own leaders, rejected by their Liberal friends as traitors and
distinctly uncomfortable among the flummery of the Primrose League, the
Liberal Unionists had to choose between principle and expedience. With
no real threat of a third Home Rule Bill after 1895 and with Chamberlain's
siren call of imperial expansion, the Party largely fell into disuse. The crucial
role that it played in bringing working men and nonconformists to support a
Conservative dominated alliance was ignored, firstly by Salisbury and then,
most seriously, by Balfour in 1902. The Liberal Unionist Party was thus
in no position to mount an effective resistance to Chamberlain's attempt to
overturn one of the central tenets of Liberalism, free trade, in 1903, at least
not outside Glasgow.[45]

The influence of Liberal Unionism, partly through the Chamberlain
dynasty, partly through the attitudes engendered by the years of constructive
Unionism of 1887–1892, has been sadly ignored. Stuart Ball and Eugenio
Biagini have recently suggested that there is a direct link between the Liberal
Unionists' ideologies and their presentation and those of the Conservatives
in the Baldwin years. Biagini believes that 'the Conservative Party took on
board the rhetoric and some of the policies of old liberalism,'[46] while Ball
quotes Hugh Cecil's metaphor for the Conservative Party in 1912: 'the waters
of which have come from many converging streams.'[47] In his view, as in
Jeremy Smith's, the twentieth-century Conservative Party's success partly lies
in its outspoken dislike of ideology and its cross-class appeal on issues such
as moderate reform, patriotism and defence of British liberties, typified by
Stanley Baldwin.[48] While these ideals have antecedents in the Conservative
Party, particularly in the rhetoric of Disraeli, the 'culture of conservatism
[which] transcended class in favour of the nation' only became convincingly
espoused by Conservatives with the alliance with Liberal Unionism, as this
culture owed more to the principles of Chamberlain and Hartington, than to
the sectarian, reactionary beliefs of Lord Salisbury.[49]

It is striking how few historians of the Conservative and Unionist Party
have given the Liberal Unionists any credit for the changing outlook of the
Tories in the early twentieth century. It was the future Poet Laureate, Alfred
Austin, who, in June 1886, asked, 'is it impossible to constitute a Party
of Common Sense?' which he foresaw as the result of the Unionist alliance

facing its first test at the polls.[50] Lord Kelvin spoke of the Unionist alliance as an example of 'government by common sense.'[51] The Liberal Unionists were the means by which the mid-Victorian tradition that the Liberals governed on behalf of the entire national community, rather than on behalf of sectional or class interests, became transmitted to the Conservatives, although it took the experience of a flirtation with protectionist dogma between 1903 and 1914 and the challenge of a global war to convince them. It is certainly true that the Conservatives needed to find a new position when faced with the challenge of Lloyd George's social reforms and the rise of the Labour Party and it was as 'the Conservative and Unionist Party' that they found this role during the First World War.[52] Jonathan Parry agrees with Gregory Phillips' conclusion that the Liberal Unionists taught the Conservatives to be 'more flexible.'[53] Parry has suggested that the Liberal Unionists provided the Conservatives with genuinely new elements in their appeal to a mass electorate. These included 'administrative probity, respect for property, individualism and economic carefulness' and Parry goes on to suggest that these new features are crucial in accounting for the Unionist Party's success in the 1920s and 1930s.[54] Austen Chamberlain continued to define himself as a Liberal Unionist, which may have contributed to his downfall as Unionist leader in 1922.[55] There is much work yet to be done on the legacy of Liberal Unionism, both on a cultural and a political level, but it cannot be denied that the imprint of the Party was still felt into the twentieth-century, both in Birmingham and beyond. [56] Exploring the connection between nineteenth century Liberalism and twentieth-century Conservatism requires advocates of the 'New Political History' to widen their perspectives and to take the Liberal Unionist Party as seriously as Parry, who has written that 'a Conservative Party guided by three Chamberlains, Churchill, Baldwin, Butler and Macmillan owed an enormous amount to Liberal Unionism.'[57]

APPENDICES

APPENDIX 1 – THE UNIONIST 'COMPACT': 'RESOLUTIONS' (N.D. – 1889) (DEVONSHIRE PAPERS 340.2205A)

1. That no seat held by a Conservative shall be attacked by a Liberal Unionist
2. That no seat held by a Liberal Unionist shall be attacked by a Conservative
3. That seats contested at the election of 1886 by Conservatives shall not be attacked by Liberal Unionists without the consent of the whips of both sections of the Unionist Party
4. That seats contested at the election of 1886 by Liberal Unionists shall not be attacked by Conservatives without the consent of the whips of both sections of the Unionist Party
5. That Gladstonian seats uncontested at the election of 1886 shall be attacked by Conservatives or Liberal Unionists as may seem most advisable having regard to local circumstances

6. That in the event of any difference the question of candidature shall, at the request of the local organisation, be referred to Mr Smith and Lord Hartington

7. That in all cases where the candidature has been decided upon, every effort shall be made to induce the electors of both sections of the Unionist Party to support the candidate

NB

It is not considered that

1. The Swansea District
2. The Mid Division of Glamorganshire
3. The Cirencester Division of Gloucestershire
4. The West Division of Edinburgh are held by Liberal Unionists.

APPENDIX 2: LIBERAL UNIONIST ORGANISING COUNCIL (*THE TIMES*, 21 MARCH 1889)

Elected Members

London , Middlesex and South-East Counties
Leedham White
W. A. Bell
W. J. Gandy
C. H. Bond

South-West Counties
Lewis Fry MP
Col. White-Thomson

Eastern Counties
R. T. Gurdon MP
W. C. Quilter MP

South Midlands
Col. Hollis
G. T. Llewellyn

West Midlands
J. Powell Williams MP
J. S. Baily

North Midlands
J. Ruston

Liverpool and Manchester
W. Oulton
H. T. Crook

Lancaster, etc
Thomas Brooks

Yorkshire
T. H. Morris
Thomas Marshall
C. W. Woodall
E. Laverack

Counties north of York and Lancaster
H. C. Howard
J. C. Backhouse

North Wales
Sir R. Cunliffe

South Wales
G. C. Thompson
Stephen Evans

Edinburgh and the North and East of Scotland
Hon. A. Elliot MP
T. D. Brodie
Captain Fletcher Campbell
Sir Donald Currie MP

Glasgow and West of Scotland
Sir William Thomson
Col. Buchanan
Alexander Cross
Robert Bird

Aberdeen and District
John Crombie jnr.

Liberal Union of Ireland
Sir R. Blennerhassett
J. T. Pim

Ulster
Thomas Sinclair
Thomas Harrison

Nominated by the Liberal Unionist Executive Committee

Lord Stalbridge
A. Craig Sellar MP
W. S. Caine MP
H. Hobhouse MP
W. Thorburn MP
James Grahame
Edwin Lawrence
H. O. Arnold-Forster
Robert Purvis
G. McCullagh

APPENDIX 3: MEMBERS PRESENT AT NATIONAL RADICAL UNION CONFERENCE, 1 JUNE 1887, BIRMINGHAM TOWN HALL (CARTWRIGHT PAPERS, C(A)1, BOX 99, UNNUMBERED BUNDLE)

MPs

J. W. Barclay
A. H. Brown
J. Chamberlain
D. H. Coghill
J. Collings
G. Dixon
Visc Ebrington
J. Goldsmid
H. James
W. Kenrick
Visc Lymington
W. Morrison
G. Pitt-Lewis
H. Story Maskelyne
H. Wiggin
J. Powell Williams

Others

H. O. Arnold-Forster
W. C. Cartwright
H. Daly
Admiral Maxse
J. Westlake
F. J. S. Foljambe
A. Cross (President of Glasgow Radical Union)
F. W. Maude
J. J. Jenkins

R. B. Martin
R. H. Elliot
E. Lawrence
R. Niven
Col. Hozier
Robert Bird (WSLUA Sec.)
Booth (Bradford LUA Sec.)

T. A. Watson (Bradford LUA chairman)
W. W. Walker (Wolverhampton LUA chairman)
W. A. Harrop (Rotherham LUA Sec.)
    Members from Radical Union branches in Glasgow, Edinburgh, Ayr, Swansea

APPENDIX 4: LIBERAL UNIONIST GENERAL ELECTION PERFORMANCES, 1886–1900

	Total LU candidates	Unopposed LU candidates	Total LU MPs returned	Total LU vote	% of national vote
1886	165	29	78	431,513	15%
1892	142	7	47	474,941	10%
1895	101	17	71	314,702	8%
1900	108	27	64	313,200	9%

APPENDIX 5: REGIONAL DISTRIBUTION OF LIBERAL UNIONIST CONSTITUENCIES, 1886–1918

South East

London

Islington West	1886–1892
Lambeth North	1895–1900
London University	1886–1906
Marylebone West	1895–1900
St. George's, Hanover Sq.	February 1887–1895
St. Pancras South	1886–1906
Mile End	January 1905–1906

South East – Excluding London

Hythe	1886–1895

East Anglia

Mid-Norfolk	1886–1892, April 1895–1895
S. Norfolk	1886–1898
Peterborough	1886–1889, 1895–1906
N. Suffolk (Lowestoft)	1886–1892
S. Suffolk (Sudbury)	1886–1906

Central

Biggleswade	1886–1892, 1895–1906
Aylesbury	1886–1918
Cirencester	1886–1892

Oxford University	1900–1914
Woodstock	1886–1891
Cricklade	1886–1892, 1895–1900

South-West

Wessex

Petersfield	1886–1892
Portsmouth	1886–1892
Southampton	1895–1906
Wilton	1886–1888

Bristol Region

Bath	1886–1906
Bristol North	1886–1892, 1895–1900
Gloucester	1895–1900
E. Somerset	1886–1906

Devon and Cornwall

Truro	1886–1906
Camborne	1895–1900
Bodmin	1886–1906
St. Ives	1886–1906
South Molton	1886-November 1891
Barnstaple	1886–1892, 1895–1900
Totnes	1886–1922
Tavistock	1886–1892

Midlands

West Midlands

Birmingham Bordesley	1886–1918
Birmingham Edgbaston	1886–1898
Birmingham Central	1886–1918
Birmingham North	1886–1918
Birmingham South	1886 1918
Birmingham West	1886–1914
Ross-on-Wye	1886–1906
Wellington	1886–1906
Ludlow	1886–1917
Burton-on-Trent	1900–1918
Handsworth	1886–1905
Lichfield	1892–1895
W. Staffordshire	1886–1906
Warwick and Leamington	1886–1906

Wolverhampton South	1886–1900
E. Worcestershire	1886–1914
Mid Worcestershire.	1886–1906
N. Worcestershire	1886–1887, 1895–1918

East Midlands

W. Derbyshire	1886–1918
Gt. Grimsby	1886–1892, March 1893–1895, August 1898– January 1910
Lincoln	1895–1906
Spalding	1895–1900
Nottingham West	1892–1895

Northern England

Peak-Don

Chesterfield	1886–1892
Doncaster	February 1888–1892

Lancastria

Barrow-in-Furness	1886-July 1890
Burnley	1886–1887
Bury	1886–1895
Northwich	1886-August 1887
Heywood	1895–1904
North Lonsdale	1895–1906
Rossendale	1886-January 1892
Liverpool Exchange	1895–1906
Manchester South	1895–1906
Newcastle-under-Lyme	1886–1892, 1900–1906
Stoke-on-Trent	1895–1900

Yorkshire

Bradford Central	1895–1906
Halifax	1900–1906
Wakefield	1895–1902
Colne Valley	1886–1892
Shipley	1895–1906
Skipton	1886–1892, 1895–1900

North England

Darlington	1895–1910
Durham	June 1898–1906
S.E. Durham	1886–1892, 1895–1898, 1900–January 1910
The Hartlepools	1886–January 1891
Tyneside	1900–1906

Wales

Carmarthen District	1895–1900
West Denbighshire	1886–1892
Mid-Glamorgan	1886–1887
Swansea District	1886–1887

Ireland

Belfast West	1892–1906
Dublin St Stephens	1892–1900
Dublin University	December 1895–1903
Londonderry South	1886–1916
S. Tyrone	1886–1916

Scotland

Scotland, Highlands and Islands

Inverness Burghs	1886–1892, 1895–1906
Invernesshire	1886–1892
Orkney and Shetland	1900–1902
Sutherlandshire	1900–1906
Wick Burghs	1892–1896, 1900–1906

Scotland, East

E. Aberdeenshire	1900–1906
Edinburgh & St. Andrews Universities	1900–1916
Edinburgh South	1895–1899, 1900–1906
Edinburgh West	1886–1887, 1892–1918
Falkirk Burghs	1886–1892, 1895–1906
Forfarshire	1886–1892
Peebles & Selkirk	1886–1906
W. Perthshire	1886–1900
Roxburghshire	1886–1892
St. Andrews Burghs	1886–1903

Scotland, West

Ayr Burghs	1886–1888
N. Ayrshire	1886–January 1910
S. Ayrshire	1886–1892, 1895–1906
Dumfriesshire	1886–1895, 1900–1906
Glasgow Camlachie	1892–1908
Glasgow St Rollox	1886–1892, 1900–1906
Glasgow Tradeston	1886–January 1910
Greenock	1886–1892, 1895–1900
Partick	1886–1906
N.E.Lanarkshire	September 1901–1904

APPENDIX 6: LIBERAL UNIONIST MPS WITH CONSTITUENCY AND DATES HELD

MP	Constituency	Dates held
Sir A. Agnew	Edinburgh South	1900–1906 (resigned)
L. S. Amery	Birmingham South	1911–1918
Sir W. R. Anson	Oxford University	1899–1914 (died)
H. T. Anstruther	St. Andrews	1886–1903 (resigned)
W. Anstruther-Gray	St. Andrews	1906- January 1910 (defeated)
		December 1910–1918
H. O. Arnold–Forster	Belfast West	1892–1906 (resigned)
	Croydon	1906–1909 (died)
Sir W. Arrol	S. Ayrshire	1895–1906 (retired)
J. W. Barclay	Forfarshire	1886–1892 (defeated)
Visc. Baring	Biggleswade	1886–1892 (defeated)
A. Barnes	Chesterfield	1886–1892 (defeated)
H. Bass	W. Staffordshire	1886–1898 (died)
H. F. Beaumont	Colne Valley	1886–1892 (retired)
W. Bickford-Smith	Truro	1886–1892 (retired)
M. Biddulph	Ross-on-Wye	1886–1900 (retired)
J. C. Bigham	Liverpool, Exchange	1895–1897 (appointed judge)
A. Bignold	Wick Burghs	1900–1906 (Con thereafter)
T. B. Bolitho	St Ives	1887–1900 (retired)
W. L. Boyle	Mid-Norfolk	Jan 1910 – 1918 (died)
J. Bright	Birmingham Central	1886–1889 (died)
J. A. Bright	Birmingham Central	1889–1895 (resigned)
A. H. Brown	Wellington	1886–1906 (retired)
T. R. Buchanan	Edinburgh West	1886–1887 (Lib thereafter)

MP	Constituency	Dates held
C. R. Burn	Torquay	Dec 1910–1923 (retired)
W. S. Caine	Barrow-in-Furness	1886–1890 (resigned)
J. Caldwell	Glasgow St Rollox	1886–1890 (Ind thereafter)
T. C. P. Calley	Cricklade	Jan–Dec 1910 (defeated)
J. Campbell	Manchester South	1895–1900 (succ. to Lords)
R. F. Campbell	Ayr Burghs	1886–1888 (died)
Lord E. Cavendish	W. Derbyshire	1886–1891 (died)
R. F. Cavendish	N. Lonsdale	1895–1906 (Lib thereafter)
S. Cavendish	Rossendale	1886–1891 (succ. to Lords)
V. C. W. Cavendish	W. Derbyshire	1891–1908 (succ. to Lords)
J. Chamberlain	Birmingham West	1886–1914 (died)
J. A. Chamberlain	E. Worcestershire	1892–1914 (resigned)
R. Chamberlain	Islington West	1886–1892 (defeated)
P. Clive	Ross-on-Wye	1900–1906, Jan 1908–1918 (killed in action)
J. A. Clyde	Edinburgh West	1909–1918
T. H. Cochrane	N. Ayrshire	1892–Jan. 1910 (defeated)
D. H. Coghill	Newcastle-under-Lyme	1886–1892 (defeated)
	Stoke-on-Trent	1895–1900 (Con thereafter)
H. A. Colefax	Manchester South West	Jan 1910–Dec 1910 (defeated)
J. Collings	Birmingham Bordesley	1886–1918
Lord A. F. Compton	Biggleswade	1895–1906 (defeated)
A. C. Corbett	Glasgow Tradeston	1886–1908 (Ind Lib therafter)
J. Corbett	Mid Worcestershire	1886–1892 (retired)
L. H. Courtney	Bodmin	1886–1899 (Ind Lib thereafter)
R. Cox	Edinburgh South	1895–1899 (died)
A. Cross	Glasgow Camlachie	1892–1909 (Lib thereafter)
S. B. Crossley	N. Suffolk (Lowestoft)	1886–1892 (retired)
	Halifax	1900–1906 (defeated)
W. Crossman	Portsmouth	1886–1892 (retired)
D. Currie	W. Perthshire	1886–1900 (retired)
L. Darwin	Lichfield	1892–1895 (defeated)
G. Dixon	Birmingham Edgbaston	1886–1898 (died)
G. Doughty	Grimsby	1898—Jan 1910 (defeated)
		Dec 1910–1914 (died)
A. R. D. Elliot	Roxburghshire	1886–1892 (defeated)
	Durham	1898—Feb 1905 (Ind Lib thereafter)
H. F. Elliot	N. Ayrshire	1886–1892 (resigned)
B. G. Falle	Portsmouth	Jan 1910–1918
H. B. Farquar	Marylebone West	1895–1898 (succ. to Lords)
R. B. Finlay	Inverness Burghs	1886–1892 (defeated)
		1895–1906 (defeated)
	Edinburgh & St. Andrews Universities	Jan 1910–1916 (ennobled)
J. F. Flannery	Shipley	1895–1906 (resigned)
H. Fortescue	Tavistock	1886–1892 (retired)
Sir M. Foster	London University	1900–1903 (Lib thereafter)

MP	Constituency	Dates held
L. Fry	Bristol North	1886–1892, 1895–1900 (retired)
J. L. Gibbons	Wolverhampton South	1898–1900 (retired)
J. Goldsmid	St Pancras South	1886–1896 (died)
J. Gordon	Londonderry South	1900–1916 (appointed judge)
G. Goschen	St George's, Hanover Sq	1887–1893 (Cons thereafter)
T. F. Grove	Wilton	1886–1888 (Lib. thereafter)
W. C. Gull	Barnstaple	1895–1900 (defeated)
R. T. Gurdon	Mid-Norfolk	1886–1892, April-July 1895
E. Hain	St Ives	1900–1904 (Lib thereafter)
Sir A. S. Haslam	Newcastle-under-Lyme	1900–1906 (defeated)
G. W. Hastings	E. Worcestershire	1886–1892 (expelled)
Sir H. Havelock-Allan	S. E. Durham	1886–1892 (defeated) 1895–1897 (retired)
A. Henderson	W. Staffordshire	1898–1906 (defeated)
E. Heneage	Grimsby	1886–1892 (defeated) 1893–1895 (defeated)
J. W. Hills	Durham	1906–1918
Sir B. Hingley	N. Worcestershire	1886–1887 (Lib thereafter)
H. Hobhouse	E. Somerset	1886–1906 (retired)
A. Hopkinson	Cricklade	1895–1898 (retired)
R. Hunt	Ludlow	1903–1918 (retired)
Sir H. James	Bury	1886–1895 (ennobled)
E. Jardine	E. Somerset	January 1910–1918
R. Jardine	Dumfriesshire	1886–1892 (retired)
Sir J. J. Jenkins	Carmarthen District	1895–1903 (Lib thereafter)
H. M. Jessel	St. Pancras South	1896–1906, Jan 1910–1918 (retired)
G. Kemp	Heywood	1895–1904 (Lib thereafter)
W. Kenny	Dublin St Stephens	1895–1898 (appointed judge)
W. Kenrick	Birmingham North	1886–1899 (retired)
F. W. Lambton	S. E. Durham	1900–Jan 1910 (defeated)
E. Lawrence	Truro	1895–1906 (defeated)
T. Lea	Londonderry South	1886–1900 (retired)
W. E. H. Lecky	Dublin University	1895–1903 (retired)
F. S. Leveson-Gower	Sutherlandshire	1900–1906 (defeated)
H. Levy-Lawson	Mile End	1905–1906 (defeated)
	Mile End	Jan 1910–1916 (succ. to Lords)
G. A. Lloyd	W. Staffordshire	Jan 1910–1918
J. Lubbock	London University	1886–1900 (ennobled)
A. Lyttelton	Warwick & Leamington	1895–1906 (defeated)
	St. George's Hanover Sq.	1906–1913 (died)
J. C. Lyttelton	Mid Worcestershire	Jan 1910–1916 (resigned)
C. Fraser Mackintosh	Invernesshire	1886–1892 (defeated)
H. J. Mackinder	Glasgow Camlachie	Jan 1910–1922 (defeated)
F. W. MacLean	Woodstock	1886–1891 (appointed judge)
A. W. Maconochie	E. Aberdeenshire	1900–1906 (defeated)

MP	Constituency	Dates held
Sir P. Magnus	London University	1906–1922 (retired)
R. B. Martin	Mid Worcestershire	1892–1906 (retired)
M. Story Maskelyne	Cricklade	1886–1892 (defeated)
W. J. Maxwell	Dumfriesshire	1892–1895 (defeated)
		1900–1906 (retired)
C. McArthur	Liverpool Exchange	1897–1906 (defeated)
L. McIver	Edinburgh West	1895–1909 (retired)
E. Meysey-Thompson	Handsworth	1906–1922
H. Meysey-Thompson	Handsworth	1892–1906 (ennobled)
J. T. Middlemore	Birmingham North	1899–1918
F. B. Mildmay	Totnes	1886–1922 (ennobled)
Sir L. W. Molesworth	Bodmin	1900–1906 (retired)
C. J. Monk	Gloucester	1895–1900 (retired)
R. J. More	Ludlow	1886–1903 (died)
Visc. Morpeth	Birmingham South	1904–1911 (succ. to Lords)
W. Morrison	Skipton	1886–1892 (defeated)
		1895–1900 (defeated)
E. F. Morrison-Bell	Ashburton	1908–Jan 1910
		Dec 1910–1918
E. Parkes	Birmingham Central	1895–1918
A. Pease	Darlington	1895–1898 (died)
H. P. Pease	Darlington	1898–Jan 1910, Dec 1910–1923
		(ennobled)
A. W. Peel	Warwick & Leamington	1886–1895 (retired)
W. R. W. Peel	Manchester South	1900–1906 (resigned)
J. Pender	Wick Burghs	1892–1896 (died)
H. Petty-Fitzmaurice	W. Derbyshire	1908–1918
G. Pitt-Lewis	Barnstaple	1886–1892 (retired)
Sir R. Pole-Carew	Bodmin	1910–1916 (resigned)
H. F. Pollock	Spalding	1895–1900 (defeated)
Sir R. Purvis	Peterborough	1895–1906 (defeated)
W. C. Quilter	S. Suffolk, Sudbury	1886–1906 (defeated)
W. E. C. Quilter	S. Suffolk, Sudbury	Jan 1910–1918
R. F. Ratcliff	Burton-on-Trent	1900–1918 (retired)
Sir W. H. Rattigan	N.E. Lanarkshire	1901–1904 (died)
E. J. Reed	Cardiff Borough	1904–1906 (retired)
T. Richardson	The Hartlepools	1886–1891 (died)
T. Richardson	The Hartlepools	1895–1900 (resigned)
F. J. de Rothschild	Aylesbury	1886–1898 (died)
L. N. de Rothschild	Aylesbury	Jan 1910–1923
L. W. de Rothschild	Aylesbury	1899–Jan 1910 (retired)
T. W. Russell	S. Tyrone	1886–1902 (Ind thereafter)
P. Rylands	Burnley	1886–1887 (died)
J. St. Aubyn	St Ives	1886–1887 (succ. to Lords)
C. Seely	Nottingham West	1892–1895 (retired)
C. H. Seely	Lincoln	1895–1906 (de-selected)

MP	Constituency	Dates held
A. C. Sellar	Partick	1886–1890 (died)
Sir J. B. Simeon	Southampton	1895–1906 (retired)
W. P. Sinclair	Falkirk Burghs	1886–1892 (defeated)
H. C. Smith	Tyneside	1900–1906 (retired)
J. P. Smith	Partick	1890–1906 (defeated)
J. W. Spear	Tavistock	1900–1906 (defeated)
		Dec 1910–1918
H. M. Stanley	Lambeth North	1895–1900 (resigned)
A. Strauss	Camborne	1895–1900 (defeated)
J. Stroyan	W. Perthshire	1900–1906 (defeated)
T. Sutherland	Greenock	1886–1900 (retired)
C. R. M. Talbot	Mid-Glamorganshire	1886–1887 (never officially joined LUs)
F. Taylor	S. Norfolk	1886–1898 (retired)
W. Thorburn	Peebles & Selkirk	1886–1906 (defeated)
Sir J. B. Tuke	Edinburgh & St. Andrews Universities	1900–1910 (retired)
R. Verdin	Northwich	1886–1887 (died)
G. R. Vernon	S. Ayrshire	1886–1892 (retired)
C. P. Villiers	Wolverhampton South	1886–1898 (died)
H. H. Vivian	Swansea District	1886–1887 (Lib thereafter)
N. Wallop	South Molton	1886–1891 (succ. To Lords)
J. L. Wanklyn	Bradford Central	1895–1906 (retired)
J. C. Wason	Orkney and Shetland	1900–1902 (Ind thereafter)
E. Watkin	Hythe	1886–1895 (retired)
W. C. de M. Wentworth-Fitzwilliam	Wakefield	1895–1902 (succ. to Lords)
W. H. Wentworth-Fitzwilliam	Doncaster	1888–1892 (defeated)
W. J. Wentworth-Fitzwilliam	Peterborough	1886–1889 (died)
W. C. West	West Denbighshire	1886–1892 (defeated)
H. Wiggin	Handsworth	1886–1892 (retired)
J. C. Williams	Truro	1892–1895 (retired)
J. Powell Williams	Birmingham South	1886–1904 (died)
Sir F. Willis	Bristol North	1900–1906 (retired)
J. Wilson	Falkirk Burghs	1895–1903 (Lib thereafter)
J. Wilson	Glasgow St. Rollox	1900–1906 (defeated)
J. W. Wilson	N. Worcestershire	1895–1903 (Lib thereafter)
A. B. Winterbotham	Cirencester	1886–1887 (Lib thereafter)
E. R. Wodehouse	Bath	1886–1906 (retired)
Visc Wolmer	Petersfield	1886–1892 (resigned)
	Edinburgh West	1892–1895 (succ. to Lords)

APPENDIX 7: LIBERAL UNIONIST BY-ELECTIONS 1886–1912 (NOT INCLUDING UNOPPOSED ELECTIONS)

* indicates LU seat before by-election
@ indicates contest against Conservative
# indicates contest against Independent
^ indicates 3 way contest between LU, Cons and Liberal
° indicates 3 way contest between LU, Lib and Labour
% indicates 3 way contest between LU, Lib and Ind
$ indicates 4 way contest between LU, Lib, Scottish Lab and Scottish Prohibition

Constituency	Date of by-election	LU Candidate	Majority
Victories			
St. George's, Hanover Sq.	9 February 1887	G. Goschen	76% (4,090)
Doncaster	23 February 1888	W. H. Wentworth-Fitzwilliam	51% (211)
Birmingham Central*	15 April 1889	J. A. Bright	68% (2,980)
Partick*	11 February 1890	J. P. Smith	51% (219)
Grimsby	6 March 1893	E. Heneage	56% (964)
Mid-Norfolk	23 April 1895	R. T. Gurdon	51% (208)
Warwick and Leamington*	23 May 1895	A. Lyttelton	56% (579)
Edinburgh West*	29 May 1895	L. McIver	55% (708)
Dublin University	6 December 1895	W. E. H. Lecky	63% (746)

St. Pancras South*	28 January 1896	H. M. Jessel	66% (1,256)
Liverpool Exchange*	10 November 1897	C. McArthur	51% (54)
Wolverhampton South*	3 February 1898	J. L. Gibbons	51% (111)
W. Staffordshire	10 May 1898	A. Henderson	55% (803)
Durham	30 June 1898	A. R. D. Elliot	51% (65)
Grimsby	2 August 1898	G. Doughty	59% (1,751)
Darlington	17 September 1898	H. P. Pease	56% (688)
Manchester South*	25 May 1900	W. R. W. Peel	61% (2,039)
London University%	6–10 February 1900	M. Foster	47% (408)
N.E. Lanarkshire°	26 September 1901	W. Rattigan	43% (904)
Warwick and Leamington	23 October 1903	A. Lyttelton	52% (190)
Ludlow*	22 Dececember 1903	R. Hunt	56% (970)
Birmingham South*	26 February 1904	Viscount Morpeth	70% (3,076)
Mile End	12 January 1905	H. Levy-Lawson	51% (78)
Ashburton	17 January 1908	E. F. Morrison-Bell	53% (559)
Ross-on-Wye	31 January 1908	P. A. Clive	56% (1,019)

Defeats

Leith Burghs%	20 August 1886	W. Jacks	21% (2,705)
Liverpool Exchange	26 January 1887	G. Goschen	49.9% (7)
St. Austell	18 May 1887	E. B. Willyams	48% (211)
Glasgow Bridgeton	2 August 1887	E. Ashley	41% (1,401)
Northwich*	13 August 1887	Lord H. Grosvenor	44% (1,129)
Edinburgh West*	18 February 1888	T. Raleigh	49.6% (46)
Dundee	16 February 1888	H. Daly	35% (3,639)
Ayr Burghs*	15 June 1888	E. Ashley	49% (53)
Dewsbury	16 November 1888	H. O. Arnold-Forster	40% (2,103)
Govan	18 January 1889	J. Pender	43% (1,101)
W. Fife	5 July 1889	R. Wemyss	44% (793)
Peterborough*	7 October 1889	R. Purvis	47% (251)
Elgin & Nairn	8 October 1889	C. B. Logan	44% (529)
Stoke-on-Trent	14 March 1890	W. S. Allen	41% (1,231)
The Hartlepools*	21 January 1891	Sir W. Gray	48% (298)
South Molton*	13 November 1891	C. Buller	42% (1,112)
Rossendale*	23 January 1892	T. Brooks	44% (1,218)
Kirkcaldy	11 March 1892	R. Cox	37% (1,066)
Newcastle-upon-Tyne	25 August 1892	P. Ralli	46% (1,739)
Luton	29 September 1892	O. T. Duke	49% (242)
E. Aberdeenshire	10 December 1892	F. S. Russell	41% (1,260)
Gateshead	24 February 1893	P. Ralli	46% (868)
Hawick Burghs	27 March 1894	R. W. M. Fullarton	44% (647)

Leith Burghs	26 March 1894	W. A. Bell	45% (131)
Lichfield*	26 February 1896	L. Darwin	47% (528)
Wick Burghs	2 June 1896	W. C. Smith	44% (212)
Halifax°	3 March 1897	S. B. Crossley	41% (412)
S.E. Durham*	3 February 1898	F. W. Lambton	49% (275)
S. Norfolk*	12 May 1898	J. S. Holmes	42% (1,330)
Launceston	3 August 1898	F. Willis	42% (1,088)
Edinburgh East	23 June 1899	H. G. Younger	38% (1,930)
Mid-Armagh@	13 February 1900	J. Gordon	36% (1,401)
Bury	10 May 1902	H. Levy-Lawson	47% (414)
Orkney and Shetland%	18–19 November 1902	T. V. S. Angier	14% (1,672)
Camborne	8 April 1903	A. Strauss	45% (689)
St. Andrews Burghs*	17 September 1903	W. Anstruther-Gray	49% (36)
Gateshead	20 January 1904	Visc Morpeth	46% (1,205)
Buteshire	3 March 1905	E. T. Salvesen	49% (34)
Bodmin	24 July 1906	G. J. Sandys	44% (1,093)
Wolverhampton East	5 May 1908	L. S. Amery	50% (8)
Dundee$	9 May 1908	G. W. Baxter	27% (2,709)
Edinburgh South	4 March 1909	H. B. Cox	46% (1,221)
Hawick Burghs	5 March 1909	H. J. Mackinder	4% (520)
E. Denbighshire	2 April 1909	F. H. Cunliffe	36% (2,721)
Edinburgh East	16 April 1909	P. J. Ford	47% (458)
South Shields	27 October 1910	R. E. Williams	38% (3,019)
Glasgow Tradeston	6 July 1911	J. H. Watts	42% (1,674)
Middleton	2 August 1911	W. A. Hewins	49% (411)
Edinburgh East	2 February 1912	J. G. Jameson	45% (925)
Glasgow St Rollox	26 February 1912	F. A. Macquisten	49% (469)

NOTES

Introduction

1. See W. Harcourt's letters to J. Chamberlain, Chamberlain Papers, Cadbury Research Room, University of Birmingham. For the Stanley split, see R. Strachey, *Millicent Garrett Fawcett* (London, 1931), pp.128–9.
2. J. St. Loe Strachey, *The Adventure of Living: A Subjective Autobiography* (London, 1922), p.9.
3. M. Jeune, *Memories of Fifty Years* (London, 1909), p.243. See also E. Fitzmaurice, *The Life of Granville George Leveson Gower, Second Earl Granville, 1815–1891, Vol. 2* (London, 1905), p.494.
4. A. E. Pease, *Elections and Recollections* (London, 1932), p.171.
5. G. R. Askwith, *Lord James of Hereford* (London, 1930), p.189.
6. *British Weekly*, 10 December 1886.
7. Askwith, *Lord James of Hereford*, p.189.
8. R. B. Brett's journal, 29 May 1886, M.V. Brett (ed.), *Letters and Journals of Reginald, Viscount Esher, Vol. 1* (London, 1934), p.126.
9. *Inverness Courier*, 20 July 1886.
10. J. Morley, *Life of W. E. Gladstone, Vols. 2 & 3* (London, 1911); J. L. Hammond, *Gladstone and the Irish Nation* (London, 1938); M. Sayers, 'Gladstone's Home Rule legacy: Philip Kerr and the making of the 1920 Government of Ireland Bill' in M. E. Daly and T. H. Hoppen (eds.), *Gladstone: Ireland and Beyond* (Dublin, 2011), pp.45–63.
11. M. Bentley, *The Climax of Liberal Politics: British Liberalism in Theory and Practice 1868–1914* (London, 1987), p.22.
12. D. G. Boyce, *The Irish Question and British Politics, 1868–1986* (Basingstoke, 2nd ed., 1996); A. O'Day, *Irish Home Rule, 1867–1921* (Manchester, 1998); D. G. Boyce and A. O'Day (eds.), *The Ulster Crisis, 1885–1921* (Basingstoke, 2006); P. Bull, '"Irish Protestants feel this betrayal deeply …": home rule, Rome rule and nonconformity' in D. G. Boyce and R. Swift (eds), *Problems and Perspectives in Irish History since 1800: Essays in honour of Patrick Buckland* (Dublin, 2004); D. G. Boyce and A. O'Day (eds.), *Defenders of the Union: A Survey of British and Irish Unionism since 1801* (London, 2001). Despite the title of the latter, the Liberal Unionist Party is dismissed in two pages, pp.105–106.

13. J. Loughlin, *Gladstone, Home Rule and the Ulster Question, 1882–1893* (London: 1986); J. Loughlin, 'Joseph Chamberlain, English Nationalism and the Ulster Question', *History*, 77, pp.202–219; J. Loughlin, *The British Monarchy and Ireland, 1800 to the Present* (Cambridge, 2007). See also, G.K. Peatling, 'Victorian Imperial theorist? Goldwin Smith and Ireland' in P. Gray (ed.), *Victoria's Ireland? Irishness and Britishness, 1837–1901* (Dublin, 2004). For an effective counter to these views, see P. Mandler, '"Race" and "nation" in Mid-Victorian thought' in S. Collini et al (eds.), *History, Religion and Culture: British Intellectual History, 1750–1950* (Cambridge, 2000), pp.242–244.

14. F. Thompson, *The End of Liberal Ulster: Land Agitation and Land Reform* (Belfast, 2001); G. Walker, *A History of the Ulster Unionist Party: Protest, Pragmatism and Pessimism* (Manchester, 2004); G. Walker, 'Thomas Sinclair, Presbyterian Liberal Unionist' in R. English and G. Walker (eds.), *Unionism in Modern Ireland: New Perspectives on Politics and Culture* (Basingstoke, 1996), pp.19–40. For a recent, more nuanced view of Irish Unionism, see A. Jackson, *Ireland 1798–1998: War Peace and Beyond* (Chichester, 2nd ed., 2010), pp.212–241.

15. J. Loughlin, 'Creating "A Social and Geographical Fact": Regional Identity and the Ulster Question 1880s-1920s', *Past and Present*, 195 (2007), pp.159–160.

16. P. Marsh, *The Discipline of Popular Government: Lord Salisbury's Domestic Statecraft 1881–1902* (Hassocks, 1978).

17. R. Shannon, *The Age of Salisbury, 1881–1902: Unionism and Empire* (London, 1996).

18. M. Bentley, *Lord Salisbury's World: Conservative Environments in late Victorian Britain* (Cambridge, 2001).

19. E. H. H. Green, *The Crisis of Conservatism: The Politics, Economics and Ideology of the British Conservative Party, 1880–1914* (London, 1995).

20. The most effective recent study of Salisbury's re-alignment of the Conservatives is F. Cammarano, *"To Save England from Decline" The National Party of Common Sense: British Conservatism and the Challenge of Democracy (1885–1892)* (Lanham, 2001).

21. D. Steele, *Salisbury: A Political Biography* (London, 1999).

22. R. Blake and H. Cecil (eds.), *Salisbury: The Man and his Policies* (Basingstoke, 1987). A. Roberts, *Salisbury: Victorian Titan* (London, 1999) has some useful anecdotes, mainly derived from the author's close association with the remaining aristocratic Tory grandees, but is not a serious academic study.

23. G. L. Goodman, 'Liberal Unionism: The Revolt of the Whigs', *Victorian Studies*, 3 (1959), p.189. See also: P. Fraser, 'The Liberal Unionist Alliance: Chamberlain, Hartington and the Conservatives, 1886–1904', *English Historical Review*, 77 (1962), pp.53–78; J. Cornford, 'The Transformation of Conservatism in the Late Nineteenth Century', *Victorian Studies*, 7 (1963), pp.35–77. This idea was perhaps encouraged by Northcote's comment in his journal in April 1880 that 'a Conservative cave may be formed on the Liberal side ... we may ... ultimately bring some of them to take part in a Conservative cabinet.' Quoted in A. Lang, *Sir Stafford Northcote, First Earl of Iddesleigh, Vol. 2* (London, 1890), p.150.

24. T. J. Spinner, *George Joachim Goschen: The Transformation of a Victorian Liberal* (Cambridge, 1973) p.122.

25. A. Hawkins, *British Party Politics 1852–1886*, (Basingstoke, 1998), p.285.

26. W. C. Lubenow, *Parliamentary Politics and the Home Rule Crisis: The British House of Commons in 1886* (Oxford, 1988), p.208. On the crisis of 1886, see also A. B. Cooke and J. Vincent, *The Governing Passion: Cabinet Government and Party Politics in Britain, 1885–86* (Hassocks, 1974).

27. See also D. Southgate, *The Passing of the Whigs, 1832–1886* (Basingstoke, 1962).

28.   R. Haggard, *The Persistence of Victorian Liberalism* (London, 2001).

29.   J. P. Parry, 'The Quest for Leadership in Unionist politics, 1886–1956' *Parliamentary History*, 12 (1993), p.300. See, for example, A. Sykes, *The Rise and Fall of British Liberalism, 1776–1988* (London, 1997).

30.   See A. V. Dicey, *England's Case against Home Rule* (London, 1886); W. E. H. Lecky, *An Irish Historian on Home Rule for Ireland* (London, 1889); Goldwin Smith, *Dismemberment No Remedy* (London, 1886). Smith is, however, condemned by Peatling for his 'intellectual inadequacies and anti-Irish prejudice'. Peatling, 'Victorian imperial theorist', p.36.

31.   For the limitations of class as an analytical tool, see D. Cannadine, *Class in Britain* (London, 1998), pp.11–17; P. J. Joyce, *Visions of the People: Industrial England and the Question of Class 1848–1914* (Cambridge, 1991); E. F. Biagini and A. Reid (eds.), *Currents of Radicalism: Popular Radicalism, Organised Labour and Party Politics in Britain, 1850–1914* (Cambridge, 1991); R. McWilliam, *Popular Politics in Nineteenth Century England*, Chap. 2, 'From the old analysis to the new' (London 1998), pp.14–29.

32.   The best is R. Jay, *Joseph Chamberlain: A Political Study* (Oxford, 1981), although the most revealing is still J. L. Garvin, *The Life of Joseph Chamberlain, Vols. 2 & 3* (London, 1933). See also P. Marsh, *Joseph Chamberlain: Entrepreneur in Politics* (London, 1994); D. Judd, *Radical Joe* (London, 1977); P. Fraser, *Joseph Chamberlain: Radicalism and Empire, 1868–1914* (London , 1966); J. E. Powell, *Joseph Chamberlain* (London, 1977); T. L. Crosby, *Joseph Chamberlain: A Most Radical Imperialist* (London, 2011).

33.   T. A. Jenkins, 'The Funding of the Liberal Unionist Party and the Honours System' *English Historical Review,* 105 (1990), pp.920–938.

34.   B. H. Holland, *The Life of Spencer Compton, Eighth Duke of Devonshire, Vols. 1 & 2* (London, 1911); P. Jackson*, The Last of the Whigs: A Political Biography of Lord Hartington* (London, 1994) was of little interest to students of Liberal Unionism.

35.   Askwith, *Lord James of Hereford.*

36.   A. R. D. Elliot, *The Life of Lord Goschen, Vols. 1 & 2* (London, 1911).

37.   J. Newton, *W.S. Caine, M.P.* (London, 1907).

38.   J. Collings and J. L. Green, *Life of the Right Hon. Jesse Collings* (London, 1920).

39.   M. C. Hurst, *Joseph Chamberlain and Liberal Reunion: the Round Table Conference of 1887* (Newton Abbot, 1970).

40.   M. Roberts, '"Villa Toryism" and Popular Conservatism in Leeds, 1885–1902, *Historical Journal,* 49 (2006), p.221. See also, M. Brodie, *The Politics of the Poor: The East End of London, 1885–1914* (Oxford, 2004); A. Windscheffel, *Popular Conservatism in Imperial London, 1868–1906* (Woodbridge, 2007); T. G. Otte, '"Avenge England's dishonour": By-elections, Parliament and the Politics of Foreign Policy in 1898', *English Historical Review*, 491 (2006), pp.385–428.

41.   Cooke and Vincent, *The Governing Passion*, p.20. Perhaps this conclusion is to be expected as Cooke and Vincent make no reference to any official or unpublished Liberal Unionist material, preferring the manuscripts of the 'high' politicians. Christopher Harvie accuses Cooke and Vincent of having 'relegated the [Liberal Unionists'] intellectuals' intervention to a booth in a sideshow.' C. Harvie, 'Ideology and Home Rule: James Bryce, A.V. Dicey and Ireland, 1880–1887', *English Historical Review*, 91 (1976), p.300.

42.   Lubenow, *Parliamentary Politics*, p.208.

43.   W. C. Lubenow, *Liberal Intellectuals and Public Culture in Modern Britain, 1815–1914* (Woodbridge, 2010), pp.192–203.

44.   E. Biagiani, *British Democracy and Irish Nationalism, 1876–1906* (Cambridge, 2007), chap. 5 'Joseph and his brethren: the rise and fall of Radical Unionism', pp.217–274.

45. T. A. Jenkins, 'Hartington, Chamberlain and the Unionist Alliance, 1886–1895', *Parliamentary History*, 11 (1992), pp.108–138.

46. P. Davis, 'The Liberal Unionist Party and the Irish Policy of Lord Salisbury's Government, 1886–1892,' *Historical Journal*, 18 (1975), pp.85–104.

47. J. D. Fair, 'From Liberal to Conservative: The Flight of the Liberal Unionists after 1886', *Victorian Studies*, 30 (1986), pp.291–314.

48. G. D. Phillips, 'The Whig Lords and Liberalism, 1886–1893', *Historical Journal*, 24 (1981), pp.167–173. Philips noted that although 4/5 of the Liberal Unionist peers were owners of vast amounts of land, there was no relationship between the social composition of the Unionist peers and their political behaviour.

49. G. R. Searle, *Country before Party: Coalition and the Idea of 'National Government, in Modern Britain, 1885–1987* (London, 1995), p.28.

50. J.M. Lawrence, 'Popular Politics and the Limitations of Party: Wolverhampton, 1867–1900', in Biagini and Reid (eds.), *Currents of Radicalism*, pp.65–87.

51. J. M. Lawrence, *Speaking for the People: Party, Language and Popular Politics in England, 1867–1914* (Cambridge, 1998).

52. C. M. M. MacDonald, 'Locality, Tradition and Language in the Evolution of Scottish Unionism: A Case Study, Paisley, 1886–1910', in C. M. M. MacDonald (ed.), *Unionist Scotland, 1800–1997* (Edinburgh, 1998), pp.52–72.

53. J. R. Moore, 'Liberal Unionism and the Home Rule Crisis in Leicester, 1885–1892', *Midland History*, 26 (2001), pp.177–197; J. R. Moore, 'Manchester Liberalism and the Unionist Secession, 1886–1895', *Manchester Regional History Review*, 15 (2001), pp.31–40.

54. I. Cawood, 'The Unionist "Compact" in West Midland Politics 1891–1895,' *Midland History*, 30 (2005), pp.92–111.

55. G. D. Goodlad, 'Liberals and the Home Rule Issue, November 1885–July 1886: The Leaders and the Rank and File with Special Reference to Certain Localities', PhD Thesis, (Cambridge, 1988), p.345.

56. C. Burness, *'Strange Associations': The Irish Question and the Making of Scottish Unionism, 1886–1918* (East Linton, 2003). See also J. T. Ward, 'Liberal Unionism in Scotland', *Contemporary Review*, 251, (1987), pp.92–96.

57. S. E. Koss, *The Rise and Fall of the Political Press in Britain, Vol. 1: The nineteenth century* (London, 1981), pp.306–339.

58. V. Barbery, 'From Platform to Polling Booth', PhD thesis (Cambridge, 2007), ii.

59. Cawood, 'The Unionist "Compact"', pp.93–95.

60. I. Cawood, 'Joseph Chamberlain, the Conservative Party and the Leamington Spa Candidature Dispute of 1895,' *Historical Research* 79 (2006), pp.554–577.

61. See also M. Fforde, *Conservatism and Collectivism, 1886–1914* (Edinburgh, 1990).

62. M. Taylor, 'The Rise and Fall of the "New Political History" 1979–2008', paper delivered at Languages of Politics conference, University of Durham, 3 April 2009.

63. For a refutation of the sociological explanation of the dominance of Unionism between 1886 and 1906, see A. Windscheffel's excellent historiographical survey in Windscheffel, *Popular Conservatism*, chap. 1, 'Relocating the "transformation" of late-Victorian Conservatism', pp.1–31.

64. Lawrence, *Speaking for the People*, p.170.

65. Most famously in the publication of the articles 'Parnellism and Crime' in 1887, despite serious doubts as to the authenticity of all the correspondence as expressed by many Liberal Unionists.

66. Most consistently: *Nineteenth Century*; *Pall Mall Gazette*; *Edinburgh Review*; *Contemporary Review*; *Annual Register*.
67. J. W. Ridgeway, 'The Liberal Unionist Party', *Nineteenth Century and After*, 342 (August 1905), pp.182–97.
68. Gladstone at Hastings, quoted in *Liberal Unionist*, 63, April 1891.
69. Gladstone at Limehouse, 15 December 1888, quoted in Newton, *W. S. Caine*, p.184.
70. A. Milner to G. Goschen, 29 December 1886, Milner Papers, Bodleian Library, Milner MS 183.
71. A. Sidgwick and E. M. Sidgwick, *Henry Sidgwick: A Memoir* (London, 1906), p.463.
72. H. W. Lucy, *A Diary of the Unionist Parliament 1895–1900* (London, 1901), p.301.
73. A. Hopkinson, *Penultima* (London, 1930), p.170.
74. Elliot, *Life of Goschen, Vol 2*, p.120; Spinner, *George Joachim Goschen*, p.177.
75. *Liberal Unionist*, 7, 11 May 1887.
76. J. Broughton, 'Working Class Conservatism and the Rise of Labour', *The Historian*, 59 (1998), pp.16–20.

1.   The Origins of the Liberal Unionist Party

1. G. L. Goodman, 'The Liberal Unionist Party, 1886–1895', PhD thesis (Chicago, 1956), p.20.
2. Lubenow, *Parliamentary Politics*, p.247.
3. This approach is condemned by John Tosh as 'an extreme example' of a 'limited' historical approach to 'a crisis with extra-parliamentary dimensions if ever there was one.' J. Tosh w. S. Lang, *The Pursuit of History* (London, 4th ed., 2006), pp.123–4.
4. P. Ghosh, 'Gladstone and Peel' in P. Ghosh and L. Goldman (eds.), *Politics and Culture in Victorian Britain: Essays in Memory of Colin Matthew* (Oxford, 2006), p.68.
5. Garvin, *Life of Joseph Chamberlain, Vol. 2*, p.137.
6. F. Nicoll, 'Gladstone, Gordon and the Sudan campaign, 1884–5', paper delivered at Gladstone Conference, St. Deniol's Library, Hawarden, 1 August 2010.
7. D. W. Bebbington, *The Mind of Gladstone: Religion, Homer and Politics* (Oxford, 2004), pp.281–82.
8. Granville at the National Liberal Club, 14 April 1886, quoted in E. Fitzmaurice, *The Life of Granville George Leveson Gower, Second Earl Granville, 1815–1891, Vol. 2* (London, 1905), pp.484–5.
9. Hawkins, *British Party Politics, 1852–1886*, p.246.
10. Derby's diary, 10 December 1885, J. Vincent (ed.), *The Later Derby Diaries: Home Rule, Liberal Unionism, and Aristocratic Life in late Victorian England* (Bristol, 1981), p.44. Parry suggests that the announcement of Home Rule, was, for Gladstone, 'a final, if flawed, attempt' to reconcile the disparate elements of the Liberal Party. J. P. Parry, 'Liberalism and Liberty' in P. Mandler (ed.), *Liberty and Authority in Victorian Britain* (Oxford, 2006), p.99.
11. 'It cannot be overstressed then, how sudden … was the split of 1886.' J. P. Parry, *The Rise and Fall of Liberal Government in Victorian Britain*, (London, 1993), p.305.
12. 'I do not believe that there exist in the country any political leaders – or if there exist political leaders, I am confident that there exists no political party, which will consent either to acquire or retain office by conceding the terms by which Mr Parnell says his alliance can be purchased.' Reported in *The Times*, 30 August 1885.
13. Hartington to Granville, 10 September 1886, quoted in Holland, *Life of Spencer Compton, Vol. 2*, p.86.

14. Hartington to Gladstone, 8 November 1885, Devonshire Papers, Chatsworth House, DP 340.1826.

15. Derby's diary, 24 January 1886, *Later Derby Diaries*, p.58.

16. Cooke and Vincent, *The Governing Passion*, p.84.

17. Morley to Chamberlain, 4 September 1885, Joseph Chamberlain papers, JC5/54/625.

18. 'I cannot admit that five millions of Irishmen have any greater inherent right to group themselves without regard to the rest of the United Kingdom than the five million inhabitants of the metropolis.' Quoted in Garvin, *Life of Joseph Chamberlain, Vol. 2*, p.64.

19. Derby's diary, 1 October 1885, *Later Derby Diaries,* p.31.

20. Derby's diary, 12 January 1886, *Later Derby Diaries,* p.53.

21. Jeune, *Memories of Fifty Years*, pp.247–8. Chamberlain described Goschen as performing 'the useful part of the skeleton at Egyptian feasts. He is there to repress our enthusiasms and to moderate our joy.' Garvin, *Life of Joseph Chamberlain, Vol. 2,* p.74.

22. Ibid., pp.97–100.

23. Spinner, *George Joachim Goschen*, p.123.

24. Goschen to A. Grey, 20 September 1885, quoted in Cooke and Vincent, *The Governing Passion*, p.101.

25. Northbrook to Hartington, 2 January 1887, DP 340.2086.

26. Quoted in H. C. G. Matthew, *Gladstone 1875–1898* (Oxford, 1995), p.240.

27. She had written to Hartington directly in October 1885, urging Hartington 'to disassociate himself from the extreme radicals and to moderate the excesses of the violent reformers.' Queen Victoria to Hartington, 3 October 1885, DP 340.1814. Hartington's response had been emollient: 'I do not think that any of the proposals which have been actually put forward by the Radical leaders can be described as revolutionary.' Hartington to Queen Victoria, 5 October 1885, DP 340.1815. Victoria had henceforward chosen to influence Hartington through surrogates.

28. Queen Victoria to Goschen, 29 December 1885, quoted in Southgate, *The Passing of the Whigs*, pp.402–3.

29. Cooke and Vincent, *The Governing Passion*, p.90.

30. Hartington to Gladstone, 16 December 1885, DP 340.1851.

31. Gladstone to Hartington, 17 December 1885, DP 340.1853.

32. Quoted in Cooke and Vincent, *The Governing Passion*, p.88.

33. Queen Victoria to Goschen, 28 January 1886, Royal Archive, Windsor Castle, B66/8.

34. Loughlin, *The British Monarchy and Ireland,* pp.188–192. Despite a chapter on 'The First Home Rule Bill: the monarchical dimension', Loughlin makes no mention of Victoria's correspondence with Goschen.

35. S. Lee, *Queen Victoria: A Biography*, (London, 1904), pp.492–493. See also Steele, *Lord Salisbury*, p.197.

36. Elliot, *Life of Goschen, Vol 2*, p.8.

37. E, Watkin to Hartington, 25 December 1885, DP 340.1871.

38. E. Heneage to Hartington, 22 January 1886, DP 340.1912.

39. Grey to Henry, 3rd Earl Grey, 22 January 1886, 3rd Earl Grey Papers, University of Durham Archives, GRE/B89.

40. Grey to Hartington, 22 January 1886, DP 340.1914.

41. Grey to Earl Grey, 29 January 1886, quoted in Cooke and Vincent, *The Governing Passion*, p.112.

42. I. Budge and C. O'Leary, *Belfast: Approach to Crisis. A Study of Belfast Politics, 1613–1970* (London, 1973), p.105.

43. A. Jackson, *Colonel Edward Saunderson: Land and Loyalty in Victorian Ireland* (Oxford, 1995), p.90.

44. Derby's diary, 14 January 1886, *Later Derby Diaries*, p.55. An indication of Victoria's continued partisan interest is that she later called on Derby at Croxteth Hall to discuss politics, which, Derby noted, 'she has not done for years: but the present agreement cancels past differences.' Derby's diary, 11 May 1886, *Later Derby Diaries,* p.68.

45. Elliot, *Life of Goschen, Vol. 2*, p.12.

46. Holland, *Life of Spencer Compton, Vol. 2*, p.127.

47. Hartington, Goschen, Sir Henry James, Courtney, Sir John Lubbock, Ebrington, Francis Egerton, St. Aubyn, Crossley, Arthur Elliot, Albert Grey, Alfred Barnes, David Davies, William Davies, Corbett, Seely, John Westlake and Wodehouse. There were also seventy-six absentees including Bright, Henry Brand, John Ramsden, and C. P. Villiers. Askwith, *Lord James of Hereford*, p.153. James was criticised by his constituency organisation in Bury for voting with the Tories. 28 January 1886, James Papers, Herefordshire Record Office, M45/150.

48. Askwith, *Lord James of Hereford*, p.155.

49. 'Every public utterance which I have ever made … has pledged me too deeply against [Home Rule].' Hartington to Gladstone, 30 January 1886, DP 340.1922.

50. Holland, *Life of Spencer Compton, Vol.2*, p.122

51. Hartington to James, 30 January 1886, M45/150.

52. Cooke and Vincent, *The Governing Passion*, p.87.

53. Ibid., pp.97–100.

54. Grey to J. Parker Smith, 13 February 1886, Parker Smith papers, Mitchell Library, Glasgow, TD1/346.

55. Salisbury to Akers-Douglas, 2 February 1886, Centre for Kentish Studies, Akers-Douglas papers, U564 C18/6.

56. Ebrington to Hartington, 1 March 1886, DP 340.1938–9.

57. Bright to James, Feb 18 1886, M45/165.

58. Elliot, *Life of Lord Goschen, Vol.2*, p.29.

59. *Liberal Unionist Association 1886: Origin and progress*, Austen Chamberlain papers, Cadbury Research Room University of Birmingham, AC2/1/1. Northbrook had expressed his objections to Derby in December 1885, with Derby noting in his diary that 'we do not see our way to Home Rule in any form.' Derby's diary, 11 December 1885, *Later Derby Diaries*, p.45. Argyll's views were similarly well known, as reported to Henry Sidgwick by Argyll's son, the Marquis of Lorne in March 1886: 'My father, I believe, is in favour of the policy of "examination and enquiry" on all matters except Home Rule.' Sidgwick and Sidgwick, *H. Sidgwick: A Memoir*, p.441. Lord Carlingford and Derby also declined office.

60. *Annual Register*, 1886, p.34.

61. Chamberlain to his electors, 5 February 1886, quoted in *Birmingham Daily Post*, 6 February 1886.

62. *The Times*, 3 February 1886.

63. *Manchester Guardian*, 3 February 1886.

64. Wolmer to Selborne, 9 February 1886, quoted in D. G. Boyce (ed.), *The Crisis of British Unionism: Lord Selborne's domestic political papers, 1885–1922* (London, 1987), p.9.

65. Derby's diary, 6 February 1886, *Later Derby Diaries*, p.62.

66. H. G. Hutchinson, *Life of Sir John Lubbock, Lord Avebury, Vol. 1* (London, 1914), p.225.

67. 'This is the first ray of hope in a most gloomy situation – you are right in supposing that the chief difficulty in getting MPs to act stoutly is their uncertainty as to Hartington's attitude.' Grey to Earl Grey, marked 'private', 1 March 1886, GRE/B89.

68. Hartington to James, 4 March 1886, quoted in Marsh, *Discipline of Popular Government*, p.109. Further evidence of Hartington's reticence can be seen in his speech to the Eighty Club on 5 March, when he refused to reveal his intentions in detail, beyond a promise of firmness and honesty in his dealings.

69. In total six ministers resigned, including Chamberlain, George Trevelyan and Edward Heneage. Heneage to J. Wintringham, 13 March 1886, Heneage Papers, Lincolnshire County Records Office, 2HEN 5/18.

70. On 13 March when Gladstone announced his intentions in cabinet, a fierce argument broke out: 'Gladstone flew into an ungovernable temper and abused [Chamberlain] without mercy. Joe retaliated and [William Harcourt] says they almost came to blows.' Lewis Harcourt Journal, 26 March 1886, P. Jackson (ed.), *Loulou: Selected Extracts from the Journals of Lewis Harcourt (1880–1895)* (Madison, 2006), p.135. Chamberlain had also felt slighted when Gladstone had attempted to reduce the salary of Chamberlain's under-secretary at the Board of Trade, Jesse Collings. 'Damn! Damn! Damn!' he wrote to Harcourt. Chamberlain to Harcourt, 8 February 1886. JC5/38/153.

71. T. H. Ford, *A.V. Dicey: The Man and his Times* (Chichester, 1985), p.152. Ford admits that he has no evidence to substantiate this claim.

72. Ibid., p.165. Lecky was not the only prominent Irish figure to oppose the policy. Argyll received a letter of support in 1886 from Daniel O'Connell's son. Douglas, *Autobiography and Memoirs, Vol. 2*, p.433.

73. Derby's diary, 21 March 1886, *Later Derby Diaries*, p.63.

74. *The Times*, 17 March 1886.

75. Balfour to Salisbury, 24 March 1886, quoted in R. Harcourt-Williams (ed.), *Salisbury-Balfour Correspondence, 1869–1892* (Hertford, 1988), pp.133–134.

76. Argyll to Hartington, 20 March 1886, DP 340.1950; Bedford to Hartington, 29 March 1886, DP 340.1952; Abercorn to Hartington', 29 March 1886, DP 340.1953.

77. Queen Victoria to Goschen, 26 March 1886, RA B66/13. She revealed her deeper motive when she wrote to Goschen in April, arguing that a union of Whigs and Conservatives was 'the only chance the country has of a strong government able to resist Democracy and Socialism.' Queen Victoria to Goschen, 11 April 1886, RA B66/19.

78. Heneage to J Wintringham, 20 March 1886, 2HEN 5/22.

79. Chamberlain to Hartington, 3 April 1886, DP 340.1958.

80. J. Bryce to Sidgwick, 3 April 1886, quoted in Sidgwick and Sidgwick, *H. Sidgwick: A Memoir*, p.444.

81. Radnor to Hartington, 22 March 1886, DP 340.1951.

82. Salisbury to Hartington, 5 April 1886, DP 340.1961.

83. Derby's diary, 23 March 1886, *Later Derby Diaries*, pp.64–5.

84. Milner to Goschen, 18 March 1886, Milner MS 183.

85. J. E. Wrench, *Alfred Lord Milner: the man of no illusions, 1854–1925* (London, 1958), p.78; J. L. Thompson, *A Wider Patriotism: Alfred Milner and the British Empire* (London, 2007), pp.43–55. The *Liberal Unionist* also paid tribute to Craig Sellar after his death in January

1890: 'When the Liberal Unionists deserted by their old chiefs and by the majority of their former associates were left without any definite organisation, his knowledge of the machinery of politics was of the greatest service.' *Liberal Unionist* 49, February 1890.

86. Elliot, *Life of Goschen, Vol. 2*, pp.81–2.

87. Cooke and Vincent, *The Governing Passion*, p.117; Milner's diary, Milner MS 60.

88. W. S. Caine to Chamberlain, n.d., JC5/10/5.

89. Caine to Chamberlain, n.d., JC5/10/6. Edmunds withdrew his candidature following his meeting with Caine.

90. Chamberlain to Bunce, 7 April 1886, JC5/8/84a.

91. Newton, *W.S. Caine* p.143.

92. Sidgwick and Sidgwick, *H. Sidgwick: A Memoir*, 13 April 1886, p.445.

93. *Manchester Guardian*, 15 April 1886.

94. *Punch*, 24 April 1886.

95. Rylands reported Hartington's naïvety about the composition of the meeting: 'I say Rylands,' Hartington muttered at the start of the meeting, 'I think we are in the midst of a great many Tories.' L. G. Rylands, *Correspondence and Speeches of Mr Peter Rylands MP, Vol. 2* (Manchester, 1890), p.238.

96. Queen Victoria to Goschen, 16 April 1886, RA B66/20.

97. Derby's diary, 16 April 1886, *Later Derby Diaries*, pp.65–66.

98. Harcourt to Chamberlain, 19 April 1886, JC5/38/46.

99. Rylands, *Correspondence and Speeches, Vol. 2*, p.238.

100. *The Times*, 27 April 1886.

101. Milner to P. Gell, 18 April 1886, Gell Papers, Derbyshire County Record Office, D3287/MIL/1/164.

102. The official title of this committee was, according to the Party record book, 'The Liberal Committee for the Maintenance of the Legislative Union between Great Britain and Ireland', though the constitution of the Party, agreed on 22 May at Westminster Palace Hotel gives its title as 'The Liberal Association for the Maintenance of the Unity and Supremacy of the Imperial Legislature', AC 2/1/1.

103. Milner to Gell, 18 April 1886, D3287/MIL/1/164.

104. See Akers-Douglas papers, U564 C261/1.

105. Grey to Earl Grey, 13 April 1886, GRE/B89.

106. Brand to Chamberlain, 22 April 1886, JC5/3/15.

107. Milner to Goschen, 28 April 1886, Milner MS 183. As Chamberlain wrote: 'for a time, I suppose, I shall have to occupy an isolated position.' Chamberlain to Jeune, 27 April 1886, quoted in Jeune, *Memories of Fifty Years*, p.286.

108. M. Barker, *Gladstone and Radicalism: The Reconstruction of Liberal Policy in Britain, 1885–1894* (Hassocks, 1975), p.49.

109. *The Times*, 22 April 1886.

110. A. W. W. Dale, *Life of R. W. Dale of Birmingham* (London, 1898), p.460.

111. In a similar fashion, William Kenrick had managed to persuade his council in North Birmingham to trust his judgement the previous night. *Birmingham Daily Post*, 21 April 1886.

112. Chamberlain to Labouchere, 17 April 1886, A. Thorold, *The Life of Henry Labouchere*, (London, 1913), p.292.

113. Chamberlain to Dilke, 6 May 1886, quoted in S. Gwynn and G. Tuckwell, *The Life of the rt. hon. Charles Dilke, MP, Vol. 2*. (London, 1917), pp.221–2.

114. Milner to Goschen, 23 April 1886, Milner MS 183.

115. Grey to Earl Grey, 22 January 1886, quoted in Cooke and Vincent, *The Governing Passion*, p.112.
116. Cooke and Vincent, *The Governing Passion*, p.105.
117. Pease, *Elections and Recollections*, p.108.
118. Milner to Goschen, 25 April 1886, Milner MS 183.
119. Goschen to Wolmer, 22 April 1886, Selborne Papers, Bodleian Library, Selborne MS 13; 5–6.
120. Milner to Goschen, 23 April 1886, Milner MS 183.
121. Milner to Goschen, 25 April 1886, Milner MS 183.
122. Milner to Goschen 28 April 1886. Milner MS 183.
123. Milner to Goschen, 25 April 1886, Milner MS 183. Milner and his group were clearly not in touch with the upper levels of Liberalism, as Derby told Hartington that the Duke of Bedford wanted to hold meetings to defend the Union in March. Derby diary, 23 March 1886, *Later Derby Diaries*, p.65.
124. Milner to Goschen, 26 April 1886, Milner MS 183.
125. *Later Derby Diaries*, p.70.
126. Cooper to Rosebery, 4 April 1886, quoted in Koss, *The Political Press, Vol. 1*, p.283.
127. Balfour to Salisbury, 24 March 1886 in Harcourt-Williams (ed.), *Salisbury-Balfour Correspondence*, pp.133–138.
128. Caine to Chamberlain, 17 April 1886, JC5/10/4.
129. Koss, *The Political Press, Vol. 1*, pp.287–8.
130. G.D. Goodman, 'Gladstone and his rivals: popular Liberal perceptions of the party leadership in the political crisis of 1885–1886' in Biagini and Reid (eds.), *Currents of Radicalism*, pp.175–182. Chamberlain also lost the support of the influential Liberal periodical, the *Birmingham Owl*.
131. West of Scotland Liberal Unionist Association (hereafter WSLUA) minute book 1, 1 December 1887, National Library of Scotland, 10424/19. Although the *Pall Mall Gazette* opposed the Government of Ireland Bill, it did so purely because of the exclusion of the Irish MPs. Once Gladstone had announced his willingness to compromise on this issue, W. T. Stead fell into line behind him and became one of the Liberal Unionists' most ruthless opponents.
132. Gell to Parker Smith, 24 April 1886, TD1/346.
133. Milner to Goschen, 26 April, Milner MS 182.
134. Craig Sellar to Parker Smith, 21 April 1886, TD1/346.
135. Maude to Parker Smith, n.d. (April 1886) TD1/346. 'List A' comprised H. F. Elliot, M. Henry, A. C. Corbett, J. Ramsay and H. Craig Sellar. 'List B' comprised R. F. F. Campbell, E. Wason, H. Watt, T. Sutherland, J. G. G. Hamilton, S. Mason, J. Finlayson, J. C. Bolton, W. B. Barbour and J. McCulloch. Scotland was clearly seen to be crucial in deciding the fate of the Home Rule Bill, as Gell noted, 'we reckon that if a dozen of the Scotch doubtful MPs can be scared, the 2nd reading will be defeated.' Gell to Parker Smith, 24 April 1886, TD1/346. Of the 'doubtful' MPs on list B, however, only Campbell and Sutherland were persuaded to vote against the second reading on 8 June, though Gell had also pencilled in the names of Borland, Duff and Buchanan, the last of whom did vote against the second reading.
136. Milner to Goschen, 28 April 1886, Milner MS 183.
137. Milner to Gell, 19 April 1886, D3287/MIL/1/165.
138. Milner to Goschen, 28 April 1886, Milner MS 183.
139. Milner to Goschen, 27 April 1886, MS 183.

140. There are conflicting accounts of when the Committee was announced. Two years later, the *Liberal Unionist*, in its history of the Association, reported that the Committee went public on 21 April. Milner's letters at the Bodleian Library and the Liberal Unionist Association Record Book, confirm the date given here.

141. *Liberal Unionist Association 1886: Origin and progress,* AC2/1/1. Only one could legitimately be described as a radical, and that was Peter Rylands. Although he did not join the Committee, Thomas Hughes, author of *Tom Brown's Schooldays*, wrote a letter of support to Argyll in 1886. Douglas, *Autobiography and Memoirs, Vol. 2,* p.447.

142. 'Liberal Unionist Work: 2 The Liberal Unionist Association,' *Liberal Unionist* 33, October 1888.

143. Jeune, *Memories of Fifty Years*, p.254.

144. *Glasgow Herald*, 1 May 1886.

145. Chamberlain to Labouchere, 30 April 1886, Thorold, *Life of Henry Labouchere,* p.299.

146. Chamberlain to Harcourt, 2 May 1886, Garvin, *Life of Joseph Chamberlain, Vol. 2,* p.223.

147. Chamberlain to Labouchere, 4 May 1886, Thorold, *Life of Henry Labouchere,* p.304.

148. H. Broadhurst, *Henry Broadhurst MP. The story of his life ... as told by himself* (London, 1901), p.196.

149. Harcourt to Hartington, 27 June 1886. Holland, *Life of Spencer Compton, Vol. 2,* p.162.

150. Harcourt to Derby, 9 January 1886, *Later Derby Diaries*, pp.152–154.

151. Powell Williams to Chamberlain, 3 June 1886, JC5/72/6.

152. Morley, *Life of W. E. Gladstone, Vol. 3*, pp.325–6.

153. Grey to Earl Grey, 11 May; 21 May, Cooke and Vincent, *The Governing Passion*, p.110.

154. *Birmingham Daily Post*, 9 June 1886.

155. Chamberlain to Collings, 10 May 1886, Garvin, *Life of Joseph Chamberlain, Vol. 2,* p.228.

156. Kate Courtney's diary, 10 May 1886, Courtney Papers, London School of Economics, XXII.

157. Chamberlain to Labouchere, 11 May 1886, Thorold, *Life of Henry Labouchere*, p.311.

158. Powell Williams to Chamberlain, 11 May 1886, JC5/72/4.

159. *The Times*, 13 May 1886.

160. *Birmingham Daily Post*, 13 May 1886.

161. *The Times*, 15 May 1886.

162. *Birmingham Daily Post*, 15 May 1886.

163. Chamberlain to Arthur Chamberlain, 15 May 1886, JC5/11/8.

164. Lord Granville informed Gladstone on 18 May that 'Hartington says in private that the agreement only consists in throwing out the bill.' A. Ramm (ed.), *Political Correspondence of Mr Gladstone and Lord Granville 1879–1886, Vol. 2* (Oxford, 1962), p.448.

165. Labouchere to Chamberlain, 17 May 1886, JC5/50/78.

166. E. H. Hamilton to Gladstone, 16 May 1886, Gladstone Papers, British Library, Add. Mss. 44191, f.69.

167. H. Gladstone's minutes on a conversation with Chamberlain on 17 May 1886, Add. Mss. 46114, f.190.

168. T. Harrison, 'Liberal Unionist Work 4: the Ulster Liberal Unionist Association,' *Liberal Unionist,* 35, December 1888.

169. *The Times*, 19 May 1886.

170. *The Times*, 20 May 1886. Salisbury had also contributed to the widening gulf between Gladstone and the Unionists with his 'Hottentot' speech at St James' Hall on 15 May. See Bentley, *Lord Salisbury's World*, p.235.

171. *The Times*, 21 May 1886.

172. *Liberal Unionist Association 1886: Origin and progress,* AC2/1/1.

173. *Scotsman*, 24 May 1886.

174. *Manchester Guardian*, 24 May 1886.

175. *The Times*, 24 May 1886.

176. Quoted in Holland, *Life of Spencer Cavendish, Vol. 2*, pp.157–8.

177. *The Times*, 28 May 1886. The attendees included J. H. Blades, Hamar Bass, H. Cozens-Hardy, Savile Crossley, R. Davies, T. F. Grove, B. Hingley, H. Hobhouse, Jacks, A. G. Kitching, Lewis McIver, W. C. Quilter, J. Ruston, Salis-Schwabe, F. Taylor, Villiers, J. Wilson. On the back of his invitation, Wolmer wrote, 'Neither I nor any other man who had made up his mind against the Bill went: only Home Rulers and wobblers.' Selborne MS 13; 7.

178. Morley, *Life of W.E. Gladstone, Vol. 3*, p.334.

179. *Birmingham Daily Post*, 28 May 1886.

180. Caine to Chamberlain, 27 May 1886, JC 5/1/20/2. He promised that 'Winterbotham, Kenrick, Powell Williams, R. Chamberlain, Dixon and myself will go with you wither you lead.'

181. Salisbury to Hartington, 30 May 1886, DP 340.1996 and Elliot, *Life of Goschen, Vol. 2*, p.72.

182. E. Alexander, *Chief Whip: The Political Life and Times of Aretas Akers-Douglas, 1st Viscount Chilston* (London, 1961), p.77.

183. WSLUA minute book 1, 29 May 1886, 10424/19.

184. J. McCaffrey, 'The Origins of Liberal Unionism in the West of Scotland', *Scottish Historical Review,* 50 (1971), pp.64–66.

185. There are allegations in three separate sources that the extra Unionists were present to ensure a motion for voting against the second reading: *The Times*, 1 June; Herbert to Henry Gladstone, 10 June 1886; and Labouchere to W. T. Stead n.d. ('3 a.m.'), quoted in Cooke and Vincent, *The Governing Passion*, pp.428–429.

186. Bright to Chamberlain, 31 May 1886, JC 5/7/41. Powell Williams commented, 'Old Bright's letter is queer but full of usefulness from what it implies.' Powell Williams to Chamberlain, JC5/72/3.

187. Ibid. For Caine's courting of Bright, see Newton, *W.S. Caine*, pp.151–152.

188. The letter was destroyed by Caine shortly after the meeting. Ibid., p.154.

189. *The Times*, 1 June 1886, Garvin, *Life of Joseph Chamberlain, Vol. 2*, p.245.

190. *Manchester Guardian*, 4 June 1886.

191. Bright to Chamberlain, 1 June 1886, quoted in R.A.J. Walling (ed.), *The Diaries of John Bright* (London, 1930), p.547.

192. R. B. O'Brien, *The Life of Charles Stewart Parnell, Vol. 2* (London, 2nd ed., 1899), p.158.

193. Cooke and Vincent, *The Governing Passion*, p.429.

194. Craig Sellar to Hartington, 3 June 1886, DP 340.1997.

195. Goschen to Milner, 26 May 1886, Milner MS 6.

196. Milner to Goschen, 29 May 186, Milner MS 6.

197. Grey to Earl Grey, 10 June 1886, GRE/B89.

198. Pease, *Elections and Recollections*, p.137.

199. H. Labouchere to J. Chamberlain, 29 May 1886, Thorold, *Life of Henry Labouchere*, pp.318–320. Heneage wrote of Unionists being 'hounded down by caucuses' during the election campaign. Heneage to J. Wintringham, 15 June 1886, 2HEN 5/13/50.

200. Kate Courtney's diary, 8 June 1886, CP XXII.

201. Lady Knightley's diary, 7 June 1886, quoted in Cooke and Vincent, *The Governing Passion*, p.433. Chamberlain was so confident that he had already prepared a draft manifesto which he had sent to Hartington, commenting that a 'joint production' was neither 'necessary or even desirable.' Chamberlain to Hartington, 7 April 1886, DP 340.1998.

202. Grey to Earl Grey, 10 June 1886, quoted in Cooke and Vincent, *The Governing Passion*, p.433. Some, such as Heneage, had expected a majority against the Bill as high as sixty. Heneage to Wintringham, 26 May 1886, 2HEN 5/13/45.

203. As identified by T. Heyck, 'Home Rule, Radicalism and the Liberal Party, 1886–1895,' *Journal of British Studies*, 13: 2 (1974), p.69.

204. Harvie, 'Ideology and Home Rule', p.302.

2.   The Ideologies of Liberal Unionism

1. Joyce, *Visions of the People*; Lawrence, *Speaking for the People*.

2. E. F. Biagini, *British Democracy and Irish Nationalism, 1876–1906* (Cambridge, 2007), p.3.

3. J. Bew, *The Glory of Being Britons: Civic Unionism in Nineteenth-Century Belfast* (Dublin, 2009), xi.

4. There were many journals and newspapers who promoted this view, most notably the *North British Daily Mail*.

5. See J.M. Hernon, 'The Use of the American Civil War in the Debate over Irish Home Rule' *American Historical Review*, 69 (1964), pp.1022–1026.

6. A.V. Dicey, *A Leap in the Dark* (London, 1893), p.104.

7. Milner to Goschen, 17 October 1886, Milner MS 183.

8. *Liberal Unionist*, 72, January 1892.

9. J. Smith 'Conservative Ideology and Representations of the Union with Ireland.' in M. Francis and I. Zweiniger-Bargielowska (eds.), *The Conservatives and British Society, 1880–1990* (Cardiff, 1996), pp.18–38. Smith, however, regards the Unionist cause as an alliance of reactionaries, ignoring the radicals and progressive Liberals within the alliance.

10. Fforde, *Conservatism and Collectivism*, p.48.

11. Harvie, 'Ideology and Home Rule,' p.298.

12. *The Times*, 4 May 1886. Huxley wrote a letter to *The Times* on 13 April strongly criticising Gladstone's policy. A. Desmond, *Huxley: Evolution's High Priest* (London, 1997), pp.167–8.

13. J. Biggs-Davison and G. Chowdharay-Best, *The Cross of St Patrick: The Catholic Unionist Tradition in Ireland* (Bourne End, 1984), pp.213–216.

14. *The Times*, 24 May 1886. I. Hutchinson, 'Lord Kelvin and Liberal Unionism', *Journal of Physics: Conference Series*, 158, (2009), pp.1–18. In much the same way that Liberal Unionism embraced different political, social and regional philosophies, Huxley and Kelvin were on opposite sides of the evolution debate. G. Jones, 'Scientists Against Home Rule', in Boyce and O'Day (eds.), *Defenders of the Union*, pp.188–202.

15. H. Emy believes that this academic revolt was against the growing power of the state and the threat of its misuse by unscrupulous politicians willing to promise unattainable treasures to an unsophisticated electorate. H. V. Emy, *Liberals, Radicals and Social Politics 1892–1914* (Cambridge, 1974), p.5. Harvie agrees, noting that 'distrust of Gladstone had always been endemic in the academic liberal community.' C. Harvie, 'Ideology and Home Rule', p.310.

16. Burness, *'Strange Associations'*, p.49.

17. *Liberal Unionist*, 16, 13 July 1887.

18. W. Miller to Gell, 28 October 1892, D3287/116/2/6.

19. One of these ten was the celebrated Rev. W. A. Spooner. D3287/116/4/12.

20. H. Paul, *The Life of Froude* (New York, 1905), p.110. In much the same way that Salisbury would appoint Alfred Austin of the *Standard* to the post of Poet Laureate as a reward for his support in 1895, Froude became Regius Professor of History at Oxford shortly before the 1892 election, despite his serious shortcomings as an academic historian. T. H. Huxley's appointment as a privy councillor in 1892 was far less controversial. Desmond, *Huxley*, pp.211–13.

21. N. Vance, 'The Problems of Unionist Literature' in Boyce and O'Day (eds.), *Defenders of the Union*, pp.176–188.

22. J. Garnett, 'Protestant Histories: James Anthony Froude, Partisanship and National Identity' in Ghosh and Goldman (eds.), *Politics and Culture in Victorian Britain*, pp.171–191. For an example of a more populist attack on the prospect of home rule, see, F. Frankfort Moore, *The Diary of an Irish Cabinet Minister: being the history of the first (and only) Irish National Administration, 1893*, (London, 1893).

23. A. V. Dicey, *Lectures on the Relation between Law and Public Opinion in England during the Nineteenth Century* (London, 1905), pp.456–457.

24. R. A. Cosgrove, *The Rule of Law: Alfred Venn Dicey, Victorian Jurist* (Basingstoke, 1980), p.113.

25. A. V. Dicey, 'Edmund Burke on Affairs with Ireland,' *The Nation*, 18 August 1881.

26. See W. Bagehot, *The Economist*, 22 April 1876, quoted in N. St. John Stevas (ed.), *The Collected Works of Walter Bagehot, Vol. 5* (London, 1974), p.132.

27. A. V. Dicey, 'How is the Law to be Enforced in Ireland?', *Fortnightly Review* (1881), pp.538–41.

28. A. V. Dicey, 'Two Acts of Union: A Contrast,' *Fortnightly Review* (1881), pp.177–8.

29. Quoted in D. G. Boyce and A. O'Day (eds.), *The Ulster Crisis* (Basingstoke, 2005) pp.23–24.

30. Ford, *Alfred Venn Dicey*, p.165.

31. See J. S. Mill, *Utilitarianism, Liberty and Representative Government* (London, 1910), pp.395–397. For popular support for this view, see *Weekly Times & Echo*, 2 February 1890. Chamberlain agreed, seeing centralisation as the means of achieving the radicals' reforming aims. E. F. Biagini, 'Radicalism and Liberty' in Mandler (ed.), *Liberty and Authority*, p.123.

32. W. C. Lubenow, 'The Liberals and the National Question: Irish Home Rule, Nationalism, and their Relationship to Nineteenth Century Liberalism', in J. A. Phillips (ed.), *Computing Parliamentary History* (Edinburgh, 1994), pp.119–142.

33. Dicey to Bryce, 10 April 1886, quoted in Cosgrove, *The Rule of Law*, p.124.

34. Dicey to Bryce, 18 May 1886, quoted in ibid., p.125.

35. Dicey, *England's Case against Home Rule*, p.2.

36. Ibid, p.20.

37. M. J. Salevouris, '*Riflemen form*': The War Scare of 1859–1860 in England* (New York, 1982).

38. *North British Daily Mail*, 20 April 1886, quoted in McCaffrey, 'The Origins of Liberal Unionism in the West of Scotland', p.567.

39. See Cammarano, '*To Save England From Decline*' and Colls, *Identity of England*, pp.50–55.

40. Dicey, *England's Case Against Home Rule*, p.45.

41. J. McCarthy, *The Case for Home Rule* (London, 1887), p.9.

42. For the most convincing account of Gladstone's motivation see J. P. Parry, *The Politics of Patriotism: English Liberalism, National Identity and Europe, 1830–1886* (Cambridge, 2006), pp.373–380.

43. Parry, *The Rise and Fall of Liberal Governments*, p.303; p.305.

44. A. V. Dicey, 'Unionists and the House of Lords,' *National Review*, 24 January 1895, pp.690–704.

45. Linda Colley has argued that the Union should be regarded as the basis for consensus among the conflicting identities of the British Isles and was well established in this position in the eighteenth century. L. Colley, *Britons: Forging the Nation, 1707–1837* (London, 1992).

46. A. O'Day, 'Defending the Union in Parliament: Parliamentary Opinions, 1869 and 1886', in Boyce and O'Day (eds.), *Defenders of the Union*, pp.90–111.

47. Quoted in Boyce and O'Day (eds.), *The Ulster Crisis*, p.286.

48. Loughlin, *Gladstone, Home Rule*; F. Thompson, *The End of Liberal Ulster: Land Agitation and Land Reform* (London, 2001); Loughlin, 'Creating a "Regional and Geographical Fact."'

49. Budge and O'Leary, *Belfast: Approach to Crisis*, p.107.

50. While Chamberlain's determination not to place Ulster under a Nationalist Irish Parliament contributed to the collapse of the 'Round Table' conference in January 1887, he had been willing to contemplate 'a separate Legislature' for the region. L. Harcourt's journal, 14 January 1887, Jackson (ed.), *Loulou*, p.147. T. W. Russell's oft-quoted speech at Grangemouth in which he referred to the Ulster Protestants, as 'bone of your bone, flesh of your flesh' was not widely reprinted until the Third Home Rule Crisis. See, for example, A. W. Samuels, *Home Rule: What is it?* (London, 1911).

51. E. Dawson, 'Shadow of the Sword', *Liberal Unionist,* 56, September 1890.

52. Dicey, *A Leap in the Dark*, pp.181–2.

53. As Phillip Gell wrote to Milner, the Liberal Unionists saw themselves as 'the party of law and order.' Gell to Milner, 4 August 1887, Milner MS 4.

54. *Irish Times*, 30 November 1887. See J. Stapleton, 'Political Thought and National Identity, 1850–1950' in Collini et al (eds.), *History, Religion and Culture*, p.252.

55. *Liberal Unionist*, 64, May 1891.

56. *Liberal Unionist*, 65, June 1891.

57. Biggs-Davison and Chowdharay-Best, *The Cross of St Patrick*, pp.245–282. On the selection of William Kenny to fight Dublin St Stephen's Green, it was noted that ' Mr Kenny belongs, as very many of the most zealous Unionists in the city of Dublin do, to the Roman Catholic Church.' *Liberal Unionist*, 70, November 1891.

58. *Liberal Unionist*, 75, April 1892.

59. *Liberal Unionist,* 76, May 1892.

60. *Liberal Unionist*, 79, August 1892.

61. 'Mr T.W. Russell on the Ulster question', *Liberal Unionist*, 76, May 1892.

62. *Liberal Unionist Association Memoranda* (hereafter *LUAM*), 1:3, March 1893.

63. *LUAM,* 1:6, June 1893.

64. *LUAM,* 1:3, March 1893.

65. See Blennerhassett's correspondence to W. C. Cartwright, Cartwright Papers, Northampton Record Office, C(A)1, box 16, bundles 7 and 14.

66. E. W. McFarland, 'The Orangeman's Unionist Vision' in MacDonald (ed.), *Unionist Scotland*, p.43. As Robert Colls has argued, the Orangeman's identity was distinct from that of the tolerant Englishman, to whom Liberal Unionism appealed. Colls, 'Englishness and the Political Culture' in Colls and Dodd (eds.), *Englishness*, p.40.

67. Hartington to Wolmer, 30 January 1892, Selborne MS II (4) 170.

68. I. Tod, *Liberal Unionist, 76,* May 1892.

69. *Liberal Unionist*, 78, July 1892. Another 100,000 Unionists processed peacefully past Balfour in Belfast during the debate on the Second Bill on 4 April.

70. P. Gibbon, *The Origins of Ulster Unionism: the formation of popular Protestant politics in nineteenth century Ireland* (Manchester, 1976), p.136. Hennessy disagrees, asserting that the Ulster Unionist enjoyed 'a multitude of identities and allegiances.' T. Hennessy, 'Ulster Unionist Territorial and National Identities 1886–1893: Province, Island, Kingdom and Empire', *Irish Political Studies*, 8 (1993), p.23. There was also a convention held at Leinster Hall in Dublin on 23 June 1892, but this received far less attention. *Irish Times*, 24 June 1892.

71. *LUAM Supplement*, March 1893.

72. *LUAM*, 1: 8, August 1893.

73. *British Weekly*, 28 July 1898.

74. *The Times*, 4 August 1898

75. R. Parkes, *Home Rule from a Liberal Unionist's Point of View* (Birmingham, 1887), p.8.

76. *The Baptist*, 25 February 1887.

77. Quoted in M. Patton, *Science, Politics and Business in the Work of Sir John Lubbock: A Man of Universal Mind* (Farnham, 2007), p.174.

78. Parkes, *Home Rule from a Liberal Unionist's Point of View*, p.2. See also *Liberal Unionist*, 76, May 1892; *Liberal Unionist*, 80, September 1892. For the popular English depiction of the Irish see L. P. Curtis, *Apes and Angels: The Irishman in Victorian Caricature* (Newton Abbot, 1971) and M. W. De Nie, *The Eternal Paddy: Irish Identity and the British Press, 1798–1882* (Madison, 2004).

79. *LUAM Supplement*, March 1893.

80. *Liberal Unionist*, 57, October 1890.

81. Some Liberal Unionists, such as Lubbock, explicitly denied that there were any ethnic distinctions between the Irish and the English. Patton, *Science, Politics and Business*, p.177.

82. For the Conservative view of Ireland, see Smith, 'Conservative Ideology', p.23.

83. Bright speaking at Birmingham, quoted in *The Times*, 2 July 1886.

84. Parry, *The Politics of Patriotism*, pp.382–384.

85. Quoted in P. O'Farrell, *England and Ireland since 1800* (Oxford, 1975), p.177.

86. Quoted in Biagini, *British Democracy*, p.242.

87. The *Baptist Magazine*, May 1886.

88. S. E. Koss, *Nonconformity in Modern British Politics* (London, 1975), p.16.

89. 'The Wesleyan dispute', *Spectator*, 24 July 1886.

90. *Methodist Times*, 12 August 1886.

91. A. Peel, *These Hundred Years: A History of the Congregational Union of England and Wales 1831–1931* (London, 1931), p.300.

92. D. W. Bebbington, *The Nonconformist Conscience: Chapel and Politics, 1870–1914* (London, 1982), pp.84–85.

93. One resolution at the Congregational Union of 1888 caused R. W. Dale of Birmingham to withdraw from the Union. Dale, *Life of R. W. Dale*, pp.584–8.

94. R. Samuel, *Island Stories: Unravelling Britain* (London, 1998), p.294.

95. Guinness Rogers claimed that the motivation for Spurgeon's opposition was his gout. G Rogers to Gladstone, 19 June 1886, quoted in Bebbington, *Nonconformist Conscience*, p.90.

96. *Christian World*, 13 May 1886. Bennet Burleigh, Liberal Unionist candidate for Glasgow Camlachie, had served with Garibaldi in Sicily, H. C. G. Matthew and B. Harrison (eds.), *Oxford Dictionary of National Biography, Vol. 8* (Oxford, 2004), pp.866–888.

97. Bebbington, *Nonconformist Conscience*, p.88.

98. Koss, *Nonconformity in Modern British Politics*, p.19. See M. Dawson, 'Liberalism in Devon and Cornwall, 1910–1931: "The old-time religion"', *Historical Journal*, 38 (1995), p.428.

99. *Baptist*, 21 May 1886.

100. See, for example, E. S. Wellhofer, *Democracy, Capitalism and Empire in Late Victorian Britain, 1885–1910* (Basingstoke, 1996), pp.82–91.
101. E. Watkin to Hartington, 25 December 1885, DP 340.1871.
102. Cartwright's address to the electors of Mid-Northampton, 18 June 1886, C(A)1, box 16, bundle 14.
103. Craig Sellar to Hartington, 28 July 1886, DP 340.2029.
104. E. Heneage to J. Wintringham, 2 January 1887, 2HEN 5/14/1.
105. Quoted in *Glasgow Herald*, 21 October 1886. See also Lubbock's address to the City of London, quoted in Patton, *Science, Politics and Business*, p.215.
106. E. Myers, 'The Unionist Alliance', *Liberal Unionist*, 33, October 1888.
107. Lubenow, 'The Liberals and the National Question', p.140.
108. The first record of this potent phrase is in the history of the Liberal Unionist Association published in the *Liberal Unionist*, 33, October 1888, though Heneage had pledged to 'stand as a Liberal on Mr Gladstone's platform of 1885' in 1886. Heneage to Wintringham, 7 June 1886, 2HEN 5/13/49.
109. *LUAM Supplement*, March 1893.
110. See Parry, 'Liberalism and Liberty', pp.71–100.
111. A. Reid (ed.), *Why I am a Liberal* (London, 1885), p.71.
112. *Liberal Unionist*, 38, March 1889.
113. *Liberal Unionist*, 37, February 1889. Burness sees the Glasgow Liberal Unionists' position on licence control as contributing to the Party's relasgve success in the west of Scotland in 1892. Burness, *'Strange Associations'*, p.94.
114. *Liberal Unionist*, 37, February 1889.
115. *Glasgow Herald*, 30 January 1890.
116. Caine wrote in his defence to Chamberlain, 'the bondage of the Tory alliance had become unbearable and their attack on the whole temperance movement ... gave me emancipation.' Caine to Chamberlain, 27 March 1892, JC 5/10/10b.
117. H. Hobhouse, 'Temperance and Party Spirit', *Liberal Unionist*, 53, June 1890.
118. WSLUA minute book I, 18 November 1890,10424/19.
119. Henry James' memoir, M45/1864, p.37.
120. *Liberal Unionist*. 54, July 1890.
121. *Liberal Unionist*, 60, January 1891.
122. *Manchester Guardian*, quoted in the *Liberal Unionist*, 55, August 1890.
123. For the best example, see 'Some facts about Home Rule,' *Weekly Times & Echo*, 30 December 1888.
124. See Patton, *Science, Politics and Business*, pp.210–11.
125. *Liberal Unionist*, 77, June 1892.
126. *Liberal Unionist*, 78, July 1892.
127. Steele, *Lord Salisbury*, pp.224–225.
128. Although the Act passed, Salisbury's majority fell from nearly 150 to 65 due to Liberal Unionist abstentions and opposition. Steele, *Lord Salisbury*, pp.308–310.
129. H. J. Hanham, *Elections and Party Management: Politics in the Time of Disraeli and Gladstone* (London, 1959), xxvi.
130. J. M. Lawrence, *Electing Our Masters: The Hustings in British Politics from Hogarth to Blair* (Oxford, 2009), pp.83–84.
131. Hawkins, *British Party Politics*, pp.268–269. See H. Berrington, 'Partisanship and Dissidence in the Nineteenth Century House of Commons' *Parliamentary Affairs*, 21 (1968), pp.338–374.

132. J. D. Fair, *British Interparty Conferences* (Oxford, 1980), p.263.

133. Hawkins, *British Party Politics*, pp.266–267.

134. H. Maine, *Popular Government* (London, 1885), p.94.

135. *Liberal Unionist, 33*, October 1888.

136. WSLUA minute book I, 4 November 1891, 10424/19.

137. Quoted in Southgate, *The Passing of the Whigs*, p.401.

138. J. B. Mackie, *The Life and Work of Duncan McLaren, Vol. 2* (London, 1888), p.248; M. Fry, *Patronage and Principle: A Political History of Modern Scotland* (Aberdeen, 1987), p.107.

139. Quoted in D. G. Boyce (ed.), *The Crisis of British Unionism*, p.11.

140. Barbery, 'From Platform to Polling Booth', p.176.

141. It was not just Liberals who resented the growing power of the party machine. See R. Wallace, *Nineteenth Century*, 37 (1895), quoted in H. J. Hanham, *The Nineteenth Century Constitution* (London, 1969), p.147; J. Owen, 'The caucus and party organization in England in the 1880s', PhD thesis (Cambridge, 2006).

142. Bright to Caine, 22 June 1886, Newton, *W.S. Caine*, p.167.

143. T. A. Jenkins, *The Liberal Ascendancy 1830–1886* (Basingstoke, 1994), p.215.

144. Reid (ed.), *Why I am a Liberal*, p.114.

145. For example, 'The Loyal Minority', *Weekly News*, 19 June 1886, reprinted in R. Douglas, L. Harte and J. O'Hara, *Drawing Conclusions: A Cartoon History of Anglo-Irish Relations, 1798–1998* (Belfast, 1998).

146. *Oxford Chronicle*, 8 May 1886.

147. *Western Mail*, 12 May 1886, quoted in M. Cragoe, *Culture, Politics and National Identity in Wales, 1832–1886* (Oxford, 2004), pp.262–263.

148. Heneage to Wintringham, 7 May 1886, 2 HEN 5/13/39.

149. Wintringham to Heneage, 6 May 1886, 2 HEN 5/13/41.

150. Hutchinson, *Life of Sir John Lubbock, Vol. 1*, p.211; Gell to Parker Smith, 24 April 1886, TD1/346. See also J. Lubbock and H. O. Arnold-Forster, *Proportional Representation: A Dialogue* (London, 1884).

151. Dicey to J. St. Loe Strachey, 29 January 1894, quoted in Searle, *Country before Party*, p.23.

152. *Liberal Unionist, 19*, 3 August 1887; Newton, *W.S. Caine*, pp.178–183.

153. J. Vernon, *Politics and the People: A Study in English Political Culture, c.1815–1867* (Cambridge, 1998).

154. Divisional Council Meeting, 14 December 1888, Birmingham West Liberal Unionist Association, Smethwick Local History Archives, NRA 4755.

155. Divisional Council Meeting, 20 March 1889, Birmingham West LUA; AGM, 16 May 1890, Birmingham West LUA, NRA 4755.

156. T. Raleigh, 'Democracy', *Liberal Unionist, 43*, August 1889.

157. Douglas, *Autobiography and Memoirs, Vol. 2*, p.418.

158. Hartington to Wolmer, 9 November 1890, Selborne MS II (4) 112.

159. Biagini, *British Democracy*, p.238.

160. M. Crackenthorpe, 'Unionism and State Socialism' *Liberal Unionist, 48*, January 1890.

161. 'Plain Words on Socialistic Problems' *Liberal Unionist, 66*, July 1891.

162. *Liberal Unionist, 66*, July 1891; 'Old Age Pensions.' *National Review*, 18 February 1892.

163. Divisional Council Meeting, 2 March 1891, Birmingham West Liberal Unionist Association, NRA 4755.

164. Chamberlain to Wolmer, 18 March 1892, Selborne MS I (8) 27–30.

165. Derby's diary, 14 March 1891, *Later Derby Diaries*, pp.139–140.

166. Chamberlain to James, 2 October 1892, M45/1718. The Royal Commission, when it finally reported in June 1894, rejected any suggestion of a statutory maximum working day for all groups, including miners.

167. *Liberal Unionist,* 41, June 1889.

168. *Liberal Unionist,* 66, July 1891.

169. 'The fruits of Liberal Unionism', *Weekly Times & Echo,* 23 October 1887.

170. P. Readman, *Land and Nation in England: Patriotism, National Identity and the Politics of Land* (London, 2008), pp.47–53.

171. *Liberal Unionist,* 73, February 1892; H. Hobhouse, 'Parish and District Councils', *Liberal Unionist,* 75, April 1892.

172. Argyll to Salisbury, 16 July 1892, Salisbury Papers, Hatfield House.

173. C. Burness, 'The Making of Scottish Unionism' in S. Ball and I. Halliday (eds.), *Mass Conservatism: the Conservatives and the Public since the 1880s* (London, 2002), p.24.

174. Chamberlain to James, 17 June 1892, M45/557. Chamberlain's active support in Lichfield may have made the difference for Darwin as the seat was won by four votes.

175. Chamberlain to Wolmer, 19 June 1892, Selborne MS I (8) 34.

176. Fforde, *Conservatism and Collectivism,* p.71.

177. Ibid., pp.44–47.

178. Chamberlain to Devonshire, 13 November 1894, DP 340.2587.

179. Chamberlain to Wolmer, 12 October 1894, Selborne MS I (8) 40.

180. Wolmer to Chamberlain, 15 October 1894, Selborne MS I (8) 42. Salisbury duly introduced a bill for 'the regulation of the immigration of destitute aliens into Great Britain' in the House of Lords on 6 July 1894.

181. Chamberlain to James, 7 November 1894, M45/1742.

182. *LUAM,* 2:10, October 1894; *LUAM,* 2: 11, November 1894.

183. Thompson, *Imperial Britain,* pp.18–19.

184. See J. Mackenzie, *Propaganda and Empire: The manipulation of British public opinion, 1880–1960* (Manchester, 1984).

185. *The Times,* 13 May 1887.

186. *The Times,* 12 April 1886.

187. *Inquirer,* 24 July 1886.

188. *The Times,* 19 June 1886.

189. Balfour to Salisbury 24 March 1886, quoted in Harcourt-Williams (ed.), *Salisbury-Balfour Correspondence,* pp.133–138.

190. *The Times,* 17 April 1887.

191. Thompson, *Imperial Britain,* p.17. This definition of Empire could prove problematic, as H. M. Stanley found in North Lambeth, when his role in the Emin Pasha expedition of 1890 was used by Liberals to discredit his candidature on humanitarian grounds and he lost the election. Windscheffel, *Popular Conservatism,* pp.167–173.

192. Parry, *The Politics of Patriotism,* pp.341–368.

193. Bentley, *Lord Salisbury's World,* p.221.

194. Koss suggests the 'imperial mission' was also of appeal to the evangelical nonconformists, such as the Wesleyan Methodists of Cornwall. S. E. Koss, 'Wesleyanism and Empire,' *Historical Journal,* 18 (1975), pp.105–18.

195. See resolutions passed at Liberal Unionist Conference at Leicester, 29 November 1899. *LUAM,* 7: 12, December 1899.

196. Loughlin, *The British Monarchy and Ireland,* p.220. He goes on to emphasise the 'Protestant' nature of the celebrations that took place in 1887; for a contrasting interpretation see W.

M. Kuhn, *Democratic Royalism: The Transformation of the British monarchy* (Basingstoke, 1996), p.88.

197. Lady Monkswell, *A Victorian Diarist 1873–1895* (London, 1944), quoted in R. Hudson, *The Jubilee Years, 1887–1897* (London, 1996), p.24.

198. D. Cannadine, 'The Context, Performance and Meaning of Ritual: The British Monarchy and the "Invention of Tradition." c.1820–1977' in E. J. Hobsbawm and T. Ranger (eds.), *The Invention of Tradition* (Cambridge, 1983), pp.101–164. The Duchess of Devonshire helped to cement the Conservative–Liberal Unionist alliance with a celebrated fancy dress ball (which Asquith famously attended, dressed as a Roundhead soldier). Hudson, *The Jubilee Years*, p.226.

199. For example, Chamberlain at the Royal Colonial Institute, *The Times*, 1 April 1897; Kuhn, *Democratic Royalism,* p.63. Chamberlain failed to get his idea of an imperial council accepted at the Colonial Conference of 1897. G. Martin, 'The Idea of "Imperial Federation"' in R. Hyam and G. Martin (eds.), *Reappraisals in British Imperial History* (London, 1975), p.132. It was also notable that southern Ireland failed to participate as fully in the Jubilee of 1897 as they had in 1887. *Annual Register*, 1897, p.237.

200. P. Williamson, 'State Prayers, Fasts and Thanksgivings: Public Worship in Britain 1830–1897,' *Past and Present*, 200 (August 2008), pp.121–174.

201. G. R. Searle, *The Liberal Party: triumph and disintegration, 1886–1929* (London, 1992), p.3.

202. Barbery, 'From Platform to Polling Booth', p.21.

203. For a similar variety of opinion in the early Labour Party see D. Tanner, *Political change and the Labour party 1900–1918* (Cambridge, 1990), pp.420–423.

204. Boyce (ed.), *The Crisis of British Unionism*, p.83.

205. Ibid., pp.84–89.

206. Smith, 'Conservative Ideology', pp.20–21.

3. The Unionist Alliance

1. Parry, *The Rise and Fall of Liberal Government*, p.302.

2. E. Sturgis, 'Wanted: a leader,' *Nineteenth Century*, 10 (August 1886), p.187.

3. For example, Searle, *Country before Party*, p.27.

4. Ibid., p.306.

5. *The Times*, 17 May 1886.

6. *The Times*, 30 April 1886.

7. *Scottish News*, 13 May 1886.

8. *Birmingham Daily Post*, 25 May 1886.

9. Hartington to James, 15 December 1886, M45/242.

10. L. Courtney to A. R. D. Elliot, 31 December 1886, CP V/43.

11. Quoted in Garvin, *Life of Joseph Chamberlain, Vol. 2*, pp.277–278.

12. L. Harcourt's journal, 28 December 1886, Jackson (ed.), *Loulou,* p.143; Hurst, *Joseph Chamberlain and Liberal reunion.*

13. Bright to Wolmer, 24 April 1887, Selborne MS II (13) 28.

14. *Bury Guardian*, 18 April 1887; *Bury Times*, 30 April 1887.

15. *Hansard*, 3rd series, 29 March 1887.

16. *Liberal Unionist*, 20, September 1887.

17. *Liberal Unionist*, 27, April 1888.

18. Chamberlain to Wolmer, 13 March 1888, Selborne MS I (8) 1.

19. *Liberal Unionist,* 80, September 1892.

20. P. Readman, 'The 1895 general election and political change in late Victorian England', *Historical Journal*, 42 (1999), pp.467–493, at pp.473–481; M. Pugh, 'Working-class experience and state social welfare, 1908–1914: Old age pensions reconsidered', *Historical Journal*, 45 (2002), pp.775–796, at p.795.
21. Salisbury to Hartington, 23 May 1887, DP 340.2131.
22. *The Times*, 7 February 1887.
23. *Birmingham Gazette*, 6 January 1892.
24. *Liberal Unionist,* 46, November 1889.
25. Quoted in K. Robbins, *Nineteenth Century Britain: Integration and Diversity* (Oxford, 1988), p.104.
26. *The Times*, 1 January 1892.
27. 'Memorandum' dated 1892, JC8/1/1.
28. Wolmer to Salisbury, 18 & 25 April 1895, Salisbury Papers. Wolmer described Balfour's action as 'a colossal blunder.'
29. *Standard*, 3 April 1895; Anon. ('Z'), 'Two Demagogues: A Parallel and a Moral', *New Review,* 12 (April 1895), pp.364–370.
30. *Leamington Spa Courier,* 27 April 1895.
31. 'Emergency' Council Meeting, 26 April 1895. Warwick and Leamington Conservative Party Association minute book. Warwick Record Office, CR1392.
32. Biagini, 'British Democracy', p.273.
33. Salisbury to Devonshire, 3 March 1895, JC6/1E/6.
34. J. H. Cooke to Boraston, 25 March 1895, JC6/6/1F/17.
35. Boraston to Chamberlain, 26 March 1895, JC6/6/1F/18.
36. 'Quousque tandem? Or one at a time', *Punch*, 6 April 1895.
37. Middleton to Akers-Douglas, 9 July 1887, quoted in Alexander, *Chief Whip,* p.135.
38. Chamberlain to Heneage, 6 July 1892, JC5/41/30.
39. Devonshire to Chamberlain, 3 March 1895, JC5/22/85.
40. JC6/6/1E/13.
41. Cawood, 'Joseph Chamberlain, the Conservative Party', pp.568–571.
42. *The Times*, 20 March 1896.
43. Hartington to Wolmer, 1 February 1890, Selborne MS II (4) 65–69.
44. 'Memoir' dated 1892, JC/8/1/1.
45. Chamberlain to James, 2 October 1892, M45/1718.
46. Harcourt-Williams (ed.), *Salisbury-Balfour Correspondence, 1869–1892,* p.292.
47. *LUAM,* 2:3, March 1894.
48. Powell Williams to Wolmer, 4 March 1894, Selborne MS II (13) 140–143.
49. *LUAM,* 2:11, November 1894.
50. *LUAM,* 2:11, November 1894.
51. Chamberlain to James, 11 December 1894, M45/1744.
52. Balfour at Newcastle, 13 November 1894, quoted in *LUAM*, 2:12, December 1894.
53. *LUAM*, 2:12, December 1894.
54. *LUAM,* 3:3, March 1895.
55. *Standard*, 27 April 1895.
56. Wolmer to Salisbury, 7 April 1895, Salisbury Papers.
57. Quoted in Roberts, *Salisbury: Victorian Titan*, p.597.
58. *LUAM,* 3:6, June 1895.
59. *LUAM,* 3:8, August 1895.
60. 14 June 1895, quoted in *LUAM*, 3:7, July 1895

61. Ibid.
62. E. Dicey, 'Alliance or Fusion', *Nineteenth Century*, 37 (June 1895).
63. Jay, *Joseph Chamberlain*, p.181.
64. Jackson, *The Last of the Whigs*, pp.95–6; Garvin, *Life of Joseph Chamberlain, Vol. 2*, p.359. L. Harcourt's journal, 30 June 1895, quoted in Jackson (ed.), *Loulou*, p.264.
65. Salisbury at Brighton, 19 November 1895, quoted in *LUAM*, 3:12, December 1895.
66. Steele, *Lord Salisbury*, p.374.
67. Devonshire at Derby, 18 September 1895, quoted in *LUAM,* 3:10, October 1895.
68. Devonshire at Leeds Liberal Unionist Federation, 30 October 1895, quoted in *LUAM,* 3:12, December 1895.
69. Pease, *Elections and Recollections*, p.274.
70. J. A. Bridges, *Reminiscences of a Country Politician* (London, 1906), pp.169–170.
71. McWilliam, *Popular Politics*, p.90.
72. 'Toryism Triumphant', *Pall Mall Gazette*, 12 June 1888.
73. Phillips, 'The Whig Lords and Liberalism', p.172.

4. Party Organisation

1. Hanham, *Elections and Party Management*; C. O'Leary, *The elimination of Corrupt Practises in British elections 1868–1911* (Oxford, 1962); J. P. King, 'Socioeconomic development and corrupt campaign practices in England' in A. J. Heidenheimer, M. Johnston and V. T. LeVine (eds.), *Political Corruption: A Handbook* (New Brunswick, 1989), pp.233–250. K. Rix, '"The Elimination of corrupt practices in British Elections?"' Reassessing the impact of the 1883 Corrupt Practices Act', *English Historical Review*, 123 (2008), pp.65–97; J. Lawrence, *Electing Our Masters*, pp.65–95.
2. Rix, '"Elimination of corrupt practises?"', p.81.
3. Windscheffel, *Popular Conservatism*, p.107; see also A. Panebianco, *Political Parties: their organisation and activity in the modern state* (Cambridge, 1988).
4. *Daily News*, 6 May 1886; Barker, *Gladstone and Radicalism*, pp.107–111.
5. Cooke and Vincent, *The Governing Passion*, p.118.
6. Kate Courtney's diary, 10 May 1886, CP XXII.
7. *The Times*, 13 May 1886.
8. Elliot, *Life of Lord Goschen, Vol. 2*, p.63; *The Times*, 24 May 1886.
9. Brand, Craig Sellar, Biddulph, Lord Rothschild, Albert Grey and Lubbock. *Liberal Unionist Association Origins and Progress*, AC 2/1/1.
10. F. W. Maude to Parker Smith, 6 May 1886, TD1/346.
11. Milner to Goschen, 3 July 1886, Milner MS 6.
12. Chamberlain to Arthur Chamberlain, 9 June 1886, JC5/11/13.
13. *Birmingham Daily Post*, 18 June 1886.
14. A. H. Brown, W. S. Caine, R. Chamberlain, A. C. Corbett, G. Dixon, Visc. Ebrington, J. Goldsmid, M. Henry, W. Kenrick, A. G. Kitching, Visc. Lymington, G. Pitt-Lewis, W. C. West, M. Story Maskelyne, H. Wiggin, A. B. Winterbotham and J. P. Williams. Chamberlain, Lord Edmond Fitzmaurice, John Jenkins and Admiral Maxse were also members of the National Radical Union (hereafter NRU).
15. Chamberlain to H. Payton, chairman of the Liberal Council of West Birmingham, n.d., quoted in *Birmingham Daily Post*, 11 June 1886.
16. *National Radical Union Conference at Birmingham, on Wednesday, June 1ˢᵗ, 1887.* C(A)1, box 99, unnumbered bundle.

17. *Liberal Unionist,* 15, 6 July 1887.
18. Heneage to Wintringham, 23 July 1886, 2 HEN 5/13/62.
19. Chamberlain to Heneage, 24 July 1886, JC5/41/21.
20. S. E. Koss, *Sir John Brunner, Radical Plutocrat 1842–1919* (Cambridge 1970), p.88.
21. Milner to Goschen, 17 October 1886, Milner MS 18.
22. Milner to Goschen, 8 June 1886, Milner MS 183.
23. *Liberal Unionist,* 36, 1 January 1889.
24. For an example see J. Ramsay to Parker Smith, 4 May 1886, TD1/346.
25. *Liberal Unionist Association: Origins and Progress,* AC 2/1/1.
26. 'That at such short notice it [the LUA] was able to grapple with [the 1886 election] was mainly due to the invaluable work of Colonel Hozier.' *Liberal Unionist,* 33, 1 October 1888.
27. Northbrook to Wolmer, 1 August 1886, Selborne MS II (13) 13–16.
28. *The Times,* 9 August 1886.
29. *Liberal Unionist Association: Origins and Progress,* AC 2/1/1.
30. Northbrook to Wolmer, 1 August 1886, Selborne MS II (13) 13–16.
31. *Liberal Unionist Association: Origins and Progress,* AC 2/1/1.
32. *Liberal Unionist,* 15, 6 July 1887; 'Liberal Unionist Work 2: The Liberal Unionist Association', *Liberal Unionist,* 33, October 1888.
33. Milner to Goschen, 28 April 1886, Milner MS 183.
34. *Liberal Unionist,* 2, 6 April 1887.
35. *Liberal Unionist,* 9, 25 May 1887.
36. *Liberal Unionist,* 19, 3 August 1887.
37. Gell to Milner, 1 August 1887, Milner MS 4.
38. Milner to Gell, 3 August 1887, Milner MS 4.
39. Gell to W. C. Cartwright, C(A)1, box 8, bundle 25; *Liberal Unionist,* 20, September 1887.
40. *The Times,* 6 September 1887.
41. He stood for election as a Liberal Unionist in the three subsequent general elections (twice in Luton and once in Stirling Burghs) and once at a by-election (Luton in September 1892). He was defeated each time.
42. *Liberal Unionist,* 75, April 1892.
43. *Liberal Unionist,* 1, 30 March 1887.
44. Courtney to Elliot, 5 January 1887, CP V/44; Caine to J. Fell, 21 March 1887, Fell Papers, Lancashire Record Office, DD Fe/1.
45. Caine to Fell, 4 February 1887, DD Fe/1.
46. Ibid.
47. *Liberal Unionist,* 15, 6 July 1887 .
48. Hartington to James, 7 October 1887, M45/289.
49. *Liberal Unionist,* 20, September 1887.
50. 'Liberal Unionist Work 2: The Liberal Unionist Association', *Liberal Unionist,* 33, October 1888.
51. J. Boyd-Kinnear, 'The Crisis of Liberal Unionism', *Liberal Unionist,* 21, October 1887.
52. Heneage to Chamberlain, 29 September 1887, JC5/41/3.
53. *Liberal Unionist,* 25, February 1888.
54. Ibid.
55. *Liberal Unionist,* 22, November 1887.
56. 'Liberal Unionist Work 2: The Liberal Unionist Association', *Liberal Unionist,* 33, October 1888.
57. E. Porritt, 'Party Conditions in England', *Political Science Quarterly,* 21 (1906), p.215.

58. *Sell's Dictionary of the World's Press* (London: 1893), quoted in Koss, *The Political Press, Vol. 1*, p.286.

59. Ibid.

60. For example, see *Weekly Times & Echo*, 4 April 1880.

61. *Weekly Times & Echo*, 1 July 1894; 7 July 1894; 15 July 1894.

62. Hartington to Salisbury, 18 May 1887, DP 340.2128.

63. 'At this dinner each guest on taking his place, found on his plate a copy of the first number.' Elliot, *Life of Goschen, Vol. 2*, p.119.

64. *Liberal Unionist, 1,* 30 March 1887.

65. *Liberal Unionist,* 31, August 1888.

66. Strachey to Chamberlain, 20 March 1887, quoted in Koss, *The Political Press,* Vol. 1, p.305

67. Strachey, quoted in ibid., p.304. It was not the association with Liberal Unionism that was the problem in Strachey's wife's opinion: 'Everybody knew, of course, that the *Liberal Unionist*, being a technical paper, could not possibly be self-supporting, and would, therefore, not survive long. No severely political, technical paper can get advertisements.' A. Strachey, *St Loe Strachey: His life and his paper* (London, 1930), p.24.

68. Ibid., p.71.

69. *Liberal Unionist,* 33, 1 October 1888.

70. Courtney to K. Courtney n.d. ('Monday night' February 1888), CP V/56.

71. *Liberal Unionist,* 27, April 1888.

72. *Liberal Unionist,* 34, November 1888.

73. *Liberal Unionist,* 27, April 1888.

74. *Liberal Unionist,* 35, December 1888.

75. *Liberal Unionist,* 32, September 1888.

76. *Liberal Unionist,* 52, May 1890.

77. J. Powell Williams, 'The Rise and Progress of the National Liberal Union,' *Liberal Unionist,* 45, October 1889.

78. It was officially stated by Wolmer at the October 1889 meeting of the Liberal Unionist Council that 'the West Midland district ... is under the special charge of the National Liberal Union of Birmingham.' *Liberal Unionist,* 46, November 1889.

79. Powell Williams, 'The Rise and Progress of the National Liberal Union', *Liberal Unionist,* 45, October 1889.

80. 'Liberal Unionist Work 12: Bradford', *Liberal Unionist,* 46, November 1889.

81. Barker, *Gladstone and Radicalism,* p.87.

82. Hartington to Wolmer, 31 October 1889, Selborne MS II (4) 47–48; Hartington to Wolmer, 2 November 1889, Selborne MS II (4) 50–51.

83. Hartington to James, 28 May 1890, M45/407.

84. *Liberal Unionist,* 74, March 1892.

85. *LUAM,* 2:3, March 1894.

86. *LUAM,* 2:10, October 1894.

87. Chamberlain at Manchester, 15 November 1898, quoted in *The Times,* 16 November 1898.

88. *Liberal Unionist,* 32, September 1888.

89. J. Boraston, ' Liberal Unionist Work 3: The Organising Committee for London', *Liberal Unionist,* 34, November 1888.

90. *Liberal Unionist,* 36, January 1889.

91. D. Dudley to R. Bickersteth, 15 May 1888, C(A)1, box 99, unnumbered bundle; Bickersteth to W. C. Cartwright, 11 June 1888. Bickersteth believed Prange's regional committees did not 'exist in anything other than name.' C(A)1, Box 16, bundle 7.

92. T. G. P. Hallett, 'Liberal Unionist Work 6: The West Country Associations', *Liberal Unionist*, 37, February 1889.

93. *Liberal Unionist*, 38, March 1889.

94. Selborne to E. P. Solomon, 4 April 1906, quoted in D. G. Boyce (ed.), *The Crisis of British Power: The Imperial and Naval Papers of the Second Earl of Selborne, 1895–1910* (London, 1990), p.260.

95. J. Chamberlain to A. Chamberlain, 15 December 1888, JC 5/12/4. For the full composition of the Liberal Unionist Organising Council, see Appendix 2.

96. *Liberal Unionist*, 39, April 1889.

97. 'I am the Hon. Sec to the Liberal Unionists.' A. Conan Doyle to A. Hoare, n.d. (1889), J. Lellenby et al (eds.), *Conan Doyle – A Life in Letters* (London, 2007), p.267.

98. A. Conan Doyle to M. Doyle, n.d. (1889), ibid., p.271.

99. Balfour to Salisbury, 23 November, 1888, quoted in Harcourt-Williams (ed.), *Salisbury-Balfour Correspondence*, p.261. Middleton too, had despaired of the Liberal Unionists' lack of activity in the constituencies, while he had tried to professionalize his Party apparatus. See A. Fawcett, *Conservative Agent* (Driffield, 1967), p.14.

100. *Liberal Unionist*, 39, April 1889.

101. *Liberal Unionist*, 40, May 1889.

102. WSLUA minute book I, 3 July 1889, 10424/19.

103. Ibid., 14 August 1889.

104. 'A Reformer'; 'Liberal Union Dinners', *Liberal Unionist*, 52, May 1890.

105. Hartington to Wolmer, 11 November 1889, Selborne MS I (6) 52.

106. Argyll to Wolmer, 15 September 1891, Selborne MS II (13) 77–80.

107. Wolmer, circular (headed 'confidential'), November 1889, uncatalogued items, Clifford Papers, Ugbrooke House.

108. R. Bickersteth to Hartington, 12 January 1891, DP 340.2266.

109. WSLUA minute book I, 9 January 1891, 10424/19.

110. *Liberal Unionist*, 60, January 1891.

111. Henry James' Memoir, M45/1864, p.75.

112. Chamberlain to James, 2 October 1892, M45/1718.

113. Selborne to Chamberlain, copy to Devonshire, 6 December 1895, DP 340.2667.

114. *Liberal Unionist*, 61, February 1891.

115. Holland, *Life of Spencer Compton*, Vol. 2, p.378.

116. Barbery, *From Platform to Polling Booth*, p.176.

117. Cooke and Vincent, *The Governing Passion*, p.437.

118. D. Howell, *British Workers and the Independent Labour Party, 1888–1906* (Manchester, 1983), vii.

119. Lawrence, *Speaking for the People*, pp.168–177.

120. *The Times*, 2 July, 1886.

121. Lord Granville to Lord Spencer, 6 July 1886, misc. correspondence, Althorp House; W. Summers, *The Liberal Unionists and their leaders* (Manchester, 1886) p.4; Sir Ughtred Kay Shuttleworth to Spencer, 12 July 1886, misc., Althorp.

122. *The Times*, 29 May 1888; Marsh, *Joseph Chamberlain: Entrepreneur in Politics*, p.273.

123. Sidgwick and Sidgwick, *H. Sidgwick: A Memoir*, p.456.

124. Liberal Unionist Association Report for 1892, D3287/116/2/9.

125. J. Powell Williams to J. Chamberlain, 10 April 1889, JC6/2/1/18; A. Chamberlain to J. Chamberlain, 10 April 1889, JC6/2/1/17.

126. J. Powell Williams to J. Chamberlain, 11 April 1889, JC6/2/1/19.

127. Lawrence, *Speaking for the People*, p.168.

128. Cawood, 'The Unionist "Compact"', passim.

129. Cawood, 'Joseph Chamberlain, the Conservative Party,' passim.

130. *Liberal Unionist*. 60, January 1891.

131. T. G. P. Hallett, 'Liberal Unionist Work 6: The West Country Associations,' *Liberal Unionist*, 37, February 1889.

132. *Liberal Unionist,* 47, December 1889.

133. E. J. Temple Willis, 'The Devon and Cornwall Liberal Federation – its History, Constitution and Work,' *Liberal Unionist,* 49, February 1890.

134. *Liberal Unionist,* 46, November 1889.

135. 'The Approaching General Election: XVI: The Western Counties', *The Times*, 2 February 1892.

136. *Liberal Unionist,* 63, April 1891.

137. See Gooch, *Life of Lord Courtney,* pp.235–328.

138. The Hon., sec of the mid-Devon LUA, W. H. Whiteway-Wilkinson described Clifford in 1913 as 'the mainspring of £.s.d. of our little band of well-wishers of England.' Whiteway-Wilkinson, to Clifford, 15 July 1913. Clifford 3 (2).

139. Mid-Devon Liberal Unionist Association, secretary's Accounts, December 1886, January 1887, February 1887, March 1887, April 1887, May 1887. Balance sheet, 1891. Clifford 3 (2).

140. Lord Clifford to Whiteway-Wilkinson, 15 May 1893. Clifford 3 (2).

141. Mid-Devon LUA report of work done in Newton Abbott, Ashburton Division, 30 December 1893–28 July 1894. Uncatalogued box marked 'Liberal Unionist', Clifford Papers.

142. Mid-Devon LUA minute book, 19 October 1904. A letter from Tom Ainge, principal agent of the Liberal Unionist Council, revealed that the Council were willing to encourage a tariff reform candidate to stand. T. Ainge to Whiteway-Wilkinson, 5 March 1905, Clifford 3 (2).

143. M. Dawson, 'Party politics and the provincial press in early twentieth century England: The case of the south west,' *Twentieth Century British History*, 9 (1998), pp.202–206.

144. *The Cornishman*, 8 December 1920. For the decline of such 'nursing' of constituencies, see Lawrence, *Electing Our Masters*, pp.92–95.

145. M. Dawson, 'Party politics and the provincial press', p.205; *The Times*, 13 July 1904.

146. *Liberal Unionist,* 17, 20 July 1887.

147. *Liberal Unionist*, 40, May 1889.

148. Hartington to Wolmer, 12 July 1890, Selborne MS II (4) 100–101. As Hartington noted to Womer, 'I am afraid there is no doubt that he was mad at one time.' Hartington to Wolmer, 2 February 1890, Selborne MS II (4) 72.

149. Chamberlain to Wolmer, 7 June 1892, Selborne MS I (8) 33.

150. 'For several years it was *my* money which kept the Durham LUA's head above water.' Durham to Devonshire, 11 January 1904. DP 340.3059. Durham resigned from the Party in protest against the Second Boer War in March 1900.

151. Ibid.

152. Moore, 'Manchester Liberalism', pp.32–34.

153. Hopkinson, *Penultima*, p.153.

154. Circular of Manchester and District LUA, 19 June 1891, Manchester Central Reference Library, Local History Collection, 329.942.
155. *Manchester Guardian*, 4 March 1889. For details of the conference, see *Report of the National Liberal Unionist Conference, Manchester, November 1891* (London, 1891).
156. J. R. Moore, *The Transformation of Urban Liberalism: Party politics and urban governance in late nineteenth-century England* (Aldershot, 2006), pp.83–87.
157. Koss, *The Political Press, Vol. 1*, p.287.
158. 'Capturing a Newspaper: The Story of a Liberal Unionist Plot', *Pall Mall Gazette*, 10 November 1887.
159. Derby's diary, 25 April 1888, *Later Derby Diaries*, p.85. Stalbridge had approached Derby to help the Liberal Unionists 'get it out of the hands of Home Rulers' but Derby appears to have thought better of it.
160. *Liberal Unionist,* 47, December 1889.
161. Ibid.
162. Wolmer to Hartington, 2 May 1890, DP 340.2232.
163. Westminster to Hartington, 21 October 1890, DP 340.2250.
164. Hartington to Wolmer, 23 October 1890, Selborne MS II (4) 111.
165. W. H. Smith to Hartington, 29 Octoer 1890, DP 340.2252.
166. Derby to Hartington, 18 January 1891, DP 340.2267.
167. Jenkins, 'The funding of the Liberal Unionist Party', p.938.
168. Wolmer to Devonshire, 5 September 1892, DP 340.2503.
169. Quoted in Koss, *The Political Press, Vol. 1*, p.291.
170. Barbery, *From Platform to Polling Booth,* pp.102–114.
171. *Liberal Unionist,* 37, February 1889.
172. *Liberal Unionist,* 42, July 1889.
173. *Liberal Unionist,* 47, December 1889.
174. Henry James' Memoir, M45/1865.
175. Manchester and District Liberal Unionist Association, M. G. Fawcett Papers, Women's Library, London Metropolitan University, 7MGF/A/2/127.
176. Moore, *The Transformation of Urban Liberalism*, pp.88–97.
177. Milner to Gell, 20 November 1886, D3287/MIL/1/176.
178. *Liberal Unionist*, 46, November 1889.
179. 'Liberal Unionist Work 15: Liberal Unionism in Leeds and the West Riding of Yorkshire,' *Liberal Unionist,* 51, April 1890.
180. *Liberal Unionist,* 57, October 1890.
181. E. S. Talbot to Devonshire, 6 May 1893, DP 340.2514.
182. N. Rowe, 'The English Press', *The Continental Monthly*, July-December 1864, p.145; W. Morrison to Devonshire, 11 May 1893, DP 340.2518.
183. Ibid. Anstruther later wrote of Morrison: 'No individual has given more money or time to the Liberal Unionist party.' Anstruther to Devonshire, 2 December 1898, DP 340.2666.
184. H. Williams, 'Liberal Unionist Work 10: Nottingham and District', *Liberal Unionist,* 43, August 1889.
185. *Liberal Unionist,* 79, August 1892.
186. Moore, *The Transformation of Urban Liberalism*, p.120.
187. Ibid., pp.106–8.
188. Moore, 'Liberal Unionism and the Home Rule Crisis in Leicester', p.191.
189. Cooke and Vincent, *The Governing Passion*, p.436.

190. Quoted in Parry, *Rise and Fall of Liberal Government*, p.306.
191. *North Wales Chronicle*, 26 June 1886, quoted in Cragoe, *Culture, Politics and National Identity in Wales*, pp.76–77.
192. *Liberal Unionist*, 32, September 1888.
193. 'Welsh Opinion on Home Rule,' *Liberal Unionist*, 44, September 1889.
194. 'The work of the Women's Liberal Unionist Association by one of its officials,' *Liberal Unionist*, 44, September 1889.
195. 'Welsh Opinion on Home Rule,' *Liberal Unionist*, 44, September 1889.
196. H. T. Evans, 'Wales and the General Election,' *Liberal Unionist*, 69, October 1891.
197. *Liberal Unionist*, 78, July 1892.
198. F. Aubel, 'The Conservatives in Wales, 1880–1935' in Francis and Zweiniger-Bargielowska (eds.), *The Conservatives and British Society*, pp.96–110.
199. R. Colls, *Identity of England* (Oxford, 2002), p.49.
200. C. Harvie, *Scotland and Nationalism: Scottish Society and Politics, 1707–1977* (London, 1977), p.33.
201. Burness, *Strange Associations*, pp.46–47.
202. D. Bebbington, 'Gladstone and Fasque', paper delivered at Gladstone Conference, St. Deniol's Library, Hawarden, 31 July 2010.
203. E&NSLUA minute books, National Library of Scotland, 10424/17; 10424/18.
204. *Liberal Unionist*, 39, April 1889.
205. E&NSLUA minute book I, 16 December 1886, 10424/17.
206. Ibid., 23 February 1887, 10 March 1887.
207. J. Chamberlain to A. Chamberlain, 3 December 1888, JC5/12/3.
208. E&NSLUA minute book I, 23 November 1888, 10424/17.
209. Ibid., 28 January 1889.
210. Ibid., 10 May 1887; November 1887.
211. Ibid., December 1889.
212. Ibid., 17 March 1890.
213. Ibid., 25 February 1891.
214. Ibid., 27 November 1891; 7 December 1891. The WSLUA minute book makes it clear that the reluctance to co-operate was entirely on the part of the E&NSLUA. WSLUA Minute Book I, 23 November 1891, 10424/19.
215. E&NSLUA minute book I, 6 April 1892, 10424/17.
216. Ibid.
217. Chamberlain to Wolmer, 17 March 1892, JC5/74/14. Fraser-Mackintosh duly lost his set to a Home Rule Crofter, Dr Donald MacGregor, whose campaign was supported by the *Highland News*, which criticised Fraser-Mackintosh as 'a man who calls himself a Liberal, yet votes, steadily and invariably to keep a Tory government in power.' *Highland News*, 9 January 1892, quoted in E. Cameron, *The Life and Times of Fraser Mackintosh, Crofter MP* (Aberdeen, 2000), pp.142–144.
218. *Scottish Highlander*, 4 August 1892.
219. WSLUA Minute Book I, 2 August 1892, 10424/19. The Association's honorary secretary, G. L. Crole, had resigned in the wake of the electoral deluge. E&NSLUA minute book I, 28 July 1892, 10424/17.
220. Ibid., 4 November 1892; 5 December 1892; 10 July 1893.
221. Ibid., 8 November 1892. In 1895, the Association collaborated with the Tories by founding a number of 'Unionist' clubs for working men. See Burness, *Strange Associations*, pp.115–119.

222. WSLUA Minute Book I, 11 July 1895, 10424/19.
223. See Burness 'The Making of Scottish Unionism', pp.20–25.
224. Hutchinson, 'Kelvin and Liberal Unionism', p.7.
225. J. G. Kellas, 'The Liberal Party in Scotland, 1876–1895,' *Scottish Historical Review,* XLIV (1965), pp.5–14.
226. WSLUA Association minute book I, 10 May 1886; 12 May 1886, 10424/19.
227. Ibid., 17 May 1886; 20 May 1886.
228. Ibid., 20 May 1886; 28 July 1886.
229. Election report, ibid., 28 August 1886.
230. *Liberal Unionist,* 36, January 1889.
231. G. Walker and D. Officer, 'Scottish Unionism and the Ulster Question' in MacDonald (ed.), *Unionist Scotland*, p.18. This is why the Duke of Argyll was not invited to be the Association's president. Hutchinson, 'Kelvin and Liberal Unionism', p.10.
232. R. Bird, 'Liberal Unionist Work 6 [sic]: the West of Scotland Liberal Unionist Association', *Liberal Unionist* 38, March 1889.
233. WSLUA minute book I, 15 November 1887, 10424/19.
234. Ibid., 1 December 1887.
235. Hutchinson, 'Kelvin and Liberal Unionism', p.8.
236. WSLUA minute book I, 1 December 1887, 10424/19.
237. Ibid., 2 April 1889.
238. AGM, ibid., 3 December 1889.
239. J. Caldwell to H. Anstruther, printed in *The Times,* 15 March 1890.
240. WSLUA minute book I, 7 May 1890, 10424/19.
241. *The Times*, 10 March 1892.
242. WSLUA minute book I, 31 March 1892; 6 April 1892, 10424/19; *The Times*, 28 May 1892.
243. WSLUA minute book I, 26 April 1892, 10424/19.
244. It was discovered after the election that there some constituency Associations, such as College, had 'practically no subscriptions.' WLSLUA minute book I, 8 October 1892, 10424/19.
245. R. Bird, quoted in ibid., 26 October 1892.
246. Ibid., 20 March 1893. By October 1894 there were fifteen organisers, clerks and canvassers working for Bird.
247. Ibid., 11 February 1893.
248. *Glasgow Herald*, 30 November 1893. The WSLUA were not satisfied, however, and sent a vice-president to meet the editor, Charles Russell, and ask for more positive reports. WSLUA Minute book I, 23 February 1894, 10424/19.
249. Parker Smith at WSLUA AGM, quoted in the *Scotsman*, 28 November 1894. His comment was not repeated in the report of the meeting published by the *Glasgow Herald* at the time.
250. WSLUA Minute Book II, 19 October 1894, 10424/20
251. WSLUA Minute Book I, 9 February 1894, 10424/19.
252. Currie, Sutherland, Corbett, Parker Smith, Cochrane, Cross and Maxwell.
253. WSLUA Minute Book II, 19 October 1894, 10424/20.
254. WSLUA constitution 1895, ibid.; *Scotsman*, 28 November 1894.
255. WSLUA Minute Book II, 10424/20, 2 August 1895.
256. Bew, *The Glory of Being Britons.*
257. *The Ulster Liberal Unionist Association: a sketch of its history, 1885–1914* (Belfast, 1913), pp.15–16.
258. Ibid., p.19.

259. Budge and O'Leary, *Belfast: Approach to Crisis,* p.105; *Liberal Unionist,* 74, March 1892.

260. N. C. Fleming 'The Landed Elite: Power and Ulster Unionism' in Boyce and O'Day (eds.), *The Ulster Crisis,* pp.92–3.

261. 'Working man and Home Rule,' *Northern Whig,* 10 May 1886.

262. Budge and O'Leary, *Belfast: Approach to Crisis,* p.121–2.

263. T. Harrison, 'Liberal Unionist Work 4: The Ulster Liberal Unionist Association,' *Liberal Unionist,* 35, December 1888.

264. *Pall Mall Gazette,* 14 September 1887; *Liberal Unionist,* 18, 27 July 1887.

265. Hartington to James, 10 July 1887, M45/282. In fact, Balfour agreed, on the grounds that Russell's demands were 'essential if Ulster is to be retained.' Balfour's memorandum on proposed legislation as it affects the Land Bill, 8 April 1887, quoted in J. Loughlin, 'T.W. Russell, the Tenant-Farmer Interest and Progressive Unionism in Ulster, 1886– 1900', *Eire-Ireland,* XXV (1990), p.49.

266. The peers backed down and Russell's announcement was withdrawn.

267. Biggs-Davison and Chowdrahay-Best, *The Cross of St Patrick,* pp.194–198.

268. *Liberal Unionist,* 74, March 1892.

269. *Northern Whig,* 29 November 1887.

270. Loughlin, 'T.W. Russell', p.55.

271. Chamberlain to Balfour, 25 May 1894, Balfour Papers, British Library, Add. MSS 49773.

272. W. Kenny to H. de F. Montgomery, 29 October 1894, quoted in Biagini, *British Democracy,* p.253.

273. W. Morrison to Devonshire, 26 July 1895, DP 340.2693.

274. Loughlin, 'T.W. Russell', pp.56–58. The Act was eventually consolidated by the 1903 Wyndham Act, affording a buy-out of Irish landowners far more expensive than that proposed by Gladstone in 1886.

275. *Northern Whig,* 3 October 1900.

276. Jackson, *Ireland 1798–1998,* p.227.

277. N. Whyte, *Science, Colonialism and Ireland* (Cork, 1999), p.97.

278. Jackson, *Ireland 1798–1998,* p.229; A. Jackson, *The Ulster Party: Irish Unionists in the House of Commons, 1884–1911* (Oxford, 1989), p.104.

279. See D. M. Jackson, *Popular Opposition to Irish Home Rule in Edwardian Britain* (Liverpool, 2009), chap. 4, pp.133–163.

280. Green, *Crisis of Conservatism,* pp.194–241.

281. Lawrence, *Electing Our Masters,* p.83.

282. M. Fawcett, (n.d.), 7MGF/A/1/230.

283. Kate Courtney's diary, 11 May 1888. CP XXIII. According to Courtney, this was because some of the women involved had 'worked in other causes' – clearly a reference to the involvement of Mrs Fawcett and the other suffragists.

284. *The Times,* 4 June 1886.

285. *Speeches on the formation of the Women's Liberal Unionist Association* (London, 1887), pp.8– 14; Strachey, *Millicent Garrett Fawcett,* p.128.

286. *Liberal Unionist,* 31, August 1888.

287. M. Luddy, 'Isabella M.S. Tod, 1836–1896' in M. Cullen and M. Luddy (eds.), *Women, power and consciousness in nineteenth century Ireland* (Dublin, 1995), pp.197–230; N. Armour, 'Isabella Tod and Liberal Unionism in Ulster 1886–1896' in A. Hayes and D. Urquhart (eds.), *Irish Women's History* (Dublin, 2004), pp.72–87.

288. *Liberal Unionist,* 41, June 1889.

289. *Liberal Unionist,* 43, August 1889.
290. *Liberal Unionist,* 44, September 1889.
291. 'Some Hints to Women on Canvassing', *Liberal Unionist,* 70, November 1891.
292. Lady Elizabeth Biddulph, quoted in *Liberal Unionist,* 43, August 1889.
293. *Liberal Unionist,* 70, November 1891.
294. *Liberal Unionist,* 79, August 1892.
295. Kate Courtney's diary, 5 July 1888, CP XXIV.
296. *Liberal Unionist,* 36, January 1889.
297. *Liberal Unionist,* 44, September 1889.
298. *Liberal Unionist,* 73, February 1892.
299. *Liberal Unionist,* 79, August 1892.
300. Quoted in *Liberal Unionist,* 44, September 1889.
301. *Liberal Unionist,* 64, May 1891.
302. M. Pugh, *March of the Women: A Revisionist Analysis of the Campaign for Women's' Suffrage, 1866–1914* (Oxford, 2002), p.132.
303. *Liberal Unionist,* 66, July 1891.
304. I. Tod, 'Lord Salisbury and Women's Suffrage,' *Liberal Unionist,* 68, September 1891.
305. M. Farrow to M. Fawcett, 11 Jan 1892, Fawcett Papers, Manchester City Archives, M50/2/1/152; M. Fawcett to M. Farrow, 12 January 1892, M50/2/1/153: L. Chamberlain to M. Fawcett, 17 January 1892, M50/2/1/155.
306. M. Fawcett, 'Women and Politics', *Liberal Unionist,* 72, January 1892.
307. *Liberal Unionist,* 72, January 1892.
308. Wolmer to M. Fawcett, 5 February 1892, M50/2/1/160. Henry James was clearly an opponent, as he was a prominent supporter of the National Women's Anti-Suffrage Association between 1907 and 1909. M45/1460.
309. Kate Courtney's diary, 10 May 1892, CP XXVI.
310. M. Fawcett, (n.d.), 7MGF/A/1/230.
311. Biagini, *British Democracy,* p.279.
312. *Liberal Unionist,* 77, June 1892.
313. Ibid.
314. *Liberal Unionist,* 78, July 1892.
315. A. Richardson to M. Fawcett, 23 February 1894, 7MGF/A/2/006.
316. *Liberal Unionist,* 77, June 1892.
317. *Report of Meeting on Proportional Representation, or Effective Voting, held {by the Women's Liberal Unionist Association} at River House, Chelsea, on Tuesday July 10th, 1894* (London, 1894).
318. Mrs Arnold-Forster to K. Courtney, 21 March 1895, CP V/18.
319. Kate Courtney's diary, 8 April 1895–20 November 1900, CP XXVIII; CP XXIX.
320. C. Rover, *Women's Suffrage and Party Politics in Britain 1886–1914* (London, 1967), pp.115–116.
321. *Daily News,* 18 April 1888.
322. Parry, *The Politics of Patriotism,* pp.112–126.
323. T. Harrison, 'Liberal Unionist Work 4: The Ulster Liberal Unionist Association,' *Liberal Unionist,* 35, December 1888.
324. *Liberal Unionist,* 35, December 1888.
325. *Liberal Unionist,* 35, December 1888.
326. 'Friends and Foes of the Union 1: Mr Bright', *Liberal Unionist,* 36, January 1889.
327. *Liberal Unionist,* 39, April 1889.
328. *Liberal Unionist,* 44, September 1889.

329. *The Times,* 31 March 1892.
330. Bebbington, *Nonconformist Conscience,* p.94.
331. *Pall Mall Gazette,* 26 May 1893.
332. Bebbington, *Nonconformist Conscience,* p.97.
333. *The Times,* 2 July 1895; H. M. Bompas, 'Nonconformists and Home Rule', *The Times,* 2 February 1894.
334. *The Times,* 20 May 1912; 21 June 1912; 26 October 1912; 25 February 1914.See also Jackson, *Popular Opposition to Irish Home Rule in Edwardian England,* p.58.
335. Collings and Green, *Life of Jesse Collings,* pp.196–202; Barker, *Gladstone and Radicalism,* pp.219–221.
336. Chamberlain to Wolmer, 13 March 1888, Selborne MS I (8) 1.
337. Steele, *Lord Salisbury,* p.233.
338. *Liberal Unionist,* 36, January 1889.
339. Collings and Green, *Life of Jesse Collings,* pp.203–205.
340. J. Collings to Wolmer, 15 June 1891, Selborne MS II (13) 67–68.
341. W. Morris, 'The Skeleton at the Feast', *Commonweal,* 127 (June 1888), p.188.
342. Derby's diary, 25 April 1889, *Later Derby Diaries,* pp.86–7.
343. Jenkins, 'The Funding of the Liberal Unionist Party', p.937.
344. 'The Report of the Labour Commission; Mr Jesse Collings' Observations', *LUAM,* 2:7, July 1894.
345. Readman, *Land and Nation in England,* pp.53–54.
346. Collings and Green, *Life of Jesse Collings,* pp.299–310.
347. For the contribution of Ferdinand Rothschild, see N. Ferguson, *The House of Rothschild, Vol. 2: The World's Banker, 1849–1999* (London, 1999), pp.327–331.
348. James' Memoir, M45/1864, p.75. James listed the principal contributors of funds as Bedford, Devonshire, Fife, Westminster, Rothschild, Revelstoke, Walter Morrison, Josslyn Pennington and Sir Horace Farquar.
349. *The Times,* 11 May 1886.
350. *Daily Telegraph,* 24 May 1886.
351. Pease, *Elections and Recollections,* p.133.
352. R. Brett's journal, 24 May 1886, quoted in Cooke and Vincent, *The Governing Passion,* p.425.
353. *Birmingham Daily Post,* 9 June 1886.
354. *Manchester Guardian,* 3 July 1886.
355. *Birmingham Daily Post,* 10 June 1886.
356. Wolmer to Hartington, 10 December 1888, DP 340, 2201.
357. *Liberal Unionist,* 58, November 1890.
358. *Liberal Unionist,* 64, May 1891.
359. Derby's diary, 20 May 1890, *Later Derby Diaries,* pp.87–8
360. *The Times,* 12 May 1892.
361. Wolmer to Devonshire, 5 September 1892, DP 340, 2503.
362. Jenkins, 'The Funding of the Liberal Unionist Party', p.937.
363. Selborne to Devonshire, 25 March 1895, DP 340, 2687.
364. James to Devonshire, 8 January 1895, DP uncatalogued.
365. Ibid.
366. Wolmer to Devonshire, 12 January 1895, DP 340.2604.
367. Chamberlain to James, 24 June 1895, M45/1755.
368. Anstruther to Wolmer, 27 June 1895, Selborne MS II (13) 144.

369. Anstruther to Devonshire, 30 September 1895, DP 340.2652.
370. Mid-Devon Liberal Unionist Association, 1891, 15 February 1892, uncatalogued items, Clifford papers.
371. W. Derbyshire LUA account book for 1906 election, Derbyshire County Record Office, D504/38/3/13.
372. Lubenow, *Liberal Intellectuals*, p.202.
373. Rix, '"The Elimination of corrupt practices in British Elections?"', pp.81–2.
374. Henry James notebook, M45/1865.

5.   Liberal Unionism and the Electorate

1. H. W. Stephens, 'The Changing Context of British Politics in the 1880s: The Reform Acts and the Formation of the Liberal Unionist Party', *Social Science History*, 1:4 (1977), pp.486–501.
2. J.P.D. Dunbabin, 'British elections in the nineteenth and twentieth centuries, a regional approach', *English Historical Review*, 375 (1980), p.254.
3. For further discussion of the impact of local personality on political behaviour see Brodie, *The Politics of the Poor*, pp.12–15.
4. There were thirty-nine challenges from Liberal Unionists in England, twenty-three in Scotland and five in Wales.
5. Those who retired were: H. G. Allen (Pembroke and Haverford West); W. S. Allen (Newcastle-under-Lyme); R. Ferguson (Carlisle); W. T. Harker (Ripon); H. C. Howard (Penrith); W. Jacks (Leith Burghs); E. A. Leatham (Huddersfield); J. Ramsay (Falkirk Burghs); H. Robertson (Merioneth); J. Ruston (Lincoln); G. Salis-Schwabe (Middleton); the Marquis of Stafford (Sutherlandshire); H. Meysey-Thompson (Brigg). Sir R. Anstruther died in July and his seat (St. Andrews Burghs) was contested by his son, Harry Anstruther. F. W. Grafton (Accrington), J. H. Blades (West Bromwich), F. T. Cobbold (Stowmarket), R. Davies (Anglesey) who had all abstained on 8 June, also retired.
6. Chamberlain to Caine, n.d. ('Sunday'), JC5/10/7.
7. Heneage to Wintringham, 15 June 1886, 2HEN 5/13/50.
8. Gell to Milner, 27 June 1886, Milner MS 4.
9. Stephens, 'The Changing Context of British Politics', p.499.
10. Alexander, *Chief Whip*, p.83.
11. A. Morley to Gladstone, 7 July 1886, Add. Mss 44253.
12. L. Morris to Lord Spencer, 20 July 1886, misc. Althorp.
13. See J. Cornford, 'Aggregate election data and British party alignments, 1885–1910' in E. Allardt and S. Rokkan (eds.), *Mass politics: Studies in Political Sociology* (New York, 1970), pp.108–109.
14. W. Harcourt to Hartington, 28 June 1886, quoted in Holland, *Life of Spencer Compton, Vol. 2*, p.163.
15. Lawrence, *Electing Our Masters*, p.73.
16. W. E. Gladstone, *The Irish Question: A history of an idea; lessons of the* election (London, 1886), p.27.
17. All statistics from *The Times,* 31 July 1886.
18. Bridges, *Reminiscences of a Country Politician,* p.167.
19. See the example of William Cartwright, defeated in Mid-Northamptonshire. C(A)1, box 16, bundle 14.

20. Heneage to Wintringham, 5 July 1886, 2HEN 5/13/56.

21. *Daily Telegraph,* 13 July 1886.

22. D. Brooks, 'Gladstone and the 1886 General Election', paper delivered at the Gladstone conference, St. Deniol's Library, Hawarden, 17 July 2011.

23. W. Tuckwell, *Reminiscences of a Radical Parson* (London, 1905), p.59.

24. Caine to Chamberlain, n.d. (July 1886?), JC5/10/5.

25. *Standard,* 14 July 1886.

26. Sidgwick and Sidgwick, *H. Sidgwick: A Memoir,* 17 July 1886, p.451.

27. C. R. Spencer to Lord Spencer, 10 July 1886, misc. Althorp.

28. Milner to Gell, 20 November 1886, D3287/MIL/1/176.

29. 'Is Liberal Reunion possible?,' *Congregational Review,* October 1886.

30. C. S. Roundell to Lord Spencer, 22 July 1886, misc. Althorp.

31. Hammond, *Gladstone and the Irish Nation,* p.557.

32. Tuckwell, *Reminiscences of a Radical Parson,* p.60.

33. E. Welbourne, *The Miners' Union of Northumberland and Durham* (Cambridge, 1923), pp.199–200.

34. *Liberal Unionist Association 1886: Origin and Progress,* AC2/1/1.

35. *Scotsman,* 7 July 1886.

36. See, for example, William Cornwallis Cartwright's correspondence with ILPU, C(A)1 Box 16 bundle 7.

37. Camperdown to Cartwright, 29 June 1886 C(A)1 Box 99, unnumbered bundle.

38. See the case of Richard Chamberlain, 'Liberal Unionist organisation', *The Liberal Unionist,* 25, February 1888.

39. O'Leary, *The elimination of Corrupt Practises in British elections,* p.208.

40. *The Times,* 28 June 1886.

41. For example in Doncaster, the wife of the Liberal Unionist candidate was injured by a rock thrown through a carriage window. On 13 July rioting broke out in Newmarket during the election, while Liberals in York were pelted with rotten fruit and eggs. Such was the level of tension that Chamberlain hired a bodyguard. Lubenow, *Parliamentary Politics,* p.292

42. *The Times,* 9 July 1886.

43. *Daily Telegraph,* 14 July 1886.

44. *Daily News,* 15 July 1886

45. *Northern Whig,* 14 July 1886; 9 August 1886. See also Budge and O'Leary, *Belfast: Approach to Crisis,* pp.87–88. Thirty-two people were killed and 371 injured.

46. D. Richter, 'The Role of Mob Riot in Victorian Elections', *Victorian Studies,* 15 (1971), pp.19–28.

47. *Liberal Unionist,* 5, 27 April 1887. Strachey was keen to bring this to his readers' attention, perhaps because he had received a black eye himself.

48. *Liberal Unionist,* 7, 11 May 1887. Violence in the capital continued, with Foster Boggis' lectures with Union Jack Van no. 1 being broken up twice in March 1890 in West Newington and Whitechapel.

49. Heneage to Wintringham, 26 April 1887, 2HEN 5/14/13.

50. H James' notebook, M45/1865.

51. P. Lynch, *The Liberal Party in Rural England 1885–1910* (Oxford, 2003), p.49.

52. Lubenow, *Parliamentary Politics,* p.286.

53. Quoted in McCaffrey, 'The Origins of Liberal Unionism in the West of Scotland', p.67.

54. For examples see *Glasgow Herald,* 27 April 1886; *Scotsman,* 1 July 1886.

55. Two of these seats remained Unionist until 1910: N. Ayrshire and Glasgow Tradeston.

56. H. Maxwell, *Evening Memories* (London, 1932), p.177.
57. E&NSLUA minute book I, 10424/17.
58. *Liberal Unionist,* 39, April 1889.
59. J. P. Grant, 'Liberal Unionist Work, 5: the East and North of Scotland Liberal Unionist Association', *Liberal Unionist,* 36, January 1889.
60. E. J. Temple Willis, 'The Devon and Cornwall Liberal Federation – its History, Constitution and Work', *Liberal Unionist,* 49, February 1890.
61. Dawson, 'Liberalism in Devon and Cornwall', p.426.
62. E. Jaggard, *Cornwall Politics in the Age of Reform* (Woodbridge, 1999), p.218; Jaggard calls the Conservative performance before 1886, 'near disastrous.' E. Jaggard, 'Small town politics in mid-Victorian Britain', *History,* 89 (2004), p.24.
63. *Liberal Unionist,* 64, May 1891.
64. F. Tillyard, 'The Distribution of the Free Churches in England', *Sociological Review,* 27 (1935), pp.1–18; Jaggard, *Cornwall Politics*, pp.184–185.
65. *Liberal Unionist,* 42, July 1889.
66. D. W. Bebbington, 'Nonconformity and Electoral Sociology 1867–1918', *Historical Journal,* 27 (1984), pp.650–651. Bebbington describes support for Liberal Unionism in the area as 'non-economic' and highlights a similar strong-hold of Wesleyan Methodism in Lincolnshire, which partially accounts for intermittent Liberal Unionist successes in the county town and Great Grimsby.
67. G. H. Chubb to Salisbury, 19 May 1887, Salisbury Papers.
68. Hartington to Salisbury, 23 May 1887, DP 340.2130; Salisbury to Hartington, 23 May 1887, DP 340.2131.
69. *Western Daily Mercury*, 1 June 1886.
70. *Western Daily Mercury*, 1 May 1886.
71. *Western Daily Mercury*, 12 June 1886.
72. J. Dingle to Courtney, 2 February 1886, CP V/9.
73. *Western Daily Mercury*, 16 June 1886.
74. *Western Morning News*, 19 June 1886.
75. Courtney to M. Fawcett, 4 July 1886, CP V/35.
76. *Western Morning News*, 2 July 1886.
77. Lynch, *The Liberal Party in Rural England*, p.49.
78. *Liberal Unionist,* 52, May 1890.
79. Dunbabin, *Rural Discontent*, chap. 10, 'The Welsh "tithe war"', pp.211–231.
80. K. O. Morgan, 'The Liberal Unionists in Wales' in K. O. Morgan, *Modern Wales: Politics, Places and People* (Cardiff, 1995), p.42.
81. Joyce, *Visions of the People*; Vernon, *Politics and the People.* For the limitations of the 'linguistic turn' in this context, see M. Bentley, 'Victorian Politics and the Linguistic Turn: Historiographical Review', *Historical Journal,* 42 (1999), pp.894–902; A. Jones, 'Word and deed: why a *post-*post-structural history is needed and how it might look', *Historical Journal*, 43 (2000), pp.537–540; P. Ghosh and L. Goldman, 'A Brief Word on "Politics" and "Culture" in Ghosh and Goldman (eds.), *Politics and Culture in Victorian Britain*, pp.1–7.
82. J. M. Lawrence, 'The dynamic of urban politics, 1867–1914' in J. Lawrence and M. Taylor (eds.), *Party, State and Society: Electoral Behaviour in Britain since 1920* (Aldershot, 1997), pp.79–105.
83. A. V. Dicey to Wolmer, 27 September 1887, Selborne MS II (13) 29–32.
84. Courtney to M. Fawcett, 4 July 1886, quoted in Gooch, *Life of Lord Courtney*, p.261.
85. *Liberal Unionist,* 12, 15 June 1887.

86. WSLUA minute book I, 1 December 1887, 10424/19.
87. Ibid., 16 April 1890.
88. *Liberal Unionist,* 32, September 1888.
89. *Liberal Unionist,* 37, February 1889.
90. 'A New Method of Canvassing', *Liberal Unionist,* 43, August 1889.
91. Heneage to Wintringham, 12 February 1892, 2HEN 5/19/3; Heneage to Wintringham 27 May 1892, 2HEN 5/19/29.
92. B. Coulbeck to Heneage, 7 March 1892, 2HEN 5/19/12.
93. Heneage to Wintringham, 13 March 1892, 2HEN 5/19/15; Heneage to Wintringham, 15 March 1892, 2HEN 5/19/17.
94. Heneage to Wintringham, 13 March 1892, 2HEN 5/19/15.
95. 'I do not trust the Tories at all.' Heneage to Wintringham, 15 March 1892, 2HEN 5/19/17; Heneage to Wintringham, 21 January 1889, 2HEN 5/16/13.
96. Heneage to Wintringham, 24 April 1892, 2HEN 5/19/24.
97. Heneage to Wintringham, 21 May 1892, 2HEN 5/19/28.
98. Heneage to Wintringham, 27 May 1892, 2HEN 5/19/29.
99. Manchester East, North, North East and South West, Rochdale, Preston, Warrington, Wigan, Widnes and Lancaster.
100. T. C. Rayner to Courtney, 21 June 1886, CP V/33; H. T. Crook 'Liberal Unionist Work 9: Manchester and District Liberal Unionist Association', *Liberal Unionist,* 41, June 1889.
101. Moore, 'Manchester Liberalism', p.37.
102. P. W. Clayden, *England under the Coalition* (London, 2nd ed., 1893), p.28.
103. James' notebook, M45/1865.
104. Hartington to Duke of Devonshire, 9 July 1886, quoted in Holland, *Life of Spencer Compton, Vol. 2,* p.163.
105. Smith, 'Conservative Ideology', p.24.
106. Sidgwick and Sidgwick, *H. Sidgwick: A Memoir,* p.559.
107. *Liberal Unionist,* 43, August 1889.
108. *Liberal Unionist,* 46, November 1889.
109. Wolmer at Leeds Conference of Liberal Unionists, November 1889, quoted in *Liberal Unionist,* 47, December 1889.
110. *Liberal Unionist,* 47, December 1889.
111. A. Richardson (Organising Sec. Oxford LUA) to Mrs Lyttelton Gell, 27 July 1894, D3287/66/4/1/55.
112. Mrs Sinclair to Mrs Gell, 17 May 1894, D3287/66/4/1/83; Mrs Sinclair to Mrs Gell, n.d. (June 1894) D3287/66/4/1/101.
113. M. Westall to Mrs Gell, n.d., (June 1894), D3287/66/4/1/96.
114. J. Boraston to J. Collings, 16 April 1886, JC8/5/3/12.
115. Mrs Sinclair to Mrs Gell, 21 March 1894, D3287/66/4/1/72.
116. Mrs Sinclair to Mrs Gell, 17 May 1894, D3287/66/4/1/83.
117. 'The Work of the Womens' Liberal Unionist Association by one of its officials', *Liberal Unionist,* 44, September 1889.
118. *Liberal Unionist,* 47, December 1889.
119. *Liberal Unionist,* 60, January 1891.
120. *Liberal Unionist,* 69, October 1891.
121. *What the Unionist Government has done for the Working Man,* Liberal Unionist Leaflet 306, (London, 1891).
122. Argyll to Wolmer, 15 March 1892, Selborne MS II (13) 123.

123. *Liberal Unionist,* 76, May 1892.
124. *Liberal Unionist,* 78, July 1892.
125. Otte '"Avenge England's dishonour"', p.386.
126. W. S. Caine, 'Organise – Educate!', *Liberal Unionist,* 1, 30 March 1887.
127. *Liberal Unionist,* 1, 30 March 1887.
128. *Liberal Unionist,* 3, 13 April 1887.
129. *Liberal Unionist,* 9, 25 May 1887.
130. *Liberal Unionist,* 16, 13 July 1887
131. Hartington to James, 18 December 1887, M45/300.
132. *Liberal Unionist,* 26, March 1888.
133. *Liberals! Liberals! Liberals!* NLF Leaflet quoted verbatim in *Liberal Unionist,* 25, February 1888.
134. *Liberal Unionist,* 35, December 1888.
135. Milner to Gell, 3 August 1887, Milner MS 4.
136. *Liberal Unionist,* 30, July 1888.
137. WSLUA minute book I, 6 December 1888, 10424/19.
138. WSLUA minute book I, 5 February 1889, 10424/19.
139. Ibid.
140. *Northern British Daily Mail,* 5 January 1889.
141. *Liberal Unionist,* 38, March 1889.
142. R. Bird, 'Liberal Unionist Work: 6. The West of Scotland', *Liberal Unionist,* 38, March 1889.
143. Quoted in Holland, *Life of Spencer Compton, Vol. 2,* p.218n.
144. *Liberal Unionist,* 46, November 1889.
145. Hartington to Wolmer, 13 September 1889, Selborne MS II (4) 41–42.
146. *Liberal Unionist,* 46. November 1889.
147. Hartington to Wolmer, 9 October 1889, Selborne MS II (4) 43–44.
148. R. MacGeah to H. de F. Montgomery, 14 February 1890, quoted in Biagini, *British Democracy,* pp.267–268.
149. TD1/129.
150. H. W. Elphiston to Parker Smith, 14 February 1890; Strachey to Parker Smith, 13 February 1890, TD1/129.
151. *Liberal Unionist,* 61, February 1891.
152. Hartington to Wolmer, 10 October 1891, Selborne MS II (4) 144.
153. A. V. Dicey to Wolmer, 11 November 1891, Selborne MS II (13) 99–102.
154. Quoted in Jay, *Joseph Chamberlain,* p.171.
155. *Bristol Mercury,* 16 November 1891; *Exeter Flying Post,* 14 November 1891.
156. E. Dawson, '"Popery" and "Clericalism"' *Liberal Unionist,* 71, December 1891.
157. 'Why Unionists lose elections in rural districts', *Liberal Unionist,* 71, December 1891.
158. Wolmer to Salisbury, 9 January 1892, Salisbury Papers.
159. *Birmingham Gazette,* 15 January 1892.
160. *Liberal Unionist,* 73, February 1892.
161. Hartington to Wolmer, 9 December 1891, Selborne MS II (4) 156.
162. Chamberlain to Wolmer, 25 January 1892, JC5/74/11.
163. Hartington to Wolmer, 9 December 1891, Selborne MS II (4) 154.
164. Lawrence, *Electing Our Masters,* p.74.
165. K. Rix, 'The Party Agent and English Electoral Culture, 1880–1906', PhD thesis (Cambridge, 2001), p.13 passim.

166. Thompson is wrong to suggest that 'campaigning vans [were] pioneered by land reform-ers in the 1890s.' J. Thompson, '"Pictorial Lies"? – Posters and Politics in Britain, c.1880–1914,' *Past and Present*, 197 (2007), p.203.
167. *Liberal Unionist,* 53, June 1890.
168. *Liberal Unionist,* 35, December 1888.
169. *Liberal Unionist,* 40, May 1889.
170. *Liberal Unionist,* 43, August 1889.
171. *Liberal Unionist,* 51, April 1890; 52, May 1890.
172. *Liberal Unionist,* 59, December 1890.
173. *Liberal Unionist,* 76, May 1892.
174. 'A Great Unionist Demonstration', *Wellow Parish Newsletter,* n.d., 1892. The activities of another Unionist van operator in the 1890s is described in K. Rix, '"Go Out into the Highways and the Hedges": The Diary of Michael Sykes, Conservative Political Lecturer, 1895 and 1907–8', *Parliamentary History,* 20 (2001), pp.209–31.
175. *Liberal Unionist,* 78, July 1892.
176. *Liberal Unionist,* 38, March 1889.
177. *Liberal Unionist,* 66, July 1891.
178. *The Times,* 9 March 1892.
179. *The Times,* 30 April 1892.
180. 'Memoir' dated 1892, JC/8/1/1.
181. See Green, *Crisis of Conservatism,* pp.131–2.
182. *The Tory,* 3, 20 September 1892, Conservative Party Archive, Bodleian Library, CPA Pub 1/1.
183. J. Bardon, *A History of Ulster* (Belfast, 2nd ed., 2005), pp.409–410.
184. 'Memoir' dated 1892, JC/8/1/1.
185. *The Times,* 31 March 1892.
186. *The Times,* 26 April 1892.
187. Moore, 'Liberal Unionism and the Home Rule Crisis in Leicester', pp.194–197.
188. South Warwickshire Conservative Association minute book, Warwickshire Record Office, CR1397.
189. Chamberlain speaking at the Liberal Unionist Club, quoted in *The Times,* 9 March 1892.
190. *The Times,* 9 March 1892.
191. *The Times,* 24 May 1892.
192. Garvin, *Life of Joseph Chamberlain, Vol. 2* pp.538–540.
193. Hurst, *Joseph Chamberlain and West Midland Politics,* p.7.
194. Pelling, *Social Geography of British Elections,* p.195.
195. Ibid., p.208.
196. Chamberlain to Wolmer, 11 July 1892, JC5/74/20.
197. Powell Williams to Chamberlain, 19 July 1892, JC5/72/14.
198. Chamberlain to Provost Wilson, 24 February 1892, JC6/6/1A/18.
199. See Devonshire to James, 2 July 1892, M45/1716.
200. Selborne MS, SP13*.
201. Jenkins, 'The funding of the Liberal Unionist Party', p.938.
202. C. G. Cooper to Wolmer, 27 July 1892, Selborne MS II (13) 124–125.
203. Harcourt-Williams (ed.), *Salisbury-Balfour Correspondence,* p.284.
204. *South Wales Daily News,* 14 October 1891.
205. See Morgan, 'The Liberal Unionists In Wales.'
206. Chamberlain to Balfour, 19 July 1892. Balfour Papers, MSS 49773.
207. Cragoe, *Culture, Politics and National Identity,* p.78.

208. 'The Approaching General Election: XVI: The Western Counties', *The Times*, 2 February 1892.

209. Bedford's behaviour had become very unpredictable following a seizure in 1887. Derby's diary, 12 September 1887, *Later Derby Diaries*, p.109.

210. *Liberal Unionist*, 46, November 1889. Purvis was standing as the previous MP, John Wentworth-Fitzwilliam, son of the fifth Earl Fitzwilliam, had died.

211. *Liberal Unionist*, 53, June 1890.

212. *Liberal Unionist*, 55, August 1890.

213. Devonshire to Salisbury, 3 May 1892, Salisbury Papers.

214. Chamberlain to Heneage, 6 July 1892, JC5/41/30.

215. Liberal Unionist Association Report for 1892, D3287/116/2/9.

216. James to Chamberlain, 16 July 1892, JC5/46/25.

217. C. H. D. Howard (ed.), *A Political Memoir: 1880–1892 by Joseph Chamberlain* (London, 1953), p.276.

218. E. Le Riche, 'The Lessons of the Elections', *Liberal Unionist*, 80, September 1892.

219. See I. Cawood, 'The 1892 General Election and the eclipse of the Liberal Unionists,' *Parliamentary History*, 29:3 (2010), pp.331–357.

220. See Smith, 'Conservative Ideology', pp.24–25; Loughlin, 'Joseph Chamberlain', pp.202–219.

221. Quoted in *The Times*, 9 March 1892.

222. Chamberlain, J. A. Bright, Meysey-Thompson and Jasper More.

223. W. Thorburn, T. W. Russell and J. Goldsmid.

224. Asquith in Commons, 8 August 1892, quoted in *The Times*, 9 August 1892.

225. Windscheffel, *Popular Conservatism*, pp.167–168. In a similar fashion, Arthur Conan Doyle and Ernest Shackleton later stood as a Liberal Unionist candidates.

226. The only victory was Heneage's return to Grimsby in March 1893.

227. Chamberlain to Devonshire, 18 April 1895, DP 340.2608.

228. *Glasgow Herald*, 30 November 1893.

229. Uncatalogued items, Clifford Papers.

230. Uncatalogued items, Clifford Papers. Mid-Devon's efforts were somewhat in vain, as only thirty-seven were returned and the Clifford archive contains at least 100 further blank copies.

231. Thompson, '"Pictorial Lies"?' p.180. Thompson only cites one example of visual propaganda from before 1900, however.

232. *The Speaker's Handbook on the Irish Question* (London, 1889); T. Hodgkin, *Think It Out: A Lecture on the question of Home Rule for Ireland* (London, 1888).

233. A. V. Dicey, *A Leap in the Dark* (London, 1893).

234. 'The Union Jack', uncatalogued items, Clifford Papers.

235. Copies of these posters and the black and white handbill versions are preserved at Ugbrooke House, Clifford 3 (2).

236. Somerset Liberal Unionist Association Annual Report, 30 April 1894., uncatalogued items, Clifford Papers. Boraston had mailed all the LUAs, asking for copies of Liberal propaganda material 'not including newspapers' so that the Liberal Unionist could respond accordingly. J. Boraston, circular, 18 April 1894, uncatalogued items, Clifford Papers.

237. 1895 Election Notes, JC 6/6/1D/4.

238. Quoted in Askwith, *Lord James of Hereford*, p.235.

239. 'Mr Chamberlain's Labour Programme', uncatalogued items, Clifford Papers.

240. Clifford 3(2); *Westminster Gazette*, 9 July 1895.

241. I. G. C. Hutchinson, *A Political History of Scotland, 1832–1924: Parties, Elections and Issues* (Edinburgh, 1986), pp.200–204.

242. W. D. Ross, 'Bradford Politics, 1880–1906', PhD thesis, (Bradford, 1977), pp.239–240; P. J. Waller, *Democracy and Sectarianism : A Political and Social History of Liverpool* (Liverpool, 1981), p.155.

243. *The Rural World*, 342 (6 July 1895), p.475.

244. Steele, *Lord Salisbury*, pp.300–301.

245. WSLUA minute book II, 27 November 1895, 10424/20.

246. Chamberlain at Stratford, reported in *The Times*, 17 July 1895.

247. Cornford, 'The Transformation of Conservatism.'

248. P. Readman, 'The 1895 General Election and Political Change in late Victorian England', *Historical Journal*, 42 (1999), p.479. See also, Brodie, *The Politics of the Poor*, p.101.

249. J. Davis, 'The Enfranchisement of the Urban poor in Late-Victorian Britain' in Ghosh and Goldman (eds.), *Politics and Culture in Victorian Britain*, pp.116–117.

250. Windscheffel, *Popular Conservatism*, pp.173–175.

251. Lewis Fry in North Bristol, Walter Morrison in Skipton, Havelock-Allen in S. E. Durham, R. B. Finlay in Inverness and William Arrol in South Ayrshire all regained their seats in 1895.

252. Uncatalogued items, Clifford Papers.

253. Uncatalogued items, Clifford Papers.

254. J. Boraston, circulars, Clifford 3 (2).

255. P. Readman, 'The Conservative Party, Patriotism and British Politics: The Case of the General Election of 1900', *Journal of British Studies*, 40 (2001), p.115.

256. Editorial, *Freeman's Journal*, 18 July 1895; *Irish Daily Independent*, 18 July 1895.

257. Sykes, *Rise and Fall of British Liberalism*, p.136.

258. Biagini, *British Democracy*, p.3.

259. Lubenow, *Liberal Intellectuals*, p.198.

260. Vernon, *Politics and the People*; L. Goldman, 'The Defection of the Middle Classes: The Endowed Schools Act, the Liberal Party and the 1874 Election' in Ghosh and Goldman (eds.), *Politics and Culture in Victorian Britain*, pp.118–135.

261. Cawood, 'The Unionist "Compact"', pp.103–104.

262. Thompson, '"Pictorial Lies"?', passim.

263. Vernon, *Politics and the People*, p.337.

264. Ridgeway, 'The Liberal Unionist Party', p.182.

6.   The Strange Death of Liberal Unionism

1. E. Hammerton and D. Cannadine, 'Conflict and Consensus on a Ceremonial Occasion: The Diamond Jubilee in Cambridge in 1897' *Historical Journal*, 24: 1 (1981), pp.112–113; A. S. Thompson, *Imperial Britain: The Empire in British Politics, c.1800–1932* (London: 2000), p.7.

2. Boraston did receive a testimonial of a silver bowl and a cheque for 1,500 guineas for his work in organising the 1895 electoral victory. *The Times*, 5 August 1896.

3. *The Times*, 3 August 1895; 13 August 1895. Chamberlain's decision was put down to 'how much closer the relations between the two sections of the National Party have become', but may have been influenced by Tory complaints that, in the allocation of government positions,

he had 'exacted his full pound of flesh. In fact he has a good deal more than he and his party are properly entitled to.' *North British Daily Mail*, 5 July 1895.

4. J. Knowles to Devonshire, 15 July 1895, DP 340.2635.

5. Devonshire to Chamberlain, 16 August 1895, DP 340.2642.

6. Chamberlain to James, 3 August 1895, M45/1768.

7. James to Devonshire, 29 November 1895. DP, uncatalogued.

8. Selborne to Chamberlain, copy to Devonshire, 6 December 1895, DP 340.2667.

9. *LUAM*, 4:2, February 1896. The letter was also circulated to all LUAs. J. Boraston, circular, 10 February 1896, Clifford 3 (2).

10. *The Times*, 24 January 1896.

11. Devonshire to James, 1 October 1896, M45/1775.

12. Hutchinson, *Life of Sir John Lubbock, Vol. 2*, pp.47–48; *LUAM*, 6:.1, January 1897.

13. James' Memoir, M45/1864, pp.89–91. For Chamberlain's career as Colonial Secretary between 1895 and 1899, see A.N. Porter, *The origins of the South Africa War: Joseph Chamberlain and the diplomacy of imperialism* (Manchester, 1980).

14. M. Bentley, *Politics Without Democracy, 1815–1914* (Oxford, 2nd ed., 1996), pp.211–212.

15. Letter from Chamberlain, 19 April 1896, published in *LUAM*, 4: 5, May 1896.

16. *LUAM*, 4:5; *LUAM*, 4:6.

17. Selborne's memoir, Selborne MS IX 191.

18. *LUAM*, 5: 2, February 1897.

19. *LUAM*, 5: 12, December 1897.

20. *LUAM*, 6: 1, January 1898.

21. WSLUA Minute Book II, 8 November 1895; AGM, 27 November 1895, 10424/20. See Burness, *'Strange Associations'*, pp.136–137.

22. WSLUA Minute Book II, 19 June 1896, 10424/20.

23. Ibid., AGM, 26 November 1896.

24. A. C. Corbett, quoted in ibid., AGM, 10 November 1897.

25. Ibid., 19 March 1897; 7 May 1897.

26. Ibid.

27. Ibid., 17 November 1897.

28. Ibid., 25 February 1898.

29. Kelvin to Matthew Arthur, 5 August 1898, recorded in ibid.

30. *Western Mail*, 21 June 1897.

31. Williamson, 'State Prayers, Fasts and Thanksgivings', pp.121–74.

32. Hammerton and Cannadine, 'Conflict and Consensus', p.113. Nationalists in Ireland either boycotted the celebrations or held a protest against Victoria's failings as monarch of Ireland.

33. Thompson, *Imperial Britain*, p.11.

34. Garvin, *Life of Joseph Chamberlain, Vol. 3*, p.186.

35. Otte, '"Avenge England's dishonour."'

36. *LUAM*, 5: 11, November 1897.

37. Sidgwick and Sidgwick, *H. Sidgwick: a Memoir*, p.555.

38. *LUAM*, 6:. 6, June 1898.

39. *LUAM*, 6: 10, October 1898.

40. *LUAM*, 6: 7, July 1898.

41. Liverpool Exchange (November 1897), Wolverhampton South (February 1898), W. Staffordshire (May 1898), Durham (June 1898), Grimsby (August 1898) and Darlington

(September 1898). Three of these were won with majorities of only 1%, however. See Otte, '"Avenge England's dishonour."'

42. The defeats were South East Durham (February 1898), South Norfolk (May 1898) and Cornwall (Launceston) (August 1898). The defeat in South Norfolk was a shock, as Francis Taylor had retained the seat in 1895 with a majority of 836, yet this was wiped out in a 13% swing to the Liberals. A letter to *The Times* from K. Kemp, chairman of the Liberal election committee, blamed this defeat on the Unionist choice of candidate, J. S. Holmes, an unpopular landowner, to replace Taylor, a popular brewer, but it may also have been due to the failure of the government to fulfil the expectations of the agricultural workers since 1895. Typical of his changed priorities, Chamberlain had made a speech on foreign policy the same day, but, Kemp noted 'the question of foreign policy did not change 200 votes.' *The Times*, 17 May 1898.

43. *LUAM*, 6: 12, December 1898.

44. *LUAM*, 6: 12, December 1898.

45. Annual report for 1897 and 1898, All Saints Ward Liberal Unionist Executive Committee Minute Book, Birmingham LUA, 1897–1914, Birmingham City Archives, Birmingham Central Library, MS 814.

46. Heneage to E. Grange, 20 November 1897, 2HEN 5/22/21.

47. Heneage to E. Grange, 4 April 1899, 2HEN 2/24/15. Parker Smith was equally dissatisfied. See letter to his brother, 31 July 1897, quoted in Lubenow, *Liberal Intellectuals*, p.214n.

48. *The Times*, 30 June 1899. The speech was not reported in *LUAM*.

49. *LUAM*, 6: 11, November 1898.

50. *LUAM*, 7: 12, December 1899.

51. Lansdowne to Devonshire, 20 September 1900, DP 340.2832.

52. Anstruther to Devonshire, 11 October 1903, DP 340.3011.

53. *LUAM*, 8: 7, July 1900.

54. Quoted in *The Times,* 24 September 1900.

55. *The Times*, 2 October 1900.

56. Chamberlain in Saltley, 29 September 1900, quoted in *The Times*, 1 October 1900.

57. Chamberlain to Parker Smith, 9 September, 1900 TD1/116.

58. *The Times*, 30 May 1901. Readman has found that although 52% of Unionist addresses mentioned old age pensions in 1895, only 20% did so in 1900. Readman, 'The Conservative Party, Patriotism and British politics', p.115.

59. Ibid., p.112. Readman suggests that imperialism's appeal in 1900 was cross-class and not wholly illiberal. Ibid., pp.134–140. For a contrasting interpretation, see R. Price, *An Imperial War and the British Working Class: Working Class Attitudes and Reactions to the Boer War, 1899–1902* (London: 1972).

60. Arthur Elliot reported in his diary that 'the largeness of the result astonished everyone'. A. Elliot diary, 1 October 1900, National Library of Scotland, 19624/106. For the impact of Liberal disunity on working-class voters, see Brodie, *Politics of the Poor*, pp.101–103. See also Sykes, *Rise and Fall of British Liberalism*, p.136.

61. E&NSLUA, Minute Book II, 26 May 1899, 10424/18.

62. See A. Conan Doyle to Mary Doyle, 27 August 1900, quoted in Lellenby (ed.), *Conan Doyle: A. Life in Letters*, p.456; A Conan Doyle to Mary Doyle, n.d. (September 1900), quoted in ibid., p.459. Boraston appears to have had a family interest in Edinburgh, which may explain his ability to bypass the E&NSLUA. Conan Doyle was based, for the duration of the campaign, at the Old Waverley Temperance Hotel, which was owned by the Boraston

family. Ibid., p.466. Conan Doyle lost by 569 votes, largely owing to a poster campaign the night before the election, which accused Conan Doyle of being a Roman Catholic (he did come from a Catholic family, but was not a Catholic himself) and an agent of the Jesuits. A. Conan Doyle to Mary Doyle, n.d. (September 1900), quoted in ibid., p.464.

63. A report into the activity of the regional LUAs in March 1898 found the following Associations were 'weak': Coatbridge; Shettleston. S. Lanark (Central) was 'defunct' as the Conservative MP objected to any Liberal Association in his constituency; N. W. Lanark (Central) had had 'only 2 attendees last meeting'; East Renfrewshire had a good Association but also 'poor attendees'; in Shawlands and Queens Park, the Associations were merely described as 'lazy.' There were on-going problems in S. Ayrshire, where the MP, Sir William Arrol, was opposed to any interference in his Association by the WSLUA. WSLUA Minute Book II, 18 March 1898, 10424/20. In Dumbarton, Argyll and Ayrshire, one Association was found to be 'defunct', nine were described as 'inactive', two more as 'dead', one as 'sleepy' and that of Newmilns as 'small, useless.' All these Associations continued to be listed on the WSLUA constitution, at least until 1900. Ibid., 1 April 1898; 25 May 1898. A serious effort to revive all these Associations was then undertaken, with varying success. See ibid., 24 March 1899.

64. Ibid., 10 January 1899. The cost of such a canvass was clearly prohibitive for the Association to bear, as they had to ask the LUA for a contribution for this activity.

65. Ibid., 17 April 1899; 19 May 1899; 7 July 1899. There is little detail in the minute book as to the methods employed by the canvassers, so it is impossible to be clear as to the rigour with which these returns were obtained.

66. J. A. Marshall to Sir A. Maclean, 26 April 1899, Partick Liberal Unionist Council Minute Book 1898–1904, Glasgow City Archives, D16.22/63.

67. Maryhill Liberal Unionist Association Minute Book, Minutes of AGM, 5 April 1900. National Library of Scotland, 10424/81.

68. W. Fleming to H. Eldred, 23 August 1900, ibid.

69. WSLUA Minute Book II, 21 April 1899, 10424/20.

70. Bird's report, Ibid., 18 October 1898.

71. The Association's funds in 1900 were not as strong as in 1895, however. Then the Association had raised £7,375, but for 1900 they had only managed £4,265 (Burness confuses these two figures). ibid., 8 August 1900. It is likely that the disarray among the Liberals in their reaction to the Boer War compensated for the relative weakness of the Party in the region that the canvass had revealed.

72. Ibid., 5 May 1899; 8 June 1900.

73. The Liberal Unionist agent in Parker Smith's seat boasted that everything was ready 'to the last envelope.' Ibid., 10 August 1900.

74. Ibid., 28 September 1900.

75. 1900 – £4,265
      1901 – £3,205
      1902 – £2,200
      Ibid., 8 August 1900; WSLUA Minute Book III, 20 November 1901, 10424/21; Ibid., 31 October 1902.

76. Ibid., 17 October 1902.

77. Ibid., 30 October 1903.

78. Ibid., 2 December 1903.

79. James' Memoir, M45/1864, p.76.

80. M Fawcett, Memo on WLUA Foreign Literature Fund, July 1902, 7MGF/A/1/230–231.

81. E. Riedi, 'Women, Gender, and the promotion of empire: the Victoria League, 1901–1914' *Historical Journal*, 45 (2002), pp.569–599.
82. F. Balfour to M. Fawcett, 24 October 1903, 9/08/199.
83. W. Fleming to J. M. Taylor, 23 February 1901, Partick Liberal Unionist Council Minute Book 1898–1904, D16.22/63.
84. W. Fleming to Whilson, 25 February 1901, ibid. As Fleming had not been informed of this proposal until two days before the meeting and, as his position as Council secretary was naturally at risk, he seems to have had no incentive to support the proposal and thus avoid this 'fiasco'.
85. W. Fleming to Russell, 28 February 1901, ibid.
86. D. Brooks, *The Age of Upheaval: Edwardian Politics, 1899–1914* (Manchester, 1995), pp.45–47.
87. In particular, see reports of the meeting of the Birmingham, Aston and Handsworth LUAs, *The Times*, 17 May 1902; Birmingham Liberal Unionist Conference, 9 October 1902, *The Times*, 10 October 1902. Perhaps understandably, Chamberlain chose to make an official visit to South Africa from November 1902 until February 1903.
88. J. Chamberlain to Devonshire, 22 September 1902, DP 340.2998.
89. Quoted in Koss, *Nonconformity in Modern British Politics*, p.46.
90. P. Readman, 'The Liberal Party and Patriotism in Early Twentieth Century Britain', *Twentieth Century British History,* 12:3, (2001), pp.273–281. See also Sykes, *Rise and Fall of British Liberalism*, p.150.
91. Porritt, 'Party Conditions in England', p.213. In Orkney and Shetland, Cathcart Wason resigned from the Party, fought and won a by-election as an independent Liberal in protest.
92. James' Memoir, M45/1864, p.95.
93. See R. A. Rempel, *Unionists Divided: Arthur Balfour, Joseph Chamberlain and the Unionist Free Traders* (Newton Abbot, 1972) for a detailed account of the divisions between the tariff reformers and Unionists free traders.
94. Searle, *Country before Party*, pp.49–50.
95. Patton, *Science, Politics and Business*, p.240.
96. Askwith, *Lord James of Hereford*, p.275.
97. Harcourt to James, 3 July, 1903, M45/1239.
98. Devonshire to James, 1 June 1903, reporting the agreement with Chamberlain. M45/1228.
99. Askwith, *Lord James of Hereford*, pp.276–7.
100. 'What is to be done as to the L.U. Association? I suppose nothing, except to suffer some resignations.' Devonshire to James, 17 September 1903, quoted in ibid., p.282.
101. Anstruther to Devonshire, 11 October 1903, DP 340.3011.
102. *The Times*, 21 October 1903. Backhouse, the honorary secretary of the LUA wrote to *The Times* confessing that, with Elliot and Lambton opposing tariff reform and Pike Pease supporting it, 'the lines of division were … most forcibly marked out.' *The Times*, 24 October 1903.
103. Devonshire to James, 15 October 1903, M45/1269.
104. Devonshire to James, 16 October 1903, M45/1272. With the refusal of Chamberlain and Powell Williams to meet him, Devonshire began to share these suspicions and suggested taking personal control of the LUA funds. Devonshire to James, 19 October, M45/1277.
105. J. Powell Williams to James, 22 October 1903, DP 340.3016; Devonshire to James, 4 December 1903, M45/1294.
106. *The Times*, 9 January 1904. James and Asquith also met on 21 December to discuss an electoral and parliamentary alliance between Liberal and Unionist free traders. M45/1299; M45/1301.

107. *The Times,* 6 January 1904; 9 January 1904; 14 January 1904. Only Elliot wrote in defence of the Duke's position. *The Times,* 16 January 1904.

108. *The Times,* 18 January 1904.

109. Devonshire to Chamberlain, 2 January 1904, DP 340.3048, The bulk of the correspondence between Chamberlain and Devonshire was published in *The Times,* 11 January 1904.

110. Durham to Devonshire, 11 January 1904, DP 340.3059. Chamberlain's enthusiasm for the cause of tariff reform may have been heightened by the impact of the 1904 Licensing Act, which drove those few nonconformist Liberal Unionists who had stomached the 1902 Education Act back to the arms of the Liberals.

111. Chamberlain to Devonshire, 3 February 1904, DP 340.3070. *The Times,* 4 February 1904.

112. *The Times,* 26 February 1904.

113. Devonshire to Chamberlain, 6 February 1904, DP 340.3072. The *LUAM* did remain uncommitted between throughout 1903, publishing the speeches of both free fooders and tariff reformers without significant editorial bias. It suspended publication with the decision to suspend the activities of the LUA, but, with Chamberlain's capture of the Council and the Club in spring 1904, it became a mouthpiece for the tariff reform movement when it resumed publication in December 1904. See J. Boraston circular, 7 November 1904. Clifford 3 (2).

114. Devonshire to Wolmer, 5 February 1904, Selborne MS II (4) 194.

115. Devonshire to James, 15 April 1904, DP 340.3081.

116. *The Times,* 17 March 1904.

117. *The Times,* 24 March 1904.

118. *The Times,* 19 May 1904.

119. *The Times,* 30 June 1904. Rempel, *Unionists Divided.,* p.147. Devonshire accepted the presidency of the Club in August 1904. Devonshire to James, 9 August 1904, M45/1320. The Unionist Free Trade Club and the Liberal Union Club held AGMs within days of each other in April 1905 and devoted more time to attacking each other than to criticising the Nationalists or Liberals. *The Times,* 11 April 1905; *The Times,* 13 April 1905.

120. *The Times,* 15 July 1904. Lord Belper, letter to the editor, *The Times,* 20 July 1904. Savile Crossley was installed as chairman and the Council secured the necessary guarantee of funding by appointing Earl Fitzwilliam as treasurer. To Devonshire's acute embarrassment, Victor Cavendish was appointed as honorary secretary.

121. *The Times,* 15 July 1904.

122. *The Times,* 13 July 1904.

123. WSLUA Minute Book III, 18 November 1904, 10424/21. For the activity of the female radical Unionists in the following years, see D. Thackeray, 'Home and Politics: Women and Conservative activism in early twentieth century Britain', *Journal of British Studies,* 49: 4 (2010), pp.826–848.

124. Devonshire to James, 17 January 1905, M45/1335; B. Turner, *Free Trade and Protection* (London, 1971), p.72.

125. A parallel made explicit in Winston Churchill's letter to Devonshire, 8 June 1903, quoted in Holland, *Life of Spencer Compton, Vol. 2,* p.310.

126. F. Trentman, *Free Trade Nation: Commerce, Consumption and Civil Society in Modern Britain* (Oxford, 2008), pp.63–68.

127. *The Times,* 4 February 1905; Devonshire to James, 17 January 1905, M45/1335; Elliot to James, 24 December 1905, M45/1427; F.W.S. Craig, *British Parliamentary Election Results, 1885–1918* (Basingstoke, 1974), p.108.

128. E. Crawford, *The Women's Suffrage Movement – A Reference Guide*, (London: 1999). M. Fawcett, (n.d.), 7MGF/A/1/230. Fawcett noted the 'free trade party' on the executive as comprising 'Lady Frances Balfour, Miss Flora Stevenson of Edinburgh, Mrs Heywood Johnstone and myself.' Clearly, Lady Gertrude Cochrane and Mrs Parker Smith (the president and hon. sec, respectively) were tariff reformers.

129. F. Balfour to M. Fawcett, 17 October 1903, 9/08/196.

130. M. Fawcett, (n.d.), 7MGF/A/1/230. Lady Balfour believed that the WLUA had only been kept going so that it could be taken over by the tariff reformers. F. Balfour to M. Fawcett, 17 October 1903, 9/08/196.

131. M. Fawcett to Lady Gertrude Cochrane (draft, n.d., 1903?), 7MGF/A/1/232a. The rebels promptly formed a 'Women's Free Trade Union.'

132. Thompson, *Imperial Britain*, p.57.

133. A copy of the agreement was published in the *Nottingham Daily Express*, 13 February 1905.

134. Mid-Devon LUA minute book, 8 February 1905, Clifford 3 (2).

135. 'I do not understand one remark in your letter where you speak of a disagreeable impression left by a previous visit to Glasgow.' Chamberlain to Parker Smith, 17 October 1903, TD1/116.

136. Lord Balfour of Burleigh to James, 3 October 1903, M45/1258. Chamberlain's meeting backfired, as Wilson rejoined the Liberals in February 1904. Asquith believed that Chamberlain's policy was making no impact on Scotland. Harcourt to James, 21 October 1903, M45/1278.

137. W. Fleming to J. Boraston, 7 July 1904, Partick Liberal Unionist Council Minute Book 1898–1904, D16.22/63.

138. WSLUA Minute Book III, 3 December 1903, 23 November 1904, 29 November 1905, 10424/21.

139. Chamberlain to Parker Smith, 2 September 1903, TD1/116. 'I should have felt more the opposition of the *Scotsman* than that of any other paper.'

140. Chamberlain to Parker Smith, 17 October 1903, ibid. This was striking as the Unionist press, including *The Times,* was converted to tariff reform very swiftly.

141. Typically, Sir William Arrol supported Chamberlain's crusade, defying the WSLUA as he had done throughout his time as MP for South Ayrshire. See Sir R. Purvis, *William Arrol* (Edinburgh: 1913), p.137.

142. Burness, 'The Making of Scottish Unionism', p.23.

143. Sir M. Foster (October 1903), T. W. Russell, J. Wilson (February 1904), G. Kemp, E. Hain (August 1904), R. Cavendish (January 1906). E. J. Reed, MP for Cardiff boroughs defected from the Liberals in support of tariff reform in December 1904.

144. *The Times*, 1 January 1906; 3 January 1906. Elliot and James even went as far as to attempt (unsuccessfully) to persuade Devonshire to issue a manifesto calling on voters to support Liberal candidates, but Balfour had already secured a promise from him 'to do as little damage to Unionism as possible.' Askwith, *Lord James of Hereford*, p.291; Elliot to James, 23 November 1905, M45/1414; Balfour to Devonshire (copy), 27 October 1905, M45/1399; Devonshire to James, 12 December 1905, M45/1419.

145. Ridgeway, 'The Liberal Unionist Party', p.197.

146. P. Williamson, 'The Conservative Party 1900–1930: From crisis to ascendancy' in C. Wrigley (ed.), *A Companion to Early Twentieth Century Britain* (Oxford, 2003), p.7.

147. The Party lost all of its Devon and Cornish seats and 75% of its MPs in Scotland. The only regional core of Liberal Unionists was now in the West Midlands (with 10 MPs),

who, through direct appeals 'to show their generous loyalty to old friends and to the old cause' and, through effective canvassing and organisation on a ward level, managed to maintain their electoral support in the face of the landslide elsewhere in the country. See S. Roberts, 'Politics and the Birmingham working class: the general elections of 1900 and 1906 in East Birmingham', *West Midland Studies,* 15 (1982), pp.12–21; Annual Report for 1904 and 1905, All Saints Ward Liberal Unionist Executive Committee Minute Book, 1897–1914. Birmingham Central Library Archive, MS 814.

148. Corbett and Cross both joined the Liberal Party before the January 1910 election. *The Times,* 13 January 1910. Lambton was defeated at S. E. Durham in January 1910, leaving F. B. Mildmay the sole Liberal Unionist free-trader in the Party. He remained an MP until raised to the peerage in 1922.

149. Disputes over the operation of the 'compact' on a constituency level still emerged. There was a dispute over the candidate for South Molton in 1907. See J. Boraston to Clifford, 17 July 1907, Clifford 3 (2).

150. As David Dutton points out, the chief reason why fusion did not take place after 1906 was because Balfour perceived it as a means whereby Chamberlain would gain control of the whole party apparatus. D. Dutton, *'His Majesty's Loyal Opposition' The Unionist Party in Opposition 1905–1915* (Liverpool, 1992), pp.127–129. The bulk of the Liberal Unionist meetings reported in *The Times* between 1906 and 1911 were held by the Midland Liberal Unionist Association and the Metropolitan Liberal Unionist Federation. The ailing Devonshire even refused to cut short his holiday in Cannes to attend the opening of Parliament in 1907. Devonshire to James, 31 January 1907, M45/1446. In November 1908, Elliot complained that 'only *two* peers, Fitzwilliam and Clifford of Chudleigh, and eight MPs and a pretty poor lot too' had attended the recent Liberal Unionist conference in Bristol. Elliot to James, 2 November 1908, M45/1520.

151. See Thackeray, 'Home and Politics'.

152. Mid-Devon Liberal Unionist Association Minute Book, Clifford 3 (2).

153. Clifford to Whiteway-Wilkinson, 2 July 1906, Clifford 3 (2).

154. Earl of Wemyss to James, 1 January 1907, M45/1444; Devonshire to James, 3 April 1907, M45/1450; Devonshire to James, 19 March 1908, M45/1504; Memo on Devonshire's political position (n.d. January 1909?), M45/1526.

155. Based on Craig's estimates, the affiliations recorded in *Dod's Parliamentary Companion* and the profiles of the individual candidates in *The Times,* it seems likely that the Liberal Unionists won twenty-nine seats in January 1910, adding a further two seats in December.

156. See Lord Lawrence's conciliatory letter to James (18 December 1909) and James' reply (n.d.), M45/1557.

157. The decision was first announced in the interim report of the Unionist Committee on Organization in April 1911 which Balfour had appointed and Arthur Steel-Maitland, the newly appointed head of the Committee, was given responsibility for achieving the task. *The Times,* 14 April 1911.

158. *The Times,* 1 November 1911; 21 February 1912.

159. *The Times,* 21 March 1912.

160. *The Times,* 16 April 1912.

161. *The Times,* 24 April 1912. The Birmingham Liberal Unionist Association also survived the amalgamation of the Midland Unionist Associations in April 1914 and only amalgamated with the local Conservatives at Neville Chamberlain's behest in January 1918. *The Times,* 24 April 1914; 28 January 1918. See also R. Self, *Neville Chamberlain: A Biography* (London, 2007), p.69.

162. *The Times*, 20 April 1912.
163. *The Times*, 10 May 1912 (my italics). Austen Chamberlain took the occasion to announce that he would simply call himself a 'Unionist' from this point and Joseph Chamberlain played his last significant political role, sending a letter which gave his 'cordial concurrence' to the achievement of fusion.
164. The name of the organisation had to be hastily changed, with the word 'Conservative' being dropped from the main title, in the face of further opposition from Birmingham. *The Times*, 6 May 1912; 10 May 1912.
165. *Daily News*, 10 May 1912.
166. *The Times*, 28 May 1912.
167. *The Times*, 28 June 1912, 20 July 1912.
168. S. Ball, 'Conservatism between the Wars: Principles, Pride and Prejudice', paper delivered at the British History 1815–1945 seminar, Institute of Historical Research, London, 13 November 2008 (full version). See also N. Keohane, *The Party of Patriotism: The Conservative Party and the First World War* (Farnham, 2010).

Conclusion

1. Phillips, 'The Whig Lords and Liberalism', p.167.
2. Henry James' Memoir, M45/1864, p.74.
3. Pease, *Elections and Recollections*, p.273.
4. 'The Black Book', *Pall Mall Gazette*, 14 September 1887.
5. *Later Derby Diaries*, p.25.
6. S. Fielding, 'Looking for the "New Political History"', *Journal of Contemporary History*, 42 (2007), p.523.
7. Cooke and Vincent, *The Governing Passion*, p.19.
8. Ibid.
9. Harvie, 'Ideology and Home Rule', p.314.
10. Barbery, 'From Platform to Polling Booth', p.177; List of Liberal Unionist officers and party workers, 1892, Bury Archives, GCP/C/4/1.
11. Barbery, 'From Platform to Polling Booth', p.179.
12. See D. P. Leighton, 'Municipal Progress, Democracy and Radical Identity in Birmingham, 1838–1886', *Midland History*, 25 (2000), pp.115–142.
13. WSLUA Minute Book II, 27 November 1895, 10424/20.
14. Quoted in Sidgwick and Sidgwick, *H. Sidgwick: A Memoir*, p.464.
15. J. Chamberlain to A. Chamberlain, 27 January 1895, JC 5/12/13.
16. Lawrence, 'Transformation of British Public Politics', pp.185–187; Lawrence, *Electing Our Masters*, pp.120–129.
17. Biagini, *British Democracy*, p.241.
18. Hopkinson, *Penultima*, p.153.
19. A. V. Dicey to Hartington, 23 December 1886, DP 340.2071.
20. Quoted in Douglas, *Autobiography and Memoirs, Vol. 2*, p.418.
21. Argyll to Granville, 22 June 1887, quoted in ibid., p.458.
22. Quoted in ibid., p.466.
23. Parry, *The Politics of Patriotism*, pp.101–102.
24. B. Hilton, 'Manliness, masculinity and the mid-Victorian temperament' in L. Goldman (ed.), *The Blind Victorian: Henry Fawcett and British Liberalism* (Cambridge, 1989), pp.60–70.

25. J. S. Mill, quoted in L. T. Hobhouse, *Liberalism* (London, 1911), p.61.

26. H. Spencer, *The Principles of Ethics, Vol. 2* (London, 1893), p.251.

27. *Irish Times*, 5 February 1921.

28. Milner to Gell, 20 May 1887, D3287/MIL/1/195.

29. Barbery, 'From Platform to Polling Booth', p.175.

30. Quoted in 'The Liberal party and coercion', *Liberal Unionist*, 30, July 1888; *Bury Guardian*, 8 October 1887.

31. Lawrence, *Electing Our Masters*, p.19.

32. J. Tosh, *Manliness and Masculinities in Nineteenth Century Britain* (London, 2005), p.2.

33. M. Roberts, 'W. L. Jackson, Exemplary Manliness and Late Victorian Political Conservatism' in M. McCormack (ed.) *Public Men: Masculinity and Politics in Modern Britain* (Basingstoke, 2007), pp.123–142.

34. Powell Williams to Chamberlain, 3 June 1886, JC5/72/6.

35. Dingle to Courtney, 2 February 1886, CP V/9.

36. Patton, *Science, Politics and Business*, p.6, pp.177–8.

37. S. Collini, 'The idea of "Character" in Victorian Political Thought,' *Transactions of the Royal Historical Society,* 5th ser., 25 (1985), pp.29–50. See also A. Jackson, 'Gladstone, Ireland, Scotland and the 'Union of heart and spirit'' in Daly and Hoppen (eds.), *Gladstone: Ireland and Beyond* , pp.23–44; Patton, *Science, Politics and Business*, p.173.

38. A. de Vere, *Medieval Records and Sonnets* (1893), pp.262–3, quoted in Biggs-Davison and Chowdharay-Best, *The Cross of St Patrick,* p.198.

39. See, for example, 'The Clan-na-Gael', *Weekly Times & Echo*, 7 July 1889 and Parkes, *Home Rule from a Liberal Unionist's Point of View*. See also De Nie, *The Eternal Paddy,* pp.267–77.

40. Loughlin, 'Joseph Chamberlain'; C. Hall, *Civilising Subjects: Metropole and Colony in the English Imagination 1830–1867* (Cambridge, 2002), pp.125–13; B. Porter, *The Absent-Minded Imperialists: Empire, Society and Culture in Britain* (London, 2004).

41. Ball, 'Conservatism between the Wars.' See also P. Williamson, *Stanley Baldwin: Conservative Leadership and National Values* (Cambridge, 1998); Stapleton, 'Political Thought and National Identity', pp.260–7.

42. Lynch. *The Liberal Party in Rural England*, p.220.

43. Lubenow, *Parliamentary Politics and the Home Rule Crisis*, p.208.

44. These were: The Clerical Tithes Bill of 1899; the second Boer War; the 1902 Education Act.

45. Burness, '*Strange Associations*', chap. 6, 'Glasgow decides not to eat imperially', pp.162–191.

46. Biagini, *British Democracy*, p.3.

47. H. Cecil, *Conservatism* (London, 1912), p.23.

48. Smith, 'Conservative Ideology', p.18.

49. McWilliam, *Popular Politics*, p.94.

50. A. Austin, 'The Revival of Common Sense', *National Review* (June 1886), p.564.

51. WSLUA Minute Book I, 1 October 1888, 10424/19.

52. Keohane, *The Party of Patriotism*.

53. Phillips, 'The Whig Lords and Liberalism', p.173.

54. Parry, *Rise and Fall of Liberal Government*, p.311.

55. R. C. Self (ed.), *The Austen Chamberlain diary letters* (Cambridge, 1995), p.197.

56. In Birmingham, Liberal Unionist identity survived into the 1920s. See D. Dilks, *Neville Chamberlain, Vol. 1, 1869–1929* (Cambridge, 2002), p.280. While the name 'Unionist' was gradually phased out by the united Party before the war, in Scotland the title 'Conservative' was not employed by the Party until the 1960s. Burness, 'The Making of Scottish Unionism', pp.31–32.

57. Parry, *The Politics of Patriotism*, p.399.

BIBLIOGRAPHY

Manuscript Collections

Liberal Unionist Party Papers

W. Birmingham Liberal Unionist Association Records, Smethwick Local History Centre.

Birmingham Liberal Unionist Association, All Saints Ward Records, Birmingham Central Library.

East and North of Scotland Liberal Unionist Association Records, National Library of Scotland.

Mid-Devon Liberal Unionist Association Records, Clifford Papers, Ugbrooke House, Newton Abbot.

West Derbyshire Liberal Unionist Association Records, Derbyshire Record Office, Matlock.

Manchester and District Liberal Unionist Association Records, Manchester Central Reference Library.

Maryhill Liberal Unionist Association Minute Book, National Library of Scotland.

Mid-Northamptonshire Liberal Unionist Association Records, Cartwright Papers, Northamptonshire Record Office.

Partick Liberal Unionist Council Minute Book, Mitchell Library, Glasgow.

West of Scotland Liberal Unionist Association Records, National Library of Scotland.

E. Worcestershire Liberal Unionist Association Records, Birmingham Central Library.

Politicians' Private Papers

Balfour Papers, British Library.

William Cartwright Papers, Northamptonshire Record Office

Joseph and Austen Chamberlain Papers, University of Birmingham.

Clifford Papers, Ugbrooke House, Newton Abbott.

Courtney Papers, London School of Economics.

Dicey Papers, Glasgow University.

Devonshire Papers, Chatsworth House.

Elliot Papers, National Library of Scotland.

Fawcett Papers, Manchester City Archives.

Fawcett Archives, Women's Library, London Metropolitan University.

Fortescue Papers, Devon Record Office.

Gell Papers, Derbyshire Record Office.

Grey Papers, Durham Record Office.

Harcourt Papers, Bodleian Library.
Herbert Gladstone Papers, British Library.
William Gladstone Papers, British Library.
Heneage Papers, Lincoln Record Office.
Henry James Papers, Hereford Record Office.
Milner Papers, Bodleian Library, Oxford.
Parker Smith Papers, Mitchell Library, Glasgow.
Salisbury Papers, Hatfield House.
Selborne Papers, Bodleian Library.
Spencer Papers, Althorp House.

Other Collections
Ballad Collection, British Library.
Barrow Election Papers, Lancashire County Record Office, Preston.
British Liberal Party Archive Vol. 1, 1884–1908, Birmingham Central Library.
Conservative Party Archive, Bodleian Library.
Warwick and Leamington Conservative Party Association Records, Warwickshire County
    Record Office, Warwick.

Newspapers/Periodicals

Annual Register.
Baptist.
Birmingham Daily Gazette.
Birmingham Daily Post.
The Birmingham Owl.
Bristol Mercury.
British Weekly.
Bury Guardian.
Bury Times.
Christian World.
Congregational Review.
Contemporary Review.
The Continental Monthly.
Daily News.
Daily Telegraph.
The Dart.
Edinburgh Review.
Exeter Flying Post.
Fortnightly Review.
Fun.
Freeman's Journal.
Glasgow Herald.
Inquirer.
Inverness Courier.
Irish Daily Independent.
Irish Times.
The Judge.
Judy.
Leamington Spa Courier.

Leeds Mercury
Liberal Unionist.
Liberal Unionist Association Memoranda.
Manchester Guardian.
Methodist Times.
The Midland Telegraph.
The Nation.
National Review.
New Review.
Nineteenth Century (and After).
North British Daily Mail.
The Northern Whig.
Oxford Chronicle.
Pall Mall Gazette.
Punch.
St Stephen's Review.
Scotsman.
The Scottish Highlander.
Scottish News.
Spectator.
South Wales Daily News.
Standard.
The Times.
The Tory.
The Town Crier.
Weekly Times and Echo.
Western Daily Mercury.
Westminster Review.

Published Primary Sources

Memoirs

M. L. Arnold-Foster, *The Rt. Hon. H.O. Arnold-Foster: A Memoir,* London: Arnold, 1910.

H. Blackburn, *Women's Suffrage: A Record of the Women's Suffrage Movement in the British Isles, with Biographical Sketches of Miss Becker,* London: Williams & Norgate, 1902.

J. A. Bridges, *Reminiscences of a Country Politician*, London: T.W. Laurie, 1906.

H. Broadhurst, *Henry Broadhurst MP. The Story of his Life from a Stoneman's Bench to the Treasury Bench as told by Himself,* London: Hutchinson & Co., 1901.

A. Chamberlain, *Down the Years* (2nd ed.), London: Cassell, 1935.

F. A. Channing, *Memories of Midland Politics 1885–1910*, London: Constable, 1918.

P. W. Clayden, *England under the Coalition* (2nd ed.), London: T. Fisher Unwin, 1893.

J. Collings and J. L. Green, *Life of the Right Hon. Jesse Collings,* London: Longman, 1920.

G. Douglas, *Autobiography and Memoirs Vol. 2*, London: John Murray, 1906.

M. G. Fawcett, *What I Remember,* London: T. F. Unwin, 1925.

A. E. Gathorne-Hardy, *Gathorne-Hardy, First Earl of Cranbrook: a Memoir Vol. 2,* London: Longman, 1910.

A. S. T. Griffith-Boscawen, *Fourteen Years in Parliament*, London: J. Murray, 1907.

M. Jeune, *Memories of Fifty Years*, London: Arnold, 1909.

A. Hopkinson, *Penultima,* London: Martin Hopkinson, 1930.

C. H. D. Howard (ed.), *A Political Memoir: 1880–1892 by Joseph Chamberlain,* London: Batchworth, 1953.

E. Lecky, *A Memoir of the Right Hon. William Edward Hartpole Lecky,* London : Longman, 1909.

H. Lucy, *Sixty Years in the Wilderness: Some Passages by the Way,* London: Smith, Elder & Co., 1909.

E. Lyttelton, *Alfred Lyttelton : An Account of his Life,* London : Longman, 1917.

T. Macknight, *Ulster as it is: or, Twenty-Eight Years' Experience as an Irish Editor* (2 vols.), Basingstoke: Macmillan, 1896.

B. Mallett, *Thomas George, Earl of Northbrook: A Memoir,* London: Longmans, Green & Co., 1908.

H. Maxwell, *Evening Memories,* London: Alexander Maclehose, 1932.

A. E. Pease, *Elections and Recollections,* London: John Murray, 1932.

R. Purvis, *Sir William Arrol: A Memoir,* Edinburgh: William Blackwood, 1913.

E. T. Raymond, *Portrait of the Nineties,* London: T.F. Unwin, 1921.

A. Sidgwick & E. M. Sidgwick, *Henry Sidgwick: a memoir,* London: Macmillan, 1906.

Goldwin Smith, *Reminiscences* (edited by A. Haultain), New York: Macmillan, 1910.

H. M. Stanley, *The Autobiography of Henry M. Stanley* (edited by D. Stanley), London: Sampson Low, Marston & Co., 1909.

A. Strachey, *St. Loe Strachey: His Life and His Paper,* London: Gollancz, 1930.

J. St. Loe Strachey, *The Adventure of Living: A Subjective Autobiography,* London: Hodder and Stoughton, 1922.

Rev. W. Tuckwell, *Reminiscences of a Radical Parson,* London: Cassell, 1905.

B. Webb, *My Apprenticeship,* Harmondsworth: Penguin, 1938.

B. Webb, *Our Partnership* (edited by B. Drake & M. I. Cole), London: Longmans, Green & Co, 1948.

Other

The Case for the Union (five series), British Library.

A Great Unionist Demonstration, Wellow Parish Newsletter, n.d., 1892.

Hansard's Parliamentary Debates, 3rd and 4th series.

Report of the National Liberal Unionist Conference, Manchester, November 1891, London: Liberal Unionist Association, 1891.

Report by the Executive of the West of Scotland Branch of the Liberal Unionist Committee for the Maintenance of the Legislative Union between Great Britain and Ireland, 1st August, 1886, Glasgow: Alex. Malcolm, 1886.

Report of Meeting on Proportional Representation, or Effective Voting, held at River House, Chelsea, on Tuesday. July 10th, 1894, London: Women's Liberal Unionist Association, 1894.

The Speaker's Handbook on the Irish Question, London: Liberal Unionist Association, 1889.

Speeches on the Formation of the Women's Liberal Unionist Association, London: Women's Liberal Unionist Association, 1887.

The Ulster Liberal Unionist Association: A Sketch of its History, 1885–1914, Belfast: Ulster Liberal Unionist Association, 1913.

D. G. Boyce (ed.), *The Crisis of British Unionism – Lord Selborne's Domestic Political Papers, 1885–1933,* Gloucester: Sutton, 1987.

D. G. Boyce (ed.), *The Crisis of British Power: The Imperial and Naval Papers of the Second Earl of Selborne, 1895–1910,* London: Historians' Press, 1990.

M. V. Brett (ed.), *Letters and Journals of Reginald, Viscount Esher Vol. 1,* London: Nicholson and Watson, 1934.

G. Brooks, *Why I Became a Liberal Unionist: Reprinted from 'Blackwood's Magazine' for February 1889,* London: Blackwood, 1889.

G. E. Buckle (ed.), *Letters of Queen Victoria, 3rd Series Vol. 1, 1886–1890,* London: John Murray, 1930.

H. Cecil, *Conservatism,* London: Butterworth, 1912

A. V. Dicey, *England's Case Against Home Rule,* London: John Murray, 1886.

A. V. Dicey, *Letters on Unionist Delusions*, London: Macmillan, 1887.

A. V. Dicey, *The Verdict: A Tract on the Political Significance of the Report of the Parnell Commission*, London: Cassell, 1890.

A. V. Dicey, *A Leap in the Dark or Our New Constitution*, London: John Murray, 1893.

A. V. Dicey, *Lectures on the Relation between Law and Public Opinion in England during the Nineteenth Century*, Basingstoke: Macmillan, 1905.

R. Douglas, L. Harte & J. O'Hara, *Drawing Conclusions: A Cartoon History of Anglo-Irish Relations, 1798–1998*, Belfast: Blackstaff Press, 1998.

F. Frankfort Moore, *The Diary of an Irish Cabinet Minister: being the history of the first (and only) Irish National Administration, 1893*, London: John Reed & Co., 1893.

W. E. Gladstone, *The Irish Question: A History of an Idea; Lessons of the Election*, London: John Murray, 1886.

T. Hodgkin, *Think It Out: A Lecture on the Question of Home Rule for Ireland*, London: Walter Scott, 1888.

P. Jackson (ed.), *Loulou: Selected Extracts from the Journals of Lewis Harcourt (1880–1895)*, Madison: Fairleigh Dickinson University Press, 2006.

H. J. Hanham (ed.), *The Nineteenth Century Constitution: Documents and Commentary*, Cambridge: Cambridge University Press, 1969.

R. Harcourt-Williams (ed.), *Salisbury-Balfour Correspondence, 1869–1892*, Hertford: Hertfordshire Record Society, 1988.

J. Harrison, *The Scot in Ulster*, Edinburgh: Blackwood, 1888.

L. T. Hobhouse, *Liberalism*, London: Thornton Butterworth, 1911

W. E. H. Lecky, *An Irish Historian on Home Rule for Ireland*, London: Liberal Unionist Association, 1889.

J. Lellenberg et al (eds.), *Arthur Conan Doyle: A Life in Letters*, London: Harper Press, 2007.

J. Lubbock and H. O. Arnold-Forster, *Proportional Representation: A Dialogue*, London: Kegan Paul, Trench & Co., 1884.

H. W. Lucy, *A Diary of the Salisbury Parliament 1886–1892*, London: Cassell, 1892.

H. W. Lucy, *A Diary of the Home Rule Parliament 1892–1895*, London: Cassell, 1896.

H. W. Lucy, *A Diary of the Unionist Parliament 1895–1900*, Bristol: J.W. Arrowsmith, 1901.

H. J. S. Maine, *Popular Government*, London: John Murray, 1885.

T. Maguire, *Reasons Why Britons Should Oppose Home Rule*, Dublin: William McGee, 1886.

H. C. G. Matthew (ed.), *The Gladstone Diaries, with Cabinet Minutes and Prime-Ministerial Correspondence Vols.11–13, 1883–1896*, Oxford: Clarendon Press, 1990–1994.

J. McCarthy, *The Case for Home Rule*, London: Chatto and Windus, 1887.

J. S. Mill, *Utilitarianism, Liberty and Representative Government*, London: Everyman, 1910.

Lady Monkswell, *A Victorian Diarist: Extracts from the Journals of Mary, Lady Monkswell* (ed. E. C. F. Collier), London: John Murray, 1944.

W. Morris, 'The Skeleton at the Feast', *Commonweal*, 4:127, June 1888.

R. Parkes, *Home Rule from a Liberal Unionist's Point of View*, Birmingham: F. Grew, 1887.

A. Ramm (ed.), *Political Correspondence of Mr Gladstone and Lord Granville 1883–1886 Vol. 2*, Oxford: Clarendon Press, 1962.

L. G. Rylands (ed.), *Correspondence and Speeches of Mr. Peter Rylands, M.P*, Manchester: Heywood, 1890.

R. C. Self (ed.), *The Austen Chamberlain diary letters*, Cambridge: Royal Historical Society, 1995.

N. St. John Stevas (ed.), *The Collected Works of Walter Bagehot Vol. 5*, London: *The Economist*, 1974.

A. W. Samuels, *Home Rule: What is it?*, London: Simpkin, Marshall & Co., 1911.

J. R. Seeley, *The Expansion of England*, Basingstoke: Macmillan, 1883.

Goldwin Smith, *Dismemberment No Remedy*, London: Cassell, 1886.

H. Spencer, *The Principles of Ethics Vol. 2*, London: Williams and Norgate, 1983.

E. C. M. Stewart & E. Satterthwaite, *Cornish Granite: Extracts from the Writings and Speeches of Lord Courtney of Penwith,* London : L. Parsons, 1925.

G. Stronach, *Twenty-Five Years of Politics; or, the Political Record of Mr. T.R. Buchanan,* Edinburgh, 1906.

W. Summers, *The Liberal Unionists and their Leaders,* Manchester. National Liberal Federation, 1886.

J. Vincent (ed.), *The Later Derby Diaries: Home Rule, Liberal Unionism, and Aristocratic Life in late Victorian England,* Bristol: University of Bristol, 1981.

R. A. J. Walling (ed.), *Diaries of John Bright,* London: Cassell, 1930.

Secondary Sources

Biographies

R. L. Q. Adams, *Balfour: The Last Grandee,* London: John Murray, 2007

B. Alderson, *Arthur James Balfour: The Man and His Work*, London: G. Richards, 1903.

E. Alexander, 3rd Viscount Chilston, *Chief Whip: The Political Life and Times of Aretas Akers-Douglas 1st Viscount Chilston,* London: Routledge and Kegan Paul, 1961.

G. R. Askwith, *Lord James of Hereford,* London: Ernest Benn, 1930.

B. Caine, *Bombay to Bloomsbury: A Biography of the Strachey Family*, Oxford: Oxford University Press, 2005

E. Cameron, *The Life and Times of Fraser Mackintosh, Crofter MP*, Aberdeen: University of Aberdeen, 2000.

G. Cecil, *Life of Robert, Marquis of Salisbury Vol. III, 1880–1886,* London: Hodder and Stoughton, 1931.

W. S. Churchill, *Lord Randolph Churchill,* London: Macmillan, 1907.

R. A. Cosgrove, *The Rule of Law: Alfred Venn Dicey, Victorian Jurist,* Basingstoke: Macmillan, 1980.

T. L. Crosby, *Joseph Chamberlain: A Most Radical Imperialist,* London: I.B. Tauris, 2011.

A. W. W. Dale, *Life of R. W. Dale of Birmingham,* London: Hodder and Stoughton, 1898.

A. Desmond, *Huxley: Evolution's High Priest,* London: Penguin, 1997.

D. Dilks, *Neville Chamberlain Vol. I, 1869–1929,* Cambridge: Cambridge University Press, 2002.

D. Dutton, *Austen Chamberlain: Gentleman in Politics,* Bolton: Ross Anderson, 1985.

A. R. D. Elliot, *The Life of Lord Goschen* (2 vols.), London: Longman, 1911.

E. Fitzmaurice, *The Life of Granville George Leveson Gower, Second Earl Granville, 1815–1891* (2 vols.), London: Longmans, Green & Co., 1905.

T. H. Ford, *Alfred Venn Dicey: The Man and his Times,* Chichester: Barry Rose, 1985.

R. F. Foster, *Lord Randolph Churchill: A Political Life,* Oxford: Oxford University Press, 1981.

P. Fraser, *Joseph Chamberlain: Radicalism and Empire, 1868–1914,* London: Cassell, 1966.

A. G. Gardiner, *The Life of Sir William Harcourt,* New York: G H Doran, 1914.

J. L. Garvin, *The Life of Joseph Chamberlain Vol. 2, 1885–1895,* Basingstoke: Macmillan, 1933.

J. L. Garvin, *The Life of Joseph Chamberlain Vol. 3, 1895–1903,* Basingstoke: Macmillan, 1933.

D. Gilmour, *Lord Curzon,* Cambridge: Cambridge University Press, 1994.

G. P. Gooch, *Life of Lord Courtney,* Basingstoke : Macmillan, 1920.

A. Grant Duff (ed.), *The Life-Work of Lord Avebury (Sir John Lubbock), 1834–1901* (2 vols.), London: Watts & Co., 1924.

J. N. Greaves, *Sir Edward Watkin, 1819–1901: The Last of the Railway Kings,* Lewes: The Book Guild, 2005.

E. H. H. Green, *Balfour,* London: Haus, 2006.

S. Gwynn and G. Tuckwell, *The Life of the rt. hon. Charles Dilke, MP* (2 vols.), London: John Murray, 1917.

B. Holland, *Life of Spencer Compton, 8th Duke of Devonshire* (2 vols.), London: Longman, 1911.

D. Hodgkins, *The Second Railway King: The Life and Times of Sir Edward Watkin, 1819–1901,* Cardiff: Merton Priory Press, 2002.

R. Huntford, *Shackleton,* London: Abacus, 1996.

H. G. Hutchinson, *Life of Sir John Lubbock, Lord Avebury* (2 vols.), Basingstoke: Macmillan, 1914.

A. Jackson, *Colonel Edward Saunderson: Land and Loyalty in Victorian Ireland,* Oxford: Clarendon Press, 1995.

P. Jackson, *The Last of the Whigs: A Political Biography of Lord Hartington,* London: Associated University Presses, 1994.

P. Jackson, *Harcourt and Son,* Madison, NJ: Fairleigh Dickinson University Press, 2004.

R. Jay, *Joseph Chamberlain: A Political Study,* Oxford: Clarendon, 1981.

R. Jenkins, *Gladstone,* Basingstoke: Macmillan, 1995.

D. Judd, *Radical Joe,* London: Hamilton, 1977.

S. E. Koss, *Sir John Brunner, Radical Plutocrat, 1842–1919,* Cambridge: Cambridge University Press, 1970.

A. Lang, *Sir Stafford Northcote, First Earl of Iddesleigh Vol. 2,* London: Blackwood, 1890.

S. Lee, *Queen Victoria: A Biography,* London: Smith, Elder & Co., 1904.

J. B. Mackie, *The Life and Work of Duncan McLaren Vol. 2,* London: T. Nelson, 1888.

P. Marsh, *Joseph Chamberlain: Entrepreneur in Politics,* London: Yale, 1994.

H. C. G. Matthew, *Gladstone, 1875–1898,* Oxford: Clarendon Press, 1995.

B. Middlemass & J. Hunt, *John Corbett: Pillar of Salt. 1817–1892* Droitwich: Saltway, 1985

J. Morley, *Life of W. E. Gladstone Vols. 2 & 3,* Basingstoke: Macmillan, 1911.

J. Newton, *W.S. Caine, M.P.,* London: James Nisbet & Co., 1907.

T. W. L. Newton, *Lord Lansdowne: A Biography,* Basingstoke: Macmillan, 1929.

R. B. O'Brien, *The Life of Charles Stewart Parnell, Vol. 2* (2nd ed.), London: Smith Elder, 1899.

M. Patton, *Science, Politics and Business in the Work of Sir John Lubbock: A Man of Universal Mind,* Farnham: Ashgate, 2007.

H. Paul, *The Life of Froude,* London: Pitman, 1905.

P. T. Phillips, *The Controversialist: An Intellectual Life of Goldwin Smith,* Wesport: Praeger, 2002.

J. E. Powell, *Joseph Chamberlain,* London: Thames and Hudson, 1977.

R. Reeves, *John Stuart Mill: Victorian Firebrand,* London: Atlantic, 2007.

A. Roberts, *Salisbury: Victorian Titan,* London: Weidenfeld and Nicholson, 1999.

R. Self, *Neville Chamberlain: A Biography,* London: Ashgate, 2007.

R. Shannon, *Gladstone Vol. 2: Heroic Minister, 1865–98,* Harmondsworth: Penguin, 2000.

T. J. Spinner, *George Joachim Goschen: The Transformation of a Victorian Liberal,* Cambridge: Cambridge University Press, 1973.

D. Steele, *Lord Salisbury: A Political Biography,* London: UCL Press, 1999.

R. Strachey, *Millicent Garrett Fawcett,* London: John Murray, 1931.

A. L. Thorold, *The Life of Henry Labouchere,* London: G.P. Putnam, 1913.

G. M. Trevelyan, *Grey of Fallodon: Being the Life of Sir Edward Grey afterwards Viscount Grey of Fallodon,* London: Longmans, Green, 1937.

E. Wallace, *Goldwin Smith: Victorian Liberal,* Toronto: University of Toronto Press, 1957.

J. E. Wrench, *Alfred Lord Milner: The Man of No Illusions, 1854–1925,* London: Eyre & Spotiswood, 1958.

Edited Collections

E. Allardt and S. Rokkan (eds.), *Mass Politics: Studies in Political Sociology,* New York: Free Press, 1970.

S. Ball & A. Seldon (eds.), *Conservative Century: The Conservative Party since 1900,* Oxford: Oxford University Press, 1994.

S. Ball & I. Holliday (eds.), *Mass Conservatism: The Conservatives and the Public since the 1880s,* London: Frank Cass, 2002.

E. F. Biagini and A. J. Reid (eds.), *Currents of Radicalism: Popular Radicalism, Organised Labour and Party Politics in Britain, 1850–1914,* Cambridge: Cambridge University Press, 1991.

R. Blake and H. Cecil (eds.), *Salisbury: The Man and his Policies,* Basingstoke: Macmillan, 1987.

D. G. Boyce and A. O'Day (eds.), *Defenders of the Union: A Survey of British and Irish Unionism since 1801,* London: Routledge, 2001.

D. G. Boyce and A. O'Day (eds.), *The Ulster Crisis: 1885–1922,* Basingstoke: Macmillan, 2005.

D. G. Boyce and R. Swift (eds.), *Problems and Perspectives in Irish History since 1800: Essays in Honour of Patrick Buckland,* Dublin: Four Courts, 2004.

R. Colls and P. Dodd (eds.), *Englishness: Politics and Culture, 1880–1920,* London: Routledge, 1986.

M. Cullen and M. Luddy (eds.), *Women, Power and Consciousness in nineteenth-century Ireland,* Dublin: Attic Press, 1995.

M. E. Daly and K. T. Hoppen (eds.), *Gladstone: Ireland and Beyond,* Dublin: Four Courts Press, 2011.

R. English and G. Walker (eds.), *Unionism in Modern Ireland: New Perspectives on Politics and Culture,* Basingstoke: Macmillan, 1996.

N. C. Fleming and A. O'Day (eds.), *Ireland and Anglo-Irish Relations since 1800: Critical Essays, Vol. 2: Parnell and his Legacy to the Treaty,* Aldershot: Ashgate, 2008.

M. Francis & I. Zweiniger-Bargielowska (eds.), *The Conservatives and British Society, 1880–1990,* Cardiff: University of Wales Press, 1996.

W. H. Fraser and I. Maver (eds.), *Glasgow Vol. 2: 1830–1912,* Manchester: Manchester University Press, 1996.

P. Ghosh and L. Goldman (eds.), *Politics and Culture in Victorian Britain: Essays in Memory of Colin Matthew,* Oxford: Oxford University Press, 2006.

L. Goldman (ed.), *The Blind Victorian: Henry Fawcett and British Liberalism,* Cambridge: Cambridge University Press, 1989.

A. Hayes and D. Urquhart (eds.), *Irish Women's History,* Dublin: Irish Academic Press, 2000

E. J. Hobsbawm and T. Ranger (eds.), *The Invention of Tradition,* Cambridge: Cambridge University Press, 1983.

C. Holmes (ed.), *Immigrants and Minorities in British society,* London: Allen and Unwin, 1978.

P. Kennedy and A. Nicholls (eds.), *Nationalist and racialist movements in Britain and Germany before 1914,* London: Macmillan in association with St Antony's College, Oxford, 1981.

J. M. Lawrence and M. Taylor (eds.), *Party, State and Society: Electoral Behaviour in Britain since 1820,* Aldershot: Scholar Press, 1997.

C. M. M. MacDonald (ed.), *Unionist Scotland 1800–1997,* Edinburgh: John Donald Publishers, 1998.

P. Mandler (ed.) *Liberty and Authority in Victorian Britain,* Oxford: Oxford University Press, 2006

M. McCormack (ed.), *Public Men: Masculinity and Politics in Modern Britain,* Basingstoke: Palgrave Macmillan, 2007.

K. O. Morgan (ed.), *Modern Wales: Politics, Places and People,* Cardiff: University of Wales Press, 1995.

J. Vernon (ed.), *Re-reading the Constitution: New Narratives in the Political History of England's long nineteenth century,* Cambridge: Cambridge University Press, 1996.

Monographs

J. Bardon, *A History of Ulster* (2nd ed.), Belfast: Blackstaff Press, 2005.

M. Barker, *Gladstone and Radicalism: The Reconstruction of Liberal Policy in Britain, 1885–94,* Hassocks: Harvester, 1975.

D. W. Bebbington, *The Nonconformist Conscience: Chapel and Politics, 1870–1914,* London: Harper Collins, 1982.

D. W. Bebbington, *The Mind of Gladstone: Religion, Homer and Politics,* Oxford: Oxford University Press, 2004.

M. Bentley, *The Climax of Liberal Politics: British Liberalism in Theory and Practice 1868–1918*, London: Hodder Arnold, 1987.

M. Bentley, *Politics Without Democracy, 1815–1914* (2nd ed.), Oxford: Blackwell, 1996.

M. Bentley, *Lord Salisbury's World: Conservative Environments in late Victorian Britain*, Cambridge: Cambridge University Press, 2001.

J. Bew, *The Glory of Being Britons: Civic Unionism in Nineteenth-Century Belfast*, Dublin: Irish Academic Press, 2009.

E. F. Biagini, *Liberty, Retrenchment and Reform: Popular Liberalism in the Age of Gladstone, 1860–1880*, Cambridge: Cambridge University Press, 1992.

E. F. Biagini, *British Democracy and Irish Nationalism 1876–1906*, Cambridge: Cambridge University Press, 2007.

J. Biggs-Davison & G. Chowdharay-Best, *The Cross of St Patrick: The Catholic Unionist Tradition in Ireland*, Bourne End: Kensal Press, 1984.

L. Black, *The Political Culture of the Left in Affluent Britain, 1951–1964: Old Britain, new Britain?*, Basingstoke: Macmillan, 2003

D. G. Boyce, *The Irish Question and British politics 1868–1986* (2nd ed), Basingstoke: Palgrave Macmillan, 1996.

A. Briggs, *The Age of Improvement, 1783–1867*, London: Longman, 1959.

M. Brodie, *The Politics of the Poor: The East End of London, 1885–1914*, Oxford: Oxford University Press, 2004.

I. Budge and C. O'Leary, *Belfast: Approach to Crisis: A Study of Belfast Politics, 1613–1970*, Basingstoke: Macmillan, 1973.

C. Burness, *Strange Associations: The Irish Question and the Making of Scottish Unionism, 1886–1918*, East Linton: Tuckwell, 2003.

D. Butler and D. Stokes, *Political Change in Britain: The Evolution of Electoral Choice* (2nd ed.), London: St. Martins Press, 1974.

B. Caine, *Victorian Feminists*, Oxford: Oxford University Press, 1992.

B. Caine, *English Feminism*, Oxford: Oxford University Press, 1997.

F. Cammarano, *"To Save England from Decline" The National Party of Common Sense: British Conservatism and the Challenge of Democracy (1885–1892)*, Lanham: University Press of America, 2001.

B. Campbell, *The Iron Ladies: Why do Women Vote Tory?*, London: Virago, 1987.

F. Campbell, *Land and Revolution: Nationalist Politics in the West of Ireland, 1891–1902*, Oxford: Oxford University Press, 2005.

D. Cannadine, *The Decline and Fall of the British Aristocracy*, Basingstoke: Macmillan, 1992.

D. Cannadine, *Class in Britain*, London: Yale, 1998

P. F. Clarke, *Lancashire and the New Liberalism*, Cambridge: Cambridge University Press, 1971.

L. Colley, *Britons: Forging the Nation, 1707–1837*, London: Yale, 1992.

S. Collini, *Public Moralists: Political Thought and Intellectual Life in Britain, 1850–1930*, Oxford: Oxford University Press, 1991.

N. Collins, *Politics and elections in nineteenth-century Liverpool*, Michigan: Scolar Press, 1994.

R. Colls, *Identity of England*, Oxford: Oxford University Press, 2002.

A. B. Cooke and J. Vincent, *The Governing Passion: Cabinet Government and Party Politics in Britain 1885–6*, Hassocks: Harvester, 1974.

K. Cowman, *'Mrs Brown is a Man and a Brother!' Women in Merseyside's Political Organisation, 1890–1920*, Liverpool: Liverpool University Press, 2004.

G. W. Cox, *The Efficient Secret: The Cabinet and the Development of Political Parties in Victorian England*, Cambridge: Cambridge University Press, 1987.

M. Cragoe, *Culture, Politics and National Identity in Wales, 1832–1886*, Oxford: Oxford University Press, 2004.

L. P. Curtis, *Coercion and Conciliation in Ireland 1880–1892: A Study in Conservative Unionism*, Princeton: Princeton University Press, 1963.

L. P. Curtis, *Apes and Angels: the Irishman in Victorian Caricature*, Newton Abbot: David and Charles, 1971.

M. W. De Nie, *The Eternal Paddy: Irish Identity and the British Press, 1798–1882*, Madison: University of Wisconsin Press, 2004.

J. P. D. Dunbabin, *Rural Discontent in Nineteenth Century Britain*, London: Faber & Faber, 1974.

D. Dutton, *'His Majesty's Loyal Opposition': The Unionist Party in Opposition, 1905–1915*, Liverpool: Liverpool University Press, 1992

H. V. Emy, *Liberals, Radicals and Social Politics, 1892–1914*, Cambridge: Cambridge University Press, 1973.

J. D. Fair, *British Interparty Conferences*, Oxford: Oxford University Press, 1980.

A. W.P. Fawcett, *Conservative Agent: A Study of the National Society of Conservative and Unionist Agents and its Members*, Driffield: East Yorkshire Printers, 1967.

N. Ferguson, *The House of Rothschild, Vol. 2: The World's Banker, 1849–1999*, London: Viking, 1999.

M. Fforde, *Conservatism and Collectivism, 1886–1914*, Edinburgh: Edinburgh University Press, 1990.

S. Fielding, *Class and Ethnicity: Irish Catholics in England, 1880–1939*, Buckingham: Open University Press, 1993.

R. F. Foster, *Paddy and Mr Punch: Connections in Irish and English History*, London: Allen Lane, 1993.

M. Fry, *Patronage and Principle: A Political History of Modern Scotland*, Aberdeen: Aberdeen University Press, 1987.

J. A. Garrard, *Democratisation in Britain: Elites, Civil Society and Reform since 1800*, Basingstoke: Macmillan, 2002.

P. Gibbon, *The Origins of Ulster Unionism: the formation of popular Protestant politics in nineteenth century Ireland*, Manchester: Manchester University Press, 1976.

A. D. Gilbert, *Religion and Society in Industrial England: Church, Chapel and Social Change, 1740–1914*, London: Longman, 1976.

L. Goldman, *Science, reform and politics in Victorian Britain: The Social Science Association, 1857–1886*, Cambridge: Cambridge University Press, 2002.

E. H. H. Green, *The Crisis of Conservatism: The Politics, Economics and Ideology of British Conservatism, 1880–1914*, London: Routledge, 1995.

R. F. Haggard, *The Persistence of Victorian Liberalism*, London: Greenwood Press, 2001.

C. Hall, *Civilising Subjects: Metropole and Colony in the English Imagination 1830–1867*, Cambridge: Polity Press, 2002.

D. A. Hamer, *Liberal Politics in the Age of Gladstone and Rosebery: A Study in Leadership and Policy*, Oxford: Clarendon Press, 1972.

J. L. Hammond, *Gladstone and the Irish Nation* (2nd ed.), London: Frank Cass, 1964.

H. J. Hanham, *Elections and Party Management: Politics in the Time of Disraeli and Gladstone*, London: Longman, 1959.

B. Harrison, *Drink and the Victorians: The Temperance Question in England, 1815 – 1872*, London: Faber, 1972.

C. Harvie, *Scotland and Nationalism: Scottish Society and Politics, 1707–1977*, London: Allen and Unwin, 1977.

A. Hawkins, *British Party Politics, 1852–1886*, Basingstoke: Macmillan, 1998.

D. Howell, *British Workers and the Independent Labour Party, 1888–1906*, Manchester: Manchester University Press, 1983.

R. Hudson, *The Jubilee Years, 1887–1897*, London: The Folio Society, 1996.

M. C. Hurst, *Joseph Chamberlain and West Midlands Politics, 1886–1895 (Dugdale Society occasional papers; no. 15)*, Oxford : Printed for the Dugdale Society by V. Ridler, 1962.

M. C. Hurst, *Joseph Chamberlain and Liberal Reunion: The Round Table Conference of 1887*, Newton Abbot: David & Charles, 1970.

I. G. C. Hutchinson, *A Political history of Scotland, 1832–1924: Parties, Elections and Issues*, Edinburgh: Donald, 1986.

K. S. Inglis, *Churches and the Working Classes in Victorian England*, London: Routledge and Kegan Paul, 1963.

A. Jackson, *The Ulster Party: Irish Unionists in the House of Commons, 1884–1911*, Oxford: Oxford University Press, 1989.

A. Jackson, *Home Rule: A History, 1800–2000*, Oxford: Oxford University Press, 2003.

A. Jackson, *Ireland 1798–1998: War Peace and Beyond* (2nd ed.) Chichester: Wiley-Blackwell, 2010.

D. Jackson, *Popular Opposition to Irish Home Rule in Edwardian Britain*, Liverpool: Liverpool University Press, 2009.

E. Jaggard, *Cornwall Politics in the Age of Reform*, Woodbridge: Boydell Press, 1999.

P. Jalland, *The Liberals and Ireland: The Ulster Question in British politics to 1914*, Brighton: Harvester, 1980.

T. A. Jenkins, *Gladstone, Whiggery and the Liberal Party, 1874–1886*, Oxford: Oxford University Press, 1988.

T. A. Jenkins, *The Liberal ascendancy, 1830–1886*, Basingstoke: Macmillan, 1994.

P. Joyce, *Work, Society and Politics,* Brighton: Harvester, 1980.

P. Joyce, *Visions of the People: Industrial England and the Question of Class, 1840–1914*, Cambridge: Cambridge University Press, 1991.

P. Joyce, *Democratic Subjects: The Self and the Social in nineteenth century England*, Cambridge: Cambridge University Press, 1994.

D. Judd, *Balfour and the British Empire: A Study in Imperial Evolution 1874–1932*, Basingstoke: Macmillan, 1968.

N. Keohane, *The Party of Patriotism: The Conservative Party and the First World War*, Farnham: Ashgate, 2010.

G. Kitson Clark, *The Making of Victorian Britain*, London: Methuen, 1962.

S. E. Koss, *Nonconformity in Modern British Politics*, London: Batsford, 1975.

S E. Koss, *The Rise and Fall of the Political Press in Britain, Vol. 1: The nineteenth century*, London: Hamish Hamilton, 1981.

S. E. Koss, *The Rise and Fall of the Political Press in Britain, Vol. 2: The twentieth century*, London: Hamish Hamilton, 1984.

W. M. Kuhn, *Democratic Royalism: The Transformation of the British monarchy*, Basingstoke: Macmillan, 1996.

J. M. Lawrence, *Speaking for the People: Party, Language and Popular Politics in England, 1867–1914*, Cambridge: Cambridge University Press, 1998.

J. M Lawrence, *Electing Our Masters: The Hustings in British Politics from Hogarth to Blair*, Oxford: Oxford University Press, 2009.

J. Loughlin, *Gladstone, Home Rule and the Ulster Question, 1882–1893*, Dublin: Gill and Macmillan, 1986.

J. Loughlin, *The British Monarchy and Ireland, 1800 to the present*, Cambridge: Cambridge University Press, 2007.

W. C. Lubenow, *Parliamentary Politics and the Home Rule Crisis: The British House of Commons in 1886*, Oxford: Clarendon Press, 1988.

W. C. Lubenow, *The Cambridge Apostles, 1820–1914 : Liberalism, Imagination, and Friendship in British Intellectual and Professional Life*, Cambridge : Cambridge University Press, 1998.

W. C. Lubenow, *Liberal Intellectuals and Public Culture in Modern Britain, 1815–1914,* Woodbridge: The Boydell Press, 2010.

P. Lynch, *The Liberal Party in Rural England, 1885–1910: Radicalism and Community,* Oxford : Clarendon Press, 2003.

P. Marsh, *The Discipline of Popular Government: Lord Salisbury's Domestic Statecraft 1881–1902,* Hassocks: Harvester, 1978

J. McCaffrey, *Scotland in the Nineteenth Century,* Basingstoke: Macmillan, 1997.

J. Mackenzie, *Propaganda and Empire: The Manipulation of British Public Opinion, 1880–1960,* Manchester: Manchester University Press, 1984.

R. McKenzie and A. Silver, *Angels in Marble: Working Class Conservatives in Urban England,* London: Heinemann Educational, 1968.

R. McWilliam, *Popular Politics in Nineteenth Century England,* London: Routledge, 1998.

J. S. Meisel, *Public Speech and the Culture of Public Life in the Age of Gladstone,* New York: Columbia University Press, 2001

J. R. Moore, *The Transformation of Urban Liberalism: Party Politics and Urban Governance in late nineteenth century England,* Aldershot: Ashgate, 2006.

A. O'Day, *Parnell and the first Home Rule Episode, 1884–1887,* Dublin: Gill & Macmillan, 1986.

A. O'Day, *Irish Home Rule 1867–1921,* Manchester: Manchester University Press, 1998.

C. O'Leary, *The Elimination of Corrupt Practises in British elections, 1868–1911,* Oxford: Clarendon, 1962.

P. O'Farrell, *England and Ireland since 1800,* Oxford: Oxford University Press, 1975.

A. Panebianco, *Political Parties: their organisation and activity in the modern state* Cambridge: Cambridge University Press, 1988.

J. P. Parry, *The Rise and Fall of Liberal Government in Victorian Britain,* New Haven, London: Yale, 1993.

J. P. Parry, *The Politics of Patriotism: English Liberalism, National Identity and Europe, 1830–1886,* Cambridge: Cambridge University Press, 2006.

A. Peel, *These Hundred Years: A History of the Congregational Union of England and Wales 1831–1931,* London: Congregational Union of England and Wales, 1931.

H. Pelling, *Social Geography of British Elections, 1885–1910* (new ed.), Aldershot: Gregg Revivals, 1994.

H. Pelling, *Popular Politics and Society in late Victorian Britain,* London: St. Martin's Press, 1968.

A. N. Porter, *The origins of the South Africa War: Joseph Chamberlain and the diplomacy of imperialism,* Manchester: Manchester University Press, 1980.

B. Porter, *The Absent-Minded Imperialists: Empire, Society and Culture in Britain,* Oxford: Oxford University Press, 2004.

R. Price, *An Imperial War and the British Working Class: Working Class Attitudes and Reactions to the Boer War, 1899–1902,* London: Routledge and Kegan Paul, 1972.

M. Pugh, *The Making of Modern British Politics* (3rd ed.), Oxford: Blackwell, 2002.

M. Pugh, *The Tories and the People,* Oxford: Blackwell, 1985.

M. Pugh, *March of the Women: A Revisionist Analysis of the Campaign for Women's Suffrage 1866–1914,* Oxford: Oxford University Press, 2002.

J. Ramsden, *An Appetite for Power: A History of the Conservative Party since 1830,* London: Harper Collins, 1998.

P. Readman, *Land and Nation in England: Patriotism, National Identity and the Politics of Land,* London: RHS, 2008.

A. J. Reid, *Social Classes and Social Relations in Britain 1850–1914,* Cambridge: Cambridge University Press, 1992.

R. A. Rempel, *Unionists Divided: Arthur Balfour, Joseph Chamberlain and the Unionist Free Traders,* Newton Abbot: David and Charles, 1972.

K. Robbins, *Nineteenth Century Britain: Integration and Diversity,* Oxford: Oxford University Press, 1988.

C. Rover, *Women's Suffrage and Party Politics in Britain 1886–1914,* London: Routledge and Kegan Paul, 1967.

M. J. Salevouris, *'Riflemen Form': The War Scare of 1859–1860 in England,* New York: Garland, 1982.

R. Samuel, *Island Stories: Unravelling Britain,* London: Verso, 1998.

M. Savage and A. Miles, *The Remaking of the British Working Class, 1840–1940,* London: Routledge, 1994.

G. R. Searle, *The Liberal Party: Triumph and Disintegration, 1886–1929,* Basingstoke: Macmillan, 1992.

G. R. Searle, *Country before Party: Coalition and the Idea of 'National Government' in Modern Britain, 1885–1987,* London: Longman, 1995.

G. R. Searle, *A New England? Peace and War 1886–1918,* Oxford: Clarendon Press, 2004.

R. Shannon, *The Age of Salisbury, 1881–1902: Unionism and Empire,* London: Longman, 1996.

D. Southgate, *The Passing of the Whigs, 1832–1886,* Basingstoke: Macmillan, 1962.

A. Sykes, *Tariff Reform in British Politics, 1903–1913,* Oxford: Oxford University Press, 1979.

A. Sykes, *The Rise and Fall of British Liberalism, 1776–1988,* London: Longman, 1997.

D. Tanner, *Political Change and the Labour Party 1900–1918,* Cambridge: Cambridge University Press, 1990.

F. Thompson, *The End of Liberal Ulster: Land Agitation and Land Reform,* Belfast: Ulster Historical Foundation, 2001.

F. M. L. Thompson, *The Rise of Respectable Society,* London: Fontana, 1988.

J. L. Thompson, *A Wider Patriotism: Alfred Milner and the British Empire,* London: Pickering and Chatto, 2007.

P. Thompson, *Socialists, Liberals and Labour: The Struggle for London, 1885–1914,* London: Routledge and Kegan Paul, 1967.

J. Tosh, *Manliness and Masculinities in Nineteenth Century Britain,* London: Pearson, 2005.

J. Tosh w. S. Lang, *The Pursuit of History* (4th ed.), London: Longman, 2006.

F. Trentman, *Free Trade Nation: Commerce, Consumption and Civil Society in Modern Britain,* Oxford: Oxford University Press, 2008.

B. Turner, *Free Trade and Protection,* London: Longman, 1971.

J. Vernon, *Politics and the People: A Study in English Political Culture, c.1815–1867,* Cambridge: Cambridge University Press, 1993.

J. Vincent, *The Formation of the Liberal Party, 1857–1868,* Constable: London, 1966.

G. Walker, *A History of the Ulster Unionist Party: Protest, Pragmatism and Pessimism,* Manchester: Manchester University Press, 2004.

P. J. Waller, *Democracy and Sectarianism: A Political and Social History of Liverpool 1868–1939,* Liverpool: Liverpool University Press, 1981.

R. Ward, *City-state and Nation: Birmingham's Political History, c.1830–1940,* Chichester: Philimore, 2005.

E. Welbourne, *The Miners' Union of Northumberland and Durham,* Cambridge: Cambridge University Press, 1923.

E. S. Wellhofer, *Democracy, Capitalism and Empire in Late Victorian Britain, 1885–1910,* Basingstoke: Macmillan, 1996.

N. Whyte, *Science, Colonialism and Ireland,* Cork: Cork University Press, 1999.

P. Williamson, *Stanley Baldwin: Conservative Leadership and National Values,* Cambridge: Cambridge University Press, 1998.

P. Williamson, *National Crisis and National Government: British Politics, the Economy and Empire, 1926–1932,* Cambridge: Cambridge University Press, 2003.

A. Windscheffel, *Popular Conservatism in Imperial London 1868–1906,* London: RHS, 2007.

Articles

F. Aalen, 'Constructive Unionism and the Shaping of Rural Ireland, c.1880–1921', *Rural History,* 4 (1993), pp.137–164.

I. d'Alton, 'Southern Irish Unionism: A Case Study of Cork Unionists, 1884–1914', *Transactions of the Royal Historical Society,* 23 (1973), pp.71–88.

M. Bentley, 'Victorian Politics and the Linguistic Turn: Historiographical Review', *Historical Journal,* 42 (1999), pp.894–902.

D. W. Bebbington, 'Nonconformity and Electoral Sociology 1867–1918', *Historical Journal,* 27 (1984), pp.633–656.

H. Berrington, 'Partisanship and Dissidence in the Nineteenth Century House of Commons', *Parliamentary Affairs,* 21 (1968), pp.338–374.

N. Blewett, 'Free Fooders, Balfourites, Whole Hoggers: Factionalism within the Unionist party, 1906–1910', *Historical Journal,* 11 (1968), pp.95–124.

D. G. Boyce, 'Dicey, Kilbrandon and Devolution', *Political Quarterly,* 46 (1975), pp.280–292.

J. Broughton, 'Working Class Conservatism and the Rise of Labour', *The Historian,* 54, (1998), pp.16–20.

P. J. Cain, 'The Conservative Party and 'Radical Conservatism', 1880–1914: Incubus or Necessity?', *Twentieth Century British History,* 7 (1996), pp.371–381.

F. Campbell, 'Irish Popular Politics and the Making of the Wyndham Land Act, 1901–1903', *Historical Journal,* 45 (2002), pp.755–773.

I. Cawood, 'The Unionist 'Compact' in West Midland Politics, 1891–1895', *Midland History,* 30 (2005), pp.92–111.

I. Cawood, 'Joseph Chamberlain, the Conservative Party and the Leamington Spa Candidature Dispute of 1895', *Historical Research,* 79:206 (2006), pp.554–577.

I. Cawood, 'The 1892 General Election and the eclipse of the Liberal Unionists', *Parliamentary History,* 29:3 (2010), pp.331–357.

S. Collini, 'The Idea of "Character" in Victorian Political Thought', *Transactions of the Royal Historical Society,* 5th ser., 35 (1985), pp.29–50.

J. Cornford, 'The Transformation of Conservatism in the Late Nineteenth Century', *Victorian Studies,* 7 (1963), pp.35–77.

J. Davis and D. Tanner, 'The Borough Franchise after 1867', *Historical Research,* 69 (1996), pp.306–327.

P. Davis, 'The Liberal Unionist Party and the Irish Policy of Lord Salisbury's Government, 1886–1992', *Historical Journal,* 18 (1975), pp.85–104.

M. Dawson, 'Liberalism in Devon and Cornwall, 1910–1931: "the old time religion"' *Historical Journal,* 38 (1995), pp.425–437.

M. Dawson, 'Party Politics and the provincial press in early twentieth century England: the case of the South-West' *Twentieth Century British History* 9 (1998), 201–218.

M. Diamond, 'Political Heroes of the Victorian Music Hall', *History Today,* 40:1 (1990), pp.33–39.

J. P. D. Dunbabin, 'British elections in the nineteenth and twentieth centuries, a regional approach', *English Historical Review,* 375 (1980), pp.241–267.

J. P. D. Dunbabin, 'Some implications of the 1885 British shift towards single-member constituencies: A note', *English Historical Review,* 109 (1994), pp.89–100

J. D. Fair, 'From Liberal to Conservative: The Flight of the Liberal Unionists after 1886', *Victorian Studies,* 29 (1986), pp.291–314.

S. Fielding, 'Looking for the "New Political History"', *Journal of Contemporary History*, 42:3 (2007), pp.515–524.

D. Fraser, 'Joseph Chamberlain's Municipal Ideal', *History Today*, 37:4 (1987), pp.33–39.

P. Fraser, 'The Liberal Unionist Alliance: Chamberlain, Hartington and the Conservatives, 1886–1904', *English Historical Review*, 77 (1962), pp.53–78.

G. D. Goodlad, 'The Liberal Party and Gladstone's Land Purchase Bill of 1886', *Historical Journal*, 32 (1989), pp.627–641.

G. L. Goodman, 'Liberal Unionism: The Revolt of the Whigs', *Victorian Studies*, 3 (1959), pp.173–189.

C. Green, 'Birmingham's Politics 1873–1891: The Local Basis of Change', *Midland History* 2, (1973), pp.84–98.

E. H. H. Green, 'Radical Conservatism: The Electoral Genesis of Tariff Reform', *Historical Journal*, 28:3 (1985), pp.667–692.

E. H. H. Green, 'The Strange Death of Tory England', *Twentieth Century British History*, 2 (1991), pp.67–88.

P. C. Griffiths, 'The Caucus and the Liberal Party in 1886', *History*, 61 (1976), pp.183–197.

M. Hampton, 'Rethinking the "New Journalism" 1850s-1930s', *Journal of British Studies*, 43 (2004), pp.278–290.

J. M. Hernon, 'The Use of the American Civil War in the Debate over Irish Home Rule', *American Historical Review*, 64 (1964), pp.1022–1026.

C. Harvie, 'Ideology and Home Rule: James Bryce, A. V. Dicey and Ireland, 1880–1887', *English Historical Review*, 91 (1976), pp.298–314.

T. Hennessy, 'Ulster Unionist Territorial and National Identities, 186–1893', *Irish Political Studies*, 8 (1993), pp.21–36.

T. Heyck, 'Home Rule, Radicalism and the Liberal Party, 1886–1895', *Journal of British Studies*, 13:2 (1974), pp.66–91.

K. T. Hoppen, 'Grammars of electoral violence in nineteenth century England and Ireland', *English Historical Review*, 109 (1994), pp.597–620.

J. Howarth, 'The Liberal Revival in Northamptonshire, 1880–1895: a case study in late 19th century elections', *Historical Journal*, 12 (1969), pp.78–118.

I. Hutchinson, 'Lord Kelvin and Liberal Unionism', *Journal of Physics: Conference Series*, 158 (2009), pp.1–19.

E. Jaggard, 'Small Town Politics in mid-Victorian Britain', *History*, 293 (2004), pp.3–29.

T. A. Jenkins, 'The Funding of the Liberal Unionist Party and the Honours System', *English Historical Review*, 105 (1990), pp.920–938.

T. A. Jenkins, 'Hartington, Chamberlain and the Unionist Alliance', *Parliamentary History*, 11 (1992), pp.108–138.

A. Jones, 'Word and Deed: why a *post*-post-structural history is needed and how it might look', *Historical Journal*, 152 (2000), pp.537–540.

J. G. Kellas, 'The Liberal Party in Scotland, 1876–1895', *Scottish Historical Review*, 44 (1965), pp.1–16.

S. Koss, 'Wesleyanism and Empire', *Historical Journal*, 18 (1975), pp.105–18

J. M. Lawrence, 'Class and Gender in the Making of Urban Toryism, 1880–1914', *English Historical Review*, 108 (1993), pp.629–652.

J. M. Lawrence, 'The Decline of Popular Politics?', *Parliamentary History*, 13 (1994), pp.333–337.

J. M. Lawrence, 'The Transformation of British Politics after the First World War', *Past and Present*, 190 (2006), pp.185–216.

D. P. Leighton, 'Municipal Progress, Democracy and Radical Identity in Birmingham, 1838–1886', *Midland History*, 25 (2000), pp.115–142.

J. Loughlin, 'Joseph Chamberlain, English Nationalism and the Ulster Question', *History*, 77 (1992), pp.202–219.

J. Loughlin, 'T.W. Russell, the Tenant-Farmer Interest and Progressive Unionism in Ulster, 1886–1900', *Eire-Ireland,* 25 (1990), pp.43–63.

J. Loughlin, 'Creating "a Social and Geographical Fact": Regional Identity and the Ulster Question 1880s-1920s', *Past and Present,* 195 (2007), pp.159–160.

W. C. Lubenow, 'Irish Home Rule and the Social Basis of the Great Separation in the Liberal Party in 1886', *Historical Journal,* 28 (1985), pp.125–142.

J. McCaffrey, 'The Origins of Liberal Unionism in the West of Scotland', *Scottish Historical Review,* 50 (1971), pp.47–71.

J. R. Moore, 'Manchester Liberalism and the Unionist Secession, 1886–1895', *Manchester Regional History Review,* 15 (2001), pp.31–40.

J. R. Moore, 'Liberal Unionism and the Home Rule Crisis in Leicester, 1885–1892', *Midland History,* 26 (2001), pp.177–197.

A. Muldoon, 'Making Irelands' Opportunity England's: Winston Churchill and the Third Irish Home Rule Bill', *Parliamentary History,* 15 (1996), pp.309–331.

J. P. Parry, 'Gladstone and the Disintegration of the Liberal Party', *Parliamentary History,* 20 (1991), pp.392–404.

J. P. Parry, 'The Quest for Leadership in Unionist Politics', *Parliamentary History,* 12 (1993), pp.296–311.

G. D. Phillips, 'The Whig Lords and Liberalism 1886–1893', *Historical Journal,* 24 (1981), pp.167–173.

E. Porritt, 'Party Conditions in England', *Political Science Quarterly,* 21 (1906), pp.206–236.

M. Pugh, 'Working-class experience and state social welfare, 1908–1914: Old age pensions reconsidered', *Historical Journal,* 45 (2002), pp.775–796.

P. A. Readman, 'The 1895 General Election and Political Change in Late Victorian England', *Historical Journal,* 42 (1999), pp.467–493.

P.A. Readman, 'The Conservative Party, Patriotism and British politics: The Case of the General Election of 1900', *Journal of British Studies,* 40 (2001), pp.107–145.

D. Richter, 'The Role of the Mob Riot in Victorian Elections, 1865–1885', *Victorian Studies,* 15, (1971), pp.19–28.

K. Rix, '"Go Out into the Highways and the Hedges": The Diary of Michael Sykes, Conservative Political Lecturer, 1895 and 1907–8', *Parliamentary History,* 20 (2001), pp.209–231.

K. Rix, 'The Elimination of Corrupt Practices in British Elections? Reassessing the Impact of the 1883 Corrupt Practices Act', *English Historical Review,* 123 (2008), pp.65–97.

M. Roberts, 'Constructing a Tory World-view: Popular Politics and the Conservative Press in late-Victorian Leeds', *Historical Research,* 79 (2006), pp.115–143.

M. Roberts, '"Villa Toryism" and Popular Conservatism in Leeds, 1885–1902', *Historical Journal,* 49 (2006), pp.217–246.

S. Roberts, 'Politics and the Birmingham Working Class: The General Elections of 1900 and 1906 in East Birmingham', *West Midland Studies,* 15 (1982), pp.12–21.

J. P. Rossi, 'Home Rule and the Liverpool By-election of 1880', *Irish Historical Studies,* 19 (1974), pp.156–168.

C. B. Shannon, 'The Ulster Liberal Unionists and Local Government Reform, 1885–98', *Irish Historical Studies,* 18 (1973), pp.407–423.

H. W. Stephens, 'The Changing Context of British Politics in the 1880s: The Reform Acts and the Formation of the Liberal Unionist Party', *Social Science History,* 1:4 (1977), pp.486–501.

D. Tanner, 'The parliamentary electoral system, the "fourth" reform Act and the rise of Labour in England and Wales', *Bulletin of the Institute of Historical Research,* 56 (1983), pp.205–219.

D. Thackeray, 'Home and Politics: Women and Conservative activism in early twentieth-century Britain', *Journal of British Studies,* 49: 4 (2010), pp.826-848.

A. S. Thompson, 'Tariff Reform: An Imperial Strategy, 1903–1913', *Historical Journal*, 40 (1997), pp.1033–1054.

J. Thompson, '"Pictorial Lies?" – Posters and Politics in Britain c.1880–1914', *Past and Present*, 197 (2007), pp.177–210.

F. Tillyard, 'The Distribution of the Free Churches in England', *Sociological Review*, 27 (1935), pp.1–18.

J. T. Ward, 'Liberal Unionism in Scotland', *Contemporary Record*, 251 (1987), pp.47–71.

P. Williamson, 'State Prayers, Fasts and Thanksgivings: Public Worship in Britain 1830–1897', *Past and Present*, 200 (2008), pp.121–174.

Chapters in Edited Collections

N. Armour, 'Isabella Tod and Liberal Unionism in Ulster 1886–1896' in A. Hayes and D. Urquhart (eds.), *Irish Women's History*, Dublin: Irish Academic Press, 2000.

F. Aubel, 'The Conservatives in Wales' in M. Francis & I. Zweiniger-Bargielowska (eds.), *The Conservatives and British Society, 1880–1990*, Cardiff: University of Wales Press, 1996.

S. Ball, 'Local Conservatism and the evolution of the party organisation' in A Seldon and S. Ball (eds.), *Conservative Century: The Conservative Party Since 1900*, Oxford: Oxford University Press, 1994.

P. Bull, 'Irish Protestants feel this betrayal deeply ... : Home Rule, Rome Rule and Nonconformity' in D.G. Boyce & R. Swift (eds.), *Problems and Perspectives in Irish History since 1800: Essays in Honour of Patrick Buckland*, Dublin: Four Courts, 2004.

D. Cannadine, 'The Context, Performance and Meaning of Ritual: The British Monarchy and the "Invention of Tradition" c.1820–1977' in E.J. Hobsbawm and T. Ranger (eds.), *The Invention of Tradition*, Cambridge: Cambridge University Press, 1983.

R. Colls, 'Englishness and the Political Culture' in R. Colls and P. Dodd (eds.), *Englishness: Politics and Culture, 1880–1920*, London: Routledge, 1986.

J. Cornford, 'Aggregate Election Data and British Party Alignments, 1885–1910' in E. Allardt and S. Rokkan (eds.), *Mass politics: Studies in Political Sociology*, New York: Free Press, 1970.

H. Cunningham, 'The Conservative Party and Patriotism' in R. Colls and P. Dodd (eds.), *Englishness: Politics and Culture, 1880–1920*, London: Routledge, 1986.

N. C. Fleming, 'The Landed Elite: Power and Ulster Unionism' in D. G. Boyce and A. O'Day (eds.), *The Ulster Crisis: 1885–1922*, Basingstoke: Macmillan, 2005.

J. France, 'Salisbury and the Unionist Alliance' in R. Blake and H. Cecil (eds.), *Salisbury: The Man and his Policies*, Basingstoke : Macmillan, 1987.

S. Gilley, 'English Attitudes to the Irish in England 1780–1900' in C. Holmes (ed.), *Immigrants and minorities in British society*, London: Allen and Unwin, 1978.

G. Jones, 'Scientists against Home Rule' in D. G. Boyce & A.O'Day (eds.), *Defenders of the Union: a survey of British and Irish Unionism since 1801*, London: Routledge, 2001.

J. P. King, 'Socioeconomic development and corrupt campaign practices in England' in A. J. Heidenheimer, M. Johnston & V. T. LeVine (eds.), *Political Corruption: A Handbook*, New Brunswick: Transaction, 1989.

J. M. Lawrence, 'The dynamic of urban politics, 1867–1914' in J.M .Lawrence & M. Taylor (eds.), *Party, State and Society: Electoral Behaviour in Britain since 1920*, Aldershot: Scholar Press, 1997.

J. M. Lawrence, 'Popular Politics and the Limitations of Party: Wolverhampton, 1867–1900' in E. F. Biagini and A. J. Reid (eds.), *Currents of Radicalism*, Cambridge: Cambridge University Press, 1991.

W. C. Lubenow, 'The Liberal and the National Question: Irish Home Rule, Nationalism, and their Relationship to Nineteenth Century Liberalism' in J. A. Phillips (ed.), *Computing Parliamentary History*, Edinburgh: Edinburgh University Press, 1994.

M. Luddy, 'Isabella M.S. Tod, 1836–1896' in M. Cullen and M. Luddy (eds.), *Women, Power and Consciousness in nineteenth century Ireland,* Dublin: Attic Press, 1995.

C. M. M. MacDonald, 'Locality, Tradition and Language in the Evolution of Scottish Unionism: A Case Study, Paisley, 1886–1910' in C. M. M. MacDonald (ed.), *Unionist Scotland 1800–1997,* Edinburgh: John Donald Publishers, 1998.

E. W. McFarland, 'The Orangeman's Unionist Vision' in C.M.M. MacDonald (ed.), *Unionist Scotland 1800–1997,* Edinburgh: John Donald Publishers, 1998.

P. Mandler, '"Race" and "Nation" in mid-Victorian thought' in S. Collini, R. Whatmore & B. Young (eds.), *History, Religion and Culture: British Intellectual History 1750–1950,* Cambridge: Cambridge University Press, 2000.

G. Martin, 'The Idea of "Imperial Federation"' in R. Hyam & G. Martin (eds.), *Reappraisals in British Imperial History,* London: Macmillan, 1975).

K. O. Morgan, 'The Liberal Unionists in Wales' in K. O. Morgan (ed.), *Modern Wales: Politics, Places and People,* Cardiff: University of Wales Press, 1995.

F. O'Gorman, 'The culture of elections in England: From the Glorious Revolution to the First World War, 1688–1914' in E. Posado-Carbo (ed.), *Elections before Democracy: The History of Elections in Europe and Latin America,* Basingstoke: Macmillan, 1996.

G. K. Peatling, 'Victorian Imperial theorist? Goldwin Smith and Ireland' in P. Gray (ed.), *Victoria's Ireland? Irishness and Britishness, 1837–1901,* Dublin: Four Courts, 2004.

D. Smith, 'Englishness and the Liberal Inheritance after 1886' in R. Colls and P. Dodd (eds.), *Englishness: Politics and Culture, 1880–1920,* London: Routledge, 1986.

J. Smith, 'Conservative Ideology and Representations of the Union with Ireland' in M. Francis & I. Zweiniger-Bargielowska (eds.), *The Conservatives and British Society, 1880–1990,* Cardiff: University of Wales Press, 1996.

D. Tanner, 'Gender, civic culture and politics in South Wales: explaining Labour municipal policy, 1918–1939' in M. Worley (ed.), *Labour's Grass Roots: Essays on the Activities and Experiences of Local Labour Parties and Members, 1918–1945,* Aldershot: Ashgate, 2005.

N. Vance, 'The Problems of Unionist Literature' in D. G. Boyce & A. O'Day (eds), *Defenders of the Union: A Survey of British and Irish Unionism since 1801,* London: Routledge, 2001.

G. Walker and D. Officer, 'Scottish Unionism and the Ulster Question' in C. M. M. MacDonald (ed.), *Unionist Scotland 1800–1997,* Edinburgh: John Donald Publishers, 1998.

G. Walker, 'Thomas Sinclair, Presbyterian Liberal Unionist' in R. English and G. Walker (eds.), *Unionism in Modern Ireland: New Perspectives on Politics and Culture,* Basingstoke: Macmillan, 1996.

L. E. Walker, 'Party Political Women: a comparative study of Liberal women and the Primrose League, 1890–1914' in J. Rendall (ed.), *Equal or Different: Women's Politics 1800–1914,* Blackwell: Oxford, 1987.

Reference Texts

F. W. S. Craig, *British Parliamentary Election Results, 1885–1918,* Basingstoke: Macmillan, 1974.

E. Crawford (ed.), *The Women's Suffrage Movement – A Reference Guide,* London: Routledge, 1999.

H. C. G. Matthew and B. Harrison (eds.), *Oxford Dictionary of National Biography (60 vols.),* Oxford: Oxford University Press, 2004.

Unpublished Theses

V. Barbery, 'From Platform to Polling Booth', PhD thesis, University of Cambridge, 2007.

C. Burness, 'Conservatism and Liberal Unionism in Glasgow 1874–1912', PhD thesis, University of Dundee, 1983.

I. Cawood, '"A Colossal Blunder", Joseph Chamberlain, the Conservative Party and the Leamington Spa Candidature Dispute of 1895', MPhil thesis, University of Birmingham, 2004.

I. Cawood, '"The Lost Party", Liberal Unionism, 1886–1895'; PhD thesis, University of Leicester, 2009.

P. G. Davis, 'The Role of the Liberal Unionist Party in British Politics, 1886–1895', PhD thesis, University of London, 1974.

G. D. Goodlad, 'Liberals and the Home Rule issue, November 1885-July 1886: The Leaders and the Rank and File with Special Reference to Certain Localities', PhD thesis, University of Cambridge, 1988.

G. L. Goodman, 'The Liberal Unionist Party, 1886–1895', PhD thesis, University of Chicago, 1956.

J. K. Lindsay, 'The Liberal Unionist Party until December 1887', PhD thesis, University of Edinburgh, 1955.

J. Owen, 'The Caucus and Party Organization in England in the 1880s', PhD thesis, University of Cambridge, 2006.

K. Rix, 'The Party Agent and English Electoral Culture, 1880–1906', PhD thesis, University of Cambridge, 2001.

W. D. Ross, 'Bradford politics, 1880–1906', PhD thesis, University of Bradford, 1977.

A. T. Sharma, 'Working Class Conservatism in Tower Hamlets and Bethnal Green, 1885–1914', BA Dissertation, University of Birmingham, 1996.

Conference Papers

S. Ball, 'Conservatism between the Wars: Principles, Pride and Prejudice', paper delivered at the British History 1815–1945 Seminar, Institute of Historical Research, London, 13 November 2008 (full version).

D. W. Bebbington, 'Gladstone and Fasque', paper delivered at Gladstone Conference, St. Deniol's Library, Hawarden, 31 July 2010.

D. Brooks, 'Gladstone and the 1886 General Election', paper delivered at the Gladstone conference, St. Deniol's Library, Hawarden, 17 July 2011.

I. Cawood, 'The Liberal Unionist Vote: The Persistence of Patronage and Localism in later Victorian Britain', paper delivered at British History 1815–1945 Seminar, Institute of Historical Research, London, 8 May 2008.

R. Gill, 'Calculating Compassion' in the South African War, 1899–1902: A Case Study in the History of the Origins of Humanitarian Relief', paper delivered at University of Sheffield Imperial History Discussion Group, 10 May 2007.

T. Little, 'Gladstone, Granville and Ireland, 1885–1886', paper delivered at Gladstone Conference, St Deniol's Library, Hawarden, 1 August 2010.

F. Nicoll, 'Gladstone, Gordon and the Sudan campaign, 1884–5', paper delivered at Gladstone Conference, St. Deniol's Library, Hawarden, 1 August 2010.

M. Taylor, 'The Rise and Fall of the "New Political History" 1979–2008', paper delivered at Languages of Politics Conference, University of Durham, 3 April 2009.

INDEX